GREAT
PERSONALITIES
of the BIBLE

Two Volumes In One

William Sanford LaSor

HENDRICKSON
PUBLISHERS

Hendrickson Publishers, Inc.
P.O. Box 3473
Peabody, Massachusetts 01961-3473

Printed in the United States of America
ISBN 1-56563-301-6

Second Printing—August 1997

Preface

THE BIBLE is a living Book because it was wrought out in life. It is a living Book, moreover, because it comes from the living God. In all the religious literature of the world, the Bible is unique in the place it gives to persons, events, places, and the significance of time and space. We call the Book "timeless"—but not because it deals with abstract principles. We say that the Bible is "universal"—but not because it is unconcerned with a particular bit of geography. This is the paradox of the Bible, that being so intimately concerned with time and space it nevertheless transcends temporal and spatial limitations.

In the works that follow, I have attempted to sketch the stories of the Old and New Testaments through the means of persons, situations, history, and geography. By selecting the characters, I have attempted to tell the story of the Bible in sequence—omitting nothing of primary significance—from the call to Abraham to set out in search of the city whose builder is God, to the description of that city and its Light and Salvation. Doubtless I have omitted some whom you would have included and I have included some whom you would have omitted. This is an author's privilege: those I have chosen were in order to tell the story I wanted to tell. It is my firm conviction that the story is true, and that in my selection of personalities I have neither taken from nor added to the story any element that affects its truth. I shall not be so bold as to make a similar claim for the way I may have handled these personalities.

After having presented one of these chapters in a church service, I was confronted by one of the congregation who said something about the "sermon" being interesting, but that I did not get into the "spiritual message." I was unable to discover exactly what he meant, but I think it has some bearing on two basic methods of Bible exposition or, rather, Bible interpretation. In former generations, Bible characters were handled almost exclusively as *types*. The *allegorical* interpretation of Scripture was considered to be the highest (or deepest) of all methods. This led to all sorts of extreme views, and brought discredit on Bible study. It is an undeniable fact that every sect claiming to be Biblical can support its position from Scripture—provided we allow its proponents to interpret or select or arrange Scripture as they wish. But this is circular reasoning of the most vicious kind. Having started from the position they hold, they have proceeded to organize the Bible so as to support that position, and then have had the effrontery to claim that their system is *the Biblical system.*

Even sincere Bible-believing Christians who are quite orthodox (using the word in relation to the great historical creeds of the church) fall into this trap, and thereby lose their defense against false systems.

If I have stressed the geographical and historical details, and have not gotten into the "spiritual message," it is because I am convinced that this is the Bible's own way of preserving its claim to authority.

God has acted and God has spoken. But it was not in spaceless, time-less, mystical experience. It was rather to men in real-life situations. Names are named. The careful historian can find many points of reference. Those who were contemporary with the Scriptural events were able to check the claims of veracity. Men who were unbelievers came to believe because they were confronted with evidence that could be verified by sensual means. This was true of Abraham and Moses; it was true of Joseph and Joshua; it was true of John the Baptist and Mary of Nazareth; it was true of Peter and Paul—in fact, it was true of every one who came to a living faith. Not one of us was born with such faith. And whether our "unbelief" was lack of faith in prayer, or distrust of God's Word, or disbelief that God would (or could) do marvelous things on our behalf, or whatever it was, we had to come to faith through being convinced.

The scoffer sometimes acts as if he were the only man on earth who refused to accept the story of God's redemptive activity without proof. Where did he get such an idea? The personalities set forth in this Book all had their questions, their moments of doubt, their request for some authenticating word or experience. Even Mary the mother of our Lord asked, "How can this be?"

As we put ourselves into the situations of these men and women of God—not idealized out of all resemblance to truth, but in the real-life situation as the Bible presents them—we find something happening to us. The God of our fathers, who met them and made known to them His saving grace, meets us. We get the "spiritual message" not by spiritualizing the story, but by reliving the situation. When Peter re-counted the events in the life and death and resurrection of Jesus, his hearers were not simply educated; they were confronted with God, and cried out, "What shall we do?" When Stephen rehearsed the story of God's works in Israel's history, his hearers did not shrug off the ancient unbelief; they rushed upon him and stoned him to death. This is the testimony of millions: as we read of God's wondrous acts with the children of men, we find that God speaks to us; and when we respond in faith, we find that He acts also in our behalf.

An author is always interested in what others think of his work. The published reviews of the first editions of these works were most interesting. Whereas one reviewer felt that my "low view" of the Bible had led me to accept Marxism, another reviewer insisted that I presented dispensationalism, typology, and an impossible view of verbal inspiration. A Protestant reviewer labeled me "Romanist," and a Catholic reviewer was repeatedly critical of my views of Mary, Peter, and the church. On the other hand, if the reviews to some extent canceled each other out, the reaction of the men and women and young people in churches, conferences, military installations, and college campuses has been generally an expression of gratitude. And that has been gratifying; for after all, the work was written for them and not for scholars. Perhaps my most cherished commendation came from a member of a high-school group which one of my former students was taking through the *Great Personalities of the Old Testament*: "We get what this guy is talking about."

For the sake of those who have not read the preface of either of the one-volume works, let me repeat that these studies were not academic. They were existential, having been prepared for and presented to Bible study classes in churches. I often spoke with a maximum of preparation and a minimum of notes, and the oral form of the messages was deliberately preserved through transcribing the recordings. Editorial work done subsequently aimed only at removing some of the most objectionable barbarisms and mental lapses and presenting documentation for many of the statements of fact. In this one-volume edition I have tried to remove the remaining errors that managed to get past a number of typists, proofreaders, and editors.

The dedication of the first volume to three laymen who encouraged me much, and of the second volume to two former teachers who taught me much, remains as cordial as when first made. Perhaps it is symbolic that I feel a debt both to those who taught me and to those I have taught. At any rate, I hope never to lose this dual sense of obligation. Others have helped to make the Bible the Book of books in my life; I hope and pray that I can help to do that for you.

WILLIAM SANFORD LASOR

Fuller Theological Seminary
Pasadena, California

VOLUME 1

GREAT PERSONALITIES OF THE OLD TESTAMENT

To

JEAN L. LAMOREAUX
PAUL C. DOEHRING AND
ROGER K. NEVIUS
whose encouragement and inspiration
over the years have meant much to me
this work is affectionately dedicated

Contents

GREAT PERSONALITIES OF THE OLD TESTAMENT

I	ABRAHAM: THE CHALLENGE *Called Out of Idolatry*	13
II	ABRAHAM: THE RESPONSE *Living by Faith*	22
III	JACOB *From Deception to Integrity*	31
IV	JOSEPH *Character That Endures*	40
V	MOSES: THE MAN *Crucial Choice*	50
VI	MOSES: THE SERVANT *Committed Completely*	60
VII	JOSHUA *Valiant Leader*	69
VIII	RUTH *God in the Commonplace*	78
IX	SAMUEL *Steadfastness in Difficult Times*	88
X	DAVID: THE MAN *Success Mingled With Failure*	98
XI	DAVID: THE KING *After God's Heart*	106
XII	SOLOMON *Splendor and Apostasy*	116
XIII	ELIJAH *Rival Altars*	126
XIV	ISAIAH *Beyond Judgment—Glory*	136
XV	JEREMIAH *As a Wall of Bronze*	145
XVI	EZEKIEL *He Taught Them to Sing*	154
XVII	DANIEL *When Worlds End*	164
XVIII	EZRA *Guardian of the Scriptures*	174
	BIBLIOGRAPHY	185
	INDEX	190

CHAPTER I

Abraham: The Challenge

IN MANY WAYS, Abraham towers above all the other men of the Old Testament. He was the outstanding pioneer of a great pioneer people. Three great religions claim him as founder: Judaism, Mohammedanism, and Christianity; almost half the population of the world traces its religious background back to this man. He is great, any way you measure him. Well was he named Abraham, "father of a multitude."

We meet him first in the eleventh chapter of Genesis where, in verse 26, we are told that "When Terah had lived seventy years, he became father of Abram." We can fit together some of the pieces of the background of Abraham partly from the facts given us in Scripture, and partly from other facts in history outside the Scriptures. We are told, for instance, in Genesis 11:28, that Haran, one of the sons of Terah and one of the brothers of Abraham, died in the land of his birth—in Ur of the Chaldeans. Now, since the birth of Abram, Nahor, and Haran is reported in a single statement, we can presume that Abraham also was born in Ur. (Many people pronounce that "Er," hence the dictionary so indicates. The modern Arabs of Iraq call it "Or." I think the correct pronunciation should be "Oor.")

However we pronounce it, Ur is not much of a place to look at today. Professor Jack Finegan, in his book *Light from the Ancient Past*, speaks of a disgruntled tourist who wrote in the register of the mud hotel at modern Ur: "No wonder Abraham left; even Job would have!"[1] In a way, you cannot blame the tourist, for Ur is now a barren place away out in the middle of the desert. About all there is to prove that there was once a city on the spot is the remains of a "ziggurat"—an imitation mountain of clay and bitumen, built by people who had come from a mountainous region, to worship their traditional deities. In addition to this ziggurat, we find, in the Iraqi Museum at Baghdad and the Uni-

[1] Jack Finegan, *Light from the Ancient Past* (Princeton: Princeton University Press, 1946), p. 12.

versity Museum at Philadelphia, the rich remains unearthed by archaeologists. From these we are able to reconstruct something of the civilization of Abraham's day.

The approximate date of Abraham's birth we can set at 2000 B.C. The
date is not important. No dates are really important, except that they
are pegs on which we hang our knowledge of the past. We will be able
to hang a few things on this one.

Suppose we try to reconstruct a little of the history of the Mesopotamia that included Ur, just before and after the year 2000 B.C. This
will enable us to fit Abraham into the picture. There is one period of
history known to the historians as the "Old Akkadian" period; they
assign the dates 2360–2180 B.C. The Old Akkadian period had its
pivotal point, its historical and geographical center, in the city of
Akkad—that is where the name "Akkadian" comes from. And the
name of the city of Akkad is usually associated with the name of the
great king, Sargon I. This king is famous, at least, for one thing: he was
the first man in history, so far as we have any record, to claim to be the
ruler of the world. Our modern dictators who have made, or hoped to
make, the same claim—Mussolini, Hitler, Stalin and the rest—are
Johnnies-come-lately, compared to Sargon I. Four thousand years before
they arrived on this earth, Sargon claimed that he had extended his
borders as far as the Upper Sea, the Cedar Forest, and the Silver Mountains. The Upper Sea would be the Mediterranean, the Cedar Forest
would be the Lebanons, and the Silver Mountains would be the Taurus
Mountains in southeastern Asia Minor. Sargon was the first to use the
title, "The King of the Four Quarters of the World."

The Old Akkadian period was one of high level in art. Some day,
I hope you may go into the museum at the University of Pennsylvania
in Philadelphia, or into the Iraqi Museum in the city of Baghdad, and
see some of the magnificent art pieces that have been dug up from the
earth of ancient Mesopotamia.[2] If and when you do, view them with
this fact in mind: many of our teachers, in their enthusiasm to prove
the constant development of art and the human being, select the worst
possible specimens of the past and the best possible of the present, to
show you how it all "progresses" from the poorer to the better. They
may be sincere, but they are wrong, in doing that. Actually, if you
were to pick out the *better* art specimens of the Akkadian period, and

[2] Some beautiful photographs can be found in Leonard Woolley, *Ur: The
First Phases* (London and New York: Penguin Books, 1946).

put them beside some of the monstrosities of "modern art," you would have a very wholesome respect for the Akkadians! Our modern artists take a bit of mud or stone or wood and give it a weird, unrecognizable shape, and call it "Madonna and Child." Looking at this "modern" exhibit, you could prove just the opposite: you could prove that we have degenerated, and not progressed at all.

In the Old Akkadian period, they had writing; they had borrowed it from the Sumerians along with a lot of other things. The Sumerians were a very ancient people; we have no knowledge of the time when they were savages. We meet them first in the fourth millennium B.C. (4000–3000 B.C.), and already they are "a civilized, metal-using people, living in great and populous cities, possessing a complicated system of writing, and living under the government of firmly established civil and religious dynasties and hierarchies."[3] The Sumerians developed the idea of *planned* cities and building, and streets. It is possible also that they developed drainage ditches to get rid of the swamplands in southern Mesopotamia, and probably used them for irrigation purposes as well. They developed the shock tactics of warfare and the phalanx. These did not come into popularity with Caesar; the Sumerians had them two thousand years before the rise of mighty Rome. They also used chariots in war, but not horses, for they had not yet been introduced.[4]

Now all these things belonged to the Sumerians and were handed on by them to the people that followed them in the Old Akkadian period. Then after a brief interlude, the Sumerians came back into power. That would be around the years 2070–1960 B.C. The great name in that period is the name of the king of Lagash, Gudea. You may have heard of him. He laid the foundations for what is known historically as the "Third Dynasty of Ur," and that is the time in which we will have to locate Abraham, so far as I have been able to fit together the facts in the case. This Dynasty wound up by being anti-Semitic; for the Semitic peoples from the Old Akkadian period were so prominent, so popular, so powerful, that the Sumerians felt that they just had to take measures to get rid of them. It has been suggested that this anti-Semitism was the occasion for Abraham's father to take his family out of Ur. It could

[3] H. R. Hall, *The Ancient History of the Near East* (London: Methuen, 1950), 11th ed., p. 172.

[4] A popular, yet scholarly, picture of the Sumerians can be gotten from S. N. Kramer, *From the Tablets of Sumer* (Indian Hills, Colo.: Falcon's Wing Press, 1956), 293 pp.

well be. In the absence of proof, I can only treat this point with a sort of sixth sense. I feel that it would have been the logical time for this separation from the land of Ur.

Following the Sumerian period, we come back into a Semite period called the "Old Babylonian"—which used to be dated around 2000 but which now is dated almost certainly at 1830–1550 B.C. The great name in this period is Hammurabi, the great lawgiver, and one of the first to develop a codified system of law in the ancient world. There were, we now know, other law codes before his.

Where are we going to fit Abraham? In the Old Akkadian period? in the Sumerian period? in the Old Babylonian period? Well, we cannot yet be positive. Scholars used to date Abraham about 2200 B.C. Then when they discovered the records of Hammurabi (who was dated at that time around 2000 B.C.), and because they concluded that the Amraphel of Genesis 14:9 must be Hammurabi, they moved Abraham's dates from 2200 to 2000 B.C. Now that we know Hammurabi lived around the end of the 1800's and the beginning of the 1700's, some scholars have changed Abraham's date again to fit Hammurabi's. Personally, I do not believe we should try to make Abraham and Hammurabi contemporary, for Amraphel and Hammurabi are completely different names, and I see no reason to try to equate them. Moreover, what little we know about Amraphel from Genesis 14 is certainly too little to identify him with the great king of the Babylonians. So if we just forget that and try to fit Abraham into the picture on the basis of other materials, I think we will probably be best satisfied with the Sumerian period just following the time of Gudea, the Third Dynasty of Ur.

We can also work *backwards,* in our Bible chronology, and come out about the same. For example, if we take the date of Solomon, which is reasonably certain, and work back to the time of the Exodus from figures that are given in the Scriptures, and then work back from the time of the Exodus through Joseph and Jacob and Isaac and Abraham, we come out somewhere in the neighborhood of 2000 B.C.

If that is so, and even if we have to give one or two hundred years either way, Abraham fits into the Babylonian civilization at a time when it was at one of its peaks of cultural and political splendor. Now, fifty years ago some critics were telling us that Abraham, "if there were such a person" (and they were not even sure that there had ever been such a person), was a nomad who came out of the desert, with no background of culture, or civilization, who knew nothing about the use of metal, who knew nothing about city life. He was just a vagrant wanderer. Today that can no longer be said. Now we know that Abraham came out of an area which for a long period of time—for four, five or six hundred years—had had a high level of civilization with writing, with fine cities, with highly developed arts, beautiful gems and carvings and very well-established law codes and legal systems; *all* of these things were his, *plus* a highly developed religious system.

According to Joshua 24:2, "Joshua said to all the people, 'Thus says the Lord, the God of Israel, "Your fathers lived of old beyond the Euphrates, Terah, the father of Abraham and of Nahor; and they served other gods." ' " I have found that some people resent the statement that Abraham's father was an idolator. They think that it is heresy to suggest that Abraham came from a line of worshipers of pagan gods. Well, here we have a statement in the Bible itself to the effect that Abraham's father and his brother and probably Abraham himself, at the beginning, were worshipers of false gods. The patron god of the city of Ur was named "Nannar" or "Nanna." (They probably did not pronounce the "r" at the end of a word.) Nanna was the moon god. We know something about the religion of Nanna; we have a lot of records from that period that tell us just how they worshiped, and we know about some of the ritual that they went through to bring honor and glory, as they thought, to the god they served.

It is an interesting fact that Abraham's father, Terah, had a name which in the Hebrew language is related to the word for "moon." It seems likely that his parents—Abraham's grandparents—named this child "Moony" because they were worshipers of Nanna the moon god; only they named him that in Hebrew rather than in Sumerian because they were good Semites.

They doubtless had the old traditions of their people. I think that it is quite likely that these Semitic peoples, who had moved into the area and come in contact with the Sumerians, had brought many stories that had been handed down from generation to generation, probably told around the campfire in front of the tent, from the days when they had lived in the desert. They probably had stories about a flood, and about creation. We know that there were various stories of the flood and various stories of the creation—Babylonian accounts, Sumerian accounts, and a Biblical account, and probably still others.

The details were different, sometimes vastly different. But there is a common denominator in the fact that *there had been a creation* when the world had come into existence by the will of the gods—or God. And there was another common denominator in the fact that there was a time when there had been a flood, and when one family was delivered from it. I suppose Abraham's father had had these traditions. It may well be that the true accounts had been handed down from father to son from the time of Noah and Shem, and that the Hebrew account, which is so different in many details from the Babylonian and Sumerian accounts, had been preserved in the family of Terah, the father of Abraham. We don't know; we are guessing now. But *somebody* must have kept the Biblical account, because it has been preserved for us in our Bible.[5]

Abraham therefore may have had a knowledge of the true God, even though his father was a worshiper of the moon god. Even though he came from a group which had degenerated—let us put it that way—from the worship of the true God to the worship of many false gods, he may still have held on to the tradition that there was a God worshiped by his ancestors who had been the preserver of the human race at the time of the flood of Noah. At any rate, we do know this: one day God called Abraham to get up and get out of that background and to go into another land and build a new civilization. It is sketched for us at the beginning of the twelfth chapter of Genesis: "Now the Lord said to Abram, 'Go from your country and your kindred and your father's house to the land that I will show you. And I will make of you a great nation, and I will bless you, and make your name great.'"

According to Acts 7:2-3, this call came when they were in Mesopotamia. The record is there in Stephen's sermon: "Brethren and fathers, hear me. The God of glory appeared to our father Abraham, when he was in Mesopotamia, before he lived in Haran, and said to him, 'Depart from your land and from your kindred, and go into the land which I will show you.'" When we read the closing verses of the eleventh chapter of Genesis, we get the impression that the call in the first part of the twelfth chapter did not come in Ur, but in Haran. So I think there may have been two calls: an earlier one that was the means whereby God got Abraham out of Ur and as far as Haran; and then the second call whereby God got Abraham "out of the rut"

[5] Unless, of course, we hold that God gave the account *de novo* to Moses. But this, to me, is an unwarranted extension of the doctrine of inspiration.

into which he had settled in Haran, and moved him down into Canaan, where God wanted him in the first place.

There is a fascinating book by a medical doctor named Penfield, entitled *No Other Gods*.[6] It is a novel about Abraham. I was rather interested to read the details in the Preface and the historical notes at the end of the book, and to learn that this book was written by a man who is not a specialist in the field, for it shows a vast amount of research and knowledge of the archaeological discoveries and the historical facts of the period. The doctor has combined these known facts with a wonderful imagination to give us a picture of the life of Abraham in the city of Ur up until the time he finally left it and started on his way to Canaan. The whole novel is written about that one area of his life. The author makes Abraham a priest of Nanna. I do not know whether that was so or not. (The author of historical fiction has at least this advantage over those of us who teach history: he can let his imagination run free once in a while and he can make up little details just so we will have a good story.) Abraham was a priest of Nanna and he became disgusted with paganism and with the ritual that he saw performed: the marriage procession of the god and goddess, the fertility rites, and all the other things that were part and parcel of it. And he felt that certainly, if there is a god who is real, who is worth worshiping, He could not be like this stone idol. The book makes Terah, the father of Abraham, not only a worshiper of false gods but a *maker* of false gods—an idol carver. One day, Terah finished his carving and said, "There, I have made you!" Abraham noticed that, and he thought about it. What kind of god is this that is only a piece of stone or wood until man gets finished and says, "There, I have made you; now you're a god"?

All this leads directly, in our novel, to the initial call of Abraham by the true God. Here is a young man with good training, and a good background, who comes to realize that this idol manufacture and worship is not true, and cannot be real. Thinking his way through, he comes later to an experience of the real God; he is "called out" by that God. Somewhere, some time, in Ur of the Chaldeans, there came a call from God to Abraham to get up and leave that place. Perhaps it was connected with the anti-Semitic movement among the Sumerians of the Third Dynasty of Ur, during which this family was expelled

[6] Wilder Penfield, *No Other Gods* (Boston: Little, Brown and Co., 1954), 341 pp.

from the city. Whatever the circumstances, they returned to the country from which their ancestors had come a generation or two before: Haran which is in Padan-Aram, up in the great bend of the River Euphrates, just south of the Armenian highland, a little east of what we know today as Asia Minor. In that region they settled down and Abraham stayed there until his father died, and perhaps a little longer. Life was so good and easy there that he seemed to forget that God had called him. So God called the second time, telling Abraham to get out of Haran and go to Canaan, where he would be safely away from the worship of the moon god, where he would have an opportunity to pioneer in the development of a nation which will know the one true God, and follow Him. "Go from your country and your kindred and your father's house to the land that I will show you. And I will make of you a great nation, and I will bless you, and make your name great." Ultimately, that blessing is to reach all men.

Here is the central thought, in this first study of Abraham: *the Hebrew faith and the Christian religion begin with a call from God.* That is a basic fact from which we cannot escape. We have no right to try to escape from it. As I understand the Scripture record, I do not see here an account of mere human curiosity. I cannot believe that simply because this young man of Semitic background became disgusted with the ways and worship of the anti-Semitic people among whom he lived he was "led to invent something better," as some have put it. I cannot believe that his religion was a product of the human mind alone. There was something beyond all that. It is the clear-cut teaching of Genesis, and of all the rest of the Bible, *that the initial move came from God, and not from Abraham.* If God had not called, he might have stayed in Ur or Haran and worshiped the moon god until he died. It was necessary that God take the initiative, that God come to him and say, "There is something better for you than what you have in this pagan world."

There was a lot of sacrifice involved, as we shall see in our next chapter on the faith of Abraham. He was leaving a well-established civilization to go out into a country that was rather backward—as he probably knew, for there had been commerce with Canaan and military expeditions to Canaan before Abraham's time in the days of King Sargon I. It was not so well civilized as Egypt or Babylon; yet Abraham was willing to give up all of his comfort and his advantages. If he were to have any children in the years to come—he did not have at that time, because "Sarah was barren"—he would have to bring them up where there were no schools and few if any of the advantages that they would have had in Ur. But God called him, and he was obedient to that call.

This is the way God deals with each one of us. He may not wait for our curiosity to get the best of us. He may not wait for us to reach the place where we are disgusted with the ways of the world.

Sometimes we are called to weigh the disadvantages of giving up the background that we have, the culture that we enjoy. It may be a question very much like the one Abraham had to face; where will our children grow up if we follow the call of God? But God calls, and He expects us to hear that call and to obey it. The man who obeys is a man of faith; the man who disobeys is a man without faith, an unbeliever. It was possible for Abraham to have a great name and become a great nation and a source of blessing to all the world only if by hearing and obeying the call of God. So it ever is for Abraham's seed.

CHAPTER II

Abraham: The Response

IN THE ELEVENTH chapter of the Epistle to the Hebrews—what someone has called "The Westminster Abbey of the Bible"—there is a roll call of the great heroes of the Hebrew faith. In this roll call, Abraham is mentioned three times. By faith Abraham heard the call of God and obeyed; by faith he sojourned in the land of Canaan; by faith he offered up his son Isaac (Hebrews 11:8, 9, 17).

We considered Abraham's call in the last chapter. It took faith to answer that call, and Abraham had faith; he "went out, not knowing where he was to go." He left Ur and Haran, which were in the land of Mesopotamia (we call it Iraq today), for Canaan. What were his thoughts? What did he know about Canaan?

Mesopotamia was in a period of a high degree of culture and well-developed civilization when Abraham shook its dust from his feet. So was Egypt. And the land of Canaan lay between Mesopotamia and Egypt. There was constant communication between these two great lands, as we know from the very detailed records now available.

Now the traveler from Egypt to Mesopotamia had to pass through the land of Canaan. We read in the records of one Egyptian traveler, an exile from the court of Pharaoh Sesotris I (1980–1936 B.C., which was about the time of Abraham), who passed through the land of milk and honey and left this written record about it: "Here are figs and grapes more wine than water; honey is plentiful, oil is all abundant; all kinds of fruit hang upon the trees. Barley and wheat grow in the fields, and there are countless herds of all types."[1] He went on to rejoice in the fact that his native language, Egyptian, was spoken in the Canaanite villages he visited. What he tells of the land was probably true of a part of the land, rather than of all of it. It was a delightful country, but still a backward country; it did not know the high level of civilization found in Egypt or Mesopotamia.

[1] The Story of Sinuhe in *Ancient Near Eastern Texts Relating to the Old Testament,* J. B. Pritchard, ed. (Princeton: Princeton University Press, 1955), 2nd ed., p. 19.

In the introduction of a fine atlas on Bible lands,[2] the editors point out a peculiar paradox about the land of Palestine. It was a land in association with the rest of the world of its day; it was the land bridge connecting the world of that day, namely: Asia Minor and the Hittite empire, Mesopotamia and the Babylonian and Sumerian civilizations, and Egypt. To get from one to the other, you had to go through Canaan, for Canaan lay at the heart of them. Literally, if you were to take a map of this world and draw an "X" across it, the crossing of the "X" would lie over Canaan, and the arms would stretch into Asia Minor and Babylonia and Egypt and the Arabian Peninsula. Canaan was the crossroads of the world—and yet, as these editors point out, it stood in *contrast* with the rest of world, in what they call "a splendid isolation." By and large the country was mountainous and not given to a network of highways. (There were two highways: one went along the coast, the other via the borderland of the Transjordanian Plateau, along the edge of the desert.) Canaan was separated from the rest of the world on the west by the sea, on the east by the desert, on the south by the desert, and on the north by mountains. So the people of Canaan, though on the trade routes connecting the rest of the world, were after all isolated by sea, desert, and mountain. They lived pretty much to themselves, and therefore their civilization was retarded, compared to the greater lands and peoples who surrounded them.

This is why, I believe, God wanted Abraham and his people in Canaan. Because, you see, when you are part of an ambitious nation in the midst of the confusion of the world, you have less chance of hearing God speak than when you are more isolated. The people of Canaan could keep up with what was going on in the world, if they wanted to. All they had to do was to ask the men in the caravans that passed through Canaan, "What's happening in Egypt? What's new in Mesopotamia?" They could keep up with the news, and yet be far enough removed from the hubbub of life to meditate, and listen for the voice of God.

Abraham was called to go and settle in this land. It took *faith,* as we have already said, for him to obey that call. The author of Hebrews tells us that "By faith Abraham obeyed. . . . By faith he sojourned in the land of promise. . . . For he looked forward to the city which has foundations, whose builder and maker is God" (Hebrews 11:8-10).

[2] *The Westminster Historical Atlas to the Bible,* G. E. Wright and F. V. Filson, eds. (Philadelphia: Westminster Press, 1956), 2nd ed., 130 pp.

It is a noteworthy fact of history that Ur perished. It fell into ruins, and the wind-driven dust of the desert buried it deep. We did not even know where it was until Sir Leonard Woolley and his archaeological expedition turned up its ruins in the 1920's and 1930's. That splendid city, capital of the magnificent Third Dynasty of Ur, was completely lost to history for nearly three thousand years. History records the same fate for Egypt. The great capital Memphis, for example—the "Noph" of the Old Testament, or "Moph," as it is sometimes called—is today little more than a few fallen statues covered with sand and weeds. But with the city whose builder and maker is God it is vastly different!

Jerusalem, to me, is a parable of this truth, for the Holy City has stood there all through the centuries; there Jerusalem shall always stand. The civilizations of Egypt and Mesopotamia have collapsed, but the faith of Abraham has endured, and been handed on down to us. Abraham had faith to believe that when God called him to leave Ur for Canaan, God meant business, and Abraham was ready to go into business with God. For this reason the Jew speaks reverently of "our father, Abraham"; for this reason the Arab calls him "the friend of God"; and for this reason the Christian looks upon him as the father of the Household of Faith (Galatians 3:7).

Abraham had a promise from God, as well as a call. The promise was that he would have a seed. We read in the twelfth chapter of Genesis: "I will make of you a great nation." And we find it mentioned again in the fifteenth chapter: "After these things the word of the Lord came to Abram in a vision, 'Fear not, Abram, I am your shield; your reward shall be very great.' But Abram said, 'O Lord God, what wilt thou give me, for I continue childless, and the heir of my house is Eliezer of Damascus?' [Eliezer was his slave.] And Abram said, 'Behold, thou hast given me no offspring; and a slave born in my house shall be my heir'" (15:1-3). That may seem strange to us, but it was the custom of the day. We know, thanks to the discovery of certain ancient clay tablets that have been dug up in Mesopotamia, that when a man was childless, a slave born in his house inherited his estate.[3] But the Lord said, "This man shall not be your heir; your own son shall be your heir. And he brought him outside and said, 'Look toward

---

[3] For this and other customs of the day, see E. Chiera, *They Wrote on Clay* (Chicago: University of Chicago Press, 1938), 233 pp. A paperback edition (Phoenix Books) was published in 1957. See also C. H. Gordon, *The Living Past* (New York: John Day Co., 1941), pp. 156-178.

heaven, and number the stars, if you are able to number them. . . . So shall your descendants be.' And he believed the Lord; and he reckoned it to him as righteousness" (15:4-6).

Abraham, we are led to believe, had faith in that promise of God, faith that God would fulfill it, and raise up from his "seed" a great multitude. Or—did he? Suppose we study it, closely.

Go back to Genesis 12 and read: "Now there was a famine in the land [that is, of course, after they reached Canaan]. So Abraham went down to Egypt to sojourn there, for the famine was severe in the land. And when he was about to enter Egypt he said to Sarai his wife, 'I know you are a woman beautiful to behold; when the Egyptians see you they will say, "This is his wife"; then they will kill me and let you live. Say you are my sister, that it may go well with me because of you, and that my life may be spared on your account' " (12:10-13).

Just think of the possibilities in all this! It was, of course, not a *complete* lie; we know that Sarai was Abraham's half-sister. But by presenting Sarai as his sister Abraham was putting God's promise into jeopardy. For if one of the Egyptians were to look upon her and fall in love with her and take her to be his wife, and if Sarai should bear a child to that Egyptian, the promise of God would come to nought. It may come to us as a surprise that God used the pagan Pharaoh to frustrate that plan.

At that particular time, Egypt had reached one of the high peaks of her history. The history of Egypt could be represented by a curved line with three or four peaks or elevations along the line; the main periods that we call the "Old Kingdom" and the "Middle Kingdom" are two of the highest peaks.[4] Like Mesopotamia, Egypt had had a history that stretched far back into antiquity. Four thousand years before Christ the Egyptians were already refining copper and making pottery; they had boats on the Nile; they lived in villages. Three thousand years before Christ they had invented a system of writing which continued to be used right on down into Christian times. The hieroglyphs on the tombs and monuments and stelae of Egypt had been invented more than a thousand years before Abraham's day.

The Great Pyramids had been built in the Old Kingdom period (2700-2200 B.C.). The greatest of the pyramids built by Cheops in the Fourth Dynasty, the "Great Pyramid of Gizeh," contains 2,300,000

[4] See G. Steindorff and K. C. Seele, *When Egypt Ruled the East* (Chicago: University of Chicago Press, 1942), 284 pp.

blocks of granite, each one of them weighing several tons. The height of the pyramid was 481 feet; its sides were 755 feet long, and according to one of the scholars who has made a comprehensive study of the pyramids,[5] the precision with which these blocks were cut and worked into shape was so accurate that when the blocks were laid up it was not necessary to put mortar between the courses—they fit precisely. The pyramid is as close to square as it is possible for any structure to be square. Modern engineering methods could not improve upon the shape and the tooling of those stones. "Precision, organized labor, planning, varied personnel (from drudges to masons and up to the master architect), and the backing of the entire economy were necessary" to establish the greatest of the seven wonders of the ancient world, says Cyrus Gordon, and he reminds us that of all of the seven wonders of the ancient world, it is the only one that exists down to the present time.[6]

This pyramid was already seven hundred years old when Abraham and his people were there, the time when Abraham lost his faith temporarily and said, "Don't say you are my wife; tell them you are my sister." And it took an Egyptian Pharaoh to remind Abraham of the moral question involved. Pharaoh called Abraham (12:18-19) and said, "What is this you have done to me? Why did you not tell me that she was your wife? Why did you say, 'She is my sister,' so that I took her for my wife? Now then, here is your wife, take her, and be gone." And he sent Abraham away.

The faith of Abraham and his wife Sarah is portrayed for us again in the story of Sarah and her handmaid, Hagar. Read the opening verses (Genesis 16:1-2): "Now Sarai, Abram's wife, bore him no children. She had an Egyptian maid whose name was Hagar; and Sarai said to Abram, 'Behold now, the Lord has prevented me from bearing children; go in to my maid; it may be that I shall obtain children by her.'"

That, too, was the custom of the time. I know that the morals involved in this offend many Christians of the twentieth century A.D., but Abraham and Sarah were not living in the twentieth century A.D. They had never heard the words of Jesus Christ. They had never read the

---

[5] I. E. S. Edwards, *The Pyramids of Egypt* ("Pelican Books"; Baltimore: Penguin Books, 1947), 256 pp.

[6] C. H. Gordon, *Introduction to Old Testament Times* (Ventnor, N. J.: Ventnor Publishers, 1953), p. 48.

Ten Commandments of Moses. They lived before those things. And they were following the custom of their day. We have marriage contracts which were dug up at Nuzu (near modern Kirkuk, Iraq), in which the details of the marriage are set down and agreed to and signed by each of the parties contracting, signed by the witnesses, and their seals rolled across the face of the tablet, to make it a marriage contract; in these contracts the woman promises to give her husband children. It is stated in some of the contracts, where the details are given more fully, that if she cannot produce children herself, she shall provide them through her handmaid.[7] Now, she signed a *contract* to do that; and I have no doubt that Sarah had agreed to a similar contract with Abraham, and was fulfilling the contract. She had no children. So she was to have a child, Ishmael, through Hagar. Of course this was lack of faith on the part both of Abraham and Sarah. We can excuse the morality of it, when we consider the customs of the day, but we cannot blame their lack of faith on the customs of the day.

In Genesis 17:15-17 we read: "And God said to Abraham, 'As for Sarai your wife, you shall not call her name Sarai, but Sarah shall be her name. I will bless her, and moreover I will give you a son by her; I will bless her, and she shall be a mother of nations; kings of people shall come from her.' Then Abraham fell on his face and laughed, and said to himself, 'Shall a child be born to a man who is a hundred years old? Shall Sarah, who is ninety years old, bear a child?'" In the eighteenth chapter, Sarah was told by the messengers of God that she was to bear a child and, remembering her age, she burst into laughter. God said to Abraham, "Why did Sarah laugh?" Sarah denied it, but God was not mocked: "But you *did* laugh!" Neither of them, you see, had the faith to believe that God could give them a child so late in life.

As we go on and read of the casting out of Hagar, after the child Ishmael was born, after Sarah had conceived in her old age and given birth to Isaac, we see another sign of lack of faith. It was all clearly covered by the laws of the time. Legally, Sarah had the right to send Hagar away; for Hagar was Sarah's property. Abraham admitted that. But the law of the day also said specifically that if the man's wife is unable to conceive, and if her handmaid does, and produces a child for the family, and then, later, the legal wife has a son of her own, the son of her handmaid takes second place. If Hagar had stayed there

[7] See C. H. Gordon, "Biblical Customs and the Nuzu Tablets," *The Biblical Archaeologist,* 3 (1940), pp. 2-3.

with Ishmael, there was no question at all about the lineage or inheritance according to the laws of the day: Ishmael would have been second to Isaac. There was no need to drive out Hagar. There was no need to drive out Ishmael. It was simply lack of faith, on the part of Abraham and Sarah.

I mention these things because I want you to see, when we are talking about a man who stands as *the* man of faith in all of history, that his faith may not always have been 100 per cent. Some of you, at times, will be discouraged because your faith is so weak. Take heart! Even Abraham, the father of all the faithful, was a man whose faith was not always quite strong enough.

In addition to numerous descendants, Abraham was also promised a land, the land of Canaan. We read in Genesis 15:13-15, "Then the Lord said to Abraham, 'Know of a surety that your descendants will be sojourners in a land that is not theirs, and will be slaves there, and they will be oppressed for four hundred years; but I will bring judgment on the nation which they serve, and afterward they shall come out with great possessions. As for yourself, you shall go to your fathers in peace; you shall be buried in good old age. And they shall come back here in the fourth generation.'" God draws the boundaries of the land in the eighteenth verse: ". . . from the river of Egypt to the great river, the river Euphrates." The river of Egypt mentioned here is not the Nile, but the little seasonal river (or wadi) in the desert south of the land of Canaan, quite a bit north of the Nile. Its modern name is Wadi el-'Arish. God determined where this land was to be, and that it was to belong to Abraham and his descendants. But—think of it!—Abraham was not to live long enough to enjoy it. He would die there. But his sons and grandsons and great grandsons would be exiled, driven out of it. It would not be theirs until the fourth generation.

Abraham actually dwelled in the new land for about a hundred years, and at the end of that time, how much of Canaan do you think he owned? Only a little burial plot he had bought of the Hittites, where he could lay Sarah's bones to rest! That was all he had. He *lived* there, but he never *owned* the land. If ever you have questioned his faith, your questions should be answered as you watch him in this experience, recorded in the twenty-third chapter.

Sarah died at Kiriath-arba in the land of Canaan; we know it better as Hebron. Grieving and heartbroken, Abraham turned to the Hittites and said to them, "I am a stranger and a sojourner among you.

Give me property among you, for a burying place." Then in true Oriental manner, they bargained: "Oh, we couldn't sell it to *you*! Just go ahead and take it." And Abraham replied, in effect, "Oh, no, gentlemen; I couldn't take it that way. How much do you want for it?" "Well, it's worth $250—but what is that among friends? Take it and bury your dead." So Abraham paid the amount suggested. According to the seventeenth verse, "the field with the cave in it, the field of Ephron and Machpelah, which was to the east of Mamre, the field with the cave which was in it and all the trees that were in the field, throughout its whole area, was made over to Abraham as a possession in the presence of the Hittites, before all who went in at the gate of his city." So he buried his wife there, in what had become his possession. It was Abraham's way of taking a pledge for four hundred years; four hundred years later his great grandchildren would come back and take over this land, and it would be theirs.

Now we come to the really great test of his faith, in Genesis 22, where God tells him to take his son—the son that he didn't have enough faith to believe he was going to have, and that Sarah didn't have enough faith to believe that she would be able to bear—he was to take this child Isaac "up unto the Mount of Moriah" (which is at the present time under the temple area in the city of Jerusalem) and offer him as a burnt offering. Genesis 22:2 says, "Take your son, your only son Isaac, whom you love. . . ." I think each phrase that God spoke to Abraham, must have stabbed another knife into his heart. "Take your son . . . your only son . . . Isaac . . . the one that you love . . . and offer him there as a burnt offering. . . ." By this time Abraham had become a man of tremendous faith. He was a man of faith before, but his faith was weak at times. This time it is great.

Try to understand what is involved. God had promised Abraham that his seed, his posterity, would be the hope of the whole world—not his slave Eliezer, not the son of his handmaid Hagar, Ishmael, but the son of Sarah would be the one who would fulfill that promise. Now God asked him to sacrifice the boy! It would have been hard enough to offer up Eliezer, who had worked for him all of those years; it would have been hard enough to offer up Ishmael, because he loved the lad and wept when he was sent away. It would have been hard enough if God had come and asked Abraham to offer his own life as a sacrifice. But, if he had offered his own life, there would still have been Isaac to carry out the promise. But God did not ask that. God put

His finger on the only person through whom the promise could be fulfilled, and said, "Offer *him* up."

If Isaac were killed, all of the promises that had been made to Abraham would become of no value. Yet Abraham was willing to go through with it. And the writer of the Epistle to the Hebrews gives us some suggestion of why. Some men say, "Abraham had faith to believe that God would not ask him to go all the way through with it; he had the feeling that God would take him up there on the mountain and then would back down and give him a second choice." *That* is not faith! The writer of Hebrews tells us that Abraham was so sure that God would be able to raise up that child *from the dead*, if necessary, that he was willing to go through and offer him up. *That* is faith!

In a way, you and I stand in the same relation to the world as Abraham did. There is a sense in which our children and our children's children have their faith because we keep ours. And the world that still needs the salvation which God provides can only hope for that salvation through those of us who have that faith. Abraham was imperfect and his faith was weak, but at the end, when he came to the last great test, he came through triumphant. You and I are expected to have that same faith that takes God at His word, faith that believes God means it when He tells us that He is going to save this world through His own Son.

I can never think about the willingness of Abraham to offer up his son Isaac without thinking of the willingness of God to offer up His Son Jesus. God provided a lamb to take the place of Isaac, but there was no lamb to take the place of Jesus. *He was the Lamb!* You and I have our life and our salvation and our hope of eternity because of what God has done for us in Christ; and the only way this world will ever come to know the salvation that we know will be by way of our faithfulness. God expects us to be faithful.

CHAPTER III

Jacob

THE THIRTY-SECOND chapter of Genesis contains the story of one of the most famous wrestling-bouts in all history. It is worth repeating.

The same night he arose and took his two wives, his two maids, and his eleven children, and crossed the ford of the Jabbok. He took them and sent them across the stream, and likewise everything that he had. And Jacob was left alone; and a man wrestled with him until the breaking of the day. When the man saw that he did not prevail against Jacob, he touched the hollow of his thigh; and Jacob's thigh was put out of joint as he wrestled with him. Then he said, "Let me go, for the day is breaking." But Jacob said, "I will not let you go, unless you bless me." And he said to him, "What is your name?" And he said, "Jacob." Then he said, "Your name shall no more be called Jacob, but Israel, for you have striven with God and with men, and have prevailed." Then Jacob said, "Tell me, I pray you, your name." But he said, "Why is it that you ask my name?" And there he blessed him. So Jacob called the name of the place Peniel, saying, "For I have seen God face to face, and yet my life is preserved." (Genesis 32:22-30)

This is Jacob, son of Isaac, grandson of the mighty Abraham. His life may be presented as a drama in three acts. The first act deals with the men he knew, and loved or despised; and the first of these men is Isaac. Isaac is hardly worth a chapter of his own in this book: he committed the sins of his father Abraham, he made no advances on the faith of that father, and he was, all in all, a rather colorless personality. And yet, in Hebrews 11:20, we read that "by faith Isaac invoked future blessings on Jacob and Esau"—and that makes him important.

If Isaac had lived in the Christian dispensation, we might call him a "second generation Christian"—that is, one who grew up knowing Christ not from his own experience but through parents who knew Him. Isaac was typical of that kind of religion. It is true, in the light of the total picture, that he did have some appreciation of spiritual values. Many Christians, you know, fail to find in the Christianity which they get from their parents a source of power for their own lives.

Isaac was not quite as bad as that. With all his weaknesses, with all his lack of color, in spite of the fact that "this world was too much with him," he still blessed Jacob and Esau and passed on to them the great spiritual blessings that were his.

Jacob was his mother Rebekah's favorite; Esau was the favorite of his father. There are several scenes proving that. You will remember that Isaac was getting along in life, and that in his old age, thinking he was near the end, he asked for a dish of venison stew. Esau, the hunter, the man of the fields could provide that; if he would bring it, Isaac said, he would give his son the parental blessing. Off goes Esau—and in comes Rebekah!

They lived in tents, in those days, and it was not hard for Rebekah to "listen in" from the other side of the goat-hair cloth, or from another part of the tent. She heard it, and she rushed to Jacob. We can almost hear her saying, "Get busy now, son, *quickly*. We'll get that blessing for you!" Jacob liked the idea—but there was one hitch. Jacob had been born with a smooth, soft skin, while his brother Esau had rough, hair-covered skin; when the blind father touched him in giving the blessing, he would know immediately that he was touching Jacob, and not Esau. "Perhaps my father will feel me," suggests Jacob, "and I shall seem to be mocking him, and bring a curse upon myself and not a blessing." That did not stop Rebekah; she covered the backs of his hands and neck with a rough goat's skin, so that when the old man touched it, he would think he was touching Esau. It was a deception that seems incredible on the part of any mother and wife.

You can lay part of the blame on Rebekah, but the larger part of the deception was Jacob's. When the father asks, "Who are you, my son?" Jacob replies, "I am Esau, your first-born. I have done as you told me; now sit up and eat of my game, that you may bless me." Isaac is suspicious: "How is it that you have found it so quickly?" Then Jacob adds blasphemy to lie: "Because the Lord your God granted me success." Still uncertain, blind Isaac would touch his son: "Come near, that I may feel you, my son. . . ." He will know the difference, thanks to his well-developed sense of touch, between smooth-skinned Jacob and rough-skinned Esau. And he touches the goat-skin, and says, pitifully, "The voice is Jacob's voice, but the hands are the hands of Esau!" He asks the question a third time: "Are you *really* my son Esau?" And again the lie: "I am."

It is an awesome picture of deception—and the guilt lies upon all three: on Jacob, for it was he who gave the direct lie; on Rebekah, for it was she who planned the lie; and upon Isaac, the overfond parent whose favoritism toward one of his sons sowed the seeds of dissension which were to wreak such havoc later in the family.

Esau, as the second man in Jacob's life, is worth careful consideration. When Jacob was born, according to the story in Genesis 25, he was born as the twin of Esau. Esau was the first-born. There was a struggle between the two in the womb of the mother and Jacob was delivered holding on to the heel of Esau, so he was named "Jacob," "a supplanter"—one who sought to take the place of his brother.

Now, of course, we know that at such an early age there could have been no decision of self-expression in the minds or wills of the children being born. Paul holds, in his argument in Romans, that this was a case of divine sovereignty and election, and not at all the choice of the child. Nevertheless, a bitterness developed between the two which ripened, in later life, into hatred. For instance, read the story of the selling of the birthright, in Genesis 25:29-34. Esau comes in from his hunting famished and finds Jacob boiling pottage. He begs for some of it. Jacob is willing to share the meal with his hungry brother, but, "First, sell me your birthright!" Esau, stabbed with pangs of hunger, says, "I am about to die; of what use is a birthright to me?" So he sells it to his brother Jacob for a mess of pottage! It sounds strange to us, especially when we know more about what that birthright was. It was the precious right of primogeniture: the first-born son had the right to take his father's place upon the father's death and become the head, the ruling member of the family.

We know from the Nuzu tablets that were discovered near Kirkuk in 1926, that one of the important elements of life in that day was the birthright, which could be bought and sold. For example, Kurpazah, the son of Hilbishuh, obtained a grove belonging to his brother Tupkitilla in exchange for three sheep.[1] Apparently Tupkitilla, too, was hungry; he wanted something to eat so badly that he was willing to sell his birthright to get it: he gave away his right to his father's fruitful orchard for a mouthful to eat!

Perhaps there is another side to this story that seems so hard to understand. It is possible that some men held the birthright so cheaply because they did not want the headache that went with it, for the birthright was not only a privilege but a responsibility. You see, from the

[1] See C. H. Gordon, *The Living Past*, p. 177.

time he became the elder in the family, the holder of the birthright had to make all decisions for the family. It was in my lifetime and yours too, that a man gave up the crown of the British Empire for the woman he loved; and many of us felt that it may have been not just for the woman he loved, but also for the desire to escape the responsibility, the burden of being tied down to the cares of the Empire. Esau was simply not interested in his birthright and what it implied—the religious heritage as well as the cultural heritage of Isaac. Esau was of the earth, earthy, a worldly man; he had no sense of values. That is illustrated again, I think, by the fact that he was so careless of his father's will that he went out and married two Hittite women, even though it was the expressed desire of the patriarch that the wives of these men should not be Canaanites or Hittites, but of the same stock as the patriarchs themselves, namely Hebrew women. Esau's whole life was a renunciation of the values of Abraham and Isaac. He just did not care about those things.

The third significant man in Jacob's life is Laban, his uncle. You remember the story of how, after the hatred between Esau and Jacob had developed to the place where it was no longer safe for Jacob to stay home, his mother sent him away, and he went to live with his Uncle Laban, his mother's brother; and of how he met Rachel and fell in love with her. He worked seven years and then another seven for her.

Now I have no certain knowledge from the Scripture itself, but I think, judging from the customs of the times, that we have here what is known as a marriage adoption. No sons of Laban are mentioned at this time; they are mentioned later. According to the custom of the day, a man who had no sons of his own to look after him in his old age, and to take over the right of primogeniture and carry on the family and the family tradition, could marry his daughter to a young man under a marriage adoption contract, in which, in exchange for giving his daughter to this young man, he took the young man as his son and conferred upon him the rights of sonship. It is further stated in those marriage documents that should a son, a *true* son, be born to the man later, that son would take the place of primogeniture and the son-in-law (the adopted son) would lose it. I think that is what must have happened in the case of Jacob with Laban, because later on we come across a reference to Laban's sons, and Laban is sending Jacob off without the rights, or the title. Jacob would have lost it entirely except for the fact that Rachel stole the teraphim, originally the

images of the family gods,[2] possession of which we know now was
guarantee to the title. The person who held the teraphim was the person
who could prove thereby that he had claim to all of the property of the
father. When Rachel stole the teraphim, it was not because she was worshiping them, but because she knew that if she did not hold on to them,
her husband Jacob would never have any legal claim on Laban's estate.[3]

Well, Laban was a hard man to work for. We read in the story that
after Jacob had served his seven years he woke up the morning after
the wedding to find that he had been given the less desirable Leah,
Rachel's older sister, instead of his beloved Rachel. Of course he objected; but Laban told him, "It is not so done in our country to give
the younger before the first-born. Complete the week of this one and
we will give you the other also—in return for serving me another
seven years" (29:26). Jacob—and how we admire him for it!—accepted
the bargain; he married Rachel at the end of the week, and he worked
seven more long years to keep her. And six years beyond that.

His wages were to be a part of Laban's flocks; he was to have every
speckled and spotted sheep and every black lamb, and every spotted
and speckled goat. Jacob worked on, in good faith, only to be double-
crossed by the crafty uncle again: the very day of the agreement, Laban
cut out of his flocks every speckled and spotted lamb, sheep, and goat,
and hid them from Jacob, putting a distance of three days' journey between himself and Jacob! It was a detestable trick—but this time Jacob
won: read Genesis 30:37-43 to see how he did it. It was one man of
guile against another, but in the end, Jacob comes off the better man.
Jacob sums up his experience with Laban in Genesis 31:41-42: "These
twenty years I have been in your house; I have served you fourteen
years for your two daughters, and six years for your flock, and you
have changed my wages ten times. If the God of my father, the God of

[2] The word *teraphim* is a Hebrew plural. If this strikes the reader as polytheism or idolatry, let us remember that there was, until the Exile, a constant
struggle between the purer form of Jehovah-worship and the idolatry and polytheism of the common people. If this had not been so, there would have been
no reason for the command, "Thou shalt have no other gods . . ." and no
reason for the preaching of the prophets. Nor would the words of Genesis 35:2
to Jacob have been necessary, "Put away the foreign gods that are among you."
[3] A different view is given in P. Heinisch, *History of the Old Testament,* W.
Heidt, trans. (Collegeville, Minn.: Liturgical Press, 1952), p. 58. This Roman
Catholic author suggests that Rachel wanted to be able to invoke the gods'
protection and deprive Laban of their power. Where Scripture is silent, the Bible
student must be content with *probable* explanations.

Abraham, and the Fear of Isaac had not been on my side, surely now you would have sent me away empty-handed. God saw my affliction and the labor of my hands, and rebuked you. . . ."

That was Laban, and that was Jacob. We can sum it up by studying the response of Jacob to the people around him. He was a man of deception; he had learned that from his mother. He *had* to deceive to get along with his father, to get along with his brother, to get along with his crafty uncle. At least, he thought he did. He was the first one of a long line to follow the principle that "the end justifies the means." Do evil that good may come!

Now look at Jacob and the women in his life. There was, of course, his mother, Rebekah, a strong character but a sly one. We have already mentioned her deception of her husband Isaac. When Jacob suggested that they might get caught, and that he would receive a curse instead of a blessing, she said, "Upon me be your curse, my son; only obey my word and go. . . ." Well, for her deception she lost her son. She was forced to send him away and she never saw him again. When he returned, she was dead.

His wife Rachel is the second important woman in his life, and with her we see Jacob in a different light. Here we have one of those facets of character that show up to tell us that Jacob is not all bad. We learn that he was a strong man. We had not known about that side of his nature until we read about how he came near to the house of Laban and saw the shepherds around the well. There was a large stone on the mouth of the well, so large that no one shepherd was able to move it. But when Jacob saw Rachel, he walked over and moved the stone all by himself. He was a big burly man, and he was going to show this beautiful young girl that he was the kind of man that she ought to marry. Then he fell in love with her. He must have really fallen in love, because he used none of his guile or craft to get her. We read in 29:20 the simple statement that Jacob "served seven years for Rachel, and they seemed to him but a few days because of the love he had for her." We see a different side of the man there. There is a tenderness of character, a depth of devotion, a real sense of value when it comes to the one truly-loved woman in his life.

There were others, of course. There were the Hittite sisters-in-law, the women whom Esau married, who gave him so much trouble. There was his daughter Dinah who was ravished by one of the men of the neighborhood, who later, but for the objections of her brothers, would have married her: the affair ended in a massacre. But Jacob was no ruthless murderer as were his sons. His response, especially in the area of the women of his life, was one of sorrow and suffering and separation.

Last of all, we come to study the relations between Jacob and his God. There are four episodes, or four scenes, here. Scene 1: Bethel. Jacob falls asleep and dreams a dream in which he sees a ladder from heaven to earth, with angels going up and coming down. God comes to him (Genesis 28:13) and repeats the promise He had made to Abraham: "I am the Lord, the God of Abraham your father, and the God of Isaac; the land on which you lie I will give to you and to your descendants; and your descendants shall be like the dust of the earth, and you shall spread abroad to the west and to the east and to the north and to the south; and by you and your descendants shall all the families of the earth bless themselves. Behold, I am with you and will keep you wherever you go, and will bring you back to this land; for I will not leave you until I have done that of which I have spoken to you" (28:13-15). It was the promise that God would always be with Jacob, that the God of his fathers was *his* God.

Scene 2: Jabbok. (Read Genesis 32:22-32.) Jacob wrestles with the angel of the Lord. Here his name is changed to Israel; it is actually the great moment of change for his whole life. All the deception and guile, all the lies and blasphemous pretense, seem to go out of his life with this event. He becomes a mellow man, touched not only in the thigh by the angel of the Lord, but in the heart by the Lord Himself. Throughout the rest of his life we find him a moderating influence trying to hold those unruly sons of his together, protesting when they rise up in the affair of Dinah, telling them, "You have brought trouble on me by making me odious to the inhabitants of the land ..." (34:30). They had. And *he* had, in the past. But the past was past. It was over and done. This is a new Jacob now. He has broken with the people and the gods of his yesterdays. He calls his family together (35:9) and tells them to put away their foreign gods and idols, the gods and idols they had brought out of Padan-Aram. He is quits with these things. He is God's man now.

Scene 3: The second episode at Bethel. In chapter 35, God renews the Bethel episode, because as I see it, between the first Bethel and the second, Jacob had moved out of the country to Mesopotamia, to Padan-Aram, and now he had come back into the land. We have here one of the clear-cut indications of Scripture that God's promise to Israel is directly associated with the land of Israel. While Jacob was in that land, God promised to bless him. When he had moved out of the land, apparently no blessing followed except through providential oversight. But when he comes back, God renews the promise and tells him that He will be with him, and that Jacob will be a means whereby the people of the world are to be blessed. God renews the statement, "Your name is . . . no longer Jacob, but Israel . . ."; and renews the promise, ". . . the land which I gave to Abraham and Isaac I will give to you, and I will give the land to your descendants after you" (35:9). I personally do not believe that the promises made to Israel can have any final fulfillment except in the land of Israel. I believe that God has tied down His promises to Israel to that particular spot of the earth, and I believe that He will keep His word and bless that region for His Name's sake.

Scene 4: Just before Jacob goes into Egypt, when he is down at Beersheba at the southern end of the land. God comes to him and says, "I am God, the God of your father; do not be afraid to go down to Egypt; for I will there make of you a great nation. I will go down with you to Egypt and I will also bring you up again; and Joseph's hand shall close your eyes" (46:1-4). That was a remarkable revelation! Up until this time His people seem to have the idea that as long as they stay in Canaan, God will be there, but when they move out of Canaan, God will not go with them. But now God says clearly, "You are going to Egypt. You are going with my permission. I am going with you." And they begin to get a bigger view of God and a better understanding of His will.

The name of Jacob appears many times in the Bible; I have read somewhere that it appears more often than any other name except the names of God. And it is interesting that God regularly calls Himself "the God of Jacob." And when the Scripture refers to "the God of Israel," it does not refer to Jacob as a person, but to Israel as a people, as the descendants of Jacob; but when God refers to a person, He calls Himself the God of Jacob: "I am the God of Abraham and of Isaac and of Jacob." For Jacob is the old fleshly name of the man, isn't it? Jacob is called Israel only after his experience with God. But God is not ashamed to be called even the God of Jacob.

I think there is a lesson for us in that. God loved Jacob not because he was already Israel, but because he was Jacob. God loves you and me not for what we can become but just *because He loves us*. He does not ask that we be perfect; He does not ask that our characters be completely purified of all their worldly elements. He did not ask that of Jacob. Jacob was in many respects as despicable a character as you could hope to find; he was crafty and shrewd and cunning and deceptive and there were many other things that you could say about him. But Jacob was also a man who was true to the faith that had been given to him by his father; and God was true to the promise that He had made to Abraham. God will bless you and He will bless me, not for what we are, but for what He is, because He is God and because He has promised to be our God and the God and Father of our children. We should be deeply grateful to Him, as Jacob came to be, for all of His blessings, and we should serve Him faithfully and well.

CHAPTER IV

Joseph

JOSEPH is one of the most lovable characters in the Old Testament; his is one of the most beautiful and best-told stories in the Book, from the standpoint of literature and storytelling, as well as containing an abundance of religious and spiritual values. For the sake of continuity and understanding, suppose we divide the story of Joseph into four parts. First: the story of Joseph and his brothers, as it is told in Genesis 37.

Joseph was a lad of seventeen at that time, and like many seventeen-year-old children he was inclined to be conceited. He thought he was "pretty good"—he had some reason to think that—and he let his brothers and his father and mother know just how good he was. There is a chip-on-the-shoulder attitude here, a little of the "fresh-kid" attitude that you would like to take out of him. As you read the story you have at the beginning almost a feeling of antagonism against this young fellow, rather than sympathy for him; you feel as though he is getting, in a way, "what's coming to him."

First, there is the dream: "Now Joseph had a dream, and when he told it to his brothers they only hated him the more. He said to them, 'Hear this dream which I have dreamed: behold, we were binding sheaves in the field, and lo, my sheaf arose and stood upright; and behold, your sheaves gathered around it, and bowed down to my sheaf.'" Well, that is *not* one of the ways to win friends and influence people! The brothers "hated him yet more for his dreams and for his words." Then he dreamed another dream and said, "Behold I have dreamed another dream; and behold, the sun, the moon, and eleven stars were bowing down to me." When he told it to his father and his brothers, "his father rebuked him and said to him, 'What is this dream that you have dreamed? Shall I and your mother and your brothers indeed come to bow ourselves to the ground before you?' And his brothers were jealous of him, but his father kept the saying in mind" (37:5-11).

Much as you feel as though you would like to shake the boy for this display of conceit, you have to realize that there was, as in the case of Jacob, an element of parental fault. Go back a little further in the thirty-seventh chapter and read verse 3, "Now Israel [that is Jacob] loved Joseph more than any other of his children, because he was the son of his old age. . . ." I am not trying to excuse Joseph. I feel that he had something coming to him, and God apparently felt so too, and saw that he got it. But we must understand that Joseph was not entirely to blame; Jacob must at least share part of the blame for making a pet of the boy—and not only for making a pet of him, but for letting the rest of the family know that Joseph was the chosen.

Jacob made him a beautiful garment. The familiar translation is "a coat of many colors." The Hebrew does not say that; rather, it seems to suggest that it was a garment with long sleeves and long legs, or at least that it came down to his ankles. The exact color and shape we do not know; but we do know that it was an indication that this boy was favored above the others. And he was comparatively a newcomer to the family! The older brothers had already won their spurs, or thought they had; and to have this young upstart suddenly given a place of favor in his father's eyes, to have the sign of his father's favor flaunted before them every time he came out of the tent wearing that coat—this was "hard to take." But, as if that were not enough, then to have him dream those dreams and come and rub *that* in was still harder to take. So they plotted to get rid of him.

We read that they were "keeping the flock," and the father said to Joseph, "You go up and see how your brothers are getting along." I wonder why he was not already up there with them, helping to take care of the flock? He was old enough to be working. David was a shepherd long before he was seventeen. Perhaps this is another indication of some of the father's favoritism that was getting Joseph into trouble.

So Joseph went up to Shechem to find out what was going on. Now the family lived in the neighborhood of Hebron, and Hebron is about twenty miles south of Jerusalem; in Joseph's day, when walking was the only way to get there, it would have been a good day's travel. Shechem is near the mountains of Samaria (Gerizim and Ebal), thirty or forty miles north of Jerusalem; so that altogether it was a journey of two or three long days of hiking. And when he got there, he found that they had moved still farther north to the area of Dothan, which is another ten or fifteen miles north of Shechem. But you realize that in those days, when people were nomadic, when they pastured their flocks wherever they could find good pasture land, it was nothing for the nomad to roam over an area two or three hundred miles long, moving back and forth with the weather, hunting pasture land for his flock.[1]

Well, when they saw this young man coming (and of course he was wearing the blazer that his father had given him, proclaiming that he was his father's pet), they said, "Let's get rid of him; let's be done with this lord of dreams." They decided to kill him. But one of the brothers intervened and instead they put him in a pit and then sold him to a caravan that came along.

One of the points at which critics have attacked the credibility of the Old Testament is in the matter of the camels. There is mention of camels in the life of Abraham, and again here in the life of Joseph; but the critics tell us that camels had not been domesticated in that part of the world that early in history. But we now have proof to the contrary. Professor Cyrus Gordon points out that "the mention of camels here in Abraham's story and elsewhere in the patriarchal narrative, is often considered anachronistic. However, the correctness of the Bible is supported by the representation of camel-riding on seal cylinders of precisely this period from North Mesopotamia."[2]

There was a widespread commerce in that day across the Middle East, from Egypt up into Asia Minor among the Hittite peoples (or the Proto-Hittite peoples), and over into Mesopotamia. And that commerce had to go, as I suggested in our first chapter, through the area that we know as Palestine or "Canaan." There was no other way from Egypt to the Hittite country; they had to skirt the eastern end of the Mediterranean—which took them through Palestine. And there was no other safe road from Egypt to Mesopotamia. It would have been possible, of course, to cut straight across the desert. I flew across that route a few years ago and could see countless caravan tracks beneath the plane. But in the patriarchal period, it would have been extremely dangerous; and even today, desert raiders make the trip hazardous. So

[1] As a matter of fact, the nomad cattle-grazer in the Middle East still follows the same habits. Property lines, fences, even international boundaries are meaningless to the nomad.

[2] *Introduction to Old Testament Times*, p. 111. Gordon gives a reference to *Iraq* 6 (1939), plate II, 9. Cf. J. P. Free, "Abraham's Camels," *Journal of Near Eastern Studies* 3 (1944), pp. 187-193. It should be added that some recent scholars tend to lower Abraham's dates to about 1500 B.C., and the mention of the camel is taken as helping to confirm this date.

caravans made the long circuitous trip by way of the "Fertile Crescent" —the fertile strip along the edge of the desert. It was because these trade routes passed through Canaan that the cultural level of Canaan had been raised. It was not as high as in Egypt or Mesopotamia, but we make a serious mistake if we think of the people of Canaan as completely ignorant. According to Professor Albright, there were four, and possibly five different systems of writing used in Canaan in the patriarchal period.[3] In Joseph's day, Canaan may have been under the control of the Egyptians—I say, "may have been," only because we cannot locate Joseph's dates precisely.

Joseph was sold to one of the caravans, which was going in the direction of Egypt. They took him along and sold him on the slave market when they got there, according to Genesis 37:28. The other sons went back home to their father with Joseph's robe, which they had dipped in the blood of a goat they had killed, and said, "We found this; is it your son's robe or not?"—and let the father draw his own conclusions.

The second scene is Joseph in Egypt, which begins in the thirty-ninth chapter of Genesis, the thirty-eighth chapter being an interlude in the story, possibly for dramatic effect.

When was Joseph in Egypt? We found, when we were talking about Abraham, that we could not be certain of the year. The Bible, for this period, does not give us statements which can be positively equated with historical dates, and as a result, we have to allow a "margin of error" of about ten per cent in our calculations. We felt that the date of 2000 B.C., plus-or-minus two hundred years, was reasonable for Abraham. Joseph would, of course, have to be put about 290 years later, according to the Biblical chronology: in other words, about 1700 B.C.

Working in ancient history is like trying to fit together the pieces of a gigantic jigsaw puzzle. Those of us who are historians work with the pieces of history from the various data preserved for us on monuments, inscriptions, letters, etc., and when they *seem* to present a recognizable picture, we feel that we may have the solution. We do not claim to have *all* the pieces, nor do we claim to have placed the known pieces with perfect finality. Recognizing these limitations, we suggest that the picture of Joseph as presented in the Bible is most consistent with the facts of history if we put him in the period of the Hyksos.

[3] W. F. Albright, *The Archaeology of Palestine* (Pelican Books; Baltimore: Penguin Books, rev. 1954), pp. 185-190.

The Hyksos period in Egyptian history is called the "Second Intermediate Age," and dated 1780-1546 B.C. The name "Hyksos" was defined by the ancient historian Manetho as "shepherd kings," and this definition can still be found in many books. Modern scholars identify the word as meaning "rulers of foreign lands." The Thirteenth and Fourteenth Dynasties of Egypt had gotten into internal strife that had weakened the country, and then the foreign rulers came in (the Fiftheenth and Sixteenth Dynasties) and took over.[4]

These Hyksos were described by the Greek historians as Phoenician. In the light of modern knowledge it seems that they were Canaanites mixed with Indo-Europeans who had come from the north (perhaps the area we know as Russian Turkestan) in the eighteenth century B.C., invaded the Bible world and conquered it. They brought with them the horse and the chariot—the first time the horse is mentioned in this region. Interestingly enough, in pictures on Egyptian walls from this period the horse appears for the first time. Likewise, in Mesopotamia, the first time that we find any word for "horse" in the language is after the Hyksos' invasion. They also introduced the composite bow. They made a military nation out of Egypt, which up until that time had been peace loving; they made an internationally-minded people out of the Egyptians, who up until that time had been very much of a home-loving people. The historians say that the Hyksos, when they came into Egypt, took the narrow Egyptian view of the world and made it a world view. Before this, Egypt had been a great empire, but without foreign holdings; after this Egypt became a great empire with holdings in other parts of the world.

Now the Hyksos, having come from Canaan, not only had charge of Egyptian affairs, but also had supervision over Syria and Palestine. It seems likely that Joseph came into the country at that time. For that was a time when he could find those who were not too far distant in relationship from him, who could speak Semitic dialects, and whose names as we know from the Egyptian monuments were Semitic names. He would find more in common with them than he would with the Egyptians who hated the Semites. Moreover, the Hyksos had located their capital in the delta region at Avaris, and that checks with the fact that when Joseph was there the capital was

---

[4] For an interesting account, see G. Steindorff and K. C. Seele, *When Egypt Ruled the East* (Chicago: University of Chicago Press, 1942), Chap. III, "The Hyksos."

down in the delta region; likewise, when his father and his brothers and their flocks came and located in the land of Goshen, they were near the capital. The fact could only be fitted into the period of Egyptian history known as the Hyksos period. So our tentative date, based on Abraham's chronology, has some confirmation in history.

Joseph came to Egypt, and he was bought by Potiphar, the captain of the guard, and taken into his home. Before long he was tempted by Potiphar's wife—a story with which I am sure you are quite familiar. Joseph was handsome; his master's wife cast her eyes upon him, and said, "Lie with me!" But he refused and said to her, "Lo, having me my master has no concern about anything in the house, and he has put everything that he has in my hand; he is not greater in this house than I am; nor has he kept back anything from me except yourself, because you are his wife; how then can I do this great wickedness, and sin against God?" (39:6-9). Repulsed, she made her next move: she tried to discredit him by claiming that he had forced his attentions upon her. And Joseph was taken from the house and put in prison.

There is a parallel here, as students of Egyptian literature know, with the Egyptian story of "The Tale of the Two Brothers."[5] It is not as delicately told as is the story in the Bible; it is crude and sensual. Actually, there is very little reason, it seems to me, to claim that the Biblical story derives from the Egyptian. This is a situation that could and did occur often in the field of ancient literature. On the other hand, there is a delicacy in the Bible story which is amazing, and beautiful. Joseph is portrayed here in a color of fidelity to God and fidelity to the man for whom he is working.

In the fortieth chapter, there is a period of two years during which Joseph accomplished nothing. He did interpret the dreams of the chief butler and the chief baker, it is true, and he asked them to remember him when the dreams were fulfilled; but they forgot, as human beings do, and he remained in prison another two years. Then, "after two whole years, Pharaoh dreamed . . ."—Joseph was still in prison—and while Pharaoh was trying to get an interpretation for his dreams, the butler remembered about the time that he was in prison; he remembered how the young Hebrew had interpreted for him, and he called that to the attention of Pharaoh; Pharaoh sent for Joseph, and Joseph interpreted the dream.

[5] *Ancient Near Eastern Texts,* pp. 23-25.

These details are familiar to us, but to get the full picture we have to mention them, and piece them together. You remember that Pharaoh had two dreams, and that Joseph pointed out that they were the one and the same; that God had given the two dreams for the sake of emphasis, and so that Pharaoh would recognize the certainty of the prediction. The story of the seven fat cows and the seven lean cows, Joseph said, portrayed seven years of plenty and seven years of famine. Joseph not only told Pharaoh what was going to happen, but advised Pharaoh to store up during the years of plenty enough to take care of the years of famine. That made sense; so Pharaoh named Joseph the "food administrator" of the government, and gave him a place in Egypt second only to that of Pharaoh himself.

Notice the details in Genesis 41:41: "And Pharaoh said to Joseph, 'Behold I have set you over all the land of Egypt.' Then Pharaoh took his signet ring from his hand and put it on Joseph's hand, and arrayed him in garments of fine linen, and put a gold chain about his neck; and he made him to ride in the second chariot; and they cried before him, 'Bow the knee!'" (or "*ab rek!*" which may mean, "Bow the heart") a sign of obedience to Joseph.

The scene shifts; we read the story of how Jacob and his sons were faring during the famine back in the land of Canaan, and of the plan to go down to Egypt where there was plenty of food. I think perhaps it may be well to point out that the land of Egypt was usually the last land to have famine when famine came upon the Middle East. The rest of the Middle East depends largely upon rainfall for its food, and if there is a bad year, of course the food supply will be bad. But Egypt depends upon the flooding of the Nile, and the flooding of the Nile is determined by the rains and the snows in equatorial Africa and Abyssinia; and so it is very seldom that there is famine in the land of Egypt. Egypt always was the breadbasket of the Middle East and in Roman times was called the "granary of Rome."

So Jacob sent his sons down to Egypt to get food. It is a delightful story how they, the brothers, come to Joseph and bow down before him with their faces to the ground; how he sees and knows them, but treats them like strangers. He says, "From where do you come?" They tell him, "From the land of Canaan to buy food." He says, "You are spies, you have come to see the weakness of the land" (42:6-9). Then he asks about the family. He elicits the fact that they have a younger brother, Benjamin, who has stayed at home—and that sets the stage for the next step of the story.

Joseph gives them food only on one condition: one of the brothers must be left behind as a hostage and they are told that they will not have any chance of getting him back or of getting further food unless and until they bring young Benjamin to him. They go back home, and Jacob's sorrow is multiplied by the loss of yet another son. They reach the place where they must go back for more food; they just cannot hold out any longer. They start to argue that they must take Benjamin back, and Jacob says, "You have bereaved me of my children: Joseph is no more and Simeon is no more, and now you take Benjamin; all this is come upon me." Then Reuben says to his father, "Slay my two sons if I do not bring him back to you" (42:36-37). (He did not say, "Slay me!" but rather, "Take my two sons and kill them!" It is always simpler to sacrifice someone else!) But they are hungry again, and they have to go back for food, and they have to take Benjamin.

Once again the story is brilliantly told. "When Joseph saw Benjamin with them he said to the steward of the house, 'Bring the men into the house and slaughter an animal and make ready, for the men are to dine with me at noon'" (43:16). Then he receives them. He asks about the father. Finally he has food served to them, but he eats in another room. (That was typical Egyptian custom. One of the noteworthy facts about these chapters of Genesis is how true they are to all we know about Egyptian custom and Egyptian life. Whoever wrote this, whether Moses or an earlier author whose work Moses was led to use, it was written only by a person who knew Egypt and who knew Egyptian customs well.) They come in to sit down, and they are amazed because they are all seated in order of their rank. How would a stranger know their rank? And then Benjamin gets a portion five times greater than all the rest.

Once again Joseph has a little fun with them. He has their sacks filled with food, as much as they could carry. He has the money put in the top of the sacks again, as he had before, and then he has a silver cup put in the sack of the youngest brother, along with the money. And when they have gone a little way, he has some of his servants overtake them and say, "Why have you returned evil for good? Why have you stolen my silver cup?" Of course, they deny it: "Far be it from thy servants that they should do such a thing!" (44:7).

They open the sacks—and find the silver cup in Benjamin's! All the time, you see, the lesson is being driven home to the sons of Jacob that their deceptions have cost them dearly. They realize that they must return to Jacob without Benjamin, and they will have to tell him, "Benjamin has been taken away, and put to death." This they cannot stand: Judah cries that his father will die at the news. Nor can Joseph stand any more. He breaks down, has the room cleared and reveals himself to his brothers. He sends them to bring his father Jacob to Egypt; Pharaoh gives them all they need for the journey, and they go home, and tell the story to Jacob. God gives His permission, in a dream, for Jacob to go to his long-lost son in Egypt. And so Israel comes to the land of Egypt.

Now, consider the relation of Joseph to the promises of God. Joseph had come to Egypt at seventeen, and immediately began to exhibit a strong character. He refused the temptation of Potiphar's wife, because he could not wrong Potiphar and—what is more important —because he could not sin against God. Through all his life he remained true to the God of Israel. He understood that he was only an interpreter of dreams, but that God was the source of the dreams; that Pharaoh has not only dreamed, but that God has revealed the truth through them to Pharaoh.

Then, when Jacob died in Egypt, Joseph had him taken back to Canaan for burial, because Joseph knew that it was the will of the patriarchs that they be buried in the land that God had given them.

As he was drawing to the close of his earthly life (read Genesis 50:24, and the verses following), Joseph repeated the promises God had made to Abraham, to Isaac, and to Jacob, saying to his brothers, "I am about to die; but God will visit you, and will bring you up out of the land to the land which he swore to Abraham, to Isaac, and to Jacob." Then he bound the Israelites by an oath to carry his bones with them, upon their return, and to bury them in the land of Canaan. And so he was embalmed and placed in a coffin until the time should come that they could take him to the land of Canaan. When the author of the Book of Hebrews mentions the faith of Joseph, he emphasizes all this and says it is by faith that Joseph made mention of the Exodus "and gave directions concerning his bones" (Hebrews 11:22).

Where did Joseph get that faith? Jacob was partly to blame for the fact that Joseph was such a fresh young boy. But Jacob was also responsible for the religious faith that Joseph had. For seventeen years Joseph had lived in his father's home before he went to the land of Egypt. That was not long. Some of us who see our teen-agers go out from our homes into the world wonder how well they will stand up against the temptations and attractions of the world. Joseph is a good lesson for us. Here is a man who only had those few years in his father's house, but the years must have been well spent. The promises which God had made to Abraham and to Isaac and to Jacob had been deeply impressed upon the mind of young Joseph, and the moral teaching of the God of Israel must also have been deeply impressed upon him, for when he got down into Egypt he never forgot these things. You and I should take a great deal of courage from that as we bring up our own young folks, as we realize that God can use the training we give them at home to carry them over their years in the world.

CHAPTER V

Moses: The Man

IN THIS CHAPTER, we turn to the study of Moses, one of the greatest persons in the Old Testament. Abraham has three references made to him in the eleventh chapter of Hebrews; Moses has four. Moses is listed in the New Testament, I think, more times than any other Old Testament character. He stands in relation to the Old Testament prophets as Christ stands in relation to the apostles in the New Testament; he stands in relation to the people of God in the Old Testament as the Deliverer, the Saviour, without whom there would have been no Israel, without whom there would have been no deliverance from Egyptian bondage. In the Bible, there are some startling expressions used in connection with Moses. For example, in Exodus 14:31 ("the people . . . believed in the Lord and in his servant Moses"), faith in Moses is placed beside faith in the Lord; and in the New Testament (I Corinthians 10:2) there is the very remarkable statement that "all were baptized into Moses in the cloud and in the sea." Above all, Moses was privileged to stand with Jesus and Elijah on the Mount of Transfiguration (Matthew 17:3).

We shall make two studies of Moses, and we are going to divide these studies so that in this chapter we are thinking about the man and his background, and in the next chapter the man and the great work which God gave him to do.

The life of Moses can be divided very conveniently into three periods of forty years each. The first period of his life is the period in Pharaoh's house; following that, the period in Midian when he was really a refugee or an outcast from Egypt; and the third is the period of forty years as the leader and law-giver of Israel, chiefly in the wilderness.[1]

Of course you will ask, unless you know the Bible story, "How

---

[1] Much valuable material on Moses and his period can be found in Henry S. Noerdlinger, *Moses and Egypt: The Documentation to the Motion Picture, "The Ten Commandments"* (Los Angeles: University of Southern California Press, 1956), 202 pp.

did Moses come to be in Pharaoh's house? How did this Hebrew lad come to be in such a situation?" The story is found in the Book of Exodus in the first and second chapters. In Exodus 1:8 we read that ". . . there arose a new king over Egypt, who did not know Joseph." This king had grown tired of the Israelites who were too many in his land and too powerful, and he decided to do something to reduce their numbers. First he increased the amount of work they had to do and, when they seemed to thrive under that, he made it more difficult for them to make bricks by taking away the straw. Incidentally, in that connection, we ought to read very carefully what it says in the Scripture. I have seen all sorts of statements about making "bricks without straw," yet I am unable to find any place in the Bible where it says that is what they did. The straw was no longer furnished them as it had been; the suggestion is that they had not only to make the bricks, but they had to go out and gather the straw *for themselves,* and to do that without decreasing the number of bricks that they made. When the severe burden of heavy labor failed to accomplish its purpose, the king decided that the male babies of the Israelites should be put to death, and he passed the word to the Hebrew midwives that they should kill the Hebrew sons and let the daughters live. That failed, too. The midwives reported that the Hebrew women were too active for them, so that by the time they could get there, in attendance, the child was already born and hidden and they had no opportunity to kill it. Thereupon, Pharaoh commanded that every Hebrew baby boy was to be cast into the Nile (Exodus 1:22).

In the midst of all this turmoil and oppression, a child was born to a family in the house of Levi, and the mother planned to outwit the command of Pharaoh. As long as the child could be hidden, she hid it; then she took it and placed it in a little basket—"an ark," it is called in the Scripture—made of reeds and daubed with pitch. She placed the baby in the ark on the bank of the Nile at a spot where Pharaoh's daughter would come down to bathe and *see* the baby—thinking in the back of her mind, I suppose, that Pharaoh's daughter would be captivated by this little baby, as she was. Read on a little further in the second chapter and you find that the sister of this baby was waiting nearby—"at a distance"—and as soon as Pharaoh's daughter came and took the basket and saw the baby in it, the sister approached and said, "Shall I go and call you a nurse from the

Hebrew women to nurse the child for you?" And who is the nurse but the mother of the baby?

So the baby is in Pharaoh's daughter's home and the baby's mother is there to nurse and take care of him. The child was given a name at that time. He probably had been named by his parents previously, but now he was given a name by Pharaoh's daughter, and the name has come into English form as "Moses."

We read in Acts 7:22 that he was brought up "in all the wisdom of the Egyptians." That is a startling statement. It becomes more amazing as we think about what is involved in the wisdom of the Egyptians at that period.[2]

Moses certainly would have had some contact with the architectural splendors of Egypt,[3] although it is impossible for us to say just how much, for again the dates are not fully certain. If Moses was in Pharaoh's house when the capital was located in the delta region at Avaris (Tanis), then he may not have had opportunity to get into Upper Egypt (i.e., the southern portion), to see Luxor and Karnak. He may not even have seen Memphis and the pyramids. On the other hand, if the capital was located at Memphis, or possibly even at Amarna, then certainly he had often seen the pyramids; for they were a thousand years old before ever Moses had been born.

Moses knew something about writing, having been brought up in Pharaoh's house. He would doubtless have learned to read and to write, using the Egyptian system of hieroglyphs—those strange pictures which we know from the tombs and temples of Egypt. He may also have known something about the cuneiform (wedge-shaped) writing of Babylonia, for this was commonly used for international correspondence. You probably have heard of the "Tell el-Amarna letters," which were discovered in Egypt, and which date from the fifteenth century B.C. These letters represent the correspondence carried on by the Pharaoh of Egypt, the kings and petty kings of the Hittite Empire in Asia Minor, and the city kingdoms in the land of Canaan and Syria. This correspondence was not conducted in Egyptian or Hittite or Canaanite, but in Babylonian, which appears to have been the language of diplomacy of the day. It is also possible that Moses may have be-

[2] The following points are suggested in the article, "Moses," in *Harper's Bible Dictionary*, p. 461.
[3] For a good introductory survey, see C. Desroches-Noblecourt, *Le style égyptienne* (Paris: Librairie Larousse, 1946), 220 pp.

come acquainted with the alphabetic-type of writing which has been discovered at Serabit el-Khadem, not far from Mount Sinai.[4]

Not more than seventy-five years ago, Old Testament scholars were telling us that Moses could not possibly have written any part of the Old Testament, because no one knew how to write in those days! How unsound such a statement was we now know, for it is now clear that men were writing fully fifteen hundred years, possibly even two thousand years before the days of Moses. By the time Moses came on the scene, Egypt had a long history of writing and a great wealth of literature behind her.

It has been suggested that Moses was educated also in the wisdom of the Egyptian philosophers. Now the Egyptian philosophers were not like those of Greece; I would not want to suggest that there was anybody in any period of Egyptian history who would be equal to such Greek philosophers as Plato or Aristotle, Socrates or Zeno, or many more we might mention. But Egypt provided its own particular type of philosophy. It was a homey type, full of aphorisms similar to the proverbs which we find in the Bible. There were many proverbs about working hard and doing your job well: you would receive a reward if you did so; if you did not, you would get beaten with a rod, or something worse would happen to you.

Then there was considerable speculation on the world to come. Someone has pointed out that, whereas the Babylonians seemed to be more interested in the past, the Egyptians were more interested in the future. The Babylonian literary remains contain many stories about creation, the flood, and other events (whether real or mythological) of the distant past. The Egyptian literary remains contain writings such as the *Book of the Dead,* dealing with the concept of life after death, or the world to come. The writings of Ptah-hotep were probably among those that Moses studied, to judge from the fact that they are quoted over and over again by other Egyptian writers.

His knowledge of the wisdom of the Egyptians probably put Moses in close contact with the magicians and their magic. Now, I am not inclined to attribute the plagues which were brought upon Egypt at the word of Moses to his knowledge of Egyptian magic. We see clearly in the Scriptural record the difference between the works of Moses

---

[4] For a bare introduction to writing, see articles: "Writing" (pp. 828-831), "Cuneiform" (pp. 121-122), and "Serabit el-Khadem" (p. 663), in *Harper's Bible Dictionary* (New York: Harper & Brothers, 1952).

and the imitations of the magicians. He could do things they could not do, for he had the power of God. On the other hand, let us not forget the fact that for forty years Moses had been brought up in Pharaoh's house. If, as we shall see in a few pages, he was being trained for the high position of the Pharaoh, then certainly he was being indoctrinated in all of the ways of the Egyptians. He probably thought very little about the God of Israel, in those days—for the Lord had to tell Moses who He was, when He called him in Midian (Exodus 3:3-15).[5]

Moses may also have learned something about monotheism in the Egyptian court. The Pharaoh known originally as Amenhotep IV became a religious rebel, overthrowing the established worship and adopting the sole worship of the solar deity. At the same time, he took the name Ikhnaton,[6] and moved the capital to Akhetaton (present-day Tell el-Amarna). Now Ikhnaton's religious revolution did not last very long, and its roots were not deep-seated. Upon his death, his young son, Tut-ankh-aton (better known to us by the name of Tut-ankh-amun) was brought up in the old ways, the views of Ikhnaton were branded as heretical, and many of the things that he had written were effaced.

But you know that when men are so deeply moved by a heresiarch, they talk. And when men talk, the heresy that one would have hushed becomes bandied about. It is like a fire that only scatters as you try to beat it out. We know today about Ikhnaton's religious ideas simply because it was impossible to kill them. And so we suggest that Moses may have been influenced by these concepts of monotheism. He may have been thus providentially prepared for the revelation that God was to give him. At any rate, we know that the religious ideas which Moses passed on to all who read his Books are not the Egyptian concepts, but the truth revealed to Moses by God, in Midian, in the Exodus deliverance, and at Sinai.

Moses was brought up in the house of Pharaoh's daughter. Who was she? I wish we knew! If we work toward the period of Moses from one

[5] Some will doubtless say, "But if Moses was not faithful to the Lord in Egypt, why would the Lord call him?" This overlooks the entire Old Testament conception of sovereign election. God did not choose anyone at any time because of that person's fidelity, wisdom, or any other quality. God's election was sovereign—based only on His will. This is the Old Testament concept, illustrated repeatedly: Jacob, the Israelites, Saul, Amos, Isaiah, Jeremiah, and many others.

[6] Or Akhnaton, or Akhenaton, 1369-1353 b.c. Obviously, if we accept the 1446 b.c. for the Exodus, the observations of this paragraph become superfluous.

set of evidence, we arrive at a date somewhere in the middle of the fifteenth century—around 1446 B.C. If, on the other hand, we use other evidence, we arrive at a date early in the thirteenth century—about 1290 B.C. Contrary to the teachings of some Old Testament scholars, this is not simply a matter of taking the evidence of "either the Bible [I Kings 6:1 supports 1446 B.C., taken mathematically] or archaeology," but it is a complex question on which the Bible itself is ambiguous. We cannot go into all the details here, but we may note that mention of the city of Raamses and location in the delta in Exodus 1:11, is at least to be looked upon as having greater possibility in the time of Rameses II (thirteenth century) than in the time of Thutmose III (fifteenth century).

But if we tentatively accept the 1446 B.C. date of the Exodus, then it might be possible to identify Pharaoh's daughter with the famous queen (she called herself "king") known as Hatshepsut (1486-1468 B.C.). She was the one who prided herself on being the first to restore the Egyptian temples after the Hyksos; she was more interested in Egypt's internal splendor than in external conquests. She built the beautiful Deir el-Bahri. She had obelisks cut from the granite quarries at Asswan and erected at Karnak. She renewed operations at the turquoise mines in Sinai and sent maritime expeditions to Punt.[7]

But whoever the daughter of Pharaoh may have been, Moses was brought up in her house, and, according to Josephus (the great Jewish historian who lived in the first century A.D.), he could have become Pharaoh. The line of succession in Egypt did not pass from father to son, but it went down through the oldest daughter. If the daughter of Pharaoh who took the baby Moses into her home was the oldest daughter of the reigning Pharaoh, and if Moses was the oldest son in her house, this would fit with what Josephus tells us. It is not beyond the realm of possibility that when Moses chose to throw in his lot with the people of God, he was renouncing all claim to the throne of Egypt. The writer of the book of Hebrews says that it was by faith that Moses chose to be reckoned with the people of God rather than to be counted as Pharaoh's daughter's son (Hebrews 11:24-25).

The second part of Moses' life was in Midian—and again you ask

[7] The fascinating story of Hatshepsut can be found in J. A. Wilson, *The Culture of Ancient Egypt* (*Phoenix Books*, P-11; Chicago: University of Chicago Press, 1956), pp. 169-177. This book was originally published under the title, *The Burden of Egypt* (1951). For Egyptian chronology I am following Wilson.

the question, "How did he get *there?*" The story is told in the second
chapter of Exodus: "One day, when Moses had grown up, he went out
to his people and looked on their burdens, and he saw an Egyptian beating a Hebrew, one of his people. He looked this way and that, and seeing no one he killed the Egyptian and hid him in the sand. When he
went out the next day, behold two Hebrews were struggling together;
and he said to the man that did the wrong, 'Why do you strike your
fellow?' He answered, 'Who made you a prince and a judge over us?
Do you mean to kill me as you killed the Egyptian?' Then Moses was
afraid, and he thought, 'Surely the thing is known.' When Pharaoh
heard of it, he sought to kill Moses. But Moses fled from Pharaoh, and
stayed in the land of Midian" (Exodus 2:11-15).

Why did he choose on this occasion to align himself with the
Hebrews? When we find him in Midian at the well of Jethro, he is
"an Egyptian." He could have passed anywhere as an Egyptian. Why
did he choose on this particular occasion to reveal himself as one of
the Hebrew people? Go back and read the story again, in the first part
of the second chapter, and see how the mother of the child was taken
to be his nurse, and how she brought him to Pharaoh's daughter. The
training of Moses in the earliest days of his childhood was under the
tutelage of his own mother, a Hebrew woman; and she did her job
so well that forty years later, when the time came for him to decide
whether he would be on the side of the Egyptians or the Hebrews, he
chose, it seems, without hesitation to be numbered with the people
of God.

This is, in my opinion, a significant lesson, and one of the great
truths of Scripture. In the Hebrew society, the home is central, and in
the home, the knowledge of the Lord. A mother's greatest work is to
bring her children up that they may know the Lord. The woman who
has already raised her children, or the woman who has no children,
may find her career outside of the home. But no career, in my opinion,
can possibly be greater than that of a mother bringing up her children
to walk in the way of the Lord. I think one of the reasons why we have
such moral deficiency among today's children is the fact that so many
of today's mothers have made the home, and the training that should
be part of the home, matters of secondary importance. Moses' mother
did her job well, and it stood up under test forty years later.

We next find Moses in Midian with Jethro the priest. In Jethro's
household he got his wife Zipporah (21:2), and from her his sons

Gershom and Eliezer. It may well be that from Jethro he learned a great deal about the worship of Jehovah. Moses, even though he had had a Hebrew mother to train him for the first few years of his life, left her to go into training in Pharaoh's house, and I doubt very much that he got any Hebrew religious training there; it is far more likely that he was trained in all of the polytheism of the Egyptians. Jethro is portrayed in the eighteenth chapter of Exodus as a worshiper of the Lord. It may well be that the knowledge of Jehovah was part of his heritage, and that in his household, Moses came to realize more about what the worship of Jehovah involves.[8] From Jethro he also got wise counsel, when the cares and the burdens of the people were upon him; Jethro warned him that he could not carry this load alone, and advised him to appoint others and turn the details over to them and just handle main policy matters. We therefore can attribute to Jethro uncommon "common sense," and we can assume that Moses may have had many occasions, during the forty years in Midian, to learn from Jethro.

While Moses was in Midian, he also had plenty of opportunity as a shepherd to learn the roads and the sources of water supply and all those other details that he would need when the time came to lead the people of God through the wilderness on a thirty-eight-year march. You just don't go out into a wilderness with a large group without any knowledge of the terrain. You could get lost and die—simply because of insufficient water. But Moses knew the area; he had spent forty years there.

The third part (and we will go over this rather quickly because we are going to talk more about it in our next chapter) shows us Moses with the people of Israel. This story divides naturally into five main scenes.

First of all there was the appearance of God in the burning bush, when God called him out of the life of a shepherd in Midian to go back and free his people from the awful oppression that had fallen upon them in the land of Egypt (Exodus 3).

Then there was the contest with Pharaoh in the fifth and the following chapters of the book of Exodus down to chapter twelve, which ends with the plagues upon the Egyptians and the death of the first-born of each house in Egypt.

---

[8] Jethro, we should remember, was a Midianite, and Midian, according to Genesis 25:1-2, was a son of Abraham by Keturah.

Next, there was the great and terrible deliverance told in the twelfth chapter of Exodus. By a mighty hand, the Lord led His people out of Egypt through the waters of the Red Sea (or the "Sea of Reeds"), into the wilderness and up to the foot of Mt. Sinai.

The fourth scene gives us that magnificent moment at Mt. Sinai when God chose to speak with Moses face to face. He spoke to other men only in figures and in dreams and in images, but with Moses, face to face. No other man ever had that privilege here on earth until the day that our Lord came to walk among men.

The last scene is a touching one. Moses, the old man, stands on Mt. Nebo looking out across the Dead Sea and over to the hills of the Promised Land, and he sees at hand the realization of the promise which God had made to Abraham so many years before. This people, which originally consisted of Abraham and Isaac and Jacob and Jacob's boys, and which was now a great multitude that had been led through the wilderness by Moses for all these years, stood poised and ready to go in and take possession of the place which God had promised. But Moses himself could not go in.

This is one of the most interesting points of the story. Things like this should give us new incentive in our own Bible study and in our own Christian lives, because we find that even the greatest of Old Testament characters are just human beings. Moses was a man. He was not a god. He was a *great* man, perhaps the greatest man of the Old Testament; but he was a *man,* and he got tired and irritated with these people who were so stubborn and backsliding, and he seems even to have lost his temper with God at times. And God said to him, "For that you cannot go in." Moses had to stand there and look into the Promised Land from afar, because once he had doubted God's word.

You and I will probably never have the opportunity to be great leaders of God's people, in the sense that Moses was. There doesn't *have* to be another Moses in this world, any more than there has to be another Jesus Christ. He served the people of God for the purpose for which God had called him. But God *does* need men and women who will be faithful in the particular task that He gives them. Sometimes they lose the blessing simply because they do not have enough faith; simply because they talk back to God in their doubt. We can learn from Moses' weakness and from his humanity to trust God, take Him at His word, and then we will have the joy of seeing what God intends to accomplish.

There are other truths that we can draw from Moses' life. We certainly can draw the lesson of the great choice which each one has to make between the world, represented by Pharaoh's household and the wealth of Egypt, and God. Moses had Egypt at his feet at a moment in Egyptian history when to be Pharaoh would have been to be one of the great characters of history; yet he chose to be God's man with God's people.

It was a terrible choice to have to make, but he made it and he made it gladly. You and I, too, should make our choice to be on God's side, no matter what we have to give up.

CHAPTER VI

Moses: The Servant

IN OUR LAST chapter we studied Moses in the light of the things that happened to him. In this chapter we will study him from a different angle: that of the servant of God, in his relation to Pharaoh, in his relation to the people of Israel, and, finally, in his relation to God. Let us see first how he looks standing side by side with Pharaoh.

Moses grew up in Pharaoh's court, as we have already mentioned, and may have been heir to the Egyptian throne. But he was forced by events and circumstances, by his own choice, and by the will of God to oppose Pharaoh. He spent years in hiding, then returned from Midian to Egypt to lead his people out of that "house of bondage," the first step in the fulfillment of God's promise to give them the land of Canaan where they were to become a great nation. The story is told in Exodus, chapters seven through twelve, and is concerned chiefly with the account of the plagues. We shall not discuss the plagues; I am sure that most of you are quite familiar with that part of the story, in which Moses performed one miracle after another, by the power of God, until at last Pharaoh let his people go.[1]

One thing is remarkable in all this: the singleness of purpose which we find in the man Moses. As he comes into conflict with Pharaoh, he has chance after chance to compromise, to settle for a little less. But he never compromises; committed completely to God, he will settle for nothing less than the unconditional release of his people and their property. Let us read over some of the account in this section of Exodus.

In Exodus 8:25, Pharaoh began to realize that he was up against a situation that was becoming too much for him. There had been four

[1] There is a marked tendency today to treat the plagues as natural phenomena. While I do not deny that God could, and on many occasions did, use natural phenomena in ways that seem to us to be "miraculous," I find the psychological elements of Exodus 7–12 difficult, if not impossible, to account for on that basis. These people, who knew Egypt and its seasons and problems, were forced to admit that Moses' God was working against the gods of Egypt—which is to say, contrary to nature, or supernatural.

60

plagues, and against all of them Pharaoh had been helpless. So he offered a compromise: the Israelites could worship their Lord, if they wished, *but within the borders of Egypt.* Moses refused the bait; it would only cause trouble with the Egyptian people. Firmly he replied: "We must go three days' journey into the wilderness and sacrifice to the Lord our God as he will command us" (8:27). Then Pharaoh offered to let the men of Israel go. Moses would not settle for that either: "We will go with our young and our old; we will go with our sons and our daughters and with our flocks and herds, for we must hold a feast to the Lord" (10:9).

Pharaoh tried again: he would let all the *people* go, all the adults and children; but the flocks and herds of Israel were to remain in Egypt. That probably seemed to him quite reasonable. Here was Moses' chance to get out, at a comparatively small cost: he need only leave their possessions behind. But God had promised Moses that when they left Egypt they would take their possessions along. What was more, they would demand and get from their Egyptian taskmasters the wages due them for all those years, all those generations of bondage. It was that, or more plagues! It took courage for Moses to stand up to Pharaoh—courage and faith. Finally, the climax was reached: the plague of the death of the first-born in all the land. Not a home escaped—for there must be a first-born in every household! Without waiting for morning, Pharaoh sent for Moses and Aaron, and gave them the exit clearance. Moses had won! The Israelites left Egypt with all they had demanded, and passed safely across the Red Sea, leaving the hosts of Pharaoh floundering, drowning, in its waters.

Moses is equally inspiring in his relation to the people of Israel. We have already mentioned the choice made by Moses, when he came to his adult life, to take the side of his people. He saw an Egyptian beating a Hebrew, and he killed the Egyptian and hid his body in the sand (see Exodus 2:11).

Now, I am not sure that what he did was right. It is not so much because he killed the Egyptian that I find fault with him, but rather because he took into his own hands the deliverance of his people. Instead of calling upon God to save the people, instead of waiting for God to do something about it, Moses sought by his own effort, by his own might, by his own wisdom, to free his people from bondage. To me, that is the major sin; that is even more of a sin than killing a man. He did something that only God had the right to do.

Then, after he had been in Midian for a while, and after he had had the vision of the burning bush (which we will consider later), he went back to Egypt, where he and his brother Aaron gathered together the elders of the people of Israel. Aaron was the spokesman. Moses had complained, you remember, that he was a stutterer and therefore not able to speak and God had given him Aaron to be his mouthpiece. So when Moses had gathered the people together, Aaron declared what the Lord had spoken to Moses, and "the people believed; and when they heard that the Lord had visited the people of Israel and that he had seen their affliction, they bowed their heads and worshiped" (4:31).

Here is an indication of the leadership potential of Moses; he was able to gather around him the elders of the people of Israel, who by this time had been in Egypt many years. The Hebrew text of Exodus 12:40 indicates that Israel had been in Egypt 430 years; on the other hand, the Samaritan and the Septuagint texts indicate that the 430 was divided into two parts, each of 215 years.[2] At any rate, whether it was 215 or 430, it was a long time. When a people settles down for 215 years, it is pretty hard to rekindle the pioneer enthusiasms. Yet Moses was able to fire the imagination of these people and elders of Israel; he was able to convince them that God was bent upon their deliverance, and he made them follow him. That is leadership!

Notice three facts about this relationship between Moses and the people of Israel. First of all, notice the long suffering which Moses had undergone for his people, and his willingness not once, but many times to intercede on their behalf when they were about to be visited by God with some punishment. The Book of Numbers is the story of the rebellion of the people, of the seeming desire of God to wipe them out, and of Moses' continued insistence that they should have another chance. But before we turn to the Book of Numbers, there is one other scene we must study, in the thirty-second chapter of Exodus.

As Moses was coming down from the mountain, having received the law from God, God told him that he was facing a bad situation. " 'They have turned aside quickly out of the way which I commanded them;—said God—they have made for themselves a molten calf, and

---

[2] Textual students will recognize at once the strength of evidence of the Samaritan agreeing with the Septuagint. Further, Galatians 3:17 seems to support the 215+215 scheme, for the 430 years are from the covenant of Abraham to the giving of the Law.

have worshiped it and sacrificed to it. . . .' And the Lord said to Moses, 'I have seen this people, and behold, it is a stiff-necked people; now therefore let me alone, that my wrath may burn hot against them and I may consume them; but of you I will make a great nation'" (32:8-10). Moses might have replied, "All right . . ."—he was tired of these people, too, by this time—"go ahead, wipe them out." But that is not Moses. Instead, he answered, " 'O Lord, why does thy wrath burn hot against thy people . . . ? Why should the Egyptians say, "With evil intent did he bring them forth to slay them in the mountains, and to consume them from the face of the earth"? Remember Abraham, and Isaac, and Israel . . .' " (32:11-13). And the Lord repented and gave them another chance.

Now turn to the Book of Numbers, chapter 14. After the spies had gone out to look over the land of Canaan, they came back and gave their report on the people of the land; it was a wonderful land, flowing with milk and honey—they brought back a huge bunch of grapes carried on a big stick by two of them, to show what the land was like—but they said the people there were big, too, and the Israelites were as grasshoppers in their sight. They would not have a chance against such giants. And God again displayed His displeasure with the lack of faith on the part of these people. "And the Lord said to Moses, 'How long will this people despise me? And how long will they not believe in me, in spite of all the signs which I have wrought among them? I will strike them with the pestilence and disinherit them, and I will make of you a nation greater and mightier than they' " (Numbers 14:11-12). And again Moses pleaded for his people: " 'The Lord is slow to anger, and abounding in steadfast love, forgiving iniquity and transgression. . . .' Pardon the iniquity of this people, I pray thee, according to the greatness of thy steadfast love [or mercy], and according as thou hast forgiven this people from Egypt even until now" (14:18-19). Again God spared the people.

A little later, we read the account of the rebellion of the sons of Korah (Numbers 16). God was once more about to visit the people with punishment, and He told Moses and Aaron to separate themselves from the congregation, "that I may consume them in a moment." Moses and Aaron fell on their faces and prayed, ". . . shall one man sin, and wilt thou be angry with *all* the congregation?" So the punishment fell only upon the sons of Korah. But there were others who had been involved in this rebellion. They, too, must be punished so God told Moses, "Get away from the midst of this congregation, that I may consume them . . ." (16:45). But Moses and Aaron rushed into the crowd and divided it, and they stood between those who had already been smitten with the punishment of God, and those who were to be preserved because of Moses' insistence that they be spared. For less than this men have been cited for courage "above and beyond the call of duty"!

Then, there had been lack of food and water, and the people murmured and rebelled again, and the Lord sent fiery serpents to smite them (Numbers 21:4-6). Once again Moses interceded and rescued them. Only once in all the wilderness journey, only *once* did Moses seem to lose his patience, and that is in the story in the twentieth chapter of Numbers where he smote the rock in impatience to bring forth the water for them. He was, indeed, a man of long-suffering and faith and intercession!

The second thing I would like to emphasize about Moses in his relationship to the people of Israel is his responsibility for their worship. Through God he was led to set up the Tabernacle and arrange its worship. The worship of the Jew today, and, to a certain extent, the worship of the Christian, stems back to Moses and the Tabernacle.

The third fact I would note is this: Moses gave them the Scriptures. So far as we know, the first Scriptures were written in the days of Moses. There were stories, probably even written records, before that time that have come down to us in the Bible, but Moses was the one who kept detailed records of the encampments, records of the events and some of the battles that were fought (Numbers 33). He gave the children of Israel the written statute of laws ("the Book of the Covenant") mentioned in the twenty-fourth chapter of Exodus. He kept a copy of his farewell address mentioned in the thirty-first chapter of Deuteronomy; and I believe that practically the whole Book of Deuteronomy is that farewell address. These things were the beginning of what we now call "the Bible"; and well are the first five books of the Bible called the Books of Moses, because he is the one who gave to Israel, and through them to us, the beginnings of sacred Scripture.[3]

[3] To argue that "unless Moses wrote the entire Pentateuch, we can no longer speak of Mosaic authorship" is, in my opinion, an unjustified extension of the truth. If we can say that "grace and truth came by Jesus Christ," even though He did not write a single word of the Gospels, certainly we can say that "the Law came by Moses." If we can say that "Moses spoke all these words," even if it was Aaron's mouth that actually did the speaking—and this is what the

Turn your thoughts now to the relationship between Moses and God, and think of it in three scenes.

First of all there was the great experience of the burning bush, when Moses was in Midian keeping the flocks of his father-in-law Jethro. Moses saw a bush and it seemed to be burning, but when he drew near to it, he found that it was not consumed. Then the angel of the Lord appeared and spoke to him. Essentially, this is a repetition of the covenant made to Abraham, plus the promise of God to deliver Israel from the Egyptians and bring them into the land of Canaan, where the covenant which God had made with their fathers would at last be fulfilled. There is also a revelation to Moses concerning the name of the Lord. When Moses said, "If . . . they [the people] ask me, 'What is his name?' what shall I say to them?" God answered, "I am who I am"[4] (Exodus 3:13-14). Thus the name "Jahweh"—or "Jehovah," as we know it in English—comes to be the *covenant* name; it is the name for God specifically as He stands in relation to Israel.

The power of God is also revealed and made available to Moses. In Exodus 4, when Moses feared to go back to Egypt because the people might not listen to him, the Lord said, "What is that in your hand?" He said, "A rod." God said, "Cast it on the ground." And it became a serpent, and Moses fled from it. Then the Lord said to Moses, "Take it by the tail"; and it became a rod in his hand. This was done for a purpose: when Moses got back to Egypt he could prove that he was acting not on his own authority, but on the authority of God.

When Moses expressed hesitation because he stuttered, God gave him a spokesman, Aaron. The next words are important: "And you shall speak to him and put the words in his mouth; and I will be with your mouth and with his mouth, and will teach you what you shall

---

Bible teaches—then we can say "Moses wrote these words," even though God may have used someone else to give us the final written form. What we need to insist upon is: (1) the historicity and veracity of the Pentateuch, (2) the essential Mosaic authorship, and (3) the plenary inspiration of the Holy Spirit for the Pentateuch in the form in which God caused it to be finally inscripturated.

[4] "Yahweh" (or Jahweh) is usually taken to be derived from the root $hwh = hyh$, meaning "to be." Whether it is to be read as "I am," "I shall be," or "I cause to be," it is almost impossible to say. More recently an effort to derive the word from the root hwy, "to say," (cf. Ugaritic hwt, "word") has gained some support. While at first glance this does not seem to be compatible with the Scriptural "I am," it does fit well with the concept of the "Word." The name, in the last analysis, is as mysterious as God Himself.

do. *He shall speak for you to the people: and he shall be a mouth for you, and you shall be to him as God*" (Exodus 4:15-16). Add to them the words in Exodus 7:1, *"See, I make you as God to Pharaoh; and Aaron your brother shall be your prophet."* Here we have one of the most important definitions of a prophet: he is God's mouth. When Moses spoke, Aaron was to say to the people what Moses said to him. This is what a prophet is supposed to do: to tell the people whatever God has told him.

That great vision, that call at the burning bush, is what sent Moses back to his people, and enabled him to lead them to freedom.

The next scene finds God and Moses at Sinai. The record begins in Exodus 19 and continues through the rest of Exodus. The people arrive at the foot of the mountain three months after leaving Egypt, and God commands them to stay there at the foot of the mountain while Moses goes up to receive the law.

Following this, we have a long series of revelations of God to Moses. In the twenty-fourth chapter of Exodus, Moses has a vision of glory; it is one of the things that you may have overlooked. I do not know how many times I read this before it stood out on the page as I had not seen it before: "Then Moses and Aaron, Nadab and Abihu, and seventy of the elders of Israel went up, and they saw the God of Israel; and there was under his feet as it were a pavement of sapphire stone, like the very heaven for clearness" (24:9-11). Moses was not the only one to go up into the mountain. Seventy-three others went with him and saw God. But Moses alone had the privilege of speaking with God face to face, so that when he came down from the mountain, his face was shining, and the people saw the glory and the splendor of God in its radiance (Exodus 34).

One day, when Moses' brother and sister, Aaron and Miriam, began to complain because of the place that Moses seemed to be taking to himself in Israel, God said to them, "Hear my words: If there is a prophet among you, I the Lord make myself known to him in a vision, I speak with him in a dream. Not so with my servant Moses; he is entrusted with all my house. With him I speak mouth to mouth clearly, and not in dark speech: and he beholds the form of the Lord" (Numbers 12:6-8). Moses is the one person in the Old Testament who had the privilege which was given to no other—the privilege of face-to-face communion with God.

Then we come to the final scene, on the mountain of Moab, Mount

Nebo, just before the death of Moses. To understand it, we must go to Numbers 20, where the people rebelled because they did not have enough food and water, and where God commanded Moses to speak to the rock that the water might come forth. Moses was tired. He had had the burden of these people for many years; he had seen rebellion upon rebellion, when they had lacked the faith to go ahead in the promises of God. "And Moses and Aaron gathered the assembly before the rock, and he said to them, 'Hear now, you rebels; shall we bring forth water for you out of this rock?' And Moses lifted up his hand and struck the rock with his rod twice; and water came forth abundantly . . ." (Numbers 20:10-11).

Some say that the sin here was in striking the rock twice; once would have been enough. That may be. But it seems to me that there is a greater sin in what Moses *said*: "Shall *we* bring forth water out of the rock?" Just once, it seems, Moses presumed to take his place on a par with God—and you can hardly blame him, with all of the experiences he had had—but just this once he seems to take to himself more than he should have. *He* was not bringing any water out of the rock; God was doing it through him. "Shall *we* bring forth water?" For that, he is told that he is not going to see the promised land.[5]

"The Lord said to Moses, 'Go up into this mountain of Abarim, and see the land which I have given to the people of Israel. And when you have seen it, you also shall be gathered to your people, as your brother Aaron was gathered, because you rebelled against my word in the wilderness of Zin during the strife of the congregation . . .'" (Numbers 27:12-14).

Moses accepted the will of God in this respect just as he had accepted it in every other respect. God had said, "You cannot go into the land." Moses was content to ask, "Well, then, let me go up and *look* at it." And he went up to the top of a high peak there on the Transjordanian plateau east of the Dead Sea, where, on a clear day, you can see not only all of the southern end of Palestine, and Jerusalem there on a hilltop very clearly, but you can see the full length of the Jordan Valley, and miles beyond, a hundred miles and more. On a rare day,

[5] I was asked, after this statement had been made, if Moses did not go to heaven just because of this one mistake. This indicates how careless we become with Scriptures. The "Promised Land" is not heaven; it is Canaan. It is not even a type of heaven, for it had to be won, it was full of sin, and the People were later exiled from it into Babylonia. That Moses did go to heaven is clear from Matthew 17:3 and Hebrews 11:23-28, 39-40.

you can even see the snow-capped peaks of Mt. Hermon.[6] ". . . Moses went from the plains of Moab to Mount Nebo, to the top of Pisgah, which is opposite Jericho. And the Lord showed him all the land, Gilead as far as Dan, all Naphtali, the land of Ephraim and Manasseh, all the land of Judah as far as the Western Sea, the Negeb, and the Plain, that is, the valley of Jericho the city of the palm trees, as far as Zoar. And the Lord said to him, 'This is the land which I swore to Abraham, and to Isaac, and to Jacob, "I will give it to your descendants." I have let you see it with your eyes, but you shall not go over there'" (Deuteronomy 34:1-4). Moses died there in the land of Moab, and we read that he was buried according to the word of the Lord, in the valley of the land of Moab. And no man knows the place of his burial to this day.

What lessons can we take from Moses for our own lives? Well, certainly we can take a lesson in faith: here is a man with tremendous faith. We can certainly take a lesson in obedience: he did what God told him to do, although at times it was at awful cost and at fearful risk. We can take a lesson in service: here is a man who for long years spent himself in the service of God on behalf of his people. And we can take a lesson in prayer: Moses prayed again and again and again for his people. We too, perhaps even more than Moses because we have Jesus Christ to intercede for us, can pray that God will spare His people.

[6] For a well-written description of this view in a popularized book, see Werner Keller, *The Bible as History* (London: Hodder & Stoughton, 1956), p. 153.

CHAPTER VII

Joshua

JOSHUA is known to us as the successor of Moses; he is the man who in the providence of God had the privilege of fulfilling the promise which God had made so long ago, to Abraham.

Four hundred years earlier, God had promised Abraham that He would give him a country. He called him out of Ur of the Chaldeans to go to another country which He would give him, and which would be the homeland of his seed, a numerous seed, as numerous as the sands of the sea or the stars of heaven. Abraham never lived to see that fulfilled; he was only a visitor, a sojourner in the land. He was told by God that it would not be his, that four hundred years later his descendants would occupy the country. Now, with Joshua, the promise is about to be fulfilled. That in itself ought to give us cause for consideration and for thanksgiving that God does not neglect His promises. Sometimes you and I feel that God has forgotten us because we do not get the answer to our prayers, perhaps in a few days or even for weeks or months. With the Israelites, it was not a matter of days or weeks or months but of generations and centuries before God fulfilled His promise. But He fulfilled it. Our God is a promise-keeping God.

Why did God use Joshua, and what is there here that will be of help to us in our Christian lives?

First of all, there was preparation. Few men, if any, step into responsible positions without preparation. Sometimes in our shortsightedness we seem to get the idea in regard to Bible characters that they come on the scene ready-made, fully prepared; here they are, God's gift to the world! They take up the work, and that is all there is to it. But if you will read more carefully you will find that usually—I think we could even say always—there is a period of preparation behind them. God lays His plans well in advance. Joshua, for instance, does not come on the scene at the crossing of the Jordan and Jericho; he had already come on the scene forty years before that.

He is described as an Ephraimite (that is, of the tribe of Ephraim) and the son of Nun. In Exodus 17:8-16, we find him at Rephidim, when the Amalekites came to fight against Israel: "And Moses said to Joshua, 'Choose for us men, and go out, fight with Amalek; tomorrow I will stand on the top of the hill with the rod of God in my hand.' " Joshua was in command of this minor skirmish; you see, already he was a man that Moses could call upon.

He was Moses' personal minister. When God told Moses to go up to the mountain where He would give him the tables of stone we are told: "Moses rose, with his servant Joshua, and Moses went up into the mountain of God" (Exodus 24:13). Joshua was Moses' personal attendant at the time that he was given the command to go to Sinai. There is some question as to whether Joshua had the privilege of being on Sinai with Moses, but he certainly was with him before he went up and after he came down; it would seem that Joshua had accompanied him part of the way, because "when Joshua heard the noise of the people as they shouted, he said to Moses, 'There is a noise of war in the camp!' " (Exodus 32:17).

Moses used to pitch the tent of meeting outside the camp, and then go out to that tent to receive instruction from the Lord. All of the men of Israel would stand in the doors of their tents and watch him as he went there. They would see the pillar of cloud come down upon the tent as Moses held his communion with God. Now notice: "when Moses turned again into the camp, his servant Joshua, the son of Nun, a young man, did not depart from the tent" (33:11). Even in the worship of Moses, Joshua was in attendance.

There came a time when a committee of twelve was sent into the land of Canaan to investigate conditions there and to see whether it was possible for the Israelites to move up from the south through the most logical entrance into the land of Canaan. Joshua was selected as one of that committee. At the time he was forty years of age, and already he had been with Moses for a year or two as his personal minister. The twelve spies went up and took a look at the land of Canaan and when they came back the majority were of the opinion that they could not go in and take the land, that the people there were too big for them. Two of the spies did not agree with that report: Joshua the son of Nun and Caleb the son of Jephunneh. In a minority report, they called upon the congregation of Israel to act on faith, to believe that God would lead them into the land and give it to them, and they begged them not to rebel against the Lord in unbelief. When the people rejected Joshua's report, God said quite bluntly that "Not one shall come into the land where I swore that I would make you dwell, except Caleb the son of Jephunneh and Joshua the son of Nun" (Numbers 14:30). The rest of them, for their faithlessness, were condemned not to enter the land, and the ten spies who brought back the false report were consumed by a plague from the Lord for their complete unbelief.

Joshua was ordained by Moses. "And the Lord said to Moses, 'Take Joshua the son of Nun, a man in whom is the spirit, and lay your hand upon him; cause him to stand before Eleazar the priest and all the congregation, and you shall commission him in their sight. You shall invest him with some of your authority, that all the congregation of the people of Israel may obey. And he shall stand before Eleazar the priest, who shall inquire for him by the judgment of the Urim before the Lord; at his word they shall go out, and at his word they shall come in, both he and all the people of Israel with him, the whole congregation'" (Numbers 27:18-21). Moses did as the Lord commanded. Then, near the end of the Book of Deuteronomy we read, "And the Lord said to Moses, 'Behold, the days approach when you must die; call Joshua, and present yourselves in the tent of meeting that I may commission him.'" So ". . . the Lord commissioned Joshua the son of Nun and said, 'Be strong and of good courage; for you shall bring the children of Israel into the land which I swore to give them: I will be with you'" (Deuteronomy 31:14-23). Joshua was not only ordained by Moses; he was also ordained by God.

That is the background. To take up the study of Joshua at the crossing of the river Jordan, just as they were ready to go into the land, without understanding that background, is to strip from the story many of its most important details. This man had had a record of faithful service and strong faith; he had had an experience in which he stood against the majority with his minority report; he had had the background of service under Moses as Moses' own personal minister; he had entered into some of the great religious experiences of Moses from time to time during that period: all this is vitally important. Now the time comes that he is to take over the leadership of the people and lead them into the land of Canaan.

Just prior to the death of Moses, there was a census of the people and it was disclosed that all of those who had been in Egypt had now died off, with the exception of Joshua and Caleb (cf. Numbers 26, especially verse 64). In other words, that generation which God swore would not enter into the land because of unbelief had passed away. So the situation is such that they can move forward: the new generation can go in. The only one remaining who does not have that privilege is Moses himself.

Joshua rises, here, to his full stature. He takes command. He gathers his host on the banks of Jordan, and cries to them, "Sanctify yourselves; for tomorrow the Lord will do wonders among you!" (Joshua 3:5).

On the banks of *Jordan!* Let us try to visualize it. There is no other river like it in all the world.[1] On either side of the valley are mountains, two thousand feet high and more. These drop rather suddenly to the valley, which is a great trench, five to thirteen miles wide. At Jericho it is the widest. But the river itself lies within another valley within the valley. The larger depression, which slopes gradually downward from the foot of the mountains to the river valley, is called by the Arabs "the Ghôr"; it is for the most part barren and flat: roads on either side of the river are on this portion. Jericho is a beautiful oasis of green in the dreary dust-brown of the Ghôr. The Jordan has cut a deeper trench within the Ghôr, which the Arabs call "the Zôr." At places, this is 150 feet deeper than the Ghôr, and a mile wide. It is thickly overgrown, and is called "the jungle [pride] of the Jordan" (Jeremiah 49:19). The Jordan itself is normally only a very small river, twenty-five or fifty feet wide, within the Zôr. When, in flood, it overflows, it spreads over the Zôr.

Near Jericho is the spot Joshua had chosen to make his crossing into Canaan. The priests bearing the Ark of the Covenant were to walk through the waters, and the men were to follow about a half-mile behind. As soon as the feet of the priests came "to the brink of the waters," God dammed up the waters above that place, and they passed through dry-shod.

Some have explained this as "a miracle of coincidence," and others claim that it is an absolute miracle apart from any coincidence. Who knows? I can tell you what the coincidence might be, although I

---

[1] Nelson Glueck, in his fascinating book, *The River Jordan* (Philadelphia: The Westminster Press, 1946), 268 pp., calls it "Earth's Most Storied River." For good photographs showing the Ghôr and the Zôr, see Figs. 2 and 4 in Glueck (pronounced "Glick").

personally am not so much inclined to that view. Less than twenty miles above the point of crossing, at what is today ed-Damiya or what in Joshua's day was called Adam, there are clay or marl banks along the Zôr. They must run fifty or a hundred feet high, and occasionally they are undermined by the water cutting away at them, and they topple over into the river. In A.D. 1267, when the Mohammedans were trying to build a bridge across the Jordan and found themselves unable to do it, they awoke one morning to discover that the river had been dammed up by an earth fall, and they hastily erected the bridge in the sixteen hours that the river's flow was stopped. In 1927, during an earthquake, the waters of the Jordan were stopped off for twenty-one hours by the falling of those mud walls.[2] There are some who believe that God, through an earthquake, through purely secondary causes, dammed up the waters at this moment by the falling of the clay walls upstream. Well, either way, at the particular moment when these people began to cross the Jordan, they were able to go through just as they had been able to go through the Red Sea. And they entered into the land.

First there was the conquest of Jericho, followed by a series of rapid conquests of the strategic cities. But let us examine the details of the story. After crossing the river, Joshua set up a base of operations at Gilgal. With his supplies across the Jordan in the rear, safe from attack, and by the constant feeding of those supplies, his whole problem of logistics was brilliantly worked out. Jericho stood in his way, guarding the roads up into the mountainous region of Canaan. Before he could capture Canaan, he must reduce Jericho. The story is told for us in the sixth chapter of Joshua. The main point to notice is the fact that the Lord gave them the city (verse 16), which resulted in thorough destruction by sword and by fire.[3]

Moving up the two valleys from Jericho, aiming at the central part of the country, Joshua conquered Ai and Bethel, moved on and took over the cities of the south, and then marched north and took the cities

[2] Cf. *Westminster Dictionary of the Bible* (Philadelphia: The Westminster Press, 1944), article on "Jordan," p. 328.

[3] Sir John Garstang excavated Jericho in the early 1930's and has "confirmed" the Biblical account. However, Miss Kathleen Kenyon has reopened the matter, with her excavations at Jericho since 1952, and has apparently invalidated some of Garstang's claims. At present, the entire matter is being restudied. Cf. K. M. Kenyon, *Digging Up Jericho* (London: Ernest Benn, 1957), 272 pp., especially pp. 256-265.

there. If you study the time references in the record, you will find that all of this took place within five years at the most. It was excellent strategy.

The mopping-up operations and the consolidation of the country took a lot longer. As a matter of fact, Joshua did not live to see it finished; it was not until David's day that the country was really unified. But Joshua's sudden invasion and quick striking at the strategic cities made it possible to take over the rest of the country at leisure. You can read the account in Joshua 6, 8, 10, and 11.

He divided the land, as Moses had told him to do, among the Twelve Tribes, so that they could settle down and take it over and make it their own. That is described in the fourteenth through the nineteenth chapters. The Levites had no land inheritance. They were not supposed to be an earthly people—they were the *spiritual* leaders of people—so they were to have forty-eight cities, four in each of the twelve tribes' apportionment. Six "cities of refuge" were set up for those who were guilty of killing—that is, not murderers, but those who involuntarily or voluntarily were guilty of *manslaughter*—that they might be spared for a fair trial (Joshua 20-21).

The organization of the land was only basic for it was not yet a unified land. The twelve tribes, through a long and bitter experience, had to be brought into a sense of unity, and finally, under the leadership of David, welded into a Kingdom. Joshua gave them only the basic organization. This done he gathered them together at Shechem (Joshua 24), and made his farewell address. And then he died at the age of 110.

Now, let us go back and pull together some of these facts, in order to evaluate Joshua. In his role as religious and military leader, the strong faith of Joshua is obvious again and again. Take, for example, the way that he captured Jericho: only a man of faith would attempt to take a city that way, to have the priests go up and march around it once a day for seven days and seven times on the seventh day, fully believing that when the people were shouting on the seventh day the city would fall. You may say "That is no way to fight a war! The whole thing is utterly ridiculous." But in the very fact that it is ridiculous we find the main lesson: it was written to prove that *the Israelites did not take that city; God took it for them!* To say that they set up a harmonic rhythm by their marching around the city, and that by marching seven days they got the ground trembling in such a way that it shook the walls down, is nonsense. You might do that on a small bridge; you could never do it on solid land. To say that with the sudden shout of the people at the end of that period of time, the sound waves went up and hit the walls and knocked the walls down is also nonsense. God was not trying to prove how smart these people were; God was trying to show them that *He* was going to take the city.

Nevertheless, as you go through the life of Joshua you will find that he used very good strategy. He was blessed by God with a military sense that is remarkable. I read some years ago that, in one of the war colleges of the world, the campaigns of Joshua are studied along with the campaigns of other great military leaders. They are recognized as sound military strategy. I am not saying this to glorify Joshua. I am pointing out, however, that God used a man with that type of genius at that particular moment in history.

Joshua established his base of operations at Gilgal, which was centrally located. It was protected from any attack from the rear; the enemy could not get at it, because the Jordan lay behind it. It was supplied by the rest of the tribes who were still over on the other side of the Jordan, where they could get plenty of foodstuffs and plenty of supplies, bring them down, get them over to the base of operations and then move them up the two valleys from Jericho to wherever the army was operating. Joshua took the center of the land first, cut the country in two, and then took each separated area. Everything about it is beautiful military strategy, however you look at it, and you realize that here was a great man in his own right, and a man who was great because of his faith in the Lord.

To say all these things about Joshua is not to overlook the fact that he made mistakes. There were at least three errors in his work and if it had not been for these the country might have been consolidated much sooner.

In the first place, Joshua was tricked into a treaty with the Gibeonites (chapter 9). The record says explicitly that he did not even wait to find out what the will of the Lord was; he entered into the treaty, and as a long-term result, the country remained disunited until the days of David. The Gibeonites, you remember, came in with their clothes in rags and their shoes worn out and their bread moldy, and they said, "We have come from a very far country ... come; now make a covenant [treaty] with us" (9:9-11). They got him to promise that he would not destroy them as he had been destroying the rest of the Canaanites. Then Joshua found out that their city was only three days away! Because of his word he could do nothing but let them stay there.[4]

Then, he allowed the Jebusites to hold Jerusalem (Joshua 15:63) the results of which plagued the tribes until David captured Jebus.

Perhaps worst of all, Joshua failed to dispossess the Philistines, as God had commanded.[5]

As a result, Judah and Simeon at the south of the country were isolated from the other tribes in the north. The country was divided across the middle by the area of Gibeon, by the city of Jebus or Jerusalem, and by the wedge occupied by the Philistines in the hill country and the Shephelah, that portion of the country that tapers down to the sea, southwest from Jerusalem. The effects of that division were never overcome. David was able to weld the tribes together, but after Solomon's time the country split apart again forming two kingdoms, north and south, and the split was right along that old line of division!

Do you look upon Joshua as a cruel man? When he took a city, he would "devote" it. To "devote" a city to the Lord meant to kill every man, woman, and child and all of the cattle in it, and take the gold and silver and put it in the temple, or in the tent of the Lord. You and I have been brought up under the New Testament code of ethics; we believe in the teaching of Jesus on the use of force. Sometimes we find it difficult to go back into the days of Joshua and understand that he was doing what was normal procedure, and that he was a child of his time.

Even more than that, I think we have to look upon Joshua as a man who was under orders. God had told him to wipe out the Canaanites, for two reasons. First, the Canaanites deserved to be punished because of their own gross sin. We know a number of facts about the Canaanites, from the discoveries of archaeology. They were one of the most grossly depraved people of ancient history. They continued to practice child sacrifice for centuries after it had been abolished in Egypt and Mesopotamia; they made their own children "to pass through the fires of Molech"—which meant burning them alive as a

---

[4] According to our way of thinking, Joshua was not obliged to keep his word, since the Gibeonites had entered into the contract fraudulently.

[5] Dawson Trotman, in a chapel address at Fuller Theological Seminary, pointed out another grave weakness in Joshua's career: he failed to train a successor!

burnt offering. Even worse was their sex perversion. They believed that they could worship their gods, their "baalim," by entering into sexual orgies in the name of religion.[6] God wanted that wiped out. He saw that if that were allowed to continue, it would ultimately destroy the people who took over that land.

He also wanted it wiped out, I think, for another reason. We have already pointed out that the land of Canaan was the center of the "X" that you drew on the map of that time, and that the influences of Canaan went out to the whole world. The religion of Canaan could not help but have its effect abroad, and it did have its effect upon the religions of Asia Minor and Egypt, Greece and Rome. God wanted this place to be a place of testimony to a holy God by a people who were holy because they served a holy God. It was preventive surgery. God saw here a cancer at the heart of the world, and He wanted it cut out no matter what the cost. The greatest charge, I think, that we could lay at the feet of Joshua and those who were associated with him in the conquest of the country was that they failed to carry out the will of God in that respect. All of the difficulties that came later in the religion of Israel—their worship on high places, their own introduction of the glorification of sex, their Baal worship—came from the Canaanites who were allowed to stay even though God had commanded that they be wiped out.

Joshua was not so great as Moses. Is it then anticlimax to study this man after we have studied Moses? I would say no, and I would call your attention to Joshua 1:1-2: "Moses my servant is dead: now therefore arise, go over this Jordan, you and all this people . . . [and] I will be with you." God expects each generation to get up on its own feet and face its own problems. God does not want us to stand around saying, "Well, now, look at Moses. *There* was a great man! We will never have another man like Moses!" And a thousand, two thousand, three thousand years later we are still looking back and saying, "Oh, what a wonderful man Moses was; there never has been another like him." Moses is dead. Great man that he was, he's dead. Get up and face the problems of your day and your age! Arise, go over this Jordan. Don't long for the past. Do the work of the present, and God says, "I will be with you." In Joshua 4:14 we read, "On that day the Lord exalted Joshua in the sight of all Israel." He gave Joshua stature commensurate with the responsibility. He will do the same for us.

[6] For the full picture, see W. F. Albright, *Archaeology and the Religion of Israel* (Baltimore: Johns Hopkins Press, 1942; 2d ed., 1953) Chap. III.

CHAPTER VIII

Ruth

MOST OF THE outstanding characters of the Bible, for one reason or another, seem to be men; only occasionally do you find a woman among them. Such selectivity makes the few even more outstanding; the very fact that a woman's name or record appears puts a special mark on her. One of the most outstanding of these women is Ruth.

Her record—and her little Book—begins with the words: "In the days when the judges ruled. . . ." That was a period in the history of Israel which seems best characterized by the word "disorganization." Young Israel was growing up. Israel had been a young child in Egypt, under the tutelage of a foreign governor. There was no leader in Israel; even Moses, whom God did indeed raise up, was destined to be not a governor, but rather a deliverer who was to free them from bondage. When they entered Canaan, in the days of Joshua, there was still no central organization; they were twelve tribes living on twelve assigned portions of the land, and that was about all. It is summed up in the statement that "In those days there was no king in Israel; every man did what was right in his own eyes" (Judges 17:6). The emphasis you place on that depends largely upon your own philosophy: to me it means that they were doing mostly what was not right in the eyes of God. The story of Israel is the reiterated story of apostasy, repentance and coming back to God, of the Lord sending a deliverer—and of a return to apostasy, as soon as the crisis is over.

In this period lies the story of Ruth; it shines out all the more brightly because of the darkness of the period in general. The story is divided into four scenes—I have often thought it would dramatize very beautifully—and the four scenes fit very nicely into the four chapters that comprise the book. In chapter one is the beautiful story of Elimelech, his wife Naomi, their sons Mahlon and Chilion, and the wives of the sons, Ruth and Orpah.

"In the days when the Judges ruled there was a famine in the land, and a certain man of Bethlehem in Judah went to sojourn in the country of Moab . . ." (1:1). Bethlehem Judah is about five miles south of Jerusalem, on the ridge of the land. Moab lies to the east on the other side of the Jordan Valley at the point where the Jordan River empties into the Dead Sea. The hills of Moab are clearly visible against a sparkling blue sky as you look across the intervening hills of the Judean wilderness, and from certain high points you can see the Dead Sea lying down there, 1292 feet below sea level. Elimelech went to Moab because there was a famine in his own land and he heard that there was food in the land on the other side.

We are told very little about his family: just their names and little else. The two boys, when they got to Moab, took Moabite wives. They lived there about ten years and then the husband of Naomi died, and not long after the sons of Naomi died. That left Naomi and her two daughters-in-law, Orpah and Ruth. It seems as though the story is almost ended before it has begun!

They decide to go back to Bethlehem; at least, Naomi decides that. It is her home; it is where her relatives would be; it is where her heart is, where her religion is. Quite commonly, in those days, people thought of their gods geographically. When they lived in one land they thought in terms of the god of that land, and when they moved to another land they thought of the god of *that* land. This is probably what Naomi meant in verse 15, when she said, "See, your sister-in-law has gone back to her people and to her gods." I suppose that was part of the decision in Naomi's mind—that she was going back to the land of Jehovah.

The girls say they will go along with her. Considering the economic and social system of the day, there was very little choice for young girls like Ruth and Orpah, who had become widowed young in life. Daughters were bought and sold as furniture or cattle or corn were sold. Once they had been "purchased" by one man, they were not very valuable in the eyes of another; frequently the widow would degenerate into a woman of the street. These girls wanted to go along with their mother-in-law hoping, I suppose, that someone would come their way to save them from such a life. But Naomi does not know what to do with them; she tells them to go to their homes (in Moab) and stay there. And they say, "No, we will return with you." Naomi asks, "Why will you go with me? Do I yet have sons in my womb that they may become your husbands?" (1:11). Even if she were to get married again that very night and have sons, would these daughters-in-law be willing to wait around for twenty years or so, until the sons grew up to marry them?

What Naomi is talking about, of course, is the institution of levirate marriage.[1] When a man died leaving a wife with no children, his brother was obligated to marry and to raise up children not to himself but to the dead brother. We find provision for such levirate marriage in the Mosaic law (Deuteronomy 25:5-10), as well as in the cuneiform tablets.[2] Naomi was talking about that custom.

Orpah saw the futility of the situation, and decided that she might just as well go back home.

But Ruth refused to leave Naomi. In one of the most poignant statements in all literature she said, "Entreat me not to leave you or to return from following you; for where you go I will go, and where you lodge I will lodge; your people shall be my people, and your God my God; where you die I will die, and there will I be buried. May the Lord do so to me and more also if even death parts me from you" (1:16-17). There is an intensely beautiful loyalty to her mother-in-law and to the family into which she had entered by marrying the son of Naomi.

So the two of them, Naomi and Ruth, come to Bethlehem. And when they enter the city gates, you can hear the women of the city saying, "Is *this* Naomi? It doesn't look like her. How she has aged! How poor she has become!" She had lost her husband and her sons, and of course the bitter experiences had left their mark upon her. To the amazed group of women Naomi says, "Do not call me Naomi [which means 'pleasant']; call me Mara [which means 'bitter']. . . ." When she had been born, her parents had given her the name "Naomi," because, I suppose, they thought she would grow up to be a pleasant little girl and a pleasant woman with a nice personality. Now she says, in effect, "That's all gone; I'm bitter now, because the Lord has dealt very bitterly with me." So she begins her life anew.

The second chapter introduces Boaz. He was a kinsman, perhaps a cousin, of Naomi's husband, a man of wealth, of the family of Elimelech.

In the first chapter of the Book of Matthew, where Matthew gives the genealogy of the Lord Jesus Christ (verse 5) we read that "Salmon

---

[1] Cf. art. "Marriage, Levirate," in *Unger's Bible Dictionary* (Chicago: The Moody Press, 1957), pp. 700-701.

[2] Cf. C. H. Gordon, *art. cit., Biblical Archaeologist* 3 (1940):10.

[became] the father of Boaz by Rahab, and Boaz the father of Obed by Ruth, and Obed the father of Jesse, and Jesse the father of David the king." The line of Jesus develops from that. Boaz was the son of Salmon by Rahab. Now there is admittedly some question as to whether this is the same Rahab that we find in the Book of Joshua. However, I do not see why her name would ever have been brought into the genealogy if she is not the well-known Rahab,[3] for Matthew lists very few women in his genealogy; those he lists must have been well known.

Let us go back to the story of Rahab, for just a minute. When Joshua and the Israelites had encamped at Gilgal after they crossed over the Jordan, the first city in their path was the city of Jericho. It had to be conquered before they could go on the rest of the way. Joshua sent two spies on ahead to find out what the situation was in Jericho and how they could get past that city to take the country beyond it. The two spies spent the night in the house of a harlot[4] whose name was Rahab. Rahab had heard about the Israelites. She knew that they served the Lord, and she knew something of the Lord's mighty works; so Rahab made them swear that they would deal kindly with her and with her father's house, and save alive her father, her mother, her brothers, her sisters and all who belonged to them. They entered into that compact with her. And they kept it. After the city of Jericho was captured, after the walls had fallen and the Israelites had moved in, they were commanded by Joshua to burn the city and to destroy everyone except Rahab (Joshua 6:22). In Hebrews, where we have the list of the great people of the faith, it is written that by faith Rahab the harlot was saved out of the destruction of Jericho (Hebrews 11:31).

If this is the same Rahab—and to my mind it is, although there is always the possibility of two persons with the same name—then Boaz

[3] A comparison of the genealogy given in Ruth 4:18 with that in Exodus 6:14-25 may be helpful in this connection. Since Aaron had married Elisheba, the daughter of Amminadab the sister of Nashon, and since Amminadab and Nashon are the immediate ancestors of Salmon and Boaz, we have an indication that Salmon belonged to the generation after Aaron (Salmon's father Nashon was Aaron's brother-in-law). The capture of Jericho certainly occurred in the generation after Aaron, and, according to Matthew 1:5, Salmon married Rahab, and their son was Boaz.

[4] According to some scholars the Hebrew word had come to mean something like "inn-keeper." This view is at least as old as Josephus (A.D. 90). But I see little reason to try to explain away the obvious moral standards of that day.

was her son. At any rate, he was the child of faith, for we find gleaming from him this vital faith in the Lord.

Ruth went to Naomi one day and said, "Let me go to the field and glean among the ears of grain after him in whose sight I shall find favor" (Ruth 2:2). According to the law of Moses, anyone was allowed to take from a field of grain as much as he could eat on the spot or as much as he could pick up after the reapers had passed. Moreover, the reaper was told that for the sake of the poor he should not cut the *corners* of the field; he should leave a little grain standing there so the poor could get it. It was a humanitarian provision of the law of God,[5] to take care of the poor of the land. Ruth was planning to go into one of the fields and get enough grain to feed Naomi and herself.

She went, and she happened to come to that part of the field belonging to Boaz (verse 3). It just "happened"—I do not believe she planned it that way. But actually, things do not "just happen" in this world. God has His hands in things; all things work together for good to them who fear God, and who try to follow His will. Ruth came to the field of Boaz, and as she was working there with the reapers, she gathered up the little bit in the corners to take home.

Boaz came from Bethlehem. He greeted the reapers with the words, "The Lord be with you"; and they answered, "The Lord bless you." He looked them over, and apparently he knew who were working for him, for he asked, "Who is this young girl?" Bethlehem was not a large city; it just had a few hundred people—too small, according to the prophet, to be listed among the thousands of Judah. All Bethlehem knew how Naomi had gone out to Moab and how she had come back with no one but her daughter-in-law. So they told Boaz, "It is the Moabite maiden; and she asked us to let her glean and gather among the sheaves, and she has been here from early morning till now, without even stopping for a rest."

Can you not hear Boaz say to Ruth, "Now listen; don't go to glean in any other field; you stay right here in mine. Stay close to my maidens. I have charged[6] the young men in this field not to molest you.

[5] Like many other elements which God led His people to preserve, this was pre-Israelite. The *kashka* in the Nuzu tablets seems to have been a portion left in the field when reaping. Cf. E. A. Speiser, "New Kirkuk Documents Relating to Security Transactions," *Journal of the American Oriental Society,* 52 (1932): 362 ff.

[6] This is an interesting verse for the study of the use of verb tenses in Hebrew. Actually, Boaz had not yet given such a command; he had only just ascertained the facts. But when an action is determined, it can be expressed "as good as done" by the past tense.

When you are thirsty, go to the water-jars and drink what the young men have drawn." In amazement and modesty she bows her face to the ground and says, "Why have I found such favor in your eyes, that you should notice me?" And Boaz says, "Well, I've heard about you. I've heard what you have done for your mother-in-law since the death of your husband, how you left your father and your mother and your native land and came to a people that you never knew before. The Lord bless you; the Lord recompense you for what you have done, and may a full reward be given you by the Lord God of Israel under whose wings you have come to take refuge!"

We like Boaz when we first meet him because he is a man with a vital religious experience. The Lord is not just a name on his lips; the Lord is a Person whom he serves, and to whom he looks for blessing and for reward.

Ruth worked until the evening, beating out what she had gleaned, and she had about an ephah of barley—about a bushel—and she took it home and showed it to her mother-in-law. Naomi asked, "Where did you glean today?" Ruth told her: "In the fields of a man named Boaz." Naomi said, "Blessed be he by the Lord, whose kindness has not forsaken the living or the dead! . . . The man is a relative of ours, one of our nearest kin" (2:19-20).

The "near kinsman" is another idea that we have to get clearly in mind to understand the story. Beside the rule of levirate marriage, which said that a man should marry his departed brother's wife and raise up children to his brother, there was also the law of the near kinsman which said in effect that in the case of a widow who had no one that she could claim in levirate marriage, the nearest male relative was under obligation to consider seriously marrying the young widow in order that she might have a place to live. It is hard for us to picture these things, because today, if a woman is left without a husband early in life, there might be some insurance to help her for a few years. She can probably find work. There is no stigma attached to her remarrying. But in Ruth's day, she could not be independent. She could not go out and get a job. She could be "redeemed"[7] by a near kinsman, or she could enter into a life of prostitution. That was about the only choice she had. Boaz was the near kinsman, and Naomi advised Ruth to stay close to him and see what would develop.

Chapter three of the Book of Ruth is the third scene in this drama—

[7] The verb "to redeem" is used to form the word ($g\acute{o}'\bar{e}l$) used for the "near kinsman." Often $g\acute{o}'\bar{e}l$ is translated "redeemer."

and by suggesting that it is a drama, I do not mean to imply that it is unhistorical. It is quite historical; but it is dramatically told, isn't it? Naomi decides that the situation needs a little pushing, and she takes it upon herself to see if she cannot do *something* about getting this young man who is a near kinsman to marry her daughter-in-law. She says, "My daughter, should I not seek a home for you, that it may be well with you? Now this Boaz, who owns the field where you are working—is he not our kinsman? See, he is winnowing barley tonight at the threshing floor" (3:1-2, paraphrased). And she tells Ruth to wash and anoint herself and put on her best clothes and go down to the threshing floor and find out where Boaz is going to sleep. When he has eaten and has had his wine for the evening and lies down to sleep, she is to crawl in at his feet.

I suppose this sounds a bit *risqué;* no respectable young lady would do that today, would she? A mother would hardly advise her daughter today to use this method of getting a man; but under the customs of ancient time, there was no reproach. We do not find Boaz reproaching this young girl; as a matter of fact, he feels rather flattered that she has not thrown her life to the young men in the field, but that she has come to him.[8]

When he had eaten and drunk, and his heart was merry, he went to lie down at the end of a heap of grain, and she came and uncovered his feet and lay down. About midnight he awoke with a start and behold "a woman lay at his feet!" He said, "Who are you?" and she answered, "I am Ruth, your maidservant; spread your skirt over your maidservant for you are next of kin" (3:9).

But, he was *not* next of kin. I do not believe *Ruth* knew that; I am not even sure that *Naomi* knew it. But *Boaz* knew it. It would seem that he had already considered his responsibility to this young girl, because he had uncovered the fact that there was another man in Bethlehem who was more closely related to her than he, and that other person must be given the right of first refusal.

So he tells Ruth that ". . . you have made this last kindness greater than the first . . . do not fear, I will do all that you ask, because [according to the Hebrew] the gate knows that you are a virtuous

[8] From time to time, I have heard an objection expressed to reading such portions of the Bible. This displays, in my opinion, a false sense of morals. After all, if God chose to include such stories in His Holy Scriptures, who art thou, O man, to criticize? These things must be understood in the light of their day. To this we might add, "Honi soit qui mal y pense."

woman." The gate is the place in the city where everything happens, where all of the gossip is passed, where all town business is transacted, where all the letters are written. Boaz says, ". . . now it is true that I am a near kinsman, yet there is a kinsman nearer than I. Remain this night and in the morning, if he will do the part of the next of kin for you, well; let him do it; but if he is not willing . . . I will do the part of the next of kin for you" (3:12-13). She stays until it is early morning. Before it is light enough to recognize anyone, Boaz sends her home; but first he fills her mantle with grain so that if anyone should see her, they would think she had gone out early in the morning to get some grain. She goes home and tells Naomi all about it.

Chapter four is the conclusion of the story; the scene is laid at the city gate. Boaz goes up to the gate and sits down; everybody has to go through that gate sooner or later during the day, so at last along comes the next of kin. We are not even told his name. Boaz collects some of the elders who are sitting around the gate—I have seen them in the East many times, the old men sitting there by the city gate; they have nothing else to do! They are supported by the younger men of the family. The word for "old man" and the word for "witness" are the same in the Babylonian language. The witnesses are the old men who sit by the gate. Boaz gets ten of these together and he says, "Sit down; you are my witnesses." Then he says to the next of kin, "Naomi who has come back from the country of Moab, is selling the parcel of land which belonged to our kinsman Elimelech. So I thought I would tell you of it and say, 'Buy it in the presence of those sitting here, in the presence of the elders of my people.' If you will redeem it, redeem it; if not, tell me, because there is no one beside you to redeem it, and I come after you." And the nearer relative says, "I will redeem it." Ah, but there is a little catch, a condition that must be met. Ruth is involved; the kinsman will have to take her with the land, in order to "restore the name of the dead." The kinsman objects. He had not thought of that, and what is more, he cannot afford it.

Why could he not afford it? Well, it was a matter of protecting his estate. Under the law, the minute he took Ruth and married her, he contracted to raise up her children not to himself, but to her dead husband! These children immediately became a drain on his resources; furthermore, they threatened the inheritance of his own children: those who were not his own children to carry on his line would threaten the inheritance of the children who were. It is too much; the next of kin backs off, saying, "I cannot redeem it [the land] for myself, lest I impair my own inheritance. Take my right of redemption yourself . . ." (4:6). Boaz must have chuckled; that was the way he wanted it!

Then they do a strange thing—at least it is strange to us. The next of kin takes off one sandal and hands it to Boaz. That seals the bargain. Boaz turns to the elders and the people standing around, and says: "'You are witnesses this day that I have bought from the hand of Naomi all that belonged to Elimelech and all that belonged to Chilion and to Mahlon. Also Ruth the Moabitess, the widow of Mahlon, I have bought to be my wife, to perpetuate the name of the dead in his inheritance, that the name of the dead may not be cut off from among his brethren and from the gate of his native place; you are witnesses this day.' Then all the people who were at the gate, and the elders said, 'We are witnesses. May the Lord make the woman, who is coming into your house, like Rachel and Leah, who together built up the house of Israel'" (4:9-11).

So Boaz took Ruth as his wife. Out of the marriage came Obed, the grandfather of David. Notice that it is Naomi who brings up the child (4:16). This act, apparently a form of adoption, put the child in the legal family genealogy, for it was Naomi who had the right to hand down the succession. She was the one, you remember, who had title to the field. Ruth, after all, was an outlander and a stranger; she would have no genealogical authority. If Naomi had not taken the child and adopted him as her very own, the line of heritage would have been broken.

It is a beautiful story, and it has a beautiful lesson which, as I see it, is this: *The ordinary event of everyday life becomes an important step in God's redemptive plan.* Just suppose Ruth had not gone to the field of Boaz. Suppose Boaz had not felt compelled to go through with the responsibility which was laid upon him as a redeeming kinsman. Or suppose Ruth had not had enough faith to go back home with Naomi; or that Naomi had not had enough faith to take her along. Can you see how God's plan would have been thwarted?

I am not suggesting that you and I, by doing some of the commonplace things of everyday life, can be the means whereby a saviour comes into the world. Our Saviour has already come. But the commonplace things of life are the means whereby God does some of the most important things He has to do. We never know, when one of these little ordinary events comes along, what the results may be. We can bring about unknown and untold good just by faithfulness in the commonplace things of every day.

CHAPTER IX

Samuel

THE PROPHET Samuel has been called the last and greatest of the judges and the first of the prophets. Many Jewish writers look upon him as the first great prophet after Moses. It was Samuel who, under God, had the responsibility of setting up the kingdom and anointing their first kings.

The period *before* the time of Samuel was a rather chaotic time in the history of Israel.[1] They had come out of the land of Egypt a subjected people who had never been responsible for handling their own affairs. For generations they had been slaves, and one of the advantages (if it *is* an advantage) of being a slave is that you do not have to plan for yourself. Everything is planned for you. You do what you are told to do, you get what you are given, and that is all there is to it. But that does not build a nation; neither does it develop independence.

In Canaan, God's promise to Abraham was to be fulfilled: the Israelites were to become a great nation and they were to have many blessings from God. But they were a disorganized people; they were twelve tribes, with intertribal jealousy and strife, and on one occasion one of the tribes was almost wiped out in an internecine quarrel. In those days, "every man did that which was right in his own eyes," and that which was right in his own eyes was not always right in the eyes of God. So God gave them judges, and those judges appeared at critical junctures in the history of the Israelites to lead them a little more steadily in the way that God intended.

Samuel was the last of the judges. Immediately preceding him was Eli; I think the best way to begin the study of Samuel is to begin with a study of Eli.

Eli was judge and his sons were priests in the land. According to I Samuel 2:12, the sons of Eli were worthless men. They had no regard for the Lord. They violated the custom and insisted upon a better

---

[1] For an interesting description of these days, see Werner Keller, *The Bible as History*, pp. 169-182.

share of the offerings. "They had treated the offering of the Lord with contempt."

Eli was not blind to the faults of his sons. It must have been a bitter experience in the life of this old man, who had been judging Israel for about forty years, to discover that his sons were so unworthy. In verse 22, we read that "Eli was very old, and he heard all that his sons were doing to all Israel, and how they lay with the women who served at the entrance to the tent of meeting. And he said to them, 'Why do you do such things? For I hear of your evil dealings from all the people. No, my sons; it is no good report that I hear the people of the Lord spreading abroad. If a man sins against a man, God will mediate for him; but if a man sins against the Lord, who can intercede for him?' But they would not listen to the voice of their father. . . ."

The time came when God had to reject this old man and his sons and tell him that although He has previously made a promise (back in the days of Moses and Aaron) that the family of Eli would be the one to continue the priesthood; yet, because of the sons' infidelity and worthlessness, God was going to break that agreement. A man of God came to Eli and told him in a cryptic way that he, Eli, would live to see the sudden death of his two sons on one day, and that his own heart would be consumed with the grief of it (2:28-31).

The punishment came about in an interesting way—quite an ordinary way, you might say. Chapter 4 tells us about it. Israel went out to battle against the Philistines; Israel was encamped at Ebenezer and the Philistines at Aphek. The battle was going against Israel, and someone got an idea: "Why don't we send for the Ark of the Covenant?" The Ark they had carried through the wilderness; it had been in the Tabernacle, representing the presence of God Himself between the cherubim; it had been carried by the priests across the Jordan so that the water dried up and they could walk dry-shod. Why not bring the Ark into battle now, so that the Lord Himself would be there? What an immature concept they had of the presence of God! If only they could get God on the battlefield they would win! So, without stopping to ask if this were the Lord's will or not, they brought the precious Ark into the battle.

But the Lord was displeased because they had not sought His will. Graphically the story is told: "A man of Benjamin ran from the battle line, and came to Shiloh the same day, with his clothes rent and earth upon his head." Eli was sitting by the side of the road watching;

he was troubled because they had taken the Ark of God down to battle without finding out the Lord's will, and he asked for news. "How did it go, my son?" The Benjamite said, "Israel has fled before the Philistines, and there has been a great slaughter among the people; your two sons also, Hophni and Phinehas, are dead, and the ark of God has been captured" (4:12-17).

The words fell upon Eli like the blows of a hammer. It was bad enough that his two sons had been killed in the battle, but when he learned that the Ark had been captured, the old man, who was sitting on a stool, fell over backward and broke his neck and died.

It was in Eli's day that Samuel was born; it was in the latter years of his judgeship that Samuel grew up, and began to fulfill the duties of the priestly office. Go back to the first chapter of I Samuel and read the account of the birth of Samuel. His father was Elkanah, of the tribe of Benjamin of Ephraim, and he had two wives: Hannah and Peninnah; Hannah had no children. Elkanah used to go up to Shiloh every year to sacrifice to the Lord of hosts—this was a century before the building of the temple at Jerusalem. There he would give portions of the sacrifices to Peninnah his wife. He loved his other wife, Hannah, but he would only give her one portion because the Lord had closed her womb.[2] That used to irritate Hannah. She would weep about it. Finally she went and prayed to the Lord and made a vow: "O Lord of hosts, if thou wilt indeed look on the affliction of thy maidservant, and remember me, and not forget thy maidservant, but wilt give to thy maidservant a son, then I will give him to the Lord all the days of his life, and no razor shall touch his head" (I Samuel 1:11). In other words, Samuel would be under the Nazirite vow.[3] If she could only *have* a son, Hannah was in effect saying, she would not even ask to keep him. The fact that she *had* a son would satisfy her.

The Lord heard her prayer and the son was born in due time; and when he was weaned (which among the Hebrews would be some time in the second year), she took him, together with an offering of a three-year-old bull, a ephah of flour, and a skin of wine, and brought them

---

[2] The verse is difficult. Others interpret it to mean that Elkanah gave Hannah a double portion. Verse 6 is also difficult to interpret: who was irritated by whom, Hannah or Peninnah? I understand it to mean that Hannah was irritated by the presence (and possibly jibes) of her husband's other wife; others interpret it to mean that Peninnah was irritated by the displays of love for Hannah by Elkanah.

[3] On the Nazirite vow, see *Westminster Dictionary of the Bible,* art. "Nazirite," p. 421.

to the house of the Lord at Shiloh, where she made her offering: "For this child I prayed; and the Lord has granted me my petition which I made to him. Therefore I have lent him to the Lord; as long as he lives, he is lent to the Lord" (1:27-28). So far as we can tell from the rest of the story, she never took the child home again. He stayed there at Shiloh and Eli in the temple and grew up in the service of the Lord.

There is another beautiful little touch in the second chapter, which tells of how his mother used to make him a little robe each year and take it to him in the temple. As the child grew, his clothing, as you mothers know, did not grow with him. So Hannah would take a larger size the next year and give him the robe as she offered the yearly sacrifice. And Eli blessed Elkanah and his wife and said, "The Lord give you children by this woman for the loan which she has lent to the Lord" (2:20). Her reward is told in the twenty-first verse: ". . . the Lord visited Hannah, and she conceived and bore three sons and two daughters. And the boy Samuel grew in the presence of the Lord."

Here then is a child who had come out of a godly home, the child of a very devout mother who was willing, if she could only have a son, to turn him over as soon as possible to the Lord's service.

The next high point in the story is the call of Samuel. He was ministering to the Lord under Eli. We do not know how old he was at this time, nor are we told how old Eli was. I suppose Samuel was in his early teens, or even younger. We are told in 3:1 that the word of the Lord was "rare" in those days. The people were living in a time when it seemed as though the heavens were shut away from them. Eli's eyesight had begun to grow dim, and he could not see; he was lying down in his place; the lamp of God had not yet quite gone out. Samuel was lying down inside the temple where the Ark of God was.

And the Lord said, "Samuel, Samuel!" And he said, "Here I am . . ."; and he ran in to Eli. Do you see how natural all of these things are? You and I do not live under the experience of those days, when God would pick out one particular person and speak to him or speak through him; we live in the dispensation of the Holy Spirit when God speaks to us by the Spirit, chiefly through His Word. But in those days it was not so. I believe that this child, who had not been through the experience before, actually heard a voice calling him by name, and went into the next room and said to Eli, "Here I am; you called me." Eli replied, "I did not call you; lie down again."

He went back and lay down and the voice came again saying, "Samuel!" And he went to Eli again and said, ". . . you called me"; and Eli denied it again. We are told that Samuel did not yet know the Lord, and that the word of the Lord had not yet been revealed to him.

Then the Lord called Samuel a third time, and he went into Eli and said, "Here I am; you called me." Eli at last perceived that the Lord was calling the boy, and he said, "Go, lie down, and if he calls you, you shall say, 'Speak, Lord, for thy servant hears.'" And he went back and lay down; and God came to him and spoke to him, and told him what was going to happen—that he was going to fulfill against Eli the things that He had spoken concerning Eli's house from the beginning to end, and that He would punish him because his sons were blaspheming God and he did not restrain them.

We cannot help but stop a moment at a verse like this to point out that there is an element of responsibility which falls upon us as parents. Eli, although he certainly could not be blamed for what his sons were doing, was blamed because he made no attempt to restrain them. He apparently was letting them go their own way. We read once of a more or less half-hearted effort to stop them, but apparently they were too far gone by that time.

It was soon after this that the Spirit of the Lord came upon Samuel, and (verse 20) "all Israel from Dan to Beersheba—from the city farthest north to the city farthest south—knew that Samuel was established as a prophet of the Lord."

This is a different situation from that which existed in the days of Eli's judgeship, when there was no frequent Word of God. Samuel becomes the means by which God can speak to His people, and it seems as though God has come back again to His land, at Shiloh, while Samuel is dwelling there.

The next step in the study of Samuel is the study of his connection with King Saul. Samuel was trying to organize the people into some kind of unity. They were still twelve tribes; still going their separate ways. One of the tribes had had an abortive effort at kingship with Abimelech, but we can scarcely refer to Abimelech as the first king of Israel. Samuel "went on a circuit year by year to Bethel, Gilgal, and Mizpah" (7:16). If you look at those places on a map, you will see that they are in the central part of the land of Canaan, lying almost in a circle. It would seem as though Samuel was making this annual tour to try to hold the people together.

The nations around them had kings, and the nations around them, especially the Philistines, were attacking the Israelites from time to time. The elders of Israel on one occasion gathered with Samuel at Ramah and said to him, "Behold, you are old and your sons do not walk in your ways; now appoint for us a king to govern us like all the nations" (8:5).

Some of our modern historians tell us that the reason why Samuel was reluctant to give the people a king was because he was an old meddler, a manipulator, and that he wanted the kingship for himself. I don't believe it! I think he was an idealist, and that he felt that to put a king over this people would be to increase their problems. He pointed out what would happen if they had a king: "These will be the ways of the king who will reign over you: he will take your sons and appoint them to his chariots to be his horsemen, and to run before his chariots; and he will appoint for himself commanders of thousands and commanders of fifties, and some to plow his ground and to reap his harvest, and to make his implements of war. . . . He will take your daughters to be perfumers and cooks and bakers. He will take the best of your fields and vineyards and olive orchards and give them to his servants. He will take the tenth of your grain and your vineyards and give it to his officers. . . . He will take your menservants and maidservants, and the best of your cattle and your asses, and put them to his work. He will take the tenth of your flocks, and you shall be his slaves" (8:11-17). Perhaps the picture was a bit overdrawn, but it is still true. When you get government, you must pay for government. In our day, we would say that "all this means increased taxation!" Samuel was saying that to his people. But they wanted a king, and God told Samuel to go ahead and give them a king.

Now this is one of the points that is often contested in Old Testament study: whether or not it was God's will that there should be a king. It *was* God's will that there should be a kingdom. He had spoken about it before this. To have a kingdom, you have to have a king; therefore, God would have given these people a king in due time, when it was His will that it should happen. I think that the sin here lies not in the desire for a king but in the fact that the people were running before God. They were crying for a king before God had chosen to give them one, and therefore the king they got turned out to be pretty much of a failure. He was not a king after God's own heart. Another had to be sent to replace him.

We come now to Saul, who was the son of Kish and a man of the tribe of Benjamin. The asses of Kish were lost and the young man and a servant were sent out to hunt for them. They covered quite a bit of ground as they hunted; they went through Ephraim, through Shalisha, through Shaalim, and through the land of Benjamin. When they came to Zuph, Saul said, "Come, let us go back, lest my father cease to care about the asses and become anxious about us." But the servant said, "There is a man of God in this city, and he is a man held in honor; all that he says comes true. Let us go there; perhaps he can tell us [where the asses are]" (I Samuel 9:5-6, slightly paraphrased).

So they went up into the city and asked if the seer were there. (Samuel was known as a "seer" at this point, not as a "prophet.") Samuel had been told by the Lord, "Tomorrow about this time I will send you a man from the land of Benjamin, and you shall anoint him to be prince over my people Israel. He shall save my people from the hands of the Philistines" (9:16). As Saul and his servant drew near, Samuel heard the voice of the Lord saying, "Here is the man of whom I spoke to you!" Saul approached Samuel and asked, "Where is the house of the seer?" Samuel answered, "I am the seer; go up before me to the high place, for today you shall eat with me, and in the morning I will let you go. . . . As for your asses that were lost three days ago, do not set your mind on them, for they have been found" (9:19-20).

Saul realized, by this time, that he was in the presence of a man who knew a lot more about what was happening than he did; meekly, he followed Samuel. As they sat down to eat, Samuel said to the cook, "Bring the portion I gave you, of which I said to you, 'Put it aside.'" When he gave Saul the choice cut of the meat Saul wondered what it was all about. Why should he be treated like this? He found out why the next day: on the outskirts of the city, Samuel told him to send his servant on ahead, so that they might be alone. There Saul knelt while Samuel poured oil on his head and rose the first king of Israel.

But something more was necessary to make the kingship complete: Saul needed the approval of the people he was to rule. Samuel took care of that, too. He called the tribes together and said in effect: "You want a king. Let's make it legal; elect a man from one of your tribes!" They did just that; they cast lots and selected the tribe of Benjamin as the one from which their king should come; from the tribe of Benjamin, the family of Kish was picked as the family from which he would come; and from that family, the choice fell on Saul. What a choice! He stood head and shoulders above any man in sight; he was handsome, courageous, looking every inch a king. Saul was just what they needed. And all the people shouted, "Long live the king!"

But even that was not enough to make Saul king. Some asked, "What's he king *of?*" Others, "He's good looking, but what will he do when a war comes?" It was not long before they found out: war with the Ammonites came, as told in chapter eleven, and Saul met the acid test; he led his people to victory over the people of Ammon. At last he was really king! He had been anointed by the prophet, chosen by lot by the people, and established as a military hero by winning a great battle. He had the goodwill of the people, the courage of a true king, the face of a god. No finer candidate for the throne could have been found in Israel—at least so it would seem.

The next person in the life of Samuel is David. There is not much to tell of David in this connection, for the Bethlehem youth was still young when Samuel died; there is just enough to round out the picture. In I Samuel 12, the old prophet called upon his people to witness to his honor and honesty; he called upon them to say whether he had ever taken anything from them fraudulently, or in oppression. They swore that he had not. Then he told them of *their* record; he reminded them of their sinfulness and disobedience and called upon them to repent. He promised that "if you still do wickedly, you shall be swept away, both you and your king" (12:25). They went on doing wickedly—both people and king.

Saul got into a battle with the Amalekites; he had previously been told by the Lord to wipe them out to the last man and the last animal. But he disobeyed; he saved some of the best animals and he allowed Agag, king of the Amalekites, to get away alive. Samuel came to Saul after the battle, heard the lowing of oxen taken alive from the enemy, and discovered the rest of Saul's disobedience. The word of the Lord came to Samuel: "I repent that I have made Saul king" (15:10).

Repent? *God* repents? How could He? I think God is speaking here in words and speech that the people can understand. It was not God's will that Saul be made king; God had, humanly speaking, given in to the wishes of the people. So, still speaking in human terms, God says, "I repent that I have made Saul king; for he has turned back from following me, and has not performed my commandments" (15:11). Samuel was angry and he cried to the Lord all night. After all, Samuel was in this thing too; he had gotten himself mixed up in

a nice mess, anointing this man as king. He did not want his reputation marred for doing that; he did not want to be repudiated, either,
by the people of God. He felt, at first, that he must defend Saul; to
turn against him would be to admit that he was wrong. But when he
heard the lowing of the oxen and discovered the king of the enemy
alive, he knew in his heart that he had anointed the wrong man: *Saul
never should have been made king.*

Samuel faces Saul in a dramatic scene, with a dramatic accusation:
"Though you are little in your own eyes, are you not the head of the
tribes of Israel? The Lord anointed you king over Israel, and the Lord
sent you on a mission, and said, 'Go, utterly destroy the sinners, the
Amalekites, and fight against them until they are consumed.' Why then
did you not obey the voice of the Lord? Why did you swoop down on
the spoil, and do what was evil in the sight of the Lord?" (15:17-19).
Saul offers his poor excuses: he *did* obey, really; he captured the king;
he took just a *little* of the spoil; it was the *people* who took most of
it! But Samuel is not impressed; he pronounces the doom of an out-
raged God upon the house of Saul, and then grieves over Saul. At last,
after the Lord has chided him for the delay, he turns to find a successor,
David. He anoints David, then returns to his house at Ramah. In a
simple, immortal statement the Scripture records his death: "Now
Samuel died; and all Israel assembled and mourned for him, and they
buried him in his house at Ramah" (25:1).

The greatness of Samuel has to be measured against the times
in which he lived. It was a chaotic period in Israel's history; those
were the formative years. We have a parallel in the colonial days in
America, before we were "the United States," in the days when we
were more divided than united, and not yet pulling together. Israel was
divided twelve ways, as the colonies were divided into thirteen. At the
head of Israel stood Saul, beset with a terrible melancholia that at
times seemed madness; no man's life was safe in his household or his
court. Division in the state, insanity at court: in the midst of this stood
Samuel, a lonely figure of tremendous stature, a man whose job it was
to start the organization of a kingdom. He did not live to see that
kingdom in its days of glory, under David and Solomon; his was only
to prepare Israel for her days of glory.

There were many obstacles. The people turned on him, demanding
a king. He gave them their king. But Saul proved to be unworthy of
the throne and not a man of God, for the simple reason that he was

chosen on the human basis of appearance and human courage, and not on the basis of spirituality or devotion to God. Through all of this, Samuel stood firmly—the one great character of the whole affair. He was the man through whom God could work His will. Eli falls, Saul falls, David is still a shepherd boy—but there stands Samuel!

There is something magnificent in being God's man in difficult times. It is not as glamorous as being God's man in the days when things are going well. But—suppose there had been no Samuel? Suppose there had been no one to hold things together, no one to guide, or counsel, or rebuke, or point out God's way? Would the kingdom then have come into existence? Perhaps so; perhaps God would have raised up someone else—but the fact remains that He raised up *Samuel,* the last of the judges and the first of the prophets, and laid great work upon him in full confidence that he would do it, and do it well. And Samuel did it well; no man can deny that.

CHAPTER X

David: The Man

DAVID is considered by many to be the greatest character in the Old Testament after Moses. I suppose, when we start talking about which one is "greatest," it is a matter of personal choice and preference, and there are many factors that enter into our decision. Each of the characters that we have been studying has some particular characteristic, some particular value, that makes him worth studying. Joshua was blessed, for example, in that he had the opportunity of leading the people into the land which God had promised Abraham; David was blessed in that he had the privilege of setting up the kingdom in that land.

God brings us back repeatedly to situations in which we can see the continuity of His whole program: the promise to Abraham is not something we study and forget; it recurs in the lives of most of these Old Testament figures. The same thing is true when we get into the New Testament; we find there that we are not starting with a whole new series of persons, but each one has some particular part in that unfolding plan of God by which He accomplishes His eternal purpose.

David was the one who set up the dynasty. Saul, of course, had been the first king of Israel, but Saul did not set up the eternal dynasty; it is not "the house of Saul," but "the house of David" which is forever. The house of David does not lack a man to sit on the throne of the kingdom: David's greater son, Jesus Christ, is of the house and lineage of David, not of Saul. So, you see, in a particular way David is the one who in God's wisdom and in God's will brought about, here on earth, in its initial stages at least, the kingdom of God which God had foretold when He made His promises to Abraham.

David's story starts in the sixteenth chapter of I Samuel, and runs through the rest of the First Book of Samuel. He was born in Bethlehem. Jesus, you will remember, was also born in Bethlehem, because He was of the house and lineage of David. Bethlehem is "the city of David."

We gather that David had a godly mother. There are, I think, two references to that in the Psalms: in the 86th and 116th Psalms, both of which are ascribed to David. In Psalm 86:16 he prays to God, "Turn to me and take pity on me; give thy strength to thy servant, and save the son of thy handmaid." Likewise in Psalm 116:16 he refers to himself as "the son of thy handmaid." We may be reading too much into it, but it is nevertheless true that David referred to his mother as "the handmaid of the Lord," at least twice in the Psalms, and the inference from that statement is substantiated by the life of David, in which we find the characteristics of a man who has been brought up by his mother to know the Lord and to trust Him.

Of course, there is a lot more to a religious life than just that. David goes through some other experiences in which he seems to lose his faith or in which it weakens or wavers, and he has still other experiences in which his faith seems to come back with a new strength. His Psalms indicate that he had passed through many such experiences. But the fact remains—we shall see it brought out over and over again in these studies—that the early training that a child has from his parents, and particularly his mother, is extremely important. We cannot overemphasize that lesson. It is one of the truths the church must insist upon in its teaching, and Christians must accept and believe and act upon.

David is described, in I Samuel 16:12, as "a ruddy lad, with beautiful eyes and handsome." Later on in life, he got into some strange situations because of his attractiveness; women ran after him, singing, "Saul has killed his thousands, but David his ten thousands," and it started a chain reaction of jealousy in the mind of Saul that led to a great deal of difficulty. David was a fine looking young man. Tradition has it that the word "ruddy" here implies that he had blue eyes and a fair complexion with blond or reddish hair.

Of course, you know that David was a shepherd. He is described in I Samuel 16:11 as keeping the sheep while the rest of the family of Jesse were at home; further on, he describes himself to Saul by saying, "Your servant used to keep sheep for his father, and when there came a lion or a bear and took a lamb from the flock, I went after him and smote him and delivered it out of his mouth; and if he arose against me, I caught him by his beard and smote him and killed him. Your servant has killed both lions and bears" (17:34-35). Some think that he is boasting, but I rather imagine there is a factual basis for it; I doubt that he was saying this to impress Saul because, after all, he was in a situation where to impress Saul was to put himself up against the giant Goliath, and there was no need for him to stick his neck out *that* far!

His bravery is emphasized again in the contest with Goliath. The Philistines were one of the thorns in the side of the Israelite kingdom in the days of Saul and in the early days of David. They lived down on the seacoast, fifty to sixty miles southwest of Jerusalem, and they extended their territory in a sort of wedge pointed northeast toward the Israelite kingdom, specifically toward Jerusalem. The wedge increased in size as the strength of the Philistines increased, and decreased whenever the Israelites grew strong. The frontier was fluid; whenever the Philistines became overstrong, they would extend their lines and stretch into Israelite territory and take more of the country; and the country in that area, we might add, is the best country in the whole land of Palestine for grape vineyards, olive orchards, and the general raising of crops.

Now the Philistines were engaged in one of those conflicts when someone got a good idea: "Why bother having a full-scale war, when we can settle it with a combat between just two men?[1] Let us pick out one of our men, and let the Israelites pick out one of theirs, and let the two of them slug it out; whichever man is victor, we'll say his side won. It will save us all a lot of trouble." That *is* a smart way to conduct a war, particularly if you happen to have a giant on your side. And the Philistines had a giant named Goliath of Gath. His height was six cubits and a span. A cubit is the length of your forearm from the point of your elbow to the tip of your long finger, usually around eighteen inches. A span is, of course, the length which you span with your fingers between the outstetched thumb and the end of the small finger—about eight inches. So a man six cubits and a span in height, would be somewhere in the neighborhood of nine feet eight inches—not an unreasonable height for a giant. Some think that this is one of the fairy tales from the days of giant killers, and they point out that there are no such giants now. But nine feet is not an incredible height for a human being; giants of the present day are known to exceed eight feet. Two years ago, if I am not mistaken, there was a basketball team in this country that could put on the floor at one time an entire team, every man above seven feet in height. So you see this is not an unreasonable story.

[1] This use of the single combat is found also in Homer's *Iliad*.

Goliath's head was covered with a helmet of bronze. He wore a coat of mail that weighed five thousand shekels of bronze—about 125 pounds. His legs were protected below the knees with greaves (thin plates) of bronze. Slung across his shoulders was a javelin of bronze, and in his hand was a spear that had a shaft like a weaver's beam and a spearhead that weighed six hundred shekels of iron—about fifteen pounds.[2] In addition to this, he had a shield-bearer who went before him. You see, Goliath had very little chance of losing when he suggested, "I'll go out there and I'll fight any representative of Israel, and whoever wins the battle will be the victor."

The Israelites took one look at him and decided it was a rather difficult assignment. They held off for days, and he taunted them. He shouted over to them, "Why have you come out to draw up for battle? Am I not a Philistine, and are you not servants of Saul? Choose a man for yourselves, and let him come down to me. If he is able to fight with me and kill me, then we will be your servants; but if I prevail against him and kill him, then you shall be our servants and serve us. . . . I defy the ranks of Israel this day; give me a man, that we may fight together" (I Samuel 17:8-10). The Israelites were dismayed. They looked around; they could find no one willing to enter into the unequal battle—until David came along and offered his services.

The story in the seventeenth chapter suggests that this had been going on for some time; there was a daily taunting by the Philistine giant, and Israel was doing nothing about it. Then David comes, looks at the situation and says immediately that he will go in and battle him. Saul says to him, "You are not able to go against this Philistine to fight with him; for you are but a youth and he has been a man of war from his youth." David replies, "The Lord who delivered me from the paw of the lion and from the paw of the bear will deliver me from the hand of this Philistine." Saul felt that if David insisted upon going into this thing, he had better be protected, and so he clothed him with his own coat of mail, and put a helmet of bronze on his head. David put on his sword, over his armor; he tried hard, but he simply could

[2] The shekel, we know from actual weights that have been recovered, varied considerably: some shekels are 2½ times as heavy as others from different places and times. I am using the value 1 shekel equals 0.4 ounce, which, in my opinion, is reasonable here. For a study of weights and measures, see G. A. Barrois, "Chronology, Metrology, etc.," in *The Interpreter's Bible* (New York and Nashville: Abingdon-Cokesbury Press, 1952ff.), Vol. I, pp. 142-164.

not use that sword, nor wear the armor. He said, "I cannot go . . . I'm not used to them."

Do you see the fix he is in? He is a young man who has been accustomed to living in the open as a shepherd with his flocks; he was probably so fleet-footed that he could race around to one side of the flock when he saw a little lamb straying off that direction, and get back to the other side quickly if he saw danger coming there. Now he is weighted down with much more than the little cloth mantle that he would wear while he was out with the flocks, and he is unable to maneuver. He takes off the armor, drops the sword, and arms himself with the weapon he knows best.

He takes his staff in his hand; it is something like a club. He chooses five smooth stones from the brook; puts them in his shepherd's bag, and takes his sling in his hand. You can still buy those slings; I bought one in the market place in Bethlehem. It is a knit affair, with two long strings coming out on each side, perhaps a foot or fifteen inches long. The center of it is woven into an almost circular shape, two or three inches across. The idea is to put a stone in the center and whirl it around several times and then let go of one end of it. The stone will travel much farther than you could throw it, because you get so much velocity at the end of the sling. In the hand of a practiced slinger it is a lethal weapon.

The Philistine came down and looked at this boy and when he saw him he said, "Am I a dog, that you come to me with sticks?" And he "cursed David by his gods." Then he taunted David, saying, "Come to me, and I will give your flesh to the birds of the air and to the beasts of the field." But David said, "You come to me with a sword and with a spear and with a javelin; but I come to you in the name of the Lord of hosts, the God of the armies of Israel, whom you have defied. This day the Lord will deliver you into my hand, and I will strike you down, and cut off your head; and I will give the dead bodies of the host of the Philistines this day to the birds of the air and to the wild beasts of the earth; that all the earth may know that the Lord saves not with sword and spear; for the battle is the Lord's and he will give you into our hands" (17:43-47).

Notice that the confidence of this young lad is not in himself; his confidence is in the Lord. He feels that the Philistines have dared to defy not only Israel; they have defied also the Lord of Israel. And David takes one of the stones and lets it go and catches Goliath in the forehead, and Goliath sinks to the ground; and while he lies stunned on the ground David runs over, takes his sword, and cuts off his head—and that is the end of Goliath.

That put the Philistines to rout, and it put David immediately in the eye of the people. As a result he came into Saul's court. There are two accounts in the Book of Samuel of how he got into the court;[3] I rather imagine both of them are true, for Saul was psychologically the kind of man who would do something and later on forget that he had done it. He probably brought David into his court and then forgot that he had him there. Lonely, the boy went back home with his father and the flocks. Later he came to the attention of the king a second time, in the conflict with Goliath, and the king asked, "Who *is* this fellow?" And he took David back into his court.

Another of David's characteristics was his musical ability. He was able to play on the harp—well, it is called a harp in our English Bibles, but actually it was a lyre.[4] The music was, I suppose, similar to what I have heard played by some of the Oriental musicians along the streets of their villages—a rather haunting kind of music. Not many of us today would have any fondness for that particular type of music, but after you have heard it for a while, after you have lived with it for two or three months, you get used to it, and there is a haunting delightfulness about it. It seems to have had therapeutic value for Saul in his moments of madness, for he would call David in and David would play this music. It "drove away the evil spirit in Saul" and helped him to compose himself. But gradually this evil in the mind of Saul built up until he became so completely jealous of David that it was impossible for David to stay there. He was forced to leave the court.

David had formed a friendship, really a deep devotion, with Jonathan, the son of Saul. It is all the more remarkable, I think, because Jonathan had come to know that Saul had been rejected by the Lord and that David would ultimately take over the throne which should, by the line of blood, go to him. Even so, he warned David of what was going

[3] The first account is told in I Samuel 16:14-23. The matter is further complicated by II Samuel 21:19, where we are told that it was Elhanan who slew Goliath. But I Chronicles 20:5 says that Elhanan slew the brother of Goliath. This is not the place to try to solve this knotty problem.

[4] For an archaeological indication of what this lyre looked like, see Fig. 76 (p. 123) in G. E. Wright, *Biblical Archaeology* (Philadelphia: Westminster Press, 1957).

on in the mind of Saul, and finally he helped David get away from Saul and find refuge in the outlying territory.

This brings us to the second period of David's life, his outlaw existence. Sometimes, when I have called David an outlaw, I have been rebuked for it. I have been told that this really is not the right word to use about a Bible character. But it is exactly what David had become. He lived off the country, by marauding and plundering; at one time he had to save his life by taking the shewbread, the bread of the presence, from the altar of the Lord. Jesus referred to that when He was rebuked by the Pharisees for breaking the Sabbath, pointing out that even David, when the circumstances required, had to go beyond what was legal to maintain his own life. The young man became not only an outlaw with reference to the laws of King Saul, but a violator of the written law of the Scriptures, in order to stay alive.

Then David accepted protection from King Achish, a Philistine king who had been an enemy of his country. If you read the story in chapter 21:1-9, you find that David seems to have lost much of his faith in the Lord. He went over to the enemy—*almost*. But he got hold of himself in time and by feigning madness he was able to get away from King Achish. Then he came to the cave of Adullam (chapter 22), where he went through an experience which I think is reflected in some of the Psalms. Psalm 34, for example, seems to contain the story of his regaining the faith: "This poor man cried, and the Lord heard him, and saved him out of all of his troubles." The Psalm goes on to say, "O taste and see that the Lord is good!" Some of the other Psalms reflect the same story.

David next gathered around himself a group of outlaws like himself, men who were not acceptable to the government of Saul. With them he succeeded in protecting the borderland of Israel against the forces of the Philistines, so that even though he and his men were not under King Saul, they were actually working in the King's interests. On two occasions at least, perhaps on three occasions, Saul went after David. David had the opportunity to kill him, but he restrained himself. He had by that time learned to depend on the Lord, not on himself. Psalm 57, I think, reflects that story. The heading of Psalm 57 is "To the choirmaster: according to Do Not Destroy.[5] A Miktam[6] of David,

[5] Possibly indicating that this Psalm is to be sung to a familiar vintage tune. Cf. Isaiah 65:8.

[6] An obscure Hebrew word, perhaps another musical notation.

when he fled from Saul, in the cave." In that Psalm David tells the story of how he cried to God and how he found his refuge in God; how he lay in the midst of lions that greedily devour the sons of men. He could say, "My heart is steadfast, O God, my heart is steadfast!" He did not seek to deliver himself; he was perfectly content to let God work this thing out in *His* own time. He refused on several occasions to do anything whatever to hasten the day when he should take over the throne from Saul.

We bring our story to a close with the reference to the Philistine war, which is told in the last few chapters of I Samuel and the death of Saul which is described in the first chapter of II Samuel. You might think this event would bring joy to the heart of young David because now he could say, "Well, Saul is out of the way; at last I can take over the throne." Instead, you find sincere mourning. Saul was God's man, although Saul had turned against God. David realized that you cannot stretch out your hand against the Lord's anointed. Then, too, Jonathan, Saul's son, had been David's best friend. The news that Saul and Jonathan had been killed broke the heart of David.

Just to study this much of his life, without going into the great events of his kingdom (which we will do in our next chapter) is to see something of the character of this man. He had gone through all sorts of adversity, all sorts of persecution; he had even wandered away from the faith which he had at the beginning, into a mild sort of unbelief. He had sought to live by his own wits, rather than by trust in God; and then in a rich, deep, spiritual experience he was brought to trust in God and to see how much God would do for him. He was willing to sit back and wait until God's time came for him to take over the kingdom. He refused to move on his own, or do anything to get rid of Saul. That was his character! We shall see even more of it as we see how he leads the nation step by step. We shall see something of the other side of his character, too, when we discover that he is a man who has sinned deeply. He knows it and his Psalms reflect it.

CHAPTER XI

David: The King

IN THE WORLD of sport we often hear the expression "color." While I cannot exactly define it, I think you understand what it is; the athlete with "color" makes his easy plays look spectacular and his mistakes are readily forgotten. The batting champion goes down swinging like a windmill, the all-American tackle fails to throw a block, the heavyweight contender leaves himself wide open—and still we love them, if they have color. Bad manners on the field are overlooked. We love them just the way they are.

David had color. I think it is for this reason the Bible can portray him in what some writers call "an honest story." The curtain is never drawn before certain episodes in his life. He stands there in full gaze, warrior or weakling, saint or sinner. We know all about David. And we love him. We have already followed the early days of his career, down to the death of Saul. In this chapter, we shall study David the King. But we shall not lose sight of David the Man—for he is the same person. His weaknesses may seem more obvious, his sins more glaring, his victories more thrilling, now that he is king. Even his name seems to take on new significance. If the evidence of the Mari tablets has been rightly interpreted, *dawîdûm* was a title, perhaps like "generalissimo,"[1] but to students of the Bible, David will always mean "beloved."

After the death of Saul, David located his capital at Hebron, in the south of the land of Palestine. Actually, he was king only of the southern part of the land known later as Judah. There was a tendency toward a division into north and south throughout the history of Israel. Only for a little while was it really united. It was one kingdom during the latter portion of David's reign and the early reign of Solomon. Then it broke apart again.

The continuing house of Saul, which had not been killed off (David

[1] G. Dossin, "Benjamites dans les textes de Mari," in *Mélanges syriens offerts à M. René Dussaud,* Vol. II (1939), p. 981.

did not follow the practice of wiping out the whole house) tried to establish a ruling dynasty in the north. For seven years David ruled in the south while the rival kingdom held forth in the north.

The first four chapters of II Samuel record the end of the house of Saul and the complete victory of David. The end came largely through the treachery of Abner, Commander of Saul's army.[2] After that, David was king over the entire country.

One of the first things that he did as king was to conquer the stronghold of the Jebusites, the city of Jebus, which we know better as Jerusalem. One advantage of Jebus was that it was centrally located, at least more centrally located than Hebron, which was twenty miles farther south. Moreover, it was neutral territory, never having been held by the south or by the north. It was in the hands of the Jebusites until it was taken by David; therefore there was no emotional tie to either north or south, hence no entering wedge that might tend to divide the kingdom again. The southerners could not say, "The capital is in *our* part of the kingdom," nor could the northerners say, "No, it is in *ours*." It was on neutral ground. Somewhat the same principle led the founding fathers of our nation to locate our capital in the District of Columbia rather than in one of the states.

The capture of Jebus is described in the fifth chapter of II Samuel. The arrogant Jebusites said that "the lame and the blind" could keep Israel from taking the city. They had reason to be arrogant: the city stood high on its hills, the valley of Kedron on one side and the Tyropoean Valley on the other; and it was well fortified. No one in the days of Joshua or since had been able to take it. David, however, did the seemingly impossible. The description of his strategy has been a puzzle until recent years. Some thought David's army went through the city water-course; but now it seems that they used hooks and scaling ropes to go up over the walls.[3]

The archaeology of Jerusalem has been somewhat discouraging, and as a result the picture is not yet too clear. Let me say briefly that it now appears that someone in the second century B.C., perhaps Simon,

---

[2] It is perhaps worth a passing note to observe that such military *coups* have always been an unstabilizing force in the Middle East, and the present day is no exception.

[3] This is discussed by W. F. Albright in "The Old Testament and Archaeology," *Old Testament Commentary*, H. C. Alleman and E. E. Flack, eds. (Philadelphia: Muhlenberg Press, 1948), p. 149. The older viewpoint has been maintained, however, in several more recent works by other authors.

as reported by Josephus, levelled the ground and dumped all previous remains into the valley.[4] But it seems certain from studying that dump that David's city was located on the southeastern side of the present-day city, overlooking the pool of Siloam. When you visit Jerusalem, they will show you the hill of Zion on the southwestern side of the old city, overlooking the valley of Hinnom. In fact, I have visited "David's tomb" there. This appears now to be certainly wrong.

David's city, you may be surprised to learn, was not large: about twelve hundred feet long and four hundred feet wide, it was only about as long as two modern city blocks and narrower than one—about eight acres. But it was a very important city and once it was taken, once it was made the capital, it became extremely important for all of the rest of the history of Israel.

David then proceeded to conquer the neighboring states. The first one he went after was that of the Philistines, because in the days of Saul they had repeatedly attacked the southwestern boundaries of the land. He defeated them so thoroughly that they never again were a serious threat to Israel, and then turned his attention to the east, to the states on the opposite side of the Jordan. He subdued the Ammonites and the Moabites, the Edomites and Amalekites, and I do not know how many others. It called for war and David went to war although he was not, strictly speaking, a man of war. He seems to me to have been, on the whole, a man of peace. But in order to establish and secure his kingdom, it was necessary for him to put down these various peoples who were disturbing the peace of the land. It is one of the ironies of history that David, who by nature would have been a peaceful man, was refused the privilege of building the temple because he had "shed much blood" (cf. I Chronicles 22:8).

Then he turned his attention to the organization of the kingdom. The organization of David's kingdom, which is described largely in I Chronicles 22-27, is very interesting. It gives us a good insight into the mind of the man. He apparently realized that the kingdom was not to be built on the personality of the king alone, but on an organization of men around him. He seems to have taken many of his ideas from the Egyptians, but whether he got them directly, or through his knowledge of the Philistines (you remember that in the days when he was an outlaw he had lived with the Philistines), we do not know. The organizational structure of his kingdom was a sort of pyramid. It had

[4] For a fuller description, see G. E. Wright, *Biblical Archaeology,* p. 126.

a broad base and narrowed toward the top, where there was just one man as king.

At the base were a number of mercenaries, or paid foreign soldiers. There was wisdom in that, because there would be no emotional tie-in on the part of these mercenaries with any particular group in the country. Above them were "The Thirty"—thirty men, although the number probably varied from time to time, chosen because of their bravery and their wisdom in leading armies. I suppose the men would be "generals" today, or perhaps, "colonels," or possibly they would be looked upon as a "cabinet." Above the thirty, "The Three"; these three would have, of course, delegated authority over the thirty. And then, at the top would be David himself. David's authority extended through this long chain of command, reaching out to the whole nation.

David also made the offices of the scribe and the recorder important and prominent in his kingdom. One of our present-day historians says that the first real historiographer was David. I suppose that statement would be challenged by many, and yet, there is truth in it. Long before the time of Herodotus or any of the other famous historians, David caused details to be recorded, and this record could be later used for the purpose of constructing an authentic history. Many of the things that we know about him and his kingdom, and many of the things that we know about the kingdom that followed the days of David, we know because David set up the office of recorder. This official was called, in Hebrew, the *mazkîr,* "the one that causes you to remember." The record was called, if we translate it literally, "The Book of the Affairs of the Days of. . . ." In other words, it was a day-book, a journal, a log-book of the important events kept day by day. We use the impressive title "Chronicles"—but "minutes" would be more meaningful. Such a record is not a history; it is the raw material from which history can be written.

You will notice, as you read through the Old Testament, frequent statements such as this: "Is it not written in the Books of the Kings of Israel and Judah?" That does not refer to the Book of Kings in the Bible; it refers to the journal, the day-book, which had been kept by the recorders in the kingdom of Israel or Judah. You also read in certain instances of kings who, when they could not sleep at night, or when they were troubled, got up and read those chronicles. They would come across the record of the work of some good man, and they would suddenly ask themselves, "What happened to that man, anyway? Was he rewarded for what he did?" The king would call in someone and ask, "Was he rewarded or not?" Perhaps it had been overlooked. That is how Mordecai happened to be honored by Ahasuerus, as we read in the Book of Esther.

In addition to introducing the *mazkîr*, which can be translated "speaker" or "chancellor" as well as "recorder," David seems to have been first to establish in Israel the office of the *sôfēr*, usually translated "scribe." This was an ancient and honorable office in Egypt. One of my favorite art objects from Egypt is the famous Scribe from Sakkara, now in the Louvre.[5] With his lifelike inlaid eyes and the color and physique of a lifeguard, he sits there ready to take dictation—and he has been sitting that way since 2500 B.C. David seems to have introduced the scribe into Israel, probably as a civic official. But we know that by the time of Jesus, the scribe had become the religious lawyer. How? By becoming first, certainly by the time of Ezra, the one charged with the copying and care of the Holy Scriptures. The modern equivalent of the *sôfēr* is the secretary. I suppose few secretaries stop to think that they belong to an honorable profession, which at one time ranked next to the king. As a matter of fact, at least two kings of ancient times boasted that they had learned to write! So, you young ladies who take dictation and punch the typewriter, lift up your heads! And just remember—even today, the highest officers in our land, beneath the President and the Vice President, are honored with the title "Secretary."

David's next move was to bring the Ark of the Covenant from Kirjath-jearim to Jerusalem. The elders, urged by the Israelites, had very foolishly taken the Ark into battle, and then the Philistines had captured it. However, that proved to be a blunder, for the Ark caused a great deal of trouble in the Philistine cities. It seems that no matter where they would take the Ark, the next morning they would find the idol of their Philistine god, Dagon, flat on his face on the ground. So finally they decided to get rid of the Ark. They sent it back to the Israelites. But the Israelites also moved it about from one place to another and it was never properly housed. Then, one day, "it was told King David, 'The Lord has blessed the household of Obed-edom and all that belongs to him, because of the ark of God.' So David went and brought up the ark of God from the house of Obed-edom to the City of David with rejoicing . . ." (II Samuel 6:12). A tent was made

---

[5] This statue can be seen pictured in many books on Egypt, and is particularly well presented in J. B. Pritchard, ed., *The Ancient Near East in Pictures*, Fig. 230.

to cover it and they ". . . set it in its place, inside the tent which David had pitched for it; and David offered burnt offerings and peace offerings before the Lord" (6:17).

Jerusalem thereupon became not only the political center of the kingdom, but the center of religious life as well. Forever after Jerusalem is looked upon not only as the city of kings, but as the city of God. The prophets three to five centuries later are talking about Zion as the place from which "the law of the Lord goes forth." Zion is the city to which the nations of the world and the kings of the world will come in order to worship Jehovah.

In connection with that worship, we read in I Chronicles 16 that David set up a musical system. He appointed certain of the Levites "as ministers before the ark of the Lord to invoke, to thank, and to praise the Lord, the God of Israel." Asaph was to sound the cymbals, Benaiah and Jahaziel the priests were to blow trumpets continually before the Ark, and others were to play harps and lyres. The seventh verse suggests that the first "Psalm" (cf. Psalm 105:1-15) was sung that day. A regular order was set up for this work, in order that there might be music and praise to God.

All this has been questioned by some historians in recent years. Starting from the conviction based on knowledge available to them that the development of music and of musical instruments was not older than the Greeks, they felt that the Biblical story could not be accurate. We know differently now, thanks to modern archaeology. In the Ugaritic materials, discovered at Ras Shamra since 1929, the same word for "singers" occurs (dating from the fourteenth century B.C.) as is used in the account of David, three centuries later. On the wall of the tomb at Beni-Ḥasan in Egypt a painting was discovered, dated about 1900 B.C., portraying thirty-seven Asiatics (Canaanites or Amorites) who had come to Egypt. One is carrying a lyre.[6] In the burials from the Third Dynasty of Ur, a magnificent lyre was found, which can be seen reconstructed, in the University of Pennsylvania Museum.[7] Music and musical instruments can therefore be traced back at least to 2000 B.C. in both Egypt and Mesopotamia; and we have already seen the great influence that these two cultural areas had on the land of Canaan.

---

[6] This can be seen in the lower register of Fig. 9, *Westminster Historical Atlas* (1945).
[7] This is reproduced in color in L. Woolley, *Ur: The First Phases* (The King Penguin Books; London: Penguin Books, 1946), plate 6.

Religious hymns were sung to the accompaniment of instruments among the Israelites as early as the time of Moses, according to Exodus 15. The elements of worship, we have seen, can be traced back to Moses and the tabernacle service. Bands of prophets in the days of Saul apparently worshiped at the "high place" with harps, tambourines, flutes, and lyres (cf. I Samuel 10:5). But it was David, according to Hebrew tradition (and there is no longer any good reason to doubt it), who was responsible for a marked development in what we might call "ritual" in the service. It was David who laid the foundations for the Book of Psalms.

Here again we must take issue with the scholars who have insisted on dating the Israelite cultural elements unduly late. No scholar, to my knowledge, has insisted that David wrote all the Psalms; and certainly no Old Testament scholar today would deny that there are "late" Psalms in the Bible—just how late, will be a matter of debate. But to deny that David is the psalmist, to deny that he, more than anyone else, is responsible for the development of this particular type of devotional literature in Israel, is sheer nonsense. Who else is there in Hebrew tradition? Certainly such a man must have left his name somewhere; and the only name that has been indelibly inscribed in tradition is the name of David. As the Law must ultimately and essentially be traced to Moses, so must the Psalms be traced to David.

David chose the Oriental king's prerogative, namely, to establish a harem. Several writers have noted that Saul had only one wife and one concubine; David, on the other hand, had a large harem, with many wives and many children. Once again, it is necessary for us to learn to judge men by the standards of their own day, rather than by the fuller light that God has given us. And once again, we must recognize that the experiences of the men and women in the past have been recorded for our benefit, so that we can see objectively the results of their moral standards. If anyone is inclined to justify polygamy on the basis that "David did it," let him weigh carefully the results that accrued to David from polygamy.

One story in particular has been preserved for us in unusual detail, and it merits our careful consideration: the story of David and Bathsheba. It is told in II Samuel 11.

Late one afternoon, David arose from the midday nap that is characteristic of life in the Middle East, and he went up on the roof of his house for a walk in the fresh air. He saw a woman bathing; and the woman, the Bible tells us, was very beautiful. David's sensual nature was aroused, and he inquired about the woman and discovered that she was the wife of one of the Hittite soldiers in his army. So David sent for her, and "she came to him, and he lay with her" (11:4).

In his book, *A History of Israel,* T. H. Robinson makes the astute observation that it would have been considered quite normal and natural, quite within his rights, for an Oriental king to take the wife of one of his subjects. It is to be looked upon as an indication of the high view of human rights in Israel that the king felt obliged to try to cover up his act.[8] Accordingly when David received the news from Bathsheba, "I am with child," he attempted to shift the blame. He called Bathsheba's husband home from battle, and tried to persuade him to take some of his "accrued leave." Uriah refused to sleep with his wife during the time of war. The taboo upon the marriage relation in time of war seems to have been rather widely observed in the Ancient Middle East. We even find it mentioned in the Dead Sea "War Scroll." Next, David wined and dined Uriah until he was drunk (verse 13); but still Uriah did not go to his own bedroom. Finally, David in desperation, sent Uriah back to war, and at the same time issued an order to Joab the commanding general, "Set Uriah in the forefront of the hardest fighting, and then draw back from him, that he may be struck down, and die" (verse 15). You can call that anything you want, but to send a man into the hottest part of the battle and then pull back all of the other troops so that he is left there alone—that is *calculated* murder. Uriah was killed, and after a "respectable" time for the weeping and the mourning period, Bathsheba was married to David.

Now when we talk about David, we say, "Here is a man after God's own heart." But some one will ask, "How can you say, 'Here is a man after God's own heart,' when he did things like that?"

Well, we have to keep two things in mind here, one of which is that God looks upon us, *not according to what we do, but according to the sincere faith in our hearts.* David was a man of God's own heart, even if he was a sinner. You say then, "Well, if God excused all of his faults, then we can go out and do anything we want and claim that we love God, and God will overlook it." Not at all! Go back and read the record again, and see what happened. David was punished *for everything he did.* As a matter of fact, David's entire life seems to change

[8] Theodore H. Robinson, *A History of Israel* (Oxford: Clarendon Press, 1932), Vol. I, p. 225.

from this moment on; the world would say, "His luck changed; from that day on, it was all bad."

Shortly after his affair with Bathsheba, David saw his home disrupted, first of all by the rape of his daughter, Tamar (13:1); then by the death of the son of Bathsheba, who was born out of this adulterous union (12:15); then by the revolt of his beloved son, Absalom (15:17), and then by the death of Absalom (18:14). Down to his dying day, David was haunted by the ghosts of his sins, for his house was divided by jealousies and schisms, his favorite wife Bathsheba was plotting an intrigue to put her son Solomon on the throne, and his sons were instigating a revolt which even involved the religious leaders. The "house of David" may have been permanently established, but certainly his home was shattered several ways.

Read through the Psalms and see the grief of this man and how his heart was torn, and you will realize that God does not let a man get away with *any* sin. I remember an illustration of this, which I heard many years ago. A father was trying to teach a boy something about the principle of forgiveness, and the boy got the idea that he could get away with wrongdoing. So the father took a board, a beautiful piece of wood that had been nicely finished, and he drove some big nails into it, and then he pulled the nails out: there were scars left in the wood. And there were scars left on David's heart; the scars were there all through his life. To read the Book of Psalms and to look at the history of David's life is to realize that he was torn and twisted all through life as the result of his own sin and his own selfishness. That is one part of the story that we *must* remember.

The other part, the greater truth—and we have a Christian church and Christian ministers proclaiming the Christian gospel only because it is true—is that God *does* forgive sin. David paid for his sin, yes. He also had his sins forgiven. You and I have our sins forgiven. God does not hold these things against us forever. Sin brings its own penalty, for the penalty of sin is built into our physical and psychological nature. But sin also has its forgiveness. God is a God of love and of redemption.

If God should measure sin, who could stand? Which of us, who so readily condemn David for what he did, would have any greater claim on the love of God? But God does not deal with us that way. The message of Calvary, the message of the New Testament, the message of the whole Bible from beginning to end, is the message of a God who deals with us, not according to the sins we commit, but in His redeeming love. If our hearts are turned toward Him, if we have a longing to live above sin, if our hearts are filled with the sincere desire to follow God, then God for Christ's sake will pardon us. The story of David and his life tells us that. The story of Jesus Christ and His death on Calvary also tells us that.

CHAPTER XII

Solomon

SOLOMON has been referred to as the wisest man who ever lived. The "wisdom of Solomon" is proverbial—and I am convinced that it is based on factual foundation; for as in the case of Moses and the Law and in the case of David and the Psalms, it is necessary for anyone who denies the tradition to put forth a more likely candidate. Who else is there? Solomon is the only man known who could have been the fountainhead of Hebrew wisdom literature.

Solomon has also been referred to as "a great son of a greater father." I rather like that description, for it tells in a few words the sad story of a son who never rose to the heights occupied by his father. In this chapter, as we examine the record of Solomon, we shall see why. The story of Solomon can be studied in three phases: his background, his reign, and his contribution to the religious life of his nation. Each of these phases, in my opinion, proves disappointing.

Some of my students get the impression, when I am teaching about the Solomonic era, that I am a bit of a "de-bunker." For some reason, Sunday school teachers and preachers have been overanxious to present the best side of Biblical characters and play down the other. At least, that has been my experience. And then, when we start to read and think for ourselves, we find that the Biblical characters are human beings like ourselves: they have feet of clay. The reaction sometimes is tragic. It is my firm conviction that we have nothing whatever to gain by altering the picture, and nothing whatever to lose by adhering to the truth. If the Bible presents a man as somewhat less than a saint, that is the best way to study him. So, with the conviction that we can learn best by seeing exactly what kind of man Solomon was, what kind of man God had to work with, and what God was able to do with and through him, we turn to the first phase, his background.

There is little more than a passing reference in the Bible to Solomon's youth. This fact in itself is odd enough to attract our attention. His mother was Bathsheba, David's favorite wife. Solomon was not the child of the sin of David and Bathsheba—that child died—but he was the next child, the fourth son born to David's wives in Jerusalem (II Samuel 5:14).

There is no evidence in Solomon's life of any early religious training. Neither is there any evidence that Bathsheba was a godly woman. At first glance this may seem strange; yet, as we think about it, does it not fit in with other details of the portrait? If she *had* been more of a godly woman, Solomon would have been more certain of the faith that was within him. There are some who feel that we have a description of Solomon's mother in the description of the godly woman in the thirty-first chapter of Proverbs. But this chapter is attributed to Lemuel; and I see no reason whatever for trying to identify Lemuel with Solomon, or for trying, on such a very doubtful basis, to construct a picture of Bathsheba from these proverbs. Her sin with David might lead some of us to the hasty conclusion that she was a completely godless woman. But let us be careful with our judgments! Her sin with David was, at least in part, David's fault. He was the king. When he ordered her to come to his house, she was in the position of a subject, and as a subject she probably had to obey. She may have been a willing subject, but at least we cannot put all of the blame on her for that episode. At most we can say that the Scripture fails to record any evidence of repentance on her part.

In the picture we have of her in the first chapter of I Kings, she seems to be pretty much of a schemer and a plotter. She arranged to have the kingship handed down to her son Solomon, rather than to the oldest son in the line of succession, Adonijah.

In addition to the fact that Solomon was the son of such a woman, he grew up in a polygamous home. David married often; the Bible records eighteen wives. We have not met a situation quite like this before—at least not so extreme a situation. Jacob, of course, did have two wives, plus the handmaid of each of those wives, in his home; and Jacob's home illustrates in small measure what David's home illustrates in large measure. The sons of Jacob were at tension, pulling against each other; and there were petty jealousies and rivalries in that home. But in David's home, where the thing was magnified all out of proportion by the large number of wives that he had in his harem, the tensions were even greater. Here were the children of all these wives fighting for position and preference. It can be established sociologically and psychologically, entirely apart from the religious viewpoint, that polygamy is not ideal, that it introduces not only the jealousy and strife of the wives in the home but the strife of the children of those wives as well. The home becomes the scene of all sorts of plots and counterplots to gain favor and to occupy places of prestige. Solomon grew up in that kind of environment.

Then, too, he grew up in the splendid days of David's kingdom. That should have been helpful to Solomon, for it is good to live in a great day. Solomon must have known that God took a small people of no significance, and brought them to a place of great importance for no other reason than that He had delighted in them and that He had *chosen* them. Solomon must have known that He had led them out of bondage of Egypt, had guided them with a strong hand through the wilderness for forty years, had fought the battles in the conquest of Canaan, had located them in the land, and at last had made them a great nation. All of that was Solomon's heritage. This boy should have grown up with a magnificent concept of the power of God—and I think he did.

But perhaps all this had certain disadvantages as well. It may have developed in him a distorted sense of the value of material things; for it seems to me that, as Solomon increased in length of reign, his emphasis upon money, wealth, and splendor increased, while his sense of the value of spiritual things diminished.

Turning to the reign of Solomon, we notice first of all that he came into the kingship through a plot. Adonijah, the son of Haggith (one of David's wives), was in line for the kingship after the death of Absalom, and Adonijah saw that David was an old man now, a bed-ridden invalid, unable to maintain his kingdom, just waiting for the end of life to come. So Adonijah decided that he was going to take over the throne. He prepared for himself chariots and horsemen, and he brought together Joab, who was commander-in-chief of David's army, and Abiathar, one of the priests; and this evil trio arranged to have a public demonstration in which Adonijah would be hailed as king. He very cleverly omitted to invite Solomon or Zadok the priest, or Benaiah the chief of David's bodyguard, or Nathan the prophet, or anyone else who was or who might be potentially on the side of Solomon. He was not going to let anyone come to this party who might come with the wrong kind of speech!

Word of the conspiracy got back to the prophet Nathan, and he went to Bathsheba with what amounted to a two-pronged attack to get David to act. In accordance with Nathan's suggestion, Bathsheba went in to David with a mincing speech that said, in effect, "Didn't you promise your little wife that Solomon would be the next king? And now Adonijah is calling himself king, and you aren't even paying attention to him; and he is planning a big coronation banquet, and he has invited your sons, and Abiathar the priest, and Joab the commander—everybody except Solomon! And the people are waiting to see what you are going to say. And if you don't name your successor before you die, Solomon and I will be put to death as disloyal to the new king!" Bathsheba had not even finished her speech when Nathan came in and asked, "Have you named Adonijah as your successor?" And he repeated the details of Adonijah's *coup d'état.* This stirred David into action; Solomon was officially named the next king, and plans were made for his anointing and his coronation. When Adonijah heard what had taken place, he faded into the background with his supporters. The time seemed ripe for revolt; but apparently Adonijah and his backers had no heart for revolution. So Solomon became king.

Soon after, Solomon started a building program, which is so amazing that it seems almost incredible, even in our times. First he built the temple which his father David had wanted to do, using forced labor, and enlisting the help of Hiram the king of Tyre,[1] and the Phoenician artisans who knew a lot more about handling bronze and stone and wood than the Israelites did. We get an idea of the cost of that temple from the fact that Solomon raised a levy of forced labor out of all Israel numbering thirty thousand men. He sent them to Lebanon at the rate of ten thousand a month—one month in Lebanon, two months at home, apparently without pay—for the purpose of cutting the famous "cedars of Lebanon." The cedars had to be transported from the heights of Lebanon to the sea, lashed together in rafts and floated down the coast, then transported overland to Jerusalem. Stones had to be cut at the quarry under Jerusalem, and we are told that the size of some of those stones was considerable (I Kings 5:13-18). By the time Solomon had finished, he had a temple twice as large in length and width and three times as high as the tabernacle.[2] Built of costly stone, it was overlaid

[1] When reading the Scriptural account, we must be careful to distinguish Hiram the King from Hiram the skilled craftsman (I Kings 5:1, 13-14). The latter is also called "Huram my father" or "Huram-abi" (II Chronicles 2:13).

[2] Although the temple was a large building for its day, it would be rather small by our standards: 90 ft. long, 30 ft. wide, and 45 ft. high, or (if we use the larger cubit) possibly about 15 per cent larger in each dimension.

with cedar so that not a stone was visible anywhere; and the interior of the holiest place was overlaid with gold on top of the cedar, and was furnished with gold cherubim and gold candlesticks. Everything was truly magnificent. Outside, in the outer court, a huge bronze altar and a bronze laver were set up. Our heads swim when we read these details, particularly when we realize that it was in the tenth century before Christ. The bronze work was cast in the Jordan valley, where there was plenty of clay, and hauled up the mountains to Jerusalem— in itself quite a feat, in view of the fact that Jerusalem is twenty-six hundred feet above sea level and the plain of the Jordan is about a thousand feet below sea level. The bronze columns ("Jachin" and "Boaz") were about 40 feet high and 6 feet in diameter, cast about 4 inches thick, with a hollow core. The bronze laver or "sea" was cast of metal of the same thickness as the columns, about 7 or 8 feet high and 15 feet in diameter, holding eighteen thousand gallons. The bronze altar was 30 feet square and 15 feet high. The skill and craftsmanship involved in making these castings is astounding, and will only be truly appreciated by those who have attempted such large castings.[3]

After Solomon built and dedicated the Lord's house, he built his own house. I think we get some idea of Solomon and of his sense of proportionate values in the seventh chapter of First Kings, where we read that he was seven years building God's house and thirteen years building his own! In other words, it was about two for Solomon to one for God. That is a pretty good way of measuring the man. He put far more time, far more money in building his own house, the Hall of the Cedars of Lebanon, the wall around the palace, and the palace for his Egyptian queen, than he did upon the building of the house of the Lord. At the same time he built stables, fortified the outposts of the nation, and spent money right and left on all sorts of "projects." Some years ago, when the New Deal was spending money, I remember that one project cost $4.8 billion. At the time it seemed to be an astronomical figure. Solomon's building projects cost about the same as

[3] The Howland-Garber model of the temple is the best reconstruction known to me. Pictures of it can be found in several publications, e.g., *Unger's Bible Dictionary*, pp. 1078-79, and a film-strip of it is available from Professor Paul L. Garber, Agnes Scott College, Decatur, Ga. I saw a full-size reproduction of the bronze sea in the new Mormon Temple in Los Angeles, but since the sanctification of the temple, this is no longer open to visitors.

that: $4.4 billion. It seems fantastic that a small kingdom should have been loaded with such a staggering cost.[4]

Down on the Gulf of Aqabah, at Ezion-geber in the southern part of his domain, Solomon had his "navy." The Israelites were never a sea-loving people, but the Phoenicians were; Solomon manned his ships with Phoenician sailors, and they sailed all over the then-known world bringing home all kinds of treasure. Once every three years they brought him cargoes of "gold, silver, ivory, apes, and peacocks" (I Kings 10:22).[5] Near Ezion-geber, at modern Tell el-Kheleifeh, Solomon built a large copper smelter. This was discovered in 1938 by Nelson Glueck and excavated during several seasons.[6] A guide, who claimed to have been Professor Glueck's guide, showed me around the remains of slag piles, blast furnaces, and workers' houses. The refinery surpasses anything known to modern discovery in the ancient world. As explained by my guide, the ore and fuel were piled in such a way as to provide flues and close contact with the heat source (probably charcoal). The blast was provided by the winds that blow almost constantly from the north.[7] Professor Albright notes that the method used for the reduction of the copper remains a mystery to specialists in metallurgy.

Solomon was a fine administrator; in this department, I think he surpassed David. He had twelve administrative districts, each one of which was required to support the court, financially, for one month of the year. When you have a harem of seven hundred wives, and three hundred concubines, and all the rest of the lavish expense at court that Solomon indulged in, you need *money*! Solomon could

---

[4] Many scholars have rejected these figures as gross exaggerations. Two facts, however, should cause us to hesitate before brushing the figures aside: Israel was in a particularly strategic position, internationally; moreover, history records the large tributes demanded of and received from Israelite kings for centuries after the Solomonic period.

[5] It was my unique good fortune to be at Eilat, the modern counterpart of Ezion-geber, in 1957, when the *Athlit* came in, the first Israeli ship since the days of Solomon to sail the Gulf of Aqabah.

[6] Glueck's description can be found in his book, *The Other Side of the Jordan* (New Haven: American Schools of Oriental Research, 1940), pp. 89-113.

[7] Modern housing in Eilat is air-conditioned by using this same phenomenon. The north side of the house is covered with a framework which is filled with desert grass over which water drips constantly. The north wind provides the breeze for an evaporator-cooler. However, two of the three days I was there, the wind was from the south (most unusual, they said!), and the cooling system was inoperative.

not very well go out and earn it, so he did the thing that politicians must always do: he had the twelve districts send in the cash. And when it came to paying off Hiram of Tyre, who was in charge of the building program, Solomon simply gave Hiram twenty cities of Galilee (I Kings 9:11-14). Already the king was selling land to finance his program. Solomon was beginning to put his kingdom in a very bad spot.

Solomon was an internationalist. In addition to his treaty with Hiram, he carried on an extensive maritime and overseas commerce (read I Kings 9—10). In the course of that commercial activity, the Queen of Sheba came to visit him. Now Sheba was a fabulous land, rich, civilized, and important to international traders.[8] The Queen brought Solomon a gift: 120 talents of gold. The talent was worth approximately $38,000—which means that the gift was worth $4,800,000. Just what it was that the Queen of Sheba wanted in exchange, we do not know; but we can have a lot of fun speculating about it. Perhaps it was a simple trade agreement.

One of the great problems of international affairs then as now was treaty-making. Treaties were made by the thousands, between big and little kings, between great kingdoms and little city-states, and for all sorts of purposes. A treaty could be made in long-drawn-out conferences and councils of state; a quicker way to do it was to arrange a marriage. Unite the king of one country with the daughter of the king in another country and presto, you had a political as well as a marriage alliance! I have no doubt that Solomon picked quite a number of his wives with one eye on political affairs and alliances. One of his wives, we know, was a daughter of the Pharaoh of Egypt: quite obviously a political marriage. I am not trying to excuse him; I am simply trying to explain how he got himself, eventually, into a sorry mess.

He did what he thought was the big-hearted, broad-minded thing, with all these wives: he allowed them to practice the rites of their own religions in his palace. He even set up places of worship outside for them, and erected idols that they might worship their own pagan gods. In the name of broad-mindedness, of good-will, of international amity and understanding, but certainly not in the name of Jehovah,

---

[8] The recent book by Wendell Phillips, *Qataban and Sheba* (New York: Harcourt, Brace, 1955), tells a fascinating story of explorations in the fabulous territory of Sheba.

he established this bedlam of foreign gods, and thereby set a cancer growing at the heart of his kingdom. He should have known better.

We turn now to the religious side of Solomon. When Solomon took over the kingdom, God said to him in a dream, "Ask what I shall give you." Solomon replied, "Thou hast shown great and steadfast love to thy servant David my father, because he walked before thee in faithfulness, in righteousness, and in uprightness of heart toward thee; and thou hast kept for him this great and steadfast love, and hast given him a son to sit on his throne this day. And now, O Lord my God, thou hast made thy servant king in place of David my father, although I am but a little child [he was about twenty at the time]; I do not know how to go out or come in. . . . Give thy servant therefore an understanding mind to govern thy people, that I may discern between good and evil; for who is able to govern this thy great people?" The Bible tells us that it pleased the Lord that Solomon had asked this, and God said to him, "Because you have asked this, and have not asked for long life or riches or the life of your enemies, but have asked for yourself understanding . . . behold, I now do according to your word. Behold, I give you a wise and discerning mind. . . ." He was also to have riches and honor, for which he did not ask, and God added, "If you will walk in my way, keeping my statutes and my commandments, as your father David walked, then will I lengthen your days" (I Kings 3:5-14).

Solomon was off to a wonderful start! This kingdom, this reign, should have been one of history's highlights. It was a magnificent hour for the kingdom—but it was completely overshadowed and lost because of what was to happen later. If we could only end the story of Solomon here, or better, with the glorious prayer he made at the dedication of the temple, asking God's help in facing apostasy, we would have a story greater than David's!

But we cannot stop here; we must go on to consider the rest of the story. The first downward step that Solomon made could be termed defection. The record reads, "Now King Solomon loved many foreign women: the daughter of Pharaoh, and Moabite, Ammonite, Edomite, Sidonian, and Hittite women, from the nations concerning which the Lord had said to the people of Israel, 'You shall not enter into marriage with them, neither shall they with you, for surely they will turn away your heart after their gods'; Solomon clung to these in love" (I Kings 11:1-2). That was the beginning of his downfall.

The second step was apostasy. That is an ugly word, and many have objected to its use with reference to Solomon. But read the record: "He had seven hundred wives, princesses, and three hundred concubines; and his wives turned away his heart. For when Solomon was old his wives turned away his heart after other gods; and his heart was not wholly true to the Lord his God, as was the heart of David his father. For Solomon went after Ashtoreth the goddess of the Sidonians, and after Milcom the abomination of the Ammonites. . . . Then Solomon built a high place for Chemosh the abomination of Moab, and for Molech the abomination of the Ammonites, on the mountain east of Jerusalem. And so he did for all his foreign wives, who burned incense and sacrificed to their gods" (11:3-8). Because he turned his heart away from God, God had to turn away from Solomon.

The final step was the loss of all that God had given him—or almost all, for God's grace spared some. "And the Lord was angry with Solomon, because his heart had turned away from the Lord, the God of Israel, who had appeared to him twice, and had commanded him concerning this thing, that he should not go after other gods; but he did not keep what the Lord commanded. Therefore the Lord said to Solomon: 'Since this has been your mind and you have not kept my covenant and my statutes which I have commanded you, I will surely tear the kingdom from you and give it to your servant. Yet for the sake of David your father I will not do it in your days, but I will tear it out of the hand of your son. However, I will not tear away all the kingdom; but I will give one tribe to your son for the sake of David my servant, and for the sake of Jerusalem which I have chosen" (11:9-13). That is exactly what happened: the prophet Ahijah came to Jeroboam, took his coat and tore it into twelve pieces and handed Jeroboam ten of them and said, "Take for yourself ten pieces . . ." or ten *tribes*! God had torn the kingdom, and he had given ten parts of it to Solomon's enemy, and only one part was left for Solomon's son.

We learn some powerful lessons here. We learn that God is faithful even though Solomon is faithless. For the sake of David and for the sake of his land, God kept a king on the throne; after Solomon's time, which was about 922 B.C., until 586 B.C., there was a king upon the throne in Jerusalem—a king of the line of David. For the sake of David, God kept His promise.

We learn at the same time that God will not tolerate apostasy and idolatry. As certainly as those elements are brought into the kingdom of Israel, so certainly God must get them out. Solomon could have been a great king—in many respects he was; as far as administration, building, national prestige and international diplomacy are concerned, he went far beyond David. But, in the one thing that was most important, the thing that was the most critical in the life of the nation, in his religious life he suffered a defection and turned away from the Lord. Therefore his kingdom was rent. You can trace a good many of the later sufferings of Israel back to that corruption.

The prophets for three hundred and fifty years after Solomon speak continually about the apostasy of the people. Well, "like king, like people." Solomon imported the wives, the wives imported the gods; Solomon tolerated it, encouraged it, built places of worship for these idolators. What can you expect the people to do but follow along? There is a terrible responsibility in being a national leader. It is a greater responsibility in the eyes of God than in the eyes of men—and the responsibility before man is great enough!

One other practical lesson we may take out of it all: that is, to remember our own national leaders and our own president. We have been charged by the Scriptures to pray for kings and those in authority: we should pray that we may have always at the head of our nation one whose primary interest is not in material splendor, but in doing the will of God, for only then can God bless our nation and use it.

CHAPTER XIII

Elijah

THE PROPHET ELIJAH stands out in the Old Testament as the typical representative of the prophets. When we speak of the Law, we think of Moses; when we speak of the prophets, we think of Elijah. He has been called "Jehovah's answer to Baal" for he came on the scene when Baal worship was at its zenith in Israel. Elijah was one of the two men in Scripture who had the privilege of being taken from this life without passing through death; Enoch was the other. And he was one of the two men granted the honor of standing on the Mount of Transfiguration with Jesus. In this chapter we will think about his times, his work, and his significance to us in the lessons we can learn from him in our own day.

Elijah was a prophet. Just what does that mean? Who were the "prophets"? We have already seen, in our study of Moses that the prophet was God's mouthpiece. If we fail to see the divine origin of the true prophetic message, we fail entirely to understand the phenomenon of prophecy. At the same time, there is a relationship of the prophets to the historical scene that must not be overlooked. The prophets were advisors to the kings. They came on the scene at the moment in history when the kingdom of Israel came into existence, and they continued only as long as that kingdom was in existence. Their primary relationship was to the kingdom.

This important fact is often overlooked, resulting in a hazy notion that prophets belong to the whole Old Testament period. Now I must admit that part of this misunderstanding stems from the fact that the word "prophet," since it basically means "one who has been called [by God to serve as His mouthpiece]," can be used of anyone so called by God, and was so used. Abraham is called a prophet (Genesis 20:7), and so is Moses (Deuteronomy 18:18); yet it would be incorrect to include Abraham and Moses in a list of the Prophets of Israel. Moreover, there were special prophets used by God (cf. Balaam, Numbers 22:35), and there were false prophets who claimed to speak

God's word (Jeremiah 23:16-32). It is equally incorrect to lump these all together and discuss them as "prophets." The prophets, strictly speaking, begin with Samuel (I Samuel 3:20; 9:9), and end with Malachi, so far as the Old Testament is concerned. Then there was a famine of the word of the Lord[1] until John the Baptist appeared in the spirit and power of Elijah to proclaim the coming of the One who would be the fulfillment of all the prophecies concerning the Davidic King. Since He was also the fulfillment of the prophecy in Deuteronomy 18:18 (the Prophet that was to come) as well as the coming King, the offices of prophet and king merge at last into one. But the very fact that Jesus is both Prophet and King serves to underscore our claim that the prophetic office is primarily related to the kingly office.

Another point that is not always clear relates to the writing activities of the prophets. We tend to think of the prophets as the men who wrote the second half of the Old Testament, from Isaiah to Malachi. But there were perhaps just as many prophets who never wrote a line of prophecy—at least, their prophecies have not been preserved for us in Scripture. Samuel, of course, we know; and if we had not thought of it in so many words, we were aware that the Books of Samuel in the Bible are not prophecies.[2] Nathan left no written prophecy; although we are quite familiar with his prophetic utterances to David. We have just read about Ahijah and his prophecy to Jeroboam—but he left no written prophecy. The same can be said for the well-known prophets Elijah and Elisha. And the lesser-known prophets, such as Micaiah ben Imlah (I Kings 22), Gad (I Samuel 22:5), and a number of nameless ones, serve to remind us that God always had His mouth-piece ready to proclaim His word to the king.

Amos is often referred to as the earliest of the writing prophets (c. 760 B.C.). But there had been kings and prophets for two centuries or more by that time. Amos even refers to them (Amos 7:14). As a matter of fact, an important shift in the prophetic office occurred in the eighth century B.C. The prophets before Amos are often called the "oral" or "non-writing" prophets; from Amos on, they are the

---

[1] This prophetic silence is mentioned in I Maccabees 4:46; 14:41; and had already been of considerable duration, I Maccabees 9:27.

[2] I am aware, of course, that in the Hebrew Bible Joshua, Judges, Samuel, and Kings (I and II) are considered as "The Former Prophets." What I have said about the difference between the "oral" and "writing" prophets can just as truly be said about the difference between the "Former" and the "Latter" Prophets.

"writing" or "literary" prophets. Did you ever ask yourself why there was this important shift from the spoken to the written word?

The prophets, we have seen, were advisors to the kings. The king of Israel was supposed to reign under divine authority, which should have been taken to mean that he was not supposed to act without first determining the will of God on the matter. The prophet was there for that purpose.[3] To make the picture complete, I should also mention the third office: the priest. These three offices, prophet, priest, and king, were supposed to be kept inviolate, each by the other.

The "oral prophets" carried on their prophetic ministry during the period (roughly the tenth and ninth centuries B.C.) when, in spite of the stubbornness of the kings, it seemed that the kingdom might be preserved. The "writing prophets" did not appear until Israel had reached that period of history when there was no longer any hope of preserving the kingdom, even in its split form. With Amos it is obvious that God had determined upon a judgment that would drive the nation into exile. This introduced a new factor: some provision must be made for the preservation of the word of the Lord in permanent form for the day when the nation, or its remnant, would be brought again into the Land. If you study this development carefully, you will notice that Elijah is like the great divide: before him, the prophets sought to advise the kings in order to preserve the kingdom; with Elijah the awful extent of national sin is laid bare. From that time on, the prophets speak of punishment, with only a remnant to be saved.[4]

Elijah appears suddenly, in the seventeenth chapter of First Kings. Without any warning, without any previous introduction, we find Elijah the Tishbite saying to Ahab the king of the Northern Kingdom

---

[3] Other scholars take a broader view of the prophetic office. The *Catholic Commentary on Holy Scripture,* in a splendid article on "Prophetical Literature," suggests on the basis of I Samuel 9:9 and other passages that the prophets were available to the general public for guidance on matters of daily life (§ 411a). Then it goes on to observe that in the *"period of extant prophetical writings . . .* it is almost certainly accidental that there is no mention of prophets being consulted about *private affairs"* (§ 412a). In my estimation, this is an unnecessary confusion arising from an initial failure to define the prophetic office with sufficient precision.

[4] It seems to me utterly unnecessary to try to remove the element of hope and restoration from the eighth century prophets. From the beginning, the writing prophets had but one message: the message of judgment and exile to be visited upon the nation; and from the beginning, the redemptive purpose was apparent in the determination of Jehovah to save the remnant.

that there will be a drought for three years. We know little about Elijah other than the work he did. We are told that he came from Tishbeh: but even the location of Tishbeh is uncertain.

Elijah's ministry was particularly to king Ahab, and it included a number of miracles. That leads us to think a little about miracles. Some of us have had a vague idea that miracles are reported to have occurred intermittently throughout the Old Testament and the New Testament. Actually, this is not so. There are only four distinct periods of miracles that have occurred, and one more yet to come, according to Scripture. In every case, miracles occurred at a time of crisis: when the nation was in bondage in Egypt and about to be exterminated by a cruel and wicked Pharaoh; when the nation was in exile and about to be swallowed up; when the Christ came into the world and was met by the onslaught of Satanic powers; and in the days of the great life-and-death struggle between the forces of Baal and the true worship of Jehovah.

It was at the time of this struggle with Baal that Elijah came on the scene; he went to the king and told him that there would be a drought—no dew or rain for three years, except by his word. And he left him to think about *that*! I suppose Ahab puzzled many times about what took place. Then Elijah went down to the Brook Cherith[5] (I Kings 17:5), and dwelt there for a while, and was ministered to by the ravens who fed him morning and evening—note the miracle! Then the word of the Lord came to Elijah and told him to leave there and go up to Zarephath, which is near Sidon on the Phoenician coast. There he was taken care of by a widow; you recall the story of how he went in and asked her to bring him a little water in a vessel and a little morsel of bread, and how she said, "I have nothing baked, only a handful of meal . . . and a little oil . . . and I am now gathering a couple of sticks, that I may go in and prepare it for myself and my son, that we may eat it, and die" (17:12). Elijah told her that they would not die; that she should feed him first, and the meal and the oil would be continuously and miraculously replenished. And so it was.

The son of the widow became ill and died. The woman did what most of us would do: she turned against Elijah and said, "What have you against me, O man of God? You have come to me to bring

[5] Pronounced *kee'rith*. With extremely few exceptions, the *ch* in Scripture names is pronounced as *k*.

my sin to remembrance, and to cause the death of my son!" (17:18). Elijah turned to God and asked why this had taken place, and then brought the son back to life again. It was an amazing miracle, the like of which we might expect to be performed by Jesus, but not by an Old Testament character. It is also noteworthy that we find very, very few miracles of such power in the Old Testament.

The time of drought had come and was nearly over, and Elijah was to go back and face the king and tell him that rain would be sent to the earth again. The famine was severe in Samaria; and when Elijah got there he found that the king and one of his servants, Obadiah,[6] were out looking for a little patch of grass that they could use to feed the king's mules. The king had gone one way and Obadiah another, and Elijah met Obadiah and told him to go and proclaim to Ahab that he had found Elijah. Obadiah said (if we may paraphrase), "Why do you want me to do that? If I go to Ahab and even mention your name, you know what's likely to happen to me: the spirit of the Lord will catch *you* up and take you off somewhere, and nobody will know where you are, and Ahab will kill me!" But he went back, nevertheless, under the persuasion of Elijah, and eventually Ahab came to Elijah and asked, "Is it you, you troubler of Israel?" (I Kings 18:11-17).

Do you know who Ahab was? He was the son of the man who had built Samaria: Omri, the greatest king of the Northern Kingdom, speaking historically. The Scripture does not look upon him that favorably, because Scripture measures a man by his religious significance, and Omri was not very significant religiously.[7] But the historical annals of the kings of Assyria for a hundred years after his day speak about the Northern Kingdom as "the House of Omri." He was an extremely important man.

When he died, his son Ahab came to the throne and inherited all of the wealth and splendor and power of that Northern Kingdom which had been built up by his father. Ahab entered into an alliance by marrying Jezebel, the daughter of the king of the Phoenicians. The account is worth careful reading: "And Ahab the son of Omri did evil in the sight of the Lord more than all that were before him. And as if it had been a light thing for him to walk in the sins of Jeroboam the son of Nebat [that was bad enough!], he took to wife

[6] Josephus identified him with the prophet Obadiah, but this is unlikely.
[7] Omri rates only a passing reference in the Bible: I Kings 16:21-27.

Jezebel the daughter of Ethbaal king of the Sidonians, and went and served Baal, and worshipped him" (I Kings 16:31).

In those days, when you brought home a wife who served a foreign god, you arranged for the worship of her god. Solomon had done that, and in doing it brought about the downfall of his kingdom; here we have another king doing the same thing. "He erected an altar for Baal in the house of Baal, which he had built in Samaria. And Ahab made an Asherah [a pole, symbolic of the goddess]. Ahab did more to provoke the Lord, the God of Israel, to anger than all of the kings of Israel who were before him." Moreover, he supported, at public expense, four hundred and fifty prophets of Baal and four hundred prophets of Asherah. They ate at the king's table while the people went hungry.

Jezebel was one of the strongest female characters of ancient history —perhaps of all time. She would almost rank with Queen Semiramis of Assyria.[8] Jezebel took it upon herself to try to exterminate the name of Jehovah and His worship from the face of the earth. She considered it her personal mission, it would seem, to get rid of all knowledge of the God of Israel and to replace it with the knowledge and worship of Baal. She almost succeeded. I am not going to suggest that the people of Israel had always hated Baal; many of them had been Baal worshipers before this. We know from the way the prophets had to cry out against Baal worship that there was a good deal of it. But for the first time, under Jezebel, Baal worship became official, and Jehovah worship was something to be stamped out. And just at that moment God set Elijah in the path of Jezebel.

Ahab summoned all the people of Israel and gathered the prophets together at Mt. Carmel for a contest between Baal and Jehovah. Elijah shouted to the people, "How long will you go limping with two different opinions? If the Lord is God, follow him; but if Baal, then follow him." The people did not answer him. And Elijah said, "I, even I only, am left a prophet of the Lord; but Baal's prophets are four hundred and fifty men. Let two bulls be given to us; and let them choose one bull for themselves, and cut it to pieces and lay it on the wood, but put no fire to it; and I will prepare the other bull

---

[8] Of Semiramis Olmstead says, "the most beautiful, most cruel, most powerful, and most lustful of Oriental queens"—A. T. Olmstead, *History of Assyria* (New York: Charles Scribner's Sons, 1923), p. 158. Semiramis was prominent about twenty-five years after Jezebel's death.

and lay it on the wood, and put no fire to it. And you call on the name of your god and I will call on the name of the Lord; and the God who answers by fire, he is God." The idea of a challenge struck a sympathetic nerve in the people; they said, "It is well spoken!" Then Elijah said to the prophets of Baal, "Choose for yourselves one bull and prepare it, first, for you are many; and call on the name of your god, but put no fire to it." They took the bull and prepared it, and they called on the name of Baal from morning until noon, saying, "O Baal, answer us!" No one answered. And they went limping about the altar which they had made. At noon Elijah taunted them, "Cry aloud, for he is a god; either he is musing, or he has gone aside,[9] or is on a journey, or perhaps he is asleep and must be awakened." So they cried louder, and cut themselves with swords and lances, until the blood gushed out upon them. The sun began to move through the western sky, and they raved on until the time of the offering of the oblation, "but there was no voice; no one answered, no one heeded."

Then Elijah called the people, at about the time of the evening offering, to come to him. He took twelve stones, according to the number of the tribes of the sons of Jacob. Now remember, the nation had already been divided into North and South, into ten tribes and two tribes; but that was not God's ultimate will. To God, Israel was still *one* people. So Elijah built an altar of stones representing one nation. Then he dug a trench about the altar "as great as would contain two measures of seed." He put the wood in place; then he cut the bull in pieces and put it on the wood, and then he said, "Fill four jars with water, and pour it on the burnt offering, and on the wood." And they did. He said, "Do it a second time." And they did it a second time. Elijah said, "Do it a third time." By that time, the water ran around the altar and filled the trench. Then Elijah prayed, "O Lord, God of Abraham, Isaac, and Israel, let it be known this day that thou art God in Israel, and that I am thy servant, and that I have done all these things at thy word." Then the fire of the Lord fell. It consumed the burnt offering and the wood and the stones and the dust, and even licked up the water that was in the trench. When the people saw it they said, "The Lord, he is God . . . ," and they fell

---

[9] This delicious bit of satire on the earthy nature of Baal is often lost through failure to understand the idiom. Elijah is suggesting that perhaps Baal has "gone to the toilet."

on their faces. Elijah said to them, "Seize the prophets of Baal, let not one of them escape." They were seized and Elijah had them taken down to the brook Kishon and killed.

Now the prophets of Baal were the worshipers of the god who was supposed to be the god of fertility. Baal worship was centered around the idea of fertility; this was the god who gave the corn and the wine and all the rest of life's good things. Hosea ridicules this concept in his prophecy: "She did not know that it was I who gave her the grain, the wine, and the oil, and who lavished upon her silver and gold which they used for Baal" (Hosea 2:8). They thought that by worshiping Baal, they could cause the earth to be fruitful; but for three years there had been no rain and the earth had dried up. The country was enduring a rigorous, terrible famine.

It was therefore not enough that the prophets of Baal be defeated. In addition, Jehovah must show that it is He and not Baal who supplies the country with rain and with food. So Elijah says to Ahab, "Go up, eat and drink; for there is a sound of the rushing of rain." Then Elijah goes up to the top of Mt. Carmel, bows himself to the earth and says to his servant, "Go up now, and look toward the sea." The servant looks and reports, "There is nothing." Elijah says: "Go again seven times." The seventh time the servant says, "Behold, a little cloud like a man's hand is rising out of the sea." Then Elijah, with terrific faith, says, "Go up and say to Ahab, 'Prepare your chariot and go down, lest the rain stop you.'" Now, it had not rained for three years, and there was only a little cloud on the horizon; but Elijah was sure that there was going to be rain before the king could get out of the way! And so there was. They race back to the capital, the rain overtakes them on the way, and they are almost bogged down in the marshy plain of the River Kishon.

There is a postscript to this in the nineteenth chapter. It is interesting because it shows us what kind of men the "heroes of the faith" really were. Here is the man who had been called by God to stand in the way of Jezebel; he had overthrown the prophets of Baal, and brought to naught all of the nonsense of Jezebel. Ahab went back and told Jezebel what Elijah had done, and Jezebel sent a messenger to Elijah and said, "So may the gods do to me, and more also, if I do not make your life as the life of one of them by this time tomorrow." And what did Elijah do? Call down fire from heaven and destroy her, as he had destroyed the messengers of the king? No.

He turned and ran! He was afraid; he fled for his life and went to Beersheba, which is as far south as you can go in that country, and then on beyond that all the way down into the wilderness of Sinai; and he stayed there.

It is amazing, isn't it? How could a man, with all of the power at his command that Elijah had, lose his nerve in the face of this wicked woman? In the still small voice God said to him, "What are you doing here, Elijah?" Elijah replied, "I have been very jealous for the Lord, the God of Hosts; for the people of Israel have forsaken thy covenant, thrown down thy altars, and slain thy prophets with the sword; and I, even I only am left; and they seek my life, to take it away." And God sent him back with a triple mission: to anoint Hazael to be king over Syria, and to anoint Jehu king over Israel, and to anoint Elisha to take his own place as prophet. And God furthermore told him, "I will leave seven thousand in Israel, all the knees that have not bowed to Baal, and every mouth that has not kissed him" (19:18).

One closing scene: Elijah's work on earth was finished. It was time for God to take him up to heaven, and for Elisha to take over as his successor. Elisha did not want to lose his friend and master, and he said, "I will not leave you." For the second time, Elijah tried to leave him, and again Elisha said, "I will not leave you." Finally, when they came down to the river Jordan, Elijah said to Elisha, "Ask what I shall do for you, before I am taken from you." And Elisha said, "I pray you, let me inherit a double share[10] of your spirit." And Elijah said, "You have asked a hard thing; yet if you see me as I am being taken from you, it shall be so for you; but if you do not see me, it shall not be so." As they were talking, behold, a chariot of fire and horses of fire separated the two of them, and Elijah went up by a whirlwind into heaven (II Kings 2:9-12).

One day, nine hundred years later, Elijah stood with Moses on the Mount of Transfiguration and talked with Jesus. What did they talk about? Luke tells us in his ninth chapter. They talked about the departure which Jesus was about to accomplish at Jerusalem (Luke 9:31). Moses had been buried on Mount Nebo let us say fourteen hundred years before that; Elijah had been translated into heaven in

---

[10] Literally, "two mouths" or two-thirds. This was the portion of the first-born (Deuteronomy 21:17). It is a misinterpretation of this text to try to prove that Elisha was twice as great as Elijah: Scripture never puts Elisha over Elijah!

a whirlwind of fire some nine hundred years before that. Now they were talking with Jesus on the Mount of Transfiguration. Israel was the same old stiff-necked and stubborn people. For fourteen hundred years they had been rejecting the law which God had given them through Moses; for centuries they had been rejecting the word of the prophets of whom Elijah is the representative, and now they were rejecting the word of Jesus. They had stoned the prophets; they had driven them out; they had sawn them asunder; and now they were about to crucify Jesus. But God had not given them up. And Elijah had the chance, as Moses had also, to see that God was still working for the redemption of His people.

CHAPTER XIV

Isaiah

ISAIAH is great for two reasons: he lived in momentous days, in critical days of international upheaval, and he wrote what many consider to be the greatest book in the Old Testament. To understand the reasons for many of the things he said, we must study him in his historic situation.

The first chapter of the prophecy of Isaiah begins with the words, "The vision of Isaiah, the son of Amoz [he is not the prophet *Amos,* but another one whose name is spelled differently in Hebrew], which he saw concerning Judah and Jerusalem in the days of Uzziah, Jotham, Ahaz, and Hezekiah, kings of Judah." To these names we can add Manasseh, for Isaiah probably lived during the first part of the reign of Manasseh. Isaiah's ministry began "in the year that king Uzziah died," and occupied about fifty years.

Those were the days when Tiglath-pileser III came to the throne in Assyria and whipped it into a mighty fighting empire which overran the whole world.[1] He did that first by winning the support of the people of Babylonia; for he did not want the Babylonian king starting a war behind his back. Having made sure of that, he moved toward the west; in a rapid campaign, he took much of Syria and some of the Phoenician cities, and dominated the roads leading to the Phoenician seaports. Israel escaped only by paying a heavy tribute (about $2,000,-000), for which Menahem was allowed to remain as "king." Later, Pekah of Israel and Rezin of Damascus attempted a revolt against Assyria, and Tiglath-pileser moved in promptly, capturing much of Israel, deporting many Israelites, and putting Judah under tribute.[2] We often forget that twelve years before the fall of Samaria, two and a half tribes were carried into captivity. Many of the details are not only

[1] For a good resumé, see *Westminster Dictionary of the Bible,* pp. 606-607.
[2] Pul and Tiglath-pileser are the same person. Hence, I Chronicles 5:26 should be translated, "So the God of Israel stirred up the spirit of Pul king of Assyria, *even* the spirit of Tiglath-pileser. . . ," as the verb in the singular indicates: "and *he* carried them away. . . ."

recorded in the Bible, but can be found in Tiglath-pileser's annals as well.[3]

Tiglath-pileser III was followed by Shalmaneser V, the king who besieged Tyre for five years and the capital of the Northern Kingdom, Samaria, for three years.[4] He was followed, upon his death, by his brother Sargon II, who records in his annals that the first thing he did, in his first year, was to capture Samaria;[5] the Northern Kingdom disappeared. Sargon was followed by Sennacherib, who took forty-six cities of the Southern Kingdom of Judah. He tells us he carried away 200,150 people; he besieged Jerusalem and shut up Hezekiah in the city "as a bird in a cage."[6]

These kings of the Assyrian empire were on the scene at the time Isaiah was carrying on his ministry in a day that was pretty much like our own, when a mighty empire is forming in another part of the world, and threatening the peace of all the world. It went beyond the threatening stage, so far as Israel was concerned.

Turning to the national scene, we have during Isaiah's life the kings Uzziah, Jotham, Ahaz, Hezekiah, and Manasseh. Uzziah had a long and a splendid reign; he was a good king. He made some mistakes, but on the whole his reign was a good one; "he did that which was good in the eyes of the Lord." Jotham was a good king, and Hezekiah was a great king; the Scripture says there was "none like him after him or even before him," probably referring only to the kings of the divided kingdom and not including David and Solomon. Ahaz was the weakest and the most wicked king of the Southern Kingdom and Manasseh had the longest reign in Judah's history and the most apostate.[7]

[3] D. D. Luckenbill, *Ancient Records of Assyria and Babylonia* (Chicago: University of Chicago Press, 1926), Vol. I, §§ 801, 815-16.

[4] For a resumé of Shalmaneser V, see *Unger's Bible Dictionary*, p. 1003.

[5] For a resumé of Sargon II, see *Unger's Bible Dictionary*, pp. 970-972. It now appears (as Olmstead argued over fifty years ago) that Sargon's claim is false, and that Shalmaneser V actually captured Samaria, as the Bible clearly states. This is discussed at length by E. R. Thiele, *The Mysterious Numbers of the Hebrew Kings* (Chicago: University of Chicago Press, 1951), pp. 122-128. For the dates of the kings of Israel and Judah, I am following Thiele.

[6] Luckenbill, *Ancient Records of Assyria and Babylonia,* Vol. II, § 240. For a resumé of Sennacherib, see *Unger's Bible Dictionary* pp. 993-995.

[7] For those who are helped by dates, we give the following:

Uzziah, as regent 791-767, as king 767-740;	Tiglath-pileser III, 745-727
Jotham, as regent 750-740, as king 740-732;	Shalmaneser V, 727-722
Ahaz, as regent 735-732, as king 732-716;	Sargon II, 722-705
Hezekiah, as regent 729-716, as king 716-687;	Sennacherib, 705-681
Manasseh, as regent 696-687, as king 687-642.	

No nation is truly strong when it goes to such extremes in the lifetime of one man. Such a condition means that things are going to pieces at the heart of the nation. It means that there is nothing to maintain it in balance, that eccentric forces are at work and it is about to fly apart.

Isaiah had his call, according to Isaiah 6:1, in the year that King Uzziah died. That would be about 740 B.C. Isaiah had been a member of the royal court of Uzziah: he had been a scribe of the king (II Chronicles 26:22). As a scribe he knew what was going on. No man in the kingdom had a greater knowledge of what was taking place than the scribe; the king would send to him for the details which it was part of his duty to record. Isaiah was a man in that strategic position. According to tradition, he was not only a scribe; he was also a relative.[8] That is only tradition; but traditions are sometimes true. He was called to his prophetic office in the year that Uzziah died, but he had been on the scene for quite a few years before that.

Let us look at just a few of the highlights of Uzziah's reign. You will find them recorded in II Kings 14 and II Chronicles 26; they are almost parallel accounts, but you should read them side by side to get all of the details.[9] Uzziah is also called Azariah; both names are used in the Scripture. He came to the throne when he was sixteen years of age and he reigned fifty-two years. We are told that he did that which was right in the eyes of the Lord; but we are also told that the high places which had been built under the influence of Baal worship, in the days of Elijah, were not taken down. Now that may seem to be a small matter. But there is an important principle involved, namely, that there is usually a lag between the leader and the followers. When the king or the prophet is good, the people will be slightly less good; when the king and the prophets are evil, the people will be (usually) more evil. Uzziah's failure to remove the high places was an occasion for the religion of the popular level to become further degraded.

In other matters, Uzziah was a great king. He built Elath on the gulf of Aqabah; he waged war against the Philistines; he built the towers of Jerusalem; he had a strong army of 307,500 men and 2600 "mighty" men. But he made one mistake: about twelve years before

---

[8] According to the Talmud, his father Amoz was a brother of King Amaziah, which would make Isaiah and Uzziah cousins. Megillah 10b.

[9] The actual references are: II Kings 14:21—15:7; II Chr. 26:1-23.

the end of his reign, he went into the temple to burn incense—and that was not his privilege. God had very clearly defined the duties of the king, the prophet, and the priest; the king was there to lead the country as a nation, and he had no right to assume the prerogative of the religious office. For this presumption Uzziah was smitten with leprosy. Because he was a leper he could not retain his throne. Jotham became regent in 750; Uzziah continued as nominal king until his death in 740 B.C.

Then followed the reign of Jotham.[10] He had been co-regent for about eleven years, and he reigned beyond that for about three more years. He "did right," according to the Scriptures; he did all that his father had done, except that he did not enter the temple. But again we read that the high places were not taken away and that the people burned incense there. There was still that disease of apostasy gnawing at the heart of the nation.

Then followed the awful days of Ahaz. Many of the prophecies of Isaiah, certainly all those of the first fourteen chapters of the Book of Isaiah, were uttered in the days of this king. To read his record is to read one of the dark pages of Old Testament history.[11] Ahaz came to the throne when he was only twenty years of age, and he reigned sixteen years. We read that he did *not* do that which was right in the eyes of the Lord, but he caused his son to "pass through the fire." To cause your son to pass through the fire meant to offer him as a burnt offering to the god Molech. Ahaz burned his son alive as an offering. He also formed molten images for the Baalim and he burned incense to foreign gods. He went to the war with Pekah, the king of the Northern Kingdom (Israel), and with Rezin, the king of Damascus. To Rezin he lost Elath, which had been built by his grandfather Uzziah. He suffered a crushing defeat.

There was also an Edomite and a Philistine invasion in the days of Ahaz, and in the face of all of this pressure from the Northern Kingdom, Damascus, the Edomites, and the Philistines, Ahaz decided that the best thing he could do was to call for help from the one nation that was strong, namely Assyria. He cried out for Tiglath-pileser to come over and help him. Well, we know what can happen when some little nations get quarrelling over territory, and one of the little nations asks a strong nation to come to its aid. We have seen

[10] For Jotham, read II Kings 15:7-38; II Chronicles 20:23—27:9.
[11] For Ahaz, read II Kings 15:38—16:20; II Chronicles 27:9—28:27.

it in our own time. Tiglath-pileser seized the opportunity; he moved immediately, and took Damascus. Ahaz made a journey from Jeru- salem to Damascus to meet with Tiglath-pileser, and Tiglath-pileser said, "Sure, we'll support you—if you pay for it." To pay out money, it was necessary for Ahaz practically to strip the temple of all of its wealth—which he did.

That was not all. While Ahaz was in Damascus, a beautiful altar caught his eye, and he had the plans copied and sent back to Jeru- salem. He had that magnificent bronze altar which Solomon had built taken out of the temple, and replaced with a copy of the heathen altar from Damascus.

Then he closed the doors of the house of the Lord. No more sacri- fices. No more offerings. No more incense burned. The people could not even worship God!

During these days, Isaiah was prophesying. He had gone to Ahaz and told him to ask a sign from the Lord against Rezin and Pekah (Isaiah 7); Ahaz refused, and Isaiah replied that God would give him a sign anyway. "Behold, a young woman[12] shall conceive and bear a son . . . (and) before the child knows how to refuse the evil and choose the good . . ." these two smoking firebrands will be extinguished. And Isaiah went to the prophetess (I understand that to refer to his wife), and she conceived and she bore a son and they called the name of the child Maher-shalal-hash-baz; and before that child had even grown to the age of knowing the difference between right and wrong, this thing was over. But Ahaz did not believe that sign; he was not a man of faith. He believed that he could work out the situation by international diplomacy.

After that came the days of Hezekiah, and it is a joy to read the record of Hezekiah after you have read the awful story of Ahaz.[13] Hezekiah did that which was right. He removed the high places. Even the brazen serpent of Moses, which had been erected in the wilderness, and which had been set up again and was being wor- shiped as an idol, Hezekiah broke in pieces. We read that "after him there was none like him." He opened the doors of the house of the

[12] I have elsewhere published my reasons in detail for the translation "young woman" rather than "virgin" in Isaiah 7:14. The sign was to be immediately valid to Ahaz—which certainly was not to be a virgin birth in his day! The virgin birth of Jesus was a greater fulfillment of this sign (for "young woman" can also apply in the case of a virgin birth).

[13] For Hezekiah, read II Kgs. 16:20; 18:1—20:21; II Chr. 28:27—32:33.

Lord (II Chronicles 29:3-19), and
out the rubbish that was there. I
the temple and when it was sp
magnificent sacrifice; he gathered
together to celebrate Passover, a fe
It was too late to have it at the
prayed the Lord that they might
following month. And he even we
the Northern Kingdom with who
at war to come to Jerusalem for t
came, and there was rejoicing and

I remember one day in 1952,
where the Samaritans were hold... their Passover. Some of the
Samaritans live on the Israeli side of the country today; most of them,
of course, live on the Arab side. There had been no crossing over that
border for five years; from 1948 on, there had been no Passover celebration for the Samaritans in Israel. But in 1952 they opened the
border for the first time. I was talking to the Samaritan high priest
and the other priests with him when the first carload of Samaritans
came through; they were squealing and laughing and singing and
going through all sorts of antics to express their joy. Here they were,
having a Passover celebration for the first time in five years! I
think something like that must have taken place on a much vaster
scale in the days of Hezekiah.

And yet it was only a year or two after this that Shalmaneser came
up and besieged the Northern Kingdom. For three years he laid siege
to Samaria, and then it fell. The Northern Kingdom was gone, the
ten tribes completely dispersed over the face of the earth. Isaiah had
a message for that. He also had a message for Hezekiah. But Hezekiah
would not listen. He staged a rebellion against the Assyrians, and
Sennacherib came and gave him a good drubbing, and once more
Israel paid tribute to the Assyrians. They stripped what was left of
the temple furnishings to pay the bill.

Then Hezekiah fell sick; and Isaiah came to tell him that it was
to be the end of his life (II Kings 20:1). But Hezekiah repented and
said, "Remember now, O Lord, I beseech thee, how I have walked
before thee in faithfulness and with a whole heart, and have done
what is good in thy sight" (verse 3). Then God gave Isaiah the
marvelous message of a sign from God that he would live another

...ow on the sundial of Ahaz moved backward
...s would happen. The sign came; God repented;
... backwards, and Hezekiah was spared.

...ah lost his head. He welcomed certain "emissaries"
...ch-baladan, king of Babylon, who had come to con-
...him on his recovery. If Hezekiah had been thinking he
...have recognized them for spies. He was not thinking; he gave
... a royal welcome, showed them everything he had—and of
...ourse they reported to Merodach-baladan that there was yet great
wealth in Jerusalem, free for the taking.

Isaiah was furious; he told Hezekiah of the blow that would fall
on his people for all this: not only would their wealth fall to Babylon
but the people themselves would go captive (Isaiah 39:1-8). And so
it was.

Isaiah saved Hezekiah, in another bad situation. Rabshakah, who
was Sennacherib's commander-in-chief, taunted the men of Hezekiah
as he stood in siege at their walls. He told them to stop asking God
to save them, for God had sent the Assyrians to punish them! In panic,
Hezekiah's captains begged the Assyrian to speak in Aramaic instead
of Hebrew, so the people would not know what was going on. It
certainly looked like the end for Hezekiah. He rushed to Isaiah
and asked, "What shall I do?" Isaiah replied in effect, "Don't worry;
the Lord will not allow him to take Jerusalem." Sennacherib himself
came and encamped outside Jerusalem, and according to his own
proud boast he had Hezekiah shut up in that city "like a bird in a
cage"—but the angel of the Lord visited Sennacherib's camp at night.
Herodotus, the Greek historian, tells us that mice came and ate all
the strings on their bows, and their shields, and they were unable to
wage their war, and they had to leave.[14] And Hezekiah was
spared.

We shall not say much about Manasseh. We do not know how far
into Manasseh's reign Isaiah lived, but we do know that not long after
Manasseh came to the throne he began to do the evil recorded of his
reign: he rebuilt the high places, and the altars of Baal. He did
what no one before him had done: he brought in all sorts of occultism
and spiritism; he worshiped idols and demons, and he shed a great
deal of blood (II Kings 21). According to Jewish tradition he had

---

[14] Some have interpreted the Scripture to mean, in the light of this reference
to mice (equals rats?), that Bubonic plague was the cause of Sennacherib's defeat.

Isaiah killed, sawed in half. It may be that Isaiah is the one who is referred to in Hebrews 11:32 where we are told that "They . . . were sawn in two."

What was the message of this man in these tremendous days? Here was the nation coming to its end, with things going to pieces all around it; the Northern Kingdom was gone, the armies of the Assyrians were encamped around Jerusalem, and forty-six cities of the country southwest of Jerusalem had been conquered by that same Assyrian king. What was Isaiah's message in the face of all this?

First of all, it was a message of the sovereignty of God. God sits on His throne and rules this world. "In the year that King Uzziah died, I saw the Lord." Uzziah was dead, but God was not. He was on His throne, high up and lifted up.

It was a message of the sinfulness of the people. The first five chapters of Isaiah's prophecy talk about that, and it is all nicely summarized at the end of the sixth chapter, when God comes to Isaiah and gives him his vision and says, "Go and tell this people." Isaiah asks, "What shall I say?" and God says (we translate freely): "Tell them that though they hear, they will not understand; that they see but they will not perceive; that their heart is fat, their ears are heavy, their eyes are shut, and they just refuse to understand." A hopeless kind of ministry, isn't it?

The third element of his message is that this sovereign God, who sits in the heavens and who reigns in spite of all that is happening here on earth, uses the Gentiles to punish Israel. He talks about that in the tenth chapter of Isaiah, and in several other chapters. God is the one who has brought the rod of the Assyrian against these people. He is the one who is using even the unbelieving pagans to smite His sinful people because of their sins.

You say it is a terrible message; is that *all* he has to say? No; in Isaiah 40 we find a message of the mercy of God. "Comfort, comfort my people, says your God. Speak tenderly to Jerusalem, and cry to her that her warfare is ended, that her iniquity is pardoned, that she has received from the Lord's hand double for all her sins." And he goes on to talk in chapters 42, 49, 50 to 53 about the "suffering servant." There is a lot of discussion about who that suffering servant is. Is it Israel? Certainly Israel was the Lord's servant; certainly Israel was suffering. But there are other passages that would seem to indicate that it is not only Israel, but one of the Israelites, one representative

Israelite, who in a supreme way is the Lord's Servant. He is the one who takes upon Himself the guilt and the burden of this people.

Isaiah's message is a message of salvation. Notice how he pulls the whole thing together. This sovereign God who uses a Gentile king to destroy His people, uses another Gentile king (Cyrus, the Persian) to bring them back again (Isaiah 45:1). He talks about the days when there will be a Son (Isaiah 9:6-7) who will be the mighty God, the everlasting Father, the Prince of Peace. There will be Immanuel, not the son of the prophetess, but the greater Immanuel, who will come to spare His people; and the suffering Servant becomes the Sin-bearer of Israel. He talks in the last few chapters (58 through 66) of the glory that will be theirs. It is a magnificent message. It is a message that starts with the sinfulness of the people and tells them that God is going to punish them double for all their iniquities; but it goes on to talk of the redemption and the glory which will come to the remnant who are faithful to the Lord.

I have already suggested that in many ways our day is like Isaiah's day. We are seeing nations collapse all about us. If we were living in England or France instead of in America, we would see it even more clearly. I do not know whether God is going to use the scourge of Russia to punish America for her godlessness and sinfulness; I am not a prophet. It may well be. He has done it before. I believe that He used the scourge of Nazi Germany to punish the unbelieving nations of Europe, and it may well be that you and I will see our nation—I pray God that we shall not!—punished by God for our sin. No nation can stand against Him and defy Him.

But if by chance that punishment should come, we have a message that looks beyond it, that tells us that the end of this world is not punishment and destruction; the end is glory and the Kingdom of God. Isaiah could look down across those years and see the nations about him falling one after another, and he could say, "This ultimately is going to come *here,* and God will carry away your sons and your daughters and the wealth of your temple." But he could also look past that and say, "The time will come when the nations will turn their swords into plowshares and their spears into pruning hooks, and when the nations will come up to Jerusalem to worship." Just so, we can look beyond the present time of crisis and say, "This is God's will, because after all, it is God who sits on the throne, and this is His world."

CHAPTER XV

Jeremiah

JEREMIAH is certainly one of the greatest of the prophets. Some consider him to be the most Christlike man to appear before the Lord Jesus Himself. I would not be honest if I failed to add that others look upon him as mentally deranged. Certainly he lived in one of the most turbulent periods of history this world has ever seen, with three large nations and countless smaller groups waging wars, conducting raids, and stirring up all sorts of intrigues. He lived under seven kings of Judah, and performed his ministry under five of them. He witnessed one of the greatest religious revivals in the history of Israel; he also witnessed three invasions of Jerusalem and the utter destruction of the city. Meanwhile, two of the great nations, Egypt and Assyria, had fallen to the third, Babylonia. And certainly Jeremiah had one of the most discouraging tasks ever handed out to man. He was commanded to persuade his people to allow themselves to be taken into captivity.

Jeremiah is often described as the "weeping prophet." As a matter of fact, his name has given us a word in the English language, "jeremiad" which means "a tale of woe," or sorrow or disappointment. We know more about Jeremiah personally than we do of any other prophet because there are so many personal references in his prophecy.

He was called to the office when he was a young man, approximately twenty years of age. But God told him, "Before I formed you in the womb I knew you, and before you were born I consecrated you, I appointed you a prophet to the nations" (1:5). Jeremiah did not have the experiences which most young men have; these were denied him because of his calling. He says, "I did not sit in the company of merrymakers, nor did I rejoice; I sat alone, because thy hand was upon me, for thou hast filled me with indignation" (15:17).

Judging from his extremely emotional and sentimental character, we would conclude that he was the kind of man who would have profited very much from having a wife and family. Yet he was forbidden to marry: "The word of the Lord came to me: 'You shall not take a wife,

145

nor shall you have sons or daughters in this place. For thus says the Lord concerning the sons and daughters who are born in this place, and concerning the mothers who bore them and the fathers who begot them in this land: They shall die with deadly diseases. They shall not be lamented, nor shall they be buried; they shall be as dung on the surface of the ground. They shall perish by the sword and by famine, and their dead bodies shall be food for the birds of the air and for the beasts of the earth'" (16:1-4). It was such a terrible, calamitous time that God in effect said to Jeremiah, "You must not enter into these experiences. You shall not have a wife and family."

Jeremiah lived in the days of the greatest revival that Israel ever knew—we shall discuss that when we consider Josiah the king. And yet, Jeremiah had a message not of joy, not of exultation because of this great revival; he had a message of gloom and doom, a message from which he himself shrank. He did not want to proclaim such words. Listen to his cry: "O Lord, thou hast deceived me, and I was deceived; thou art stronger than I, and thou hast prevailed. I have become a laughingstock all the day; everyone mocks me. For whenever I speak, I cry out, I shout, 'Violence and destruction!' For the word of the Lord has become for me a reproach and derision all day long. If I say, 'I will not mention him, or speak any more in his name,' there is in my heart as it were a burning fire shut up in my bones, and I am weary with holding it in, and I cannot. For I hear many whispering. Terror is on every side! 'Denounce him! Let us denounce him!' say all my familiar friends, watching for my fall. . . . But the Lord is with me as a dread warrior" (20:7-11). He asked God why he should force him to give a message such as this. The whole twentieth chapter is a chapter of lament. "Cursed be the day on which I was born! The day when my mother bore me, let it not be blessed! Cursed be the man who brought the news to my father! . . ."

He just did not want to be responsible for a message such as this; and yet God had laid it upon him, and it is to his credit that he proclaimed the message faithfully. In fact, when reading Jeremiah we have to distinguish between the complaints of Jeremiah and the message of God: "If you return, I will restore you, and you shall stand before me. If you utter what is precious, and not what is worthless, you shall be as my mouth. They shall turn to you, but you shall not turn to them. And I will make you to this people a fortified wall of bronze; they will fight against you, but they shall not prevail over you, for I am with you to save you and deliver you, says the Lord (15:19-20). When we are reading this prophecy, we must keep in mind that some of the words in the book are the prophet's own objections to the message he has to give: they are the outpourings of his own feelings; the rest of the time—most of the time—it is the message which God has laid upon him.

It was only after he had preached for many years that his message was put into writing. Chapter 36 tells us about that. In the fourth year of Jehoiakim, which was many years after he had started to preach, the word came to Jeremiah from the Lord, "Take a scroll and write on it all of the words that I have spoken to you against Israel and Judah and all the nations. . . ." Jeremiah dictated it to Baruch the scribe, and it was then read to the king. As the king heard it, column by column, he ordered it to be cut up and thrown in the fire, until the whole thing was burned. He wanted nothing to do with a message like that. But at the word of the Lord the entire thing was written all over again, with certain additions, before it came into the form that we have now in the Scriptures.

Jeremiah saw the captivity which took place when Nebuchadrezzar,[1] the king of Babylon, invaded Jerusalem and carried off the nobles of the people and the vessels from the temple. But because he had preached to the people to yield to Babylon (he recognized that it was God's will that they should go into captivity) Jeremiah was granted certain privileges: "Nebuchadrezzar . . . gave command concerning Jeremiah through Nebuzaradan, the captain of the guard, saying 'Take him, look after him well and do him no harm, but deal with him as he tells you'" (39:11). He gave Jeremiah his choice: he could go to Babylon or he could stay in Jerusalem. He chose to stay in Jerusalem, and he had the protection of the king of Babylon there not because he was selling out to the Babylonians, but because he had proclaimed the message of God that there was no use trying to fight against this. It was God's will that the people should be taken into Babylon and into captivity.

He preached a message of "life as usual." In the days when the Babylonian flag was flown over Jerusalem, there was a false prophet named Hananiah who said, "Thus saith the Lord of hosts, the God of

[1] Both "Nebuchadnezzar" and "Nebuchadrezzar" are found in the Bible, the latter in Jeremiah. The difference is apparently due to a dialectal dissimilation which need not concern us here. Jeremiah's form more nearly reflects the Babylonian *Nabû-kudurri-uṣur*.

Israel: I have broken the yoke of the king of Babylon. Within two years I will bring back to this place all the vessels of the Lord's house, which Nebuchadnezzar, king of Babylon took away from this place ... I will also bring back Jeconiah..., and all the exiles ..." (28:2-4). Jeremiah would have gladly said "Amen" to that, but he said, "Let us wait and see." At the end of two years, it had not happened. It was a false message that God had not given to Hananiah, and Hananiah died for uttering such rebellion. Jeremiah gave the true message in the next chapter: "Thus says the Lord of hosts, the God of Israel, to all the exiles whom I have sent into exile from Jerusalem to Babylon: Build houses and live in them; plant gardens and eat their produce. Take wives and have sons and daughters; take wives for your sons, and give your daughters in marriage...; multiply there, and do not decrease." And he goes on to say, "When seventy years are completed for Babylon, I will visit you, and I will fulfill to you my promise and bring you back to this place" (29:4-10).

Jeremiah was so convinced that this was true—that God was going to bring His people back at the end of seventy years—that he himself caused a plot of ground to be purchased at Anathoth, which would be used for those who would return from the captivity. He reminds us somewhat of Abraham, in that respect: Abraham knew that his descendants would be slaves in a foreign land for four hundred years, and yet he bought a plot of ground as a burial place for his wife and himself against the day when his family would come back to that land, and when it would be theirs.

In the days of Jeremiah, the closing days of the kingdom, there was a pro-Egypt party. They felt that their hope was Egypt, that they could stand off the forces of Babylonia if they would unite with Pharaoh. Jeremiah had not gone along with that idea, because he knew that God's will was otherwise and that God had explicitly said that they should not trust in Egypt. The pro-Egypt party felt that he was a traitor, that he was selling out. They left the land, finally, after an unsuccessful attempt to overthrow the Babylonian puppet on the throne, and they took Jeremiah to Egypt with them. He tells us about it in the forty-third chapter. He was then about sixty years of age, and he had been prophesying for perhaps forty years. He was in Egypt for a few years, but we know practically nothing about him during that time. He prophesied a bit more; and then he died there, a man hated by his fellow countrymen, a man whose life was lived under terrific pressure of saying

things he did not want to say, a man ridiculed by the people and repudiated by the king; even Josiah—the great king, the king who was responsible for the great revival—seems to have turned against him at
one time. Jeremiah was a lonely man, but a man of God.

Let us look closely at the day in which he lived. He came to the
prophetic office when Josiah was king. Josiah had acceded to the throne
at the age of eight, and had been converted in the eighth year of his
reign and had become "out and out for the Lord." It was in the
thirteenth year of the reign of Josiah that Jeremiah was called to the
prophetic office at twenty years of age; Josiah was about the same age
and his great efforts to clean up the country were getting into full
swing. If I were to be called by God to be a prophet, I could want nothing better than to come to my job at a time when the leadership of the
nation was undergoing a real spiritual revival and the nation was beginning to cleanse itself; I would consider that to be a most auspicious
moment to begin a prophetic task. It would seem as though I could not
fail; I could join hands with a king of my own age and we could go
ahead and sweep the nation into a glorious revival. That was the potential of the moment. In the eighteenth year of Josiah—that would be
five years after Jeremiah had come on the scene—his workmen, in
cleaning out the temple, discovered the Law: the Law of Moses which
had been lost in the rubbish! You can imagine how low the spiritual
character of the nation had fallen when the rubbish that cluttered up
the temple had buried even the copy of the Law. When they read it to
Josiah, he broke into tears; he realized that God must certainly punish
the nation for having failed to obey the Law which He had given (cf.
II Kings 22:1-13).

Recognizing the great sin, Josiah sent to Huldah the prophetess to
ask her what was going to happen now; she assured him that God certainly would punish these people, but that it would not happen in his
day because of his true penitence and his desire to walk in the way of
the Lord. In gratitude, Josiah put down the idolatrous priests, destroyed
the altar which Jeroboam had built at Bethel, banished the mediums
and the wizards and the idols and abominations, and held a Passover
such as had not been held since the days of Samuel: apparently, it even
exceeded the glory of the one that Hezekiah had held in Isaiah's day
(cf. II Kings 23:1-25).

But Josiah, somewhere along the line, got out of contact with
Jeremiah and with the will of God, and he very foolishly tried to inter-

fere with an invasion of Pharaoh-Neco, the king of Egypt;[2] he was killed at Megiddo by Neco's archers. He was succeeded by Jehoahaz; all we can say about him is that he did evil, and that Neco deposed him and carried him off to Hamath, and thence to Egypt. Jehoahaz was succeeded by Jehoiakim, a puppet whom Neco had placed on the throne, who also did evil; he laid the whole land under tribute to Egypt. It was in his days that Nebuchadrezzar first invaded the country and made Jehoiakim his vassal, replacing him three years later, when he attempted to revolt, with Jehoiachin, another puppet. He also did evil. He was carried away by Nebuchadrezzar, who then put Zedekiah, yet another puppet, on the throne (II Kings 24:1-20).

We read in the closing verses of Jeremiah that when Evil-merodach succeeded to the throne of Babylon after the days of Nebuchadrezzar, he took Jehoiachin out of prison and he fed him daily rations (Jeremiah 52:31-34). For a long, long time, that statement was suspect; no king of Babylon would do a thing like that! But not too many years ago a cuneiform tablet was discovered in the gate of the city of Babylon, which contained the orders of King Evil-merodach, to grant daily portions to Yaukin, the King of Judah (that is Jehoiachin), and to his sons.[3] So we have archaeological confirmation that this element of the story is historical. Zedekiah lived through the days when all of the wealth and the best men of the city were carried to Babylon: the princes, the mighty men, the craftsmen. No one was left but the poorest. Finally, when Zedekiah tried to revolt, Nebuchadrezzar sent his troops to sack the city, burning the temple, the palace, and every great house, and tearing down the walls. Zedekiah was blinded and carried in chains to Babylon. Jeremiah's prophecies were largely in the days of Josiah and Zedekiah. As you read through the book you will notice that these are the names most often mentioned.

[2] There has been some confusion concerning Neco's purpose and why Josiah got himself involved. The best suggestion is that Neco was going not "against" but "to the aid of" Assyria (II Kings 23:29). Nineveh had already fallen to the Medes and Babylonians and Neco was either attempting to aid the remaining Assyrian forces, or (more likely) trying to take some territory for Egypt. Just why Josiah attempted to interfere is not clear; a simple explanation would be that he was trying to protect his own land against an Egyptian land-grab.

[3] Described by W. F. Albright, "King Joiachin in Exile," *Biblical Archaeologist*, Vol. 5 (1942), pp. 51-55. The tablets had been discovered and taken to Berlin in the early part of this century, but had not been read until E. F. Weidner made this remarkable discovery in 1933. The translation is in Pritchard, *Ancient Near Eastern Texts*, p. 308.

This gives you a pretty good idea of Jeremiah's day. It was a day when the forces of Egypt and the forces of Assyria were slugging it out for supremacy; actually, the forces of Babylonia were the winners, because all that Egypt and Assyria did was weaken each other, and Babylonia was able to come in and pick up the pieces. It was a day when the nation of Judah was having its last chance before God, and when God had decided that Judah must pay the penalty for its idolatry, its apostasy, its bloodshed, and its evil. Jeremiah came on the scene with a message—a message which so completely oppressed him that there are some who think that Jeremiah was a psychopathic case. I was present in New York a few years ago at the meeting of a learned society, when one of the papers read at the meeting attempted to psychoanalyze Jeremiah. I do not know enough about psychiatry to give the details but I am certain that if Jeremiah had not been the Lord's servant, he might well have been a neurotic. Anyone who had to face situations such as he faced and deliver the messages he delivered certainly would be torn by the pressures of all sorts of emotions! You have no doubt heard the claim from time to time that there are more people in mental hospitals because of religion than any other single reason. I do not know whether there are figures to substantiate such a claim. But this much, I think, is clear: such cases do not develop in persons who are certain that they *are* doing God's will; rather it is the persons who are torn with fears that they have *not* done God's will who break down. Professor Hyatt has well observed, with reference to Jeremiah: "On account of his deep faith in God, and because he did not hesitate to give vent to his feelings of despair and bitterness, the tension of his inner life did not cause him to break down."[4]

Turning to Jeremiah's message, we can say that it was a message of denunciation. In chapter 7, he declares that God wants obedience. The Judeans were practicing a formal kind of religion. He says, "Thus says the Lord of hosts, the God of Israel: 'Add your burnt offerings to your sacrifices, and eat the flesh. For in the day that I brought them out of the land of Egypt, I did not speak to your fathers or command them concerning burnt offerings and sacrifices. But this command I gave them, "Obey my voice, and I will be your God, and you shall be my people; and walk in all the way that I command you that it may be well with you." '" He goes on to point out that they did not walk in His way; they did not obey. They backslid; they went their own

[4] *Interpreter's Bible*, Vol. 5, p. 783.

way. "From the day that your fathers came out of the land of Egypt to this day, I have persistently sent all my servants the prophets to them, day after day; yet they did not listen to me, or incline their ear, but stiffened their neck. They did worse than their fathers" (Jeremiah 7:21-25). God did not want formality; He wanted obedience.

Some would have us believe that Jeremiah represented an anti-priest movement in Judah. The "Book of the Law," discovered in Josiah's temple-cleaning, they tell us, was a newly-written document (known to us as Deuteronomy), that was an attempt to get "Scriptural" backing for the rising priesthood. It is clear, they point out, that Jeremiah was opposed to burnt offerings and sacrifices. But this would have been impossible, they remind us, if the Law of Moses had already been written including these things, for then Jeremiah would have been branded as a false prophet. Of course we might ask, If the priestly caste became powerful enough to impose its will on the Jewish people, how did the prophetic message manage to survive? Most of the prophets, it seems to me, oppose what Jeremiah is opposing. Or we might ask, How did the priestly caste ever get started? The prophets from Amos on opposed meaningless ritual. The best answer is the easiest answer, for it is clear that the prophets were voicing God's protest against form without content, ritual without true religion, offerings without obedience. The priestly ritual was not something new; it was something old, so old that it had become cold, meaningless formality. God hates such ritual (Amos 5:21). He wants worship that stems from the heart (Micah 6:6-8). Jeremiah was uttering this same message, which God's servants the prophets had been proclaiming for more than a century.

Jeremiah reminded them that God had never intended it to be a matter of religious furniture: "And when you have multiplied and increased in the land, in those days, says the Lord, they shall no more say, 'The ark of the covenant of the Lord'" (Jeremiah 3:16). It is a matter of something deeper than that; it reaches to the depths of the heart: "O Jerusalem, wash your heart from wickedness, that you may be saved. How long shall your evil thoughts lodge within you?" (4:14). It is the heart that is wicked. It is the heart that needs to be changed. We are told sometimes that this is a New Testament message; perhaps it is. Jeremiah in some respects comes closest to the New Testament message with his attitude toward religion. He talked about the day when there would be a new covenant: "Behold, the days are coming, says the Lord, when I will make a new covenant with the house of

Israel and the house of Judah, not like the covenant which I made with their fathers when I took them by the hand to bring them out of the land of Egypt. . . . But this is the covenant which I will make with the house of Israel after those days, says the Lord: I will put my law within them, and I will write it in their hearts; and I will be their God, and they shall be my people. And no longer shall each man teach his neighbor and each his brother, saying, 'Know the Lord,' for they shall all know me, from the least of them to the greatest . . ." (31:31-33). And again: "I will give them one heart and one way, that they may fear me forever, for their own good and the good of their children after them" (32:39). That summarizes the message of Jeremiah. It is a message of punishment and gloom and doom, but it is also a message of hope and restoration and a day when God will take away all of the formal aspects of religion and put a genuine heart-religion in His people.

One day Jesus said to His disciples, "Who do men say that the Son of Man is?" And they said, "Some say . . . Jeremiah." Well, there were qualities of Jesus that were like the qualities of Jeremiah. He too wept over Jerusalem. He too was crushed in His heart by the sins of the people. But I think there is one outstanding difference between them —and it is a difference that we should not overlook when we try to evaluate Jeremiah the prophet. Jeremiah had only words of vengeance for his enemies. For example, "O Lord of hosts, who judgest righteously, who triest the heart and the mind, let me see thy vengeance upon them, for to thee have I committed my cause" (11:20); or again: "O Lord, thou knowest; remember me and visit me, and take vengeance for me on my persecutors . . ." (15:15). But Jesus, when He was persecuted, turned and prayed to the Father, "Father, forgive them, for they know not what they are doing." In Jeremiah we see a great man; we do not see completely the love of the Son of God. He approaches it; in many respects he approaches it more than any other in the Old Testament. But he comes just so far, and then falls short.

CHAPTER XVI

Ezekiel

To MANY, Ezekiel is a little-known person, and his book an unknown book. If we look for the reason, we have only to read the first chapter of Ezekiel with its four-faced creatures and its wheels within wheels. If that is not convincing, to read the gloomy prophecies of judgment and destruction that occupy the first half of the book will certainly deter many from finishing the book. However, as in the case of Daniel and Revelation (with which Ezekiel has much in common), we must learn to fasten upon the understandable rather than to be confused by the enigmatic; we must learn to look at the glorious outcome, rather than to be repelled by (or possibly gloat over) the scenes of judgment. When we learn to read these books in such a way, then we shall find that they are truly great books. Of such, Charles R. Erdman, dean of American Bible expositors, writes as the opening words of his book on Ezekiel, "Blessed are those poets and prophets who have taught the people of God to sing songs in the night."[1]

Ezekiel was the prophet whose lot it was to live with his people in captivity. It was his burden to have to foretell in detail the destruction of Jerusalem. It was his sad experience to see, in a vision, the glory of the Lord departing from the temple, and it was his happy experience to see that same glory returning to the new temple. One day, many years later, when the church of the Lord Jesus Christ was facing the black night of persecution by the Roman emperors, when the aged John was sitting in exile on the isle of Patmos, he had a vision of the horrors of judgment and the glories of the triumph and he wrote the book of Revelation. There can be little doubt that he found the source of much of his hope in the prophecy of Ezekiel.

What do we know about the prophet Ezekiel? He was the son of Buzi, he was a priest, and he was with the exiles in Tel-Abib[2] in

---

[1] C. R. Erdman, *The Book of Ezekiel* (Westwood, N. J.: Fleming H. Revell Co., 1956), p. 9.

[2] The dictionary authorizes the pronunciation *tell-ă'-bĭb* for this name; however, since it has been taken for the name of the modern Israeli city of Tel Aviv, I see no reason why we should not give it the modern pronunciation of *tell-ă-veev'*.

154

Babylonia (1:1-3; 3:15). Ezekiel had been exiled with the group that had been taken captive with Jehoiachin: a group that is described as princes, mighty men of valor, craftsmen and smiths, officials and chief men of the land (II Kings 24:14). He therefore had a place of some prominence in his nation. If the opening reference to "the thirtieth year" refers to his age at the time of his call—which seems the best of all explanations given—we can say that Ezekiel was born about 621 B.C., and that he was twenty-five years old when he was taken into captivity. For a man of thirty, Ezekiel was unusually mature, probably due to the fact that he had lived through thirty hectic years. By the time Ezekiel was fourteen, his nation was paying tribute to Egypt. During the next ten years he saw four kings on the throne, and the controls passed from Egypt to Babylonia; he saw two kings deposed, and at least one severely punished for trying to lead a revolt. He saw the golden furnishings and then the golden decoration of the temple stripped away to pay tribute to the foreign governments. Finally, he himself was taken to Babylonia in captivity.

What was life in exile like? Those who were exiled by the Assyrians (the Northern Kingdom, for example) were scattered abroad, and, so far as we can ascertain, soon lost their identities. On the other hand, the Babylonians seem to have allowed their displaced persons to settle in communities and to pursue a rather normal existence. They built houses, planted vineyards, pursued their crafts, and so forth. Jeremiah had been instructed to advise the Jews to do just these things (Jeremiah 29:4-7). Some of the Jews in exile quickly grew to like their new surroundings. They were probably impressed with the fertile plains well watered by the system of canals then in existence,[3] in contrast to the stony hills of Palestine from which man could scarcely wrest his existence. They must have liked the cultural factors, especially the opportunities for business enterprise, for within a generation we find records of business houses having Jewish names.[4] Since they accumulated considerable wealth, as evidenced by the handsome contributions made for rebuilding the temple (cf. Ezra 2:68-69), we can suppose that the burden of taxation was not excessive. These factors must have

[3] The river Chebar (1:3) might be translated "The Grand Canal."
[4] H. Gressmann, *Altorientalische Texte zum Alten Testamente* (Berlin and Leipzig, 1926), pp. 434f. For a good picture of the living conditions among the exiles, read P. Heinisch, *History of the Old Testament* (Collegeville, Minn.: The Liturgical Press, 1952), pp. 310-314.

entered into the decision of many Jews not to return to Palestine when they had the opportunity under Cyrus the Great. History since the days when Abraham went out from Ur, seems to have come around the cycle. Will God be able to get His people out of Mesopotamia a second time?

One of the distinctly depressing features of the exile, at least to the more religious of the deportees, was the feeling that they were absent from the Lord. It is hard for us to realize that the people of God had not yet learned the great truth of the universality or omnipresence of God. As it was in the case of Naomi and her daughters-in-law, so it was with the exiles in Ezekiel's day: to leave the land of promise was to leave the Lord who had given them that land.

> By the waters of Babylon,
>   there we sat down and wept,
>   when we remembered Zion.
> On the willows there
>   we hung up our lyres.
> For there our captors
>   required of us songs,
> and our tormentors, mirth, saying,
>   "Sing us one of the songs of Zion!"
> How shall we sing the Lord's song
>   in a foreign land?   (Psalm 137:1-4)

That they learned to sing the Lord's song in the land of exile, that they learned the great truth that the Lord was with them, was due in large measure to the prophet who taught them to sing.

Several scholars have noted the large number of parallels between Ezekiel's prophecy and the book of Leviticus.[5] In my estimation, much of this discussion is now obsolete, since the archaeological discoveries of the past fifty years have certainly made it unnecessary to give the institution of priestly ritual a late date. If we accept an essentially Aaronic (or Mosaic) origin for the book of Leviticus, and the tradi-

---

[5] The picture is sometimes obscured to the layman due to the fact that the scholars insist on talking about "H" (or "the Holiness Code," Leviticus 17-26) and "P" (or "the Priestly Code," which may be roughly approximated to the rest of Leviticus for our present purpose). To make the matter still more difficult, scholars are not at all agreed upon the date they assign to the final writing of Ezekiel, nor to the exact relationship between H and P and the editorial work on Ezekiel.

tional view of sixth century authorship of Ezekiel,[6] we get the following picture, which in my opinion is self-consistent and compatible with the known facts.

Ezekiel was a priest, schooled in the priestly office, therefore thoroughly familiar with the Levitical legislation. He used its phraseology often.[7] Now, what was the purpose of the Levitical legislation? It was to establish the people of Israel as a "peculiar people." Repeatedly the expression is used, "you shall be holy." The basic idea in the word "holy" is *separation*. It comes to have an ethical meaning—and we certainly lose the great purpose behind the Law if we lose sight of the ethical significance. "You shall be holy; for I the Lord your God am holy" (Leviticus 19:2), does not mean that God is aloof from the sinful world; it means that He is morally straight or "righteous." A careful reading of the Levitical laws should make that clear. But in protecting the ethical connotation, let us not lose the basic idea of separation. These people were about to go into the land of the Canaanites, the land of gross idolatry and gross sin. They were to be a peculiar people, set apart from the Canaanites by peculiar rituals, peculiar garb, peculiar dietary laws, particularly by the Sabbaths, all designed to mark out the separation. Their sin, as proclaimed by all the prophets—and Ezekiel is certainly no exception!—had been due to the loss of this sense of separation and the concomitant loss of holiness. Now, as they are about to go into the land of Babylonia (in fulfillment of Leviticus 26:14-45, we might note) where they might easily be swallowed up forever, it is necessary for God to remind them once more of His purpose for them. Ezekiel is His servant, and the Levitical Law is at the heart of his message. These people must be reminded that they belong to the Lord. Notice how many times Ezekiel echoes the familiar words of Leviticus, "I am the Lord."

We have already given some indication of the days in which Ezekiel lived. For the first thirty-five years of his life he was contemporary with Jeremiah. The three great powers (today, I suppose, we would call them "the Big Three"), Egypt, Assyria, and Babylonia, were going

[6] This latter point is ably defended by C. G. Howie, *The Date and Composition of Ezekiel* (Philadelphia: Society of Biblical Literature, 1950), note pp. 100-102.

[7] "The parallels with Lev. 26:3ff. are peculiarly numerous and striking, including several expressions not occurring elsewhere in the Old Testament," says S. R. Driver, *An Introduction to the Literature of the Old Testament* (9th ed., Edinburgh: T. & T. Clark, 1913), p. 147, and then he lists 27 of these expressions.

through a time of transition. Egypt had temporarily risen to strength after a few centuries of impotence. Assyria was on the way out. Babylon was rising to the top—but would not stay there long. The smaller nations were feeling growing pains and small wars were breaking out in many places. How much like our own day it was! About 626 B.C. the Scythians had broken through from the north, and had moved toward Egypt. We do not know much about them—they are not mentioned by name in the Old Testament—other than the fact that they came from the region around the Black Sea.[8] Probably they are the background for the figure used in the prophets, especially Jeremiah, Ezekiel, and Zephaniah, of the scourge to come from the north. I do not mean to say that the Scythians fulfill these prophecies; I simply mean that such an invasion of a hitherto-unknown people, being fresh in the minds of the people of Israel, would be an apt figure to drive home the truth of a prophecy of future trouble out of the north.

It has been suggested that this Scythian invasion may have been the event that triggered the reform in the days of Josiah five years later, the year Ezekiel was born. It is possible that Josiah was deeply impressed by his escape from some unknown fate when the Scythians were bribed by Pharaoh Psamtik to go back home. God uses various ways of touching the hearts of men. However, splendid as the reform of Josiah was, it apparently had no deep roots in the lives of the people. Soon they were paying Egypt for protection—with an Egyptian puppet on the throne; then they were paying Babylonia for protection—with a Babylonian puppet on the throne. And hardly anyone remembered that their best protection was the Lord of hosts; and He should be on the throne. Ezekiel reminded them.

Ezekiel's message can be divided into three main sections, covering the Fall of Jerusalem (chapters 1—24), the Judgment upon the Nations (chapters 25—32), and the Restoration of the City (chapters 33—48). The first section can be further subdivided into three parts, or three "cycles of threats."[9] It is as though God has drawn up a bill of particulars setting forth the reasons for the judgment that is to fall, and that Ezekiel is commissioned to read the horrible details.

[8] Recently an advocate of the British-Israel theory was trying to convince me that the Scythians (the Saxons, he pointed out, with some fanciful etymological equations) were the "Lost Tribes." When I asked him how they managed to be threatening Egypt less than a hundred years after they had been taken into captivity, he seemed to be completely ignorant of this detail of history.
[9] This expression I have taken from *A Catholic Commentary on Holy Scripture,* p. 602.

The first "cycle of threats" (chapters 1—11) begins with the mysterious visions of chapter one. Living creatures with four faces and wheels within wheels: someone has suggested that they represent second causes, both living and inorganic; but over them was a throne and over the throne One like us in form. He is the Prime Mover, all else are second causes. Historians try to explain the rise and decline of nations; the prophet knows that it is God in the last analysis who is accomplishing His will.

It is an indication of the spiritual level of our own day, I think, that we fail to understand that Israel's worst sin was the sin of idolatry, apostasy, turning from the true God. "What is so bad about that?" we ask. We would be much more impressed if God had specified a list of crimes: gas chambers, concentration camps, broken treaties, the use of poison gas or flame throwers or nuclear weapons; child marriage, polygamy, sweat shops, slave labor; gluttony and drunkenness, and the like. Some of the prophets do enumerate such social sins—and they are more frequently quoted and better understood today. But Israel's worst sin was turning from God! Until we understand the awful depth of that sin, we ourselves are under condemnation; for until we thoroughly believe that God is supreme in this universe and act upon that faith, we have denied to Him the honor that is His right and we have rebelled against His authority.

Ezekiel saw the glory of God move from the cherubim in the Holy Place to the threshold (9:3), and then from the threshold to the east gate (10:19), and then from the midst of the city to the mountain on the east side (the Mount of Olives) (11:23). The glory of the Lord's presence that had filled the house when Solomon dedicated it (II Chronicles 5:13-14) had departed, because Solomon and his successors had failed to heed the Lord's warning: "If you turn aside and forsake my statutes and my commandments which I have set before you, and go and serve other gods and worship them, then I will pluck you up from the land which I have given you; and this house, which I have consecrated for my name, I will cast out of my sight . . ." (II Chronicles 7:19-22).

There was mercy there, too, for God had put a mark on the foreheads of the men who were truly penitent (Ezekiel 9:4), and the Lord's ministers of judgment spared those who were marked (cf. Revelation 7:3; 14:1).

Ezekiel was appalled by the threat, and he cried out, "Ah Lord God! wilt thou make a full end of the remnant of Israel?" Then God told him of the regathering of the exiles, of the new heart of flesh, and added "they shall be my people, and I will be their God" (11:13-20).

The second "cycle of threats" (chapters 12—19) begins by singling out the false prophets and prophetesses, and laying upon them the burden of guilt for misleading the people (chapter 13). God names the sins, and says that even if the three most righteous men of old were in the city (it reminds us of how Abraham had pled for the sparing of Sodom for Lot's sake), they could only succeed in sparing themselves (14:14). Then God rehearses the history of Israel in a touching story (chapter 16).

This people was like an unwanted girl, cast out to die when God found her and took her. He cared for her in the days of her childhood, and when she came to maturity He "spread his skirt" over her (remember Ruth and Boaz?), He married her, He made her a beautiful queen, famous throughout the world. Then this wife proved unfaithful. With the Egyptians, the Assyrians, and the Babylonians (or Chaldeans), she played the harlot. Her sins were many, and they were deep. Yet, God would remember His covenant with her in the days of her youth, and the time would come, He told her, when she would "remember and be confounded, and never open your mouth again because of your shame, when I forgive you all that you have done" (16:63). That is the greatest love theme of all time—the love of God for His faithless and sinful people.

The idea that personal responsibility was lost in corporate existence must be set straight. "What do you mean by repeating this proverb concerning the land of Israel, 'The fathers have eaten sour grapes, and the children's teeth are set on edge'?" (Ezekiel 18:2). "Behold, all souls are mine," says God; "the soul of the father as well as the soul of the son is mine: the soul that sins shall die" (18:4). And God makes it clear and simple that each man must stand on his own feet. Spiritual life is a matter of personal responsibility before God. Church membership does not save, any more than does physical Israelite lineage; each man stands before God on the basis of his own relationship to God (18:20). But over and above this truth is the greater truth: *God does not take pleasure in the death of the wicked!* (18:23). "Why will you die, O house of Israel? For I have no pleasure in the death of anyone, says the Lord God; *so turn, and live*" (18:31-32).

In the third cycle of threats, God reminds them of the statutes and ordinances which they have failed to observe, especially the Sabbaths (20:12). We get an insight into the heart of God when He remarks, "I will be king over you" (20:33). He promises to bring them out from the countries where they have been scattered: "And you shall know that I am the Lord, when I deal with you for my name's sake, not according to your evil ways, nor according to your corrupt doings, O house of Israel, says the Lord God" (20:44).

Then, on the very day that Jerusalem was taken, God took away the delight of Ezekiel's eyes, his beloved wife—and told him that he could not even express his grief in proper mourning. This was to be a sign to the people (24:24).

We pass over the judgments upon the nations (chapters 25—32) with the observation that nations used by God as instruments of His judgment do not themselves escape judgment. Judgment begins at the house of the Lord and with the elders of His people (Ezekiel 9:6); but it does not stop until all have been judged. The picture of the judgment of Tyre especially fascinates us (chapters 26—28): first, because it is the finest extant picture of the maritime mercantile life of the Ancient Middle East; but especially because it is so markedly similar to the judgment upon Babylon in Revelation 18. Likewise, the picture of hell is striking, with the roll call of those who are there (Ezekiel 32:18-32). We would probably like to add a few more recent nations to the list!

With chapter 33, and the news that the city has fallen, God repeats the charge to Ezekiel and His desire that men repent and turn to Him. Now the message turns to hope and assurance.

False shepherds who have been interested only in their own security have let the nation get into this mess. God not only says, "I am against the shepherds; and I will require my sheep at their hand"; He goes on to say, "I myself will search for my sheep . . . I myself will be the shepherd of my sheep." And He promises to restore the line of David (34:10-23). How can anyone miss this amazing prophecy? How can anyone think that it is just another son of David, or David himself come back from the dead, of whom Ezekiel speaks? No more human shepherds, says God. I myself. "If David thus calls him Lord, how is he his son?" (Matthew 22:45). "And you are my sheep, the sheep of my pasture, and I am your God, says the Lord God" (Ezekiel 34:31). "I am the good shepherd; I know my own and my own know me," says the Lord Jesus Christ (John 10:14).

Why does God restore His people? Is it because of some good that is in them? some intrinsic worth? "It is not for your sake, O house of Israel, that I am about to act, but for the sake of my holy name . . . I will take you . . . gather you . . . bring you. . . . I will sprinkle clean water upon you. . . . A new heart I will give you. . . . I will put my spirit within you. . . . It is not for your sake that I will act, says the Lord God; let that be known to you" (36:22-32). This is what theologians call "grace"—undeserved love. "God shows his love for us in that while we were yet sinners Christ died for us" (Romans 5:8).

Is Ezekiel now talking of the church? Is the church the fulfillment of God's promises to Israel? Though many will disagree, I must say that I do not think so. The thirty-seventh chapter of Ezekiel is talking about Israel (37:11, 19). The same Israel that was scattered and dead, like dead bones in a very dry valley: this is the Israel that God revives. The same two sticks that were Joseph and Judah in captivity are united by God to be one stick. Only the most forced exegesis can get rid of the clear teaching of this passage; and only the most forced exegesis can get rid of the same clear teaching in Romans 11.

But the prophet's eye seems to confuse the near and the distant.[10] He sees the restored Israel in the land at the same time as he sees the everlasting Davidic prince (Ezekiel 37:25). God has not let him see clearly the interval which our Lord called "the times of the Gentiles" (Luke 21:24).

Charles Erdman has pointed out that "Ezekiel is absolutely unique among all the Old Testament prophets in predicting another invasion of their land after the people of Israel have been restored and are dwelling in peace and security under the will of their Good Shepherd."[11] The language of the thirty-eighth chapter of Ezekiel is so clearly similar to the language of the Book of Revelation, particularly portions of the nineteenth and twentieth chapters, that I am forced to consider them together when I am interpreting either book. It therefore seems to me that Ezekiel is speaking of a time, after the glorious messianic promises have begun to be fulfilled, when the godless forces of the world shall make one last effort against the people of God in the land of promise.

[10] This is sometimes called "prophetic foreshortening," or "prophetic perspective." Catholic scholars may refer to it as "compenetration" resulting in a lack of chronological perspective. Its existence in Scripture is responsible for the fact that Jesus' contemporaries were looking for elements of the Second Advent (as we know it) mixed with the elements of the First Advent.

[11] *The Book of Ezekiel*, p. 117.

And that time, God Himself will enter the battle and bring to an end such human madness (Ezekiel 38:19-23).

There is little else I would say. Just as the seer of Patmos saw the New Jerusalem, so Ezekiel was granted the vision. I am not convinced that we should attempt to press all the physical details in either case, for God's word is concerned with the souls of men rather than with architecture or real estate. Imagery and symbolism may turn out to be closer to the real than we had thought, and if so, we have not lost a thing. But if we miss the spiritual truth behind the image, then we have lost all. The size of the New Jerusalem is less important than the kind of people who are in it. It is not big enough for godless men (Revelation 21:8). Whether the streets are of real gold is less important than the fact that the river of life flows through the city, with healing for the nations growing on its banks (22:2). Whether there was a temple or not (John did not see it), is less important than the fact that its temple is the Lord God Almighty and the Lamb (21:22).

So it is with Ezekiel's vision. The height of the walls is not great enough for either defense or display (Ezekiel 40:5); but it serves to remind us that only holiness can get in (43:12). Whether the temple will be rebuilt to Ezekiel's dimensions, I do not know (it is interesting to remember that Zerubbabel did not attempt it); what matters is that Ezekiel saw the glory of the Lord returning by the eastern gate, and filling the temple (43:5). Whether an actual river will flow from Jerusalem into the Ghôr to sweeten the waters of the Dead Sea, I cannot say with great conviction; but I am sure of this: Jerusalem will be the source of life and health and abundance (47:10-12). "But how," someone will ask, "can you be so sure of this, if you are not sure about these other matters?" The reason is simple: "the name of the city henceforth shall be, The Lord is there" (48:35).

The Lord is there, but will you be there? Israel's story is given to us as a lesson. As God spared not Israel, but required of her double for all her sins, so will He not spare any who have turned from Him. But why will you die? God has no pleasure in the death of the wicked; all He wants is the recognition that He is supreme, and submission to His will. You give this to human rulers; why will you not give it to the Lord of heaven and earth?

CHAPTER XVII

Daniel

DANIEL's book is dark and mysterious, and there are many who do not know it, and some who do not like it, and some do not understand it. Whether the Book of Daniel is interesting to you or not, the man whose name it carries is an interesting character and an important one.

Daniel was from the princely line of Judah and he was carried into captivity from Jerusalem to Babylon in the first captivity under Nebuchadnezzar[1] (605 B.C.). According to tradition, he was about twelve or fifteen at the time. When he got to the city of Babylon, he was included in a group which was chosen to be trained as statesmen. The king commanded his chief eunuch "to bring some of the people of Israel, both of the royal family and of the nobility, youths without blemish, handsome and skillful in all wisdom, endowed with knowledge, understanding, learning, and competent to serve in the king's palace, and to teach them the letters and language of the Chaldeans"[2] (1:3-4). They were to be educated for three years and at the end of that time they were to stand before the king. In other words, the king saw here a group of young men that he could use in his court: and Daniel was one of them. Now if this group was taken captive in 605 B.C., and if Daniel was still serving when the empire fell to Cyrus in 539 B.C., you can readily see that Daniel served in that court for more than sixty years.

In the modern Hebrew Bible, Daniel's book is not listed among the "Prophets," but rather among the "Writings." This has led some to object to any reference to the book as a "prophecy." Perhaps it will help us to understand something of the man as well as something of his book, if we take time to discuss this point. In the story of Samuel we came across the statement, "he who is now called a prophet was for-

[1] The form Nebuchadnezzar is used in this chapter because it is the form used in Daniel; see note 1 on page 147, above.
[2] "Chaldeans" is a name used for the Neo-Babylonian empire, probably arising from the fact that the dominant race in the empire was from Chaldea (southern Babylonia). In Herodotus the name becomes synonymous with the priests of Marduk (or Bel).

merly called a seer" (I Samuel 9:9). There were, then, two terms, "prophet" and "seer."[3] The terms are used somewhat interchangeably, which leads to further confusion. But as I understand them, the word "prophet" stresses the idea that God has spoken that which is being delivered, whereas the word "seer" stresses the idea that God has given a revelation in a dream or vision. Prophets could be seers, as the example of Samuel clearly proves; and prophets, as we know from Amos and Ezekiel and others, could receive their message from visions. When the vision was given by the Lord as the basis for a message to the people Israel, the seer was acting as a prophet. But—and here, I think, is the important point to remember when we are studying Daniel —when the vision was not the basis for a message to Israel, then the seer was not acting as a prophet.[4] So far as I can discover, Daniel does not claim that God spoke to him; he received his revelations in the forms of dreams and visions. And so far as I can discover, Daniel does not address the people Israel. He never uses the words, "Thus said the Lord."

There is another fact that has to be brought into this discussion. Daniel's ministry seems to have been not to the people of Israel immediately (although ultimately it was, because the message was written in a book and sealed up until the proper time), but to the Gentile kings under whom he was serving. It makes him unique among the Old Testament characters, that his ministry was immediately directed not toward the chosen people but toward that nation which held the chosen people in captivity.[5] While they were in exile God had a message for the ones who were holding them, and Daniel was the man who gave them that message.

He lived in Jerusalem, as we have already said, when Nebuchadnezzar carried the first group into captivity. God had spoken through the prophets to His people; He had chastised them because of their unbelief and their apostasy, and had threatened to punish them, but they

---

[3] Actually there are three terms, for two Hebrew words, *rô'êh* and *hôzêh,* are translated "seer"; as far as I can determine, these two were completely synonymous.

[4] Some scholars see a difference between the "prophetic office" and the "prophetic gift"; Daniel, they tell us, had the latter, but not the former. Cf. E. J. Young, *The Prophecy of Daniel* (Grand Rapids: Wm. B. Eerdmans Publishing Co., 1949), pp. 20-21.

[5] The contrast between Ezekiel and Daniel has often been pointed out: Ezekiel was the prophet of the Lord to the Jews in exile; Daniel was the Lord's servant in the court of the Gentile power that held the Jews captive.

had not repented. The long-awaited punishment of God fell at last on the Southern Kingdom; and it came in three stages, as though God were loath to move all the way through with this thing. He took away their king and the vessels from the temple in 605; He struck them again with another wave of punishment about 597; and finally in 586 the city was wiped out entirely, and the temple was burned.

Nebuchadnezzar, the king of Babylon from 605 to 562, whose reign is described as one of the longest and most brilliant in human history, was the man used by God to take the Southern Kingdom into captivity. The Neo-Babylonian empire had come into being only a few years before that; Nineveh, the capital of Assyria, fell in 612 b.c. The collapse of Assyria had come about not because Babylonia was so strong but because they had united with a couple of other kingdoms and, united they were able to overthrow this great Assyrian empire. But what happens when a coalition of powers overthrows a powerful enemy? Those who unite with you for the destruction of your common foe—as we have had occasion to learn since 1945—may turn against you as soon as the enemy has been defeated. The Babylonian empire was destined to be short-lived: it had too many enemies.

Nebuchadnezzar built Babylon. I visited it several years ago and found nothing but a heap of mounds, as the prophet Ezekiel said it was going to be: a dwelling place of jackals. But I could see the remains of the ancient city in the ruins, far and wide, everywhere I looked. The guide would say, "You see that big mound over there? Well, that was the tower of Marduk." And looking the other way he would say, "That is all that remains of the city gate." There were great walls around Babylon. According to Herodotus, the Greek historian who lived about a century later, the city was built like a huge square, with walls about fourteen miles long on each side (a later historian agrees that the city was fourteen miles long, but makes the circumference only forty-two miles), fifty great cubits wide (about eighty-four feet), and two hundred great cubits high (about 333 feet). Herodotus further tells us that first a wide and deep moat had been dug, the earth of which had been used to make bricks for the wall, and then the moat had been filled with water from the river. The river itself flowed through the midst of the city. On top of the wall were two rows of buildings, one at each edge, and between them was a place wide enough to drive four-horse chariots. There were one hundred bronze gates in the wall.[6]

Even if we allow for considerable exaggeration, the picture that

[6] Herodotus, Book I, § 178.

Herodotus gives is impressive. But if you could walk around the ruins and see the unusually large buildings, if you could look at the remains of the famous Ishtar Gate (the most beautiful part, the blue-glazed tile façade, was taken to Berlin by the excavator, Koldewey), if you could walk the length of the walls for even the part that has been discovered, you would wonder whether Herodotus *has* exaggerated.[7] But this is only part of the story.

Nebuchadnezzar had a wife who came from the mountainous country of Persia, and she longed for mountains; so he built for her what have been known as the hanging gardens, one of the seven wonders of the ancient world. Actually they were not hanging gardens, but artificial mountains constructed in the city and planted over with trees, so that his queen, looking out at them, would have a memory of the mountains she had left behind when she moved to that monotonously flat land. He also built a reservoir at Sippara which, we are told, had a circumference of 160 miles, and was 180 feet deep, to supply the country with water for its agriculture. He built canals between the Euphrates and the Tigris so that the country could be irrigated. And he built a dock system down on the Persian Gulf. A tremendous king! Imagine being advisor to a king like that!

Nebuchadnezzar had a dream, and he called in the court magicians and wise men. Notice the way he put the problem to his wise men: You tell me what I dreamed and what it means. Anyone could make up an interpretation of a dream; only a truly wise man could tell him what he had dreamed. And of course, they were unable to do what he commanded. Then Daniel was brought in and the same request was made of him: "Are you able to make known to me the dream that I have seen and its interpretation?" Daniel replied frankly, "No wise men . . . can show to the king the mystery which the king has asked, but there is a God in heaven who reveals mysteries . . ." (2:26-28), and he gave the interpretation. Nebuchadnezzar had dreamed of an image with four parts: the first of these four parts was the Babylonian empire; following that would be three successive empires, and at last the image was struck with a stone which is not cut by human hands,

---

[7] For splendid photographs of reconstructions of the tower of Marduk, the Ishtar Gate, and Procession Street with the Hanging Gardens, see H. Schmökel, *Ur, Assur und Babylon* (in *Grosse Kulturen der Frühzeit*; Stuttgart: Gustav Kilpper Verlag, 1955), plates 114-115. Color plates of a large enamelled-brick lion from the Procession Street and of the elaborately decorated wall of the throne-room can be found in H. Schäffer und W. Andrae, *Die Kunst des alten Orients* (Berlin: Propyläen-Verlag, 1925), plates XXIX-XXX.

and the whole thing was smashed; but the stone that had smashed it became a great mountain. We will talk about the interpretation of it later.

Of course the king was greatly impressed with Daniel's ability to describe and interpret this vision, and he gave him honors and gifts, and a place of prominence (2:46-48).

In the fourth chapter Nebuchadnezzar has another dream, and again Daniel has to interpret. The dream is of a tree which had grown very large, and then was cut down, stripped of its branches and its leaves, its fruit was scattered, and only the stump was left. Daniel interprets it to mean that the king was to be visited with severe punishment, "till you know that the Most High rules the kingdom of men and gives it to whom he will" (4:24-27).

The outcome of it is described at the end of the chapter. The king was walking along the roof of the royal palace, looking at this immense city with its great gates, its great walls, its hanging gardens, and all the rest of it, and he said, in a moment of pride: "Is not this great Babylon which I have built by my mighty power?" And there came a voice from heaven, "O King Nebuchadnezzar, to you it is spoken, the kingdom has departed from you. . . ." The king became subject to a disease known as lycanthropy, in which he imagined himself to be a beast; he went out and ate grass in the field like an ox, and he lost the right of his kingdom for seven years. At the end of that time he came to realize that his dominion was only his because God had given it to him, and that God's dominion is an everlasting dominion.

Two lesser kings succeeded him, and then Nabonidus came to the throne. Nabonidus was a rather strange character; he apparently was more interested in vacations than in being king. He spent almost all of his reign, according to his royal letters, in an oasis out in the desert named Tema. He put his son Belshazzar on the throne as co-regent; in the book of Daniel he is called King, although in the letters he is simply called the king's first son. The king was actually absent from the throne, though, out there in the desert halfway to Egypt, and the son had all of the responsibilities of the kingdom; it was his lot to reign for the closing days of the Babylonian empire and to see it collapse before the Persian thrust.[8]

---

[8] A thorough discussion of this whole problem will be found in R. P. Dougherty, *Nabonidus and Belshazzar* (*Yale Oriental Series;* New Haven: Yale University Press, 1929), 216 pp.

There is not a great deal to be told about either Belshazzar or Nabonidus. Their days were not splendid days; they were days when the force of the other kingdoms which had united with Babylonia against Assyria was turned against their former ally. If it had been glorious to be advisor to the king in the days of Nebuchadnezzar, I suppose it must have been disappointing to be his advisor in the days that followed when it was only a matter of time before the kingdom collapsed. It must have been especially bitter to see how little interest the king took in the kingdom. He was warned repeatedly for three years that the Persians were advancing, but he did nothing about it. At last he rushed into the city to try to save what little he could, but it was too late.[9]

In the days of Belshazzar, Daniel dreamed a dream: a dream of four beasts, and it should be placed beside the dream of Nebuchadnezzar of the four-part image, for both of these dreams teach the same general lesson. The story, you will note, is not told in chronological order. Chapter 5 tells of the end of Belshazzar's reign; chapter 6, the beginning of the Persian reign; and chapter 7 takes us back to the days of Belshazzar, prior to the end of his kingdom. I think we should also note that chapter 7 begins the second half of Daniel, and that its form is different from that of the first half: the second half consists of dreams and visions which Daniel had and which he wrote down in a book— a book "shut up and sealed until the time of the end." The four beasts of Daniel's dreams represented "four kings who shall arise out of the earth" (7:17). I shall come back to them a bit later. The fact of primary significance is expressed in the verse that follows: "But the saints of the Most High shall receive the kingdom, and possess the kingdom, for ever and ever." The kingdoms of this world are great and terrible. God's people know that, especially when they come under the heel of these kingdoms. But the kingdoms of this world are not eternal. The dominion that is an everlasting dominion, and the kingdom that shall not be destroyed belongs to the One whom Daniel saw coming with the clouds of heaven, One like a son of man (7:13-14).

The Babylonian empire had been the instrument in God's hands to punish faithless Israel. But it was not going to last forever. Its end was

[9] It is perhaps unfair to suggest that it was only pleasure that attracted Nabonidus to Tema. Dougherty thinks that it may have had strategic value, and that Nabonidus was seeking allies against Persia. But prolonged absence (five years, possibly nine) hardly seems necessary for such a purpose.

at hand. For that, we go back to the fifth chapter. Belshazzar made a great feast for a thousand of his lords. God had tried to make Nebuchadnezzar understand that he was on the throne of Babylon and the Babylonian empire was strong only because God had allowed it. He had allowed it as a means of punishment against His people Israel. The punishment that fell upon Nebuchadnezzar was due to the fact that he had failed to recognize that he was king only under God. Belshazzar went a step further than Nebuchadnezzar: he not only forgot that he was on the throne by virtue of God's will, but he dared to take the golden vessels that had been captured by Nebuchadnezzar in Jerusalem, the sacred vessels that had been used only in the worship of Jehovah in the temple—he dared to take these and use them as drinking vessels for his drunken party. "Immediately the fingers of a man's hand appeared and wrote on the plaster of the wall of the king's palace, opposite the lampstand; and the king saw the hand as it wrote. Then the king's color changed, and his thoughts alarmed him; his limbs gave way, and his knees knocked together. The king cried aloud to bring in the enchanters, the Chaldeans, and the astrologers . . ." (5:5-6), to find out what the hand had written. None of them was able to interpret it.

The queen remembered that there was a Jew at that court who could interpret dreams; the king brought in Daniel and said, "if you can read the writing and make known to me its interpretation, you shall be clothed with purple, and have a chain of gold about your neck, and shall be the third ruler in the kingdom" (5:14-16).[10]

Daniel told him to keep his gifts, but ". . . nevertheless I will read the writing"; and he read the four words: "MENE, MENE, TEKEL and PARSIN." Now those are quite common words, and we may well ask, Why could the king not understand them? There are several possible reasons. The words are Aramaic, and the king was Babylonian—although we know that Aramaic was widely used as a diplomatic language just following that period, and we suppose some of the men of the court could speak it. Aramaic however is written with just the consonants, and the same group of consonants may be read two or three

[10] For years they wondered why Belshazzar, who was named as king in this book, would make Daniel *third* in the kingdom; why not make him second? It is only since we have learned that Nabonidus was the true king and that Belshazzar his son was reigning in his place as second in the kingdom that we have understood why Daniel could only be named third. Belshazzar could not name him second, because that would have put him in the place of Belshazzar himself.

ways. For example, these words could be read as sums of money: Mina, Tekel (Shekel), and Fractions (Half-shekels). Now suppose suddenly you saw the words on the wall before you, "Dollar, dollar, dime, and nickels"—what would you understand by them? The wise men may have recognized the words; but they were unable to read (understand) or interpret them. Or again, the words could be read as forms of common verbs: Weighed, numbered, divisions. But what did that mean? Daniel chided the king for his pride and presumption, and then interpreted the words: "God has numbered the days of your kingdom and brought it to an end . . . you have been weighed in the balances and found wanting . . . your kingdom is divided and given to the Medes and Persians" (5:26-28). That very night, while the king feasted in confidence that his city could not be taken in twenty years, the Persian troops succeeded in diverting the river into the moats around the city, marched in by the river-bed, and took Babylon "without firing a shot."[11] Belshazzar was killed; how, we do not know.

The king of the Persian empire was Cyrus, but he himself did not enter the city of Babylon that night; his minister, one of his governors named Darius or Gobyrus (Ugbaru), led the capture. Cyrus was proud of the fact that when he took a country he liberated his prisoners, and he writes in his annals that he looked upon himself as a liberator of the gods. When they captured a country, it was the custom to take the gods from the temples and bring them to the victor's country as proof that the dominion over the conquered country extended even to its gods. Cyrus says that he sent these gods back to their homes. But above all, he sent the Israelites home; their captivity was over.

Now let us set the message of Daniel against his day, and see what it says to us. His message came when Israel was in captivity. But more than that, it came at the time when a world came to its end. The night that the Persian forces turned aside the Euphrates and marched into Babylon, that night the dominion of the world passed from East to West. Up until that moment, the great empires of the world had been Oriental empires. From that moment until this present day, the empires of the world have been Indo-European, non-Semitic empires; Persian, Greek, Roman, British.

[11] The Nabonidus Chronicle says simply, "On the sixteenth day Ugbaru the governor of Gutium and the troops of Cyrus without fighting entered Babylon"; and Cyrus says, "Without any battle he [i.e. Marduk] made him [Cyrus] enter his town Babylon, sparing Babylon any calamity." The documents may be seen in Dougherty, *Nabonidus and Belshazzar*, pp. 170, 176.

But worlds come to an end slowly. And people who live in the end of an age probably have no idea at all that epochal events are occurring. That is why the prophet of God is essential for interpretation. Daniel's interpretations of the image of four parts and the four beasts are important because they help us understand what was taking place in the world. Four successive world empires came into existence in this world. The first was the Neo-Babylonian Empire of Nebuchadnezzar. That the interpretation must begin here is clearly indicated, for Daniel said to Nebuchadnezzar, "You are the head of gold." The second was the Persian Empire under Cyrus, the Achaemenian dynasty. The third was the Macedonian Empire under Alexander the Great, and the fourth the Roman Empire.[12] Daniel says that in the day of the fourth kingdom a stone that had not been fashioned by human power smashed the image. What is he saying? He is saying that the world empires, the empires established by the hands of Nebuchadnezzar and Cyrus and Alexander and the Caesars, are only here for a limited time. They are tolerated by God. God has them here for a purpose. But they shall not last forever.

There is a greater kingdom to come: "In the days of those kings the God of heaven will set up a kingdom which shall never be destroyed, nor shall its sovereignty be left to another people. It shall break in pieces all these [previous] kingdoms and bring them to an end, and it shall stand forever" (Daniel 2:44-45). And again, "I saw in the night visions, and behold, with the clouds of heaven there came one like a son of man, and he came to the Ancient of Days and was presented before him. And to him was given dominion and glory and kingdom, that all peoples, nations, and languages should serve him; his dominion is an everlasting dominion, which shall not pass away, and his kingdom one that shall not be destroyed" (7:12-14).

You and I are living in the day of the end of the kingdoms, as Daniel prophesied. I am not a fanatic; I am not saying the end of the

[12] Another school of interpretation holds: (1) Neo-Babylonian, (2) Medes, (3) Persians, (4) Greek. But this is impossible, for the Medes and the Persians were never two great empires. Therefore a third school is growing that interprets: (1) Neo-Babylonian, (2) Medo-Persian, (3) Macedonian (Alexander), (4) the successors of Alexander (Seleucids and Ptolemies). The main argument is that the fourth empire is destroyed before the messianic kingdom is established (Daniel 7:11-13). But this argument fails when the messianic kingdom is viewed in its first- and second-advent aspects. The fact remains: it was in the fourth kingdom that the messianic kingdom arose—and that was in the Roman Empire!

world is coming tomorrow, or the day after tomorrow. I am simply saying that we have already gone through the four parts of the image of the second chapter and four beasts of the seventh chapter; therefore certainly we are living in the end of the days of this image. We are living in the days when the One like the Son of Man has come, and when the kingdom which was not made with human hands has come and struck the kingdoms of the world; and we have this message: that *the kingdoms of this world cannot stand, but the Kingdom of God is forever.* In a day when armies seem to be on the march again and when we are afraid to read tomorrow's headlines for fear they will say that another war has broken out, we can thank God that we belong to a Kingdom which has no end.

CHAPTER XVIII

Ezra

EZRA was not a prophet but a priest and a scribe. The kingdom was over, at least for the moment, hence the prophetic voice was stilled. Haggai had been sent to encourage the people to rebuild the temple; the temple, Zerubbabel, and Joshua, in his prophecy are all strongly typical of the Messiah to come. Zechariah had carried on the typology of Zerubbabel, and then abandoned it to speak directly of the Messiah and His coming. Malachi had been sent to answer the questions that Jews were asking: questions about the love and justice of God; and to tell them of the coming judgment that is an inevitable part of justice, and the coming possession that is an inevitable result of love. Then God was silent. But the Law and the Prophets were still there (remember how Jesus turned aside the request for a convincing sign with the statement, "They have Moses and the prophets; let them hear them"? Luke 16:29), and men needed only to be taught the Scriptures. Hence, in the providence of God, the priesthood, and especially the office of the scribe, came into prominence.

Ezra is traditionally looked upon as the first of the scribes, and in a sense he might be looked upon as the founder of Judaism. What would have happened to Judaism if it had not been for Ezra and the men of the Great Synagogue?[1] And, humanly speaking, how could Christianity have gotten started in the world if there had not been the Scriptures preserved and studied by the scribes, and the Pharisees with their meticulous zeal to keep the Law, and the seed of David of which the Christ was born according to the flesh? So in a very special way Ezra is the link between the old and the new. Coming at the time when the Old Testament was complete,[2] he stands in a unique place with

[1] See G. F. Moore, *Judaism* (Cambridge, Mass.: Harvard University Press, 1927), Vol. I, 29-47, for an authoritative discussion of Ezra, the Great Synagogue, and the scribes.

[2] It is obvious that I reject the idea of late post-Exilic writings in the Old Testament. One of the strong arguments against this idea, it seems to me, is the lack of *creative* writing in the last pre-Christian centuries. It was the nature of the

reference to Judaism and to Christianity. He is a fitting personality, I believe, to bring to a close our series of studies.

Ezra was born and raised in Babylonia in the days of the captivity. He traces his lineage to Aaron through Zadok and Phinehas (Ezra 7:2, 4). It would indeed be difficult to prove that these men contributed physically to Ezra's heritage at such great distance; but it is not unreasonable to say that they contributed psychologically. The very fact that he was proud to trace his line back to them may suggest that he desired to have something in common with them, that, even though it may have been subconsciously, he tried to be like them.

Zadok was one of the priests who went with the leaders of the tribes of Israel to David when he was at Hebron, to offer to him the kingship and to turn the kingdom from Saul to David. Zadok stayed with David through all the turbulent episodes of his career. At the end, when there was an abortive attempt to get the succession away from David's favorite son Solomon, when Abiathar the priest cast in his lot with the plot of Joab, Zadok remained loyal to David and backed Solomon. For this, his line, rather than the line of Abiathar, was established in the priestly succession (see I Kings 1—2). Zadok was the name henceforth that suggested loyalty to the Davidic line.[8]

Phinehas, whom Ezra also mentions, takes our thoughts back to the time of Moses and his elder brother Aaron and the sin of the Israelites at Baal-peor. The sin is described in the twenty-fifth chapter of Numbers. The Israelites were joining with the Moabites in the worship of Baal, and "the anger of the Lord was kindled against Israel." One of the Israelites took one of the Midianite women in the sight of Moses and in the sight of the whole congregation of the people of Israel, to commit with her the abomination which was called "worship" of the god of Baal, and Phinehas took his spear and thrust it through the man and the woman in the act of sin. A plague had come upon the people

scribes and the great teachers to be *interpretative*. Other writings are *imitative*. But where are the creative writers, other than in the Scriptures? These cannot be used to support a circular argument.

[8] It is interesting to note that the Sadducees, in the formative days when they took (or received) their name, were called Zadokites (of which Sadducees is a corruption). Some years later, in a reform movement, the group that split off called themselves "the true sons of Zadok." This group finally located at the place we know as Qumran, and gave us the materials we call "The Dead Sea Scrolls." Reasons for some of the statements I have made here, together with a sketch of the historical development, can be found in my volume, *Amazing Dead Sea Scrolls* (Chicago: The Moody Press, 1956), pp. 195-200, 222-224.

of Israel as punishment for sin they were committing; but the plague was stayed. "And the Lord said to Moses, "Phinehas the son of Eleazar, son of Aaron the priest, has turned back my wrath from the people of Israel [and I think this is an amazing statement] in that he was jealous with my jealousy among them, so that I did not consume the people of Israel in my jealousy" (Numbers 25:10-11). Phinehas so completely entered into the feelings of God that his act was equivalent to the act of God. God goes on to say, "Behold, I give to him my covenant of peace; and it shall be to him, and to his descendants after him, the covenant of a perpetual priesthood, because he was jealous for his God, and made atonement for the people of Israel" (25:12).

Phinehas who was jealous with the Lord's jealousy for the purity of the people, and Zadok who was intensely loyal to the Davidic kingship, and Ezra who had elements of both: this is the heritage of the priesthood. It was because of faithful representatives that the line continued; and it is equally true today that because of faithful people of God the work of God is done.

Ezra is called a "scribe" by the Persian king. The word scribe, at that time, had a technical meaning that we must attempt to understand. In David's kingdom the office of scribe was one of political significance. In the New Testament, the scribe was more concerned with the minutiae of legalistic ritual, which probably developed under the aegis of Pharisaism. Just after Ezra's day, the scribe was a member of a professional class that seems to have had a broad field of interests: perhaps something like the European scholar of bygone generations. Jesus ben Sirach describes him in Ecclesiasticus 38:24—39:11. I rather imagine Ezra was a scribe of this kind. The main interest of the scribe was the interpretation of the Law and the Prophets.

Ezra tells us that he requested permission to go from Babylon to Jerusalem: He had heard disconcerting reports about what was happening in Jerusalem in those days, and in accordance with his request, he was sent to Jerusalem by Artaxerxes the king, in order to look into the welfare of the people and to bring about a reform movement.

In order to understand Ezra, we must go back and fit him into his day, for there is no man who is not to a large extent the child of his own time. After we have understood Ezra and have seen what he did of permanent value, then we can learn from him for our own lives. He went to Jerusalem in the seventh year of Artaxerxes (Ezra 7:7). That would have been Artaxerxes I (Longimanus)—Artaxerxes of the Long

Hand—and the date 457 B.C.[4] Cyrus the Great had entered Babylon in 539 B.C. In some ways, Cyrus is unique among political rulers in history. He discontinued the cruel practices of the Semitic tyrants before him, and took pride in the fact that he was a beneficent ruler. He says, "My numerous troops advanced into the heart of Babylon peaceably. . . . In Babylon and all the outlying regions I strove for peace. . . . The yoke which was not honorable I removed from them. Their run-down houses I repaired. . . . The gods . . . I caused to return, their hearts to their places I returned and caused to dwell in an eternal habitation. All their people I assembled and I returned to their habitations."[5] Every report we have shows that Cyrus was as good as his word. One tradition has it that since he could not send the gods of the Jews back to Jerusalem (since they had no idols), he sent the furnishings of the temple instead. His decree permitting the Jews to return to Jerusalem and to rebuild the temple is recorded in Ezra 6:3-5 About fifty thousand persons returned to Jerusalem at that time.

Ezra also tells us a little about the rebuilding of the temple which had been destroyed by the Babylonians in 586; "When the builders laid the foundation of the temple of the Lord, the priests in their vestments came forward with trumpets, and the Levites, the sons of Aspah, with cymbals, to praise the Lord, according to the directions of David king of Israel. . . . But many of the priests and Levites and heads of fathers' houses, old men who had seen the first house, wept with a loud voice when they saw the foundations of this house being laid, though many shouted aloud for joy" (3:10-12). I suppose that we should point out that there were three returns from exile: the first, to which Ezra is referring here, was led by Sheshbazzar, and took place in 538 B.C.; the second was led by Ezra in 457 B.C.; the third by Nehemiah in 445 B.C. Men of twenty who had gone into captivity in 586 B.C. would have been seventy years old when they returned; some of the elders among the returnees could remember the glorious days of the magnificent temple of Solomon, and they looked upon the foundations of the new temple as nothing compared to the old. In Haggai we get something of their attitude and their longing "for the good old days" (Haggai 2:3).

There had been attempts to halt the work. Ezra tells us about an

[4] Many scholars today identify him with Artaxerxes II (Mnemon), 404-358 B.C. The best summary of the arguments for the later date, together with replies to them, so far as I know, is in *A Catholic Commentary on Holy Scripture*, pp. 377-378.

[5] Cyrus Cylinder, 24-33.

effort on the part of the Samaritans to put an end to the building. They sent a letter to the king pointing out that this was a rebellious people, and that when they got the city rebuilt, they would stop paying their taxes and revolt, etc., etc. (Ezra 4:11-16). The king was swayed by the letter—he did not realize that he was violating a decree which had already been established by his father—and he halted the work for a while.

Then Haggai and Zechariah came along, and Zerubbabel and Joshua (about 520 b.c.), and under this new leadership and inspiration construction was begun anew. A second effort was made to stop the work, and a full report was forwarded to the Persian king, who by that time was Darius.[6] He searched the records, and found the decree of Cyrus, which read: "In the first year of Cyrus the king, Cyrus the king issued a decree: Concerning the house of God at Jerusalem, let the house be rebuilt, the place where sacrifices are offered and burnt offerings are brought; its height shall be sixty cubits and its breadth sixty cubits. . . . And also let the gold and silver vessels of the house of God, which Nebuchadnezzar took out of the temple that is in Jerusalem . . . be restored . . ." (6:3-5). That allowed them to continue the work.

Now that was about sixty-three years before Ezra's return. The people had spent fifty to seventy years in Babylonia. They had come back to the land and had started the rebuilding of the temple and they had been discouraged, but finally they had completed it. Another sixty years went by, and by that time a cold indifference had settled down over the people. There was even rebellion against the Lord. Some were completely fed up with the whole thing. They had been taken out of their land because they had worshiped God—at least, that was the way they looked at it—then they had been brought *back* into the land, and they had gone through all sorts of opposition and persecution, and they just frankly did not see any sense in the whole performance. Read Malachi to get some of the reaction.

Let us try to find out why. Israel had been taken captive into Babylonia in three stages in 605, 597, and 586; approximately every ten years a group had been taken out of the land, until at last only the poor and the ignorant were left in the land. All of the golden and silver vessels of the temple had been hauled away; everything of any value had been taken, and there was just nothing left but the poor people, and

[6] Darius Hystaspis (521-486 b.c). I often hear the name Darius mispronounced; it should be *dă-rye'-us*.

very little to maintain them. And what had happened to the Hebrew people in Babylonia? They were there for fifty, sixty, or seventy years. The children of those who had been taken into exile from Jerusalem were now old men and old women, and their children had grown up, and their grandchildren and maybe even some of their great grandchildren had been born in Babylon. They had laid out farms and plowed them, they had established their homes; many of them had gone into business.

Ezekiel, the prophet who lived among the exiles, says in his prophecy, "Yet you say, 'The way of the Lord is not just.' Hear now, O house of Israel; Is my way not just? Is it not *your* ways that are not just?" (Ezekiel 18:25). Ezekiel would never had said that if the people had not been complaining against the justice of the Lord. They had reached the point where they thought that God had not treated them fairly. Again, Ezekiel says, "with their lips they show much love, but their heart is set on their gain." The people had moved slowly but surely into a materialistic viewpoint. Then Cyrus came along and said, "All right; you can go back home!" And what did they do? Fifty thousand of them went back; and the rest of them stayed there in Babylon! Why? Because they were more interested in the material things which they had gotten, their businesses and their farms, than they were in going back to the land that God had given to them. And those that had gone back to their land, I suppose, in many cases were the poorer ones. Those who were well established in the land of Babylon probably stayed. There is evidence that even many of the priests did not go back.

That was the situation in Palestine, in Ezra's day. There were those who had not been taken into captivity because they were too poor, because they had no elements of leadership, because the Babylonians just had nothing to fear by leaving them there—possibly fifty to eighty thousand it has been estimated. There were also the returnees who probably were not very successful in business and worldly ventures in Babylon. These two groups started a half-hearted rebuilding program; they started in with a lot of enthusiasm but it died out rather quickly.

Then there were the Samaritans, who wanted to join with them but were rejected. They were not told the exact reason—that their men had intermarried with the Gentiles and that they had not been true to the law of Moses—but they were given another reason: "Cyrus gave us the permission to come back here and rebuild; he did not give *you* any such permission. You would get us into trouble if we brought you in on the deal . . ."; and the Samaritans immediately turned hostile and tried to stop the work.

Further opposition is described in the Book of Nehemiah. In Nehemiah 4 there is the story of the opposition of Sanballat. It became so serious that the Jews, when they were rebuilding the walls, had to designate certain men to carry spears and shields and bows, and those who were carrying burdens were laden in such a way that they worked with one hand and held their weapons with the other; each of the builders on the wall had a sword girded on his side. They had to be ready for an attack from the opposition at all times.

The whole picture is one of a disagreeable time. The people had gotten into such a mess that in 445 b.c., twelve years after Ezra had gone into the land, Nehemiah, who was the cupbearer to the king back in Babylon, asked permission to go to Jerusalem and try to straighten it out. He was made governor of Palestine, in order to do just that.

Ezra's work, briefly, was to renew the spiritual power of Israel. They had almost forgotten their God in their pursuit of worldly gain; they had nearly lost their faith. Ezra called them to build on something more substantial, to rekindle the ancient spiritual fire, and to rebuild the nation. These are the reasons why he went back. He took with him fifteen hundred men; altogether he had not more than five thousand people. They went back at government expense, and took with them the vessels that belonged in the temple.

How do you explain the attitude of the Persian king? May I offer one suggestion? Esther had been the queen of the king who preceded King Artaxerxes known as Ahasuerus or Xerxes. Ahasuerus, according to secular records, was not much of a king. He was more interested in his harem than he was in the welfare of the kingdom. Could it be that Esther had so influenced Ahasuerus that when his able son Artaxerxes came to the throne he demonstrated his gratitude to the Jewish people by giving this privilege to Ezra and to those with him? I do not know; I suppose we shall never know in this life; but it could well be that Esther's influence in that home had brought all this about. I know of no other reason that will explain the gracious treatment of Ezra. When Ezra had finished quoting the king's letter, he said, "Blessed be the Lord, the God of our fathers, who put such a thing as this into the heart of the king, to beautify the house of the Lord which is in Jerusalem, and who extended to me his steadfast love before the king and his counsellors . . ." (Ezra 7:27-28).

Ezra called the people together and read to them from the book of
Moses. He had thirteen Levites assist him, to help the people to understand, "and they read from the book, from the law of God, clearly;
and gave the sense, so that the people understood the reading"[7]
(Nehemiah 8:8). As a result, the people came to realize just how great
their sin was, and they confessed their sin and prayed, "Now, therefore,
our God, the great and mighty and terrible God, who keepest covenant
and steadfast love, let not all the hardship seem little to thee that has
come upon us, upon our kings, our princes, our priests, our prophets,
our fathers, and all thy people, since the time of the kings of Assyria
until this day. Yet thou hast been just in all that has come upon us. . . ."
Do you remember how Ezekiel said that the people complained that
God was not just? Now at last they realize their sin, and they confess:
"Yet thou hast been just in all that has come upon us, for thou hast
dealt with us faithfully and we have acted wickedly; our kings, our
princes, our priests, and our fathers have not kept thy law or heeded
thy commandments and thy warnings which thou didst give them"
(Nehemiah 9:32-34).

Ezra made two questionable decisions. He decided at one time to rebuild the walls of Jerusalem. Now he had not been commissioned to
do that. Maybe it was a good thing, but it made him at once a target
for opposition, and the Samaritans quickly seized the opportunity; they
sent a letter back to the king, and they said in effect, "You did not tell
him to do this: he is building the walls, and the next thing you know,
he will revolt against you." That lowered Ezra's prestige for a while.

His second questionable decision came when he insisted that all of
the men of Israel who had married foreign wives should divorce them.
There is no question about the danger that they had gotten into by
marrying the foreign wives. Nehemiah points it out very well, when he
says, "Did not Solomon king of Israel sin on account of such women?
Among the many nations there was no king like him, and he was beloved by his God, and God made him king over all Israel; nevertheless
foreign women made even him to sin" (Nehemiah 13:25-27). There is
no question that there was real danger in the situation. But here were
families that had been established for years, and Ezra insisted that *all*
of the men divorce their wives. Of course, not all of them went along
with it; many of them refused. But this was a questionable decision

[7] According to Jewish interpretation, this was the beginning of the Targums or
Aramaic translation of the Hebrew Bible.

on Ezra's part. We never hear any more of him after that; he seems to have lost his prestige and his authority with the people for good. Nehemiah seems to have modified the rule, to prevent future mixed marriages without dissolving the existing ones.

Not only was Ezra there to call the people back to a renewed spiritual life; in the providence of God he was there to do something of even greater value for them and for us. He rewrote the Scriptures. What does that mean? Writing, as we have seen, has a long history. In what form, for example, did Moses write? Did he write in cuneiform (the Amarna letters were so written)? Did he write in Egyptian hieroglyphs (he had been trained in Pharaoh's court)? It is inconceivable that he wrote the Pentateuch in the form in which we have it today: the shapes of the letters, the spelling, and other items, underwent changes in the course of a thousand years. In what form did David's scribe write? He probably used the old "Phoenician" alphabet, similar to the Moabite stone—the letters look quite similar to Greek turned around backwards.[8] Someone, at some time, *must* have put the ancient writings in the later form in which they were preserved for us. Jewish tradition attributes this to Ezra and the men of the Great Synagogue. I understand that to mean that all of the existing Scriptures were cast in "modern" spelling, "square" letters, perhaps with some of the explanatory notes (such as, "and it is there even to this day," etc.), and other editorial elements. Jewish tradition moreover says that it was done by the inspiration of the Lord. I understand that to mean that the Lord inspired Ezra in such a way that the inspiration imparted to the original authors was not destroyed by Ezra's editorial work. But whether my interpretations are accurate or not, it is certain that the Old Testament, as we have it today, came into existence about or not long after the time of Ezra. To whom else shall we attribute it? Where is there any other name of a man of sufficient stature to accomplish the task? Until such can be presented, I am content to say that Ezra was the man raised up of God to bring the restored exiles back to His word, to inaugurate the office of scribe for preservation and interpretation of the Scriptures, and to put into their hands the Old Testament in its final form.

Down through the history of the Hebrew nation, God was using individual men and women. We have studied together fifteen of these great Old Testament personalities. They were great not alone because

[8] Actually, Greek letters are Phoenician, turned around.

of great things they did, certainly not because of their sinlessness, and not because they did not make mistakes—every one of them made mistakes, and every one of them was guilty of some sin or other. They were great because they were faithful when God called them. They did the work that He had for them to do.

God does not just work through a nation collectively; He does not just work through a big church or a big Sunday school class collectively; He works *through individual men and women who are faithful in their work.*

Bibliography

BIBLE DICTIONARIES (articles on persons, places, items, etc.)

The Westminster Dictionary of the Bible, edited by John D. Davis, revised and rewritten by Henry Snyder Gehman, Philadelphia: The Westminster Press, 1944. 658 pp., XVI plates. [An excellent Bible Dictionary revised by a careful scholar; if I could have only one, it would be this.]

Harper's Bible Dictionary, edited by Madeleine S. Miller and J. Lane Miller. New York: Harper & Brothers, 1952. 851 pp., XVI plates. [Particularly strong in modern archaeological discoveries; sometimes disappointing in theological or critical views.]

Unger's Bible Dictionary, edited by Merrill F. Unger. Chicago: The Moody Press, 1957. 1192 pp. [Many good articles on Old Testament subjects, from an extremely "Conservative" viewpoint. Although the title page does not show it, much of this dictionary is reprinted without substantial revision form the 1900 edition of C. R. Barnes, *Bible Encyclopaedia.*]

The International Standard Bible Encyclopaedia, edited by James Orr, *et al.,* revised by Melvin Grove Kyle. Chicago: The Howard-Severance Co., 1930. 5 vols. Reprinted by Wm. B. Eerdmans, Grand Rapids, Mich. [An excellent work that deserves careful revision throughout by well-qualified editors and publication in handsome format.]

BIBLE GEOGRAPHIES AND ATLASES

L. H. Grollenberg, *Atlas of the Bible*; translated and edited by Joyce M. H. Reid and H. H. Rowley. New York: Thomas Nelson & Sons, 1956. 165 pages, 37 maps, 408 photographs. [My first choice; a splendid work in every way.]

The Westminster Historical Atlas to the Bible, edited by G. Ernest Wright and Floyd V. Filson. Revised edition. Philadelphia: The Westminster Press, 1956. 130 pp., 18 maps. [A close second to the above; many prefer this. In either case a hearty recommendation!]

George Adam Smith, *The Historical Geography of the Holy Land.* 25th edition. New York and London: Harper & Brothers, 1931. 744 pp., 8 maps. [Long the classical and still the only *historical* geography of the Holy Land. Excellent literary style; careful observations that have withstood the test of sixty-four years. Earlier editions are in places not reliable.]

Denis Baly, *The Geography of the Bible.* New York: Harper & Brothers, 1957. 304 pp., 48 maps and diagrams. [In spite of its subtitle, this is not a historical geography; it is however a valuable physical geography.]

Atlante storico della Bibbia, edited by Paulin Lemaire and Donato Baldi. Turin: Marietti, 1955. 322 pp., 56 maps in text, 13 full-page maps, many photographs. [A beautiful and excellent historical atlas—if you can read Italian.]

ART AND ARCHITECTURE (for pictures and reconstructions)

James B. Pritchard, *The Ancient Near East in Pictures* Relating to the Old Testament. Princeton: Princeton University Press, 1954. 351 pp., 769 plates. [A magnificent work covering just about everything significant as defined in the title.]

Henri Frankfort, *The Art and Architecture of the Ancient Orient.* (The Pelican History of Art.) Baltimore: Penguin Books, 1954. 279 pp., 192 plates. [A fine work, chiefly on Mesopotamian art, with Asia Minor, the Levant, and Persia as "Peripheral Regions," but without Egypt.]

Heinrich Schäfer and Walter Andrae, *Die Kunst des alten Orients.* (Propyläen-Kunstgeschichte, 2). 3d edition. Berlin: Propyläen-Verlag, 1925. 762 pp. (616 of which are pictures), XXXII plates (some of which are in color). [Excellent coverage, including Egypt. The German text is simply a descriptive catalog of the pictures.]

Christiane Desroches-Noblecourt, *Le style égyptien.* (Arts, styles et techniques.) Paris: Librairie Larousse, 1946. 220 pp., 64 plates. [Popular, inexpensive, and reliable for an introduction to Egyptian art and architecture.]

ARCHAEOLOGY

G. Ernest Wright, *Biblical Archaeology.* Philadelphia: The Westminster Press, 1957. 288 pp. [A beautifully produced work, written by a foremost expert in the subject.]

William F. Albright, *The Archaeology of Palestine* (Pelican Books, A199.) Revised edition. Baltimore: Penguin Books, 1954. 271 pp., 30 plates. [An excellent, inexpensive work by the dean of American archaeologists.]

J. A. Thompson, *Archaeology and the Old Testament.* (A Pathway Book.) Grand Rapids: Wm. B. Eerdmans Publishing Co., 1957. 121 pp. [Brief, simply told, reliable.]

Merrill F. Unger, *Archeology and the Old Testament*. Grand Rapids: Zondervan Publishing House, 1954. 339 pp. [An excellent selection of material integrated with Biblical history. At times the author lets his convictions overshadow the evidence.]

Seton Lloyd. *Foundations in the Dust*. (Pelican Books, A336.) Baltimore: Penguin Books, 1955. 256 pp. [Originally published in 1947; a reliable and interesting account of Mesopotamian archaeology.]

Seton Lloyd, *Early Anatolia*. (Pelican Books, A354). Baltimore: Penguin Books, 1956. 231 pp., 32 plates. [A most interesting work. I carried it on 6,000 miles of study throughout Turkey and can vouch for its reliability.]

Millar Burrows, *What Mean These Stones?* (Living Age Books, 7.) New York: Meridian Books, 1957. 306 pp. [Originally published in 1941; written by a careful and well-qualified scholar.]

Chester Charlton McCown, *The Ladder of Progress in Palestine*. New York: Harper & Brothers, 1943. 387 pp. [A most stimulating work with a selected bibliography.]

CHRONOLOGY

Robert W. Ehrich, ed., *Relative Chronologies in Old World Archeology*. Chicago: University of Chicago Press, 1954. 154 pp. [Experts in each area present the basic materials for a universal chronology. The work is difficult —but necessary!]

P. van der Meer, *The Chronology of Ancient Western Asia and Egypt*. 2d revised edition. Leiden: E. J. Brill, 1955. 95 pp. [Again, difficult, but necessary.]

Edwin R. Thiele, *The Mysterious Numbers of the Hebrew Kings*. Chicago: The University of Chicago Press, 1951. 298 pp. [The author has succeeded in harmonizing the chronologies of the kings of Israel and Judah to the satisfaction of most scholars. No one working in the field can ignore this book.]

THE ANCIENT NEAR EAST

Jack Finegan, *Light from the Ancient Past*. Princeton: Princeton University Press, 1946. 500 pp., 204 plates. [A carefully written, thoroughly documented account of the archaeological and historical matters that pertain to the Biblical record.]

H. R. Hall, *The Ancient History of the Near East*. Eleventh edition. London: Methuen & Co., 1950. 620 pp., 33 plates. [First edition 1913; a standard reference work.]

Sabatino Moscati, *Ancient Semitic Civilizations*. London: Elek Books, 1957. 254 pp. [A delightful and valuable work by a man who writes equally well in several languages.]

Cyrus H. Gordon, *The Living Past*. New York: The John Day Company, 1941. 232 pp., 27 plates. [A popularized treatment of the results of archaeology by an excellent scholar.]

Cyrus H. Gordon, *Introduction to Old Testament Times*. Ventnor, N. J.: Ventnor Publishers, 1953. 312 pp. [A delightful presentation of the background of the Old Testament reconstructed from modern historical research.]

V. Gordon Childe, *What Happened in History*. (Pelican Books, A108.) Baltimore: Penguin Books, 1954. 288 pp. [First published in 1942, revised after several printings. A fascinating survey of man from Palaeolithic savagery to the end of the ancient world.]

William F. Albright, *From the Stone Age to Christianity*. Second edition. Baltimore: Johns Hopkins Press, 1957. 432 pp. [Since it first appeared in 1940, this has been recognized as a most important work. It is not easy reading.]

James B. Pritchard, editor, *Ancient Near Eastern Texts* Relating to the Old Testament. Second edition. Princeton: Princeton University Press, 1955. 544 pp. [This volume contains practically all of the relevant texts that throw light on the Old Testament, translated by world-renowned experts in each field, well annotated.]

OLD TESTAMENT HISTORY

W. O. E. Oesterley and T. H. Robinson, *A History of Israel*. Oxford: Clarendon Press, 1932. 2 vols. [Vol. I, by Robinson, covers the period from the Exodus to the Fall of Jerusalem, 586 b.c. (496 pp.); Vol. II, by Oesterley, from the Fall of Jerusalem to the Bar-Kokhba Revolt, a.d. 135 (516 pp.). The work follows the critical viewpoint, but has a wealth of valuable material.]

Paul Heinisch, *History of the Old Testament,* translated by William Heidt. Collegeville, Minn.: Liturgical Press, 1952. 492 pp. [Revised from the German edition of 1949, this Roman Catholic work is both rich and reverent. As a general rule, Roman Catholic works do not follow the extremes of critical scholarship. This work has a vast number of excellent references.]

Werner Keller, *The Bible as History;* Archaeology Confirms the Book of Books; translated by William Neil. London: Hodder & Stoughton, 1956. 429

pp. [Well told in understandable language, with a wealth of material. One gets the impression at times that in his desire to support the subtitle of his book, he has not presented all sides of some questions.]

THE MODERN ATTEMPT AT SYNTHESIS

H. H. Rowley, *The Re-discovery of the Old Testament.* London: James Clarke & Co., 1945. 224 pp. [Stimulating.]

G. Ernest Wright, *The Old Testament Against its Environment.* (Studies in Biblical Theology, 2.) London: SCM Press, 1950. 116 pp. [A work that is quoted repeatedly.]

H. H. Rowley, editor, *The Old Testament and Modern Study.* Oxford: Clarendon Press, 1951. 405 pp. [Twelve outstanding scholars discuss the impact of modern discovery upon the various fields of Old Testament study. An extremely significant book, worth repeated careful reading, with excellent bibliographies.]

Quite a few additional pertinent titles are listed, with comments, in my *Basic Semitic Bibliography* (Wheaton, Ill.: Van Kampen Press, 1950; 56 pp.). Other titles are sprinkled in the footnotes of the preceding pages. And I am fully aware that I have omitted many books of outstanding merit, not a few of which I use constantly. But there are space limitations which I must observe.

Index

Adonijah, 118f
adoption, 34, 86
Ahab, 128ff
Ahasuerus, 180
Ahaz, 137, 139ff
Ahijah, 124
Akkadian Period, 14f
Amarna, 52
Amenhotep IV, 54
Amos, 127f
anti-priest, 152
architecture, Egyptian, 52
art, Akkadian, 14
Artaxerxes I, 176
Assyria, 136f, 141ff, 145, 151, 155, 166
Avaris, 44, 52
Azariah, 138

Baal worship, 77, 126, 131ff, 175
Babylon, 166f, 171, 179
Babylonia, 142, 145, 151, 155, 166
Babylonian, Neo-, 164, 166, 172
Babylonian, Old, 16
Baruch, 147
Bathsheba, 112ff, 116ff
Belshazzar, 168ff
Beni-Ḥasan, 111
Benjamin, 47
Bethlehem, 79, 98
Bethel, 37
birthright, 33f

camel, 42
Canaan, 22f, 42, 63, 77, 157
Canaanites, 76
Chaldeans, 164
Cheops, 25
civilization, Egyptian, 25f, 111
civilization, Mesopotamian, 14ff, 22, 111
commerce, 42
copper, 121
corners of the field, 82
cubit, 100

cuneiform, 52
customs, Nuzu, 24, 26f, 33f, 80, 83
Cyrus the Great, 156, 171, 176

Darius Hystaspis, 178
David, 95f, 117, 175
Dead Sea Scrolls, 175
"devote," to, 76
"double portion," 134

Egypt, 43ff, 51f, 145, 148, 151, 155
Egypt, River of, 28
election, 54
Eli, 88ff
end of world, 171ff
Esau, 32f
Esther, 180
Evil-merodach, 150
exile, 155, 179
Exodus, date of, 55
Ezion-geber, 121

Fertile Crescent, 43

gate, the, 84f
Ghôr, 72
Gibeonites, 75
gố'ēl, 83
Goliath, 100ff
Gudea, 15

Haggai, 174, 178
Hammurabi, 16
Hananiah, 147f
Hannah, 90f
Hatshepsut, 55
Hezekiah, 137, 140ff
hieroglyphic, 25, 52
Hiram, King, 119, 122
historiography, 109
holy, 157
horse, 44
Hyksos, 43f
hymns, 112

music, 103, 111

idolatry, 159
Isaac, 29f, 31f
Israel, 37, 162

Jabbok, 37
Jacob, 41
Jebus, 107
Jeconiah, 148
Jehoahaz, 150
Jehoiachin, 150, 155
Jehoiakim, 147, 150
Jehovah, 65
Jericho, 72ff, 81
Jerusalem, 107, 111, 154f
Jethro, 56f
Jezebel, 130ff
Jordan River, 71ff
Josiah, 146, 149, 158
Jotham, 137, 139
Judaism, 174
Judges, the, 88f

kashka, 82
kingdom, 93, 126, 172f
Kingdom, Southern, 166
Kingdom, Northern, 124, 130, 139, 141, 155
kinsman, near, 83ff

Laban, 34f
Land Promised, 28, 37f, 48, 63, 67, 69ff, 148, 156, 178
levirate marriage, 80, 83
Leviticus and Ezekiel, 156f
lyre, 103, 111

Macedonian Empire, 172
Malachi, 174, 178
Manasseh, 137, 142f
Mari tablets, 106
marriage adoption, 34
marriage alliance, 122
marriage contracts, 27
marriage, levirate, 80
mazkîr, 109
Menahem, 136
Merodach-baladan, 142
miracles, 129f
Molech, 76, 139
monotheism, 54
Moses, 70f, 77, 112, 175

Nabonidus, 168, 171
Nathan, 127
Nazirite, 90
Nebuchadnezzar (Nebuchadrezzar), 147, 164ff, 166
Neco, 150
Nehemiah, 177, 180f
Nuzu, 24, 27, 33, 80, 82

Omri, 130

Palestine, see Canaan
Pekah, 136, 139f
Pentateuch, Mosaic authorship, 64f
Persians, 169, 171f
Philistines, 100
philosophy, Egyptian, 53
Phinehas, 175f
polygamy, 117f
post-exilic writings, 174
priest, 152, 154, 157, 174, 176
primogeniture, 33f
prophet, 66, 92, 126ff, 152, 164f, 172
prophetic perspective, 162
prophets, non-writing (oral), 127f
prophets, writing (literary), 127f
Proverbs, Solomonic authorship, 116
Psalms, Davidic authorship, 112
Pul, 21
Pyramids, 25f, 52

Rachel, 33f, 36
Rahab, 81
Rebekah, 32, 36
recorder, 109
redeemer, kinsman, 83
Rezin, 136, 139f
Roman Empire, 172

Sadducees, 175
Samaria, 130, 137, 141
Samaritans, 178ff
Samuel, 127
Sarah, 25ff
Sargon I, 14
Sargon II, 137
Saul, 92
scribe, 110, 138, 174, 176
Scriptures, 64, 182
Scythians, 158

seer, 94, 165
Sennacherib, 137, 141f
Shalmaneser V, 137, 141
Sheba, 122
shekel, 101
Sheshbazzar, 177
Sinuhe, Tale of, 22
sôfēr, 110
Sumerian, 15

"Tale of Two Brothers," 45
Targums, 181
Tell el-Amarna, 52, 54
temple, 119f, 140, 163, 177
teraphim, 34f
Tiglath-pileser III, 136, 139
trade routes, 43
tradition, 17f

Ugaritic tablets, 111
Ur, 13, 14f, 24, 111
Uzziah, 137f

wisdom literature, 116
worship, 64, 111f
writing, 15, 25, 52, 182

Xerxes, 180

Yahweh, 65

Zadok, 175f
Zechariah, 174, 178
Zedekiah, 150
Zion, 108, 111
Zôr, 72

VOLUME 2

GREAT PERSONALITIES
OF THE NEW TESTAMENT

To
HENRY SNYDER GEHMAN
AND
OTTO A. PIPER
this work
is gratefully dedicated

Contents

GREAT PERSONALITIES OF THE NEW TESTAMENT

I	THE FULLNESS OF TIME	13
II	JOHN THE BAPTIST	23
III	MARY THE MOTHER OF JESUS	32
IV	JESUS THE SON OF MAN	41
V	ANDREW THE FIRST DISCIPLE	50
VI	LAZARUS, MARY, AND MARTHA	60
VII	SIMON BAR-JONAH	70
VIII	PETER THE ROCK	79
IX	STEPHEN THE PROTOMARTYR	89
X	SAUL OF TARSUS	98
XI	PAUL THE APOSTLE	108
XII	BARNABAS AND MARK	118
XIII	LUKE THE BELOVED PHYSICIAN	128
XIV	PRISCILLA AND AQUILA	138
XV	TIMOTHY AND TITUS	147
XVI	THOMAS WHO BELIEVED	156
XVII	JOHN THE THEOLOGIAN	165
XVIII	THE TRIUMPHANT CHRIST	175
	BIBLIOGRAPHY	185
	INDEX	190

CHAPTER I

The Fullness of Time

IF YOU WERE going to launch a world-wide movement, when would you do it? You would probably wait until the political factors were just right. The ideal time would be when there was no war, and when communication was easy to all parts of the world. You would wait until the cultural factors were right. You would desire a minimum language barrier. You would look for ease in the spreading of ideas. And if the movement you were to launch happened to be a religious movement, you would feel that even the religious scene needed to be prepared.

In the letter to the Galatians, Paul says, "But when the time had fully come"—or as it is in the King James Version, "when the fullness of the time was come"—"God sent forth his Son, born of woman, born under the law, to redeem those who were under the law, so that we might receive adoption as sons" (Galatians 4:4f). In other words, Paul is saying that the advent of Jesus Christ occurred at that moment of history that could be described as "the fullness of time."[1] Jesus Himself suggested that the fullness of time had come when He began His public ministry with the words, "The time is fulfilled, and the kingdom of God is at hand" (Mark 1:15).

It is fitting as we begin our series on the Great Personalities of the New Testament that we try to understand something of the significance of this concept, *the fullness of time*. God works in history. God is the Lord of history. These sayings are so commonplace that they have become clichés. Yet in a very real sense these commonplace sayings are true. For centuries God had been preparing the world for the advent of the Redeemer. Without ever being aware of it, nations moved on and off the scene, fulfilling the parts that were determined for them: is this not what Paul was trying to tell the learned men of Athens (cf. Acts 17:24-26)? Only one nation in the world had

[1] For a stimulating discussion of "the fullness of time," see Otto Piper, *God in History* (New York: The Macmillan Company, 1939), pp. 1-40.

13

an intimate acquaintance with God and knew something of His purposes: that was the nation Israel. But it is written very clearly in the pages of the Old Testament that Israel was not the only nation in which God was active or through which God was bringing to pass His purpose. Through His prophets He made it very clear, as indeed He had done in the first promise to Abraham, that all of the nations of the world were involved in His redemptive activity (cf. Genesis 12:3; Isaiah 60:1-3).

All the nations of the world were involved—how?[2] Students of the Bible are familiar enough with the Egyptians and the Assyrians, the Babylonians and the Persians, and the parts they played in the divine plan. But the story of the Old Testament ends approximately in the middle of the fifth century B.C. It is a gross mistake to suppose that God's activity ended at that same time and did not begin again until the annunciations of the births of John the Baptist and Jesus of Nazareth. Some of the most important preparation of the world was taking place in the centuries between the Old Testament and the New Testament.

The political preparation. Instead of thinking of the Biblical world as spreading over parts of three continents, think of it as a geographical and cultural entity bordering on the eastern half of the Mediterranean Sea. Because of the mountains that extend across the northern portion from the Alps to the Himalayas, and the desert that stretches across the southern portion, plus the desert and seas of the eastern portion, communication between those parts of Europe, Asia, and Africa that border on the Mediterranean was far less difficult than communication to the remaining parts of any of the continents. This single area is the Bible world. Yet, it is still true that there are three distinct parts of the Bible world. There were Asiatics, Europeans, and Egyptians (to the last of which should be added, of course, the Libyans, Ethiopians, and others). Although the Egyptians were of great importance in the earlier portion of Old Testament history, by the time of the last centuries before Christ Egypt was no longer of primary importance. The struggle was between the Asiatics and the Europeans.

[2] I have tried to show something of the historical activity of God in my previous volume, *Great Personalities of the Old Testament* (Westwood, N.J.: Fleming H. Revell Company, 1959).

It is possible to trace a shift of power, first from the Semitic peoples in Asia to the non-Semitic, and specifically to the Indo-European peoples in Asia; then from the Asiatic Indo-Europeans to the European Greeks. The night Babylon fell before the forces of Cyrus the Great the hegemony of Semitic empires came to an end. When Darius the Third was conquered by Alexander the Great, the world-empires of the Asiatic peoples came to an end and the world-empires of the Europeans began. Since that time, only twice in history have Asiatics seriously threatened the supremacy of the European powers: first in the time of Mohammed, when the Islamic forces spread across northern Africa and into the Iberian Peninsula, only to be stopped by Charles Martel at Tours (A.D. 732); the second time when Genghis Kahn[3] swept westward into Europe to the Dnieper River in the early thirteenth century A.D. Both of these attempts, it will be noted, are considerably later than the time of Christ, and both of them failed.[4]

The rise of world empires is undoubtedly part of the political preparation employed in the idea of the fullness of time. At the end of the third millenium B.C., Sargon of Akkad had ideas of world empire when he called himself, "king of the four quarters of the earth." But this amounted to little more than a self-conferred honorary degree. The idea, however, seems to have been present in the minds of rulers who succeeded him, and at last in the days of the second Assyrian Empire it began to take on reality. Tiglath-pileser I (c.1118-1078 B.C.) provided considerable stimulus for its development, but the carrying out belongs really to the dynasty of Tiglath-pileser III (c.745-727 B.C.), including Shalmaneser V (c.727-722 B.C.), Sargon II of Assyria (722-705 B.C.), and Sennacherib (705-681 B.C.).[5] The Assyr-

[3] Pronounced jĕng'gĭs kän'—it is a common mistake to pronounce the first g hard.

[4] This is of course not to imply the superiority of the European over the Asiatic, nor for that matter over the African. The historian knows that there is no assurance that the European empires (or powers, as we now call them) will continue to maintain a relative supremacy in the world; in fact, the decline of the West was apparent to some historians years ago. But to discuss this would be to get away from our present purpose.

[5] It is debatable whether this succession of kings should be called a dynasty. According to most scholars, Sargon was a usurper of the throne; on the other hand, van der Meer lists him as a brother of Shalmaneser V (cf. P. van der Meer, *The Chronology of Ancient Western Asia and Egypt* [2d ed.; Leiden: E. J. Brill, 1955], p. 76). Unfortunately, van der Meer does not document this, and I have been unable to find the record in which the relationship is expressed.

ian empire was indescribably cruel, and maintained its grasp not so much by means of wise and efficient government as by sheer brute force. With the destruction of Nineveh in 612 B.C., it was replaced by the Babylonian empire of Nebuchadnezzar; but this empire was doomed to fall even before it arose, for it had come into existence by a coalition of powers and was unable to maintain the loyalty of its allies.

The Medo-Persian empire came into being by the destruction of Babylon in 539 B.C., and proceeded to establish a system of government which should have furnished sufficient cohesion to hold together an empire stretching from the Aegean Sea to the Indus River and including Egypt. But the Medo-Persian empire probably overextended itself by attempting to subdue the Scythians along the Danube, and later by attempting to conquer Athens and other parts of Greece. At the same time, we must recognize the fact that another power had arisen that was able to conquer the Medo-Persian empire.

Alexander the Great of Macedon had come to the throne and succeeded in whipping together the peoples of Greece, who had hitherto shown no remarkable unity. Moreover, he had established an ideal which struck fire. Quickly he moved across the world of his day, conquering the Medo-Persian empire and attempting even to extend its boundaries. Alexander died young, before the empire was really unified, and he bequeathed his empire to his four generals who soon reduced it to four and then three parts. By the end of the fourth century B.C. it would seem that the idea of world empire had come to an end.

This, however, was not to be. A new power had arisen in the west which, after it had overcome its only western rival, Carthage, on the northern coast of Africa,[6] turned its attention to the east, and by 63 B.C., Rome had taken over the lands of the eastern Mediterranean. While it is true that the Roman empire did not reach its greatest extent until the rule of Trajan (A.D. 117), it is also true that Roman rule extended over enough of the world of Jesus' day that it could be called "the whole world" (Luke 2:1).

The Romans were able to give to the world that unity and strength of government which was necessary for peace and for the rapid spread of the gospel. *Pax Romana* (Roman peace) was not only an ideal; it was a fact. Perhaps for the only time in the history of the world there

[6] In the three Punic Wars, 264-241, 218-201, and 149-146 B.C.

was an extended period of universal peace. If Jesus Christ had come into the world one hundred years either side of the actual time of His advent, the story, from the historian's point of view, would have been far different. Alongside *Pax Romana* was *Lex Romana* (Roman law). The Roman empire in some way had learned to balance local autonomy and central authority, the rights of individuals and the rights of the state. So well was Roman law developed that the legal systems of the western world are largely drawn from it.

We would not suggest that there were no problems. In order to maintain peace, the Roman empire had a standing army of a quarter-million men. True, the citizen army maintained by conscription had been replaced by a professional army. But armed forces are expensive, and taxes were imposed in the forms of customs, excise, inheritance, and sales taxes, usually collected by men who bought the office as a concession and then charged what they could get. Once every fourteen years a census or poll-tax was levied. These things were sources of annoyance and an occasional riot. But all-in-all, it was a time of peace and prosperity.

The cultural preparation. The empires which had preceded that of Alexander the Great were dead. It would not be possible to speak of a continuing Babylonian or Persian ideal, or any other. But the ideal of Alexander the Great, with the establishment of the Roman empire, was far from dead. That ideal can be summarized in one word: Hellenism. While this term can be used, and has been used, to cover many things, it will help us to think of it as the desire to give to the world the best of Greek life and thought. Alexander wanted to establish all over his empire centers of Greek culture, libraries that would house Greek writings, theaters that would present Greek drama and music. Cities named "Alexandria" sprang up all over the empire, and anyone who travels in the Near East will be duly impressed by the magnificence and geographical extent of Greek ruins. The library in Alexandria, Egypt, possessed over 500,000 volumes, and this was not the only library in the empire, for when it caught fire, Antony gave to Cleopatra 200,000 volumes from the library at Pergamum as replacement. It was Alexander's ideal also that a common language should unite the empire, and, of course, that would be Greek. One of the most dramatic ways in which Alexander attempted to put into effect his ideal was a mass wedding ceremony, held at Susa (one of the capitals of the Medo-Persian empire), where Alexander and his generals, and ten thousand of his soldiers, attempted to symbolize the marriage of Europe and Asia by taking Persian wives.[7] In some ways Alexander's expedition could be looked upon as scientific, somewhat as was Napoleon's expedition to Egypt many centuries later. Alexander took with him scholars, historians, geographers, and botanists. He built a fleet of ships at the mouth of the Indus River which was to explore the coast of the Persian Gulf; and he had other ideas which were considerably in advance of his day.[8] And the most completely Hellenized part of the empire outside Greece itself was Syro-Palestine![9]

When the Roman empire achieved supremacy, it is fortunate, or we prefer to say, providential, that there was no spirit of pan-Romanism. No effort seems to have been made to overthrow the Hellenistic ideals, to replace the Greek language with the Latin, or to develop an indigenous Roman culture. To expect the world to adopt a second universal language so soon would be to expect the impossible. Greek continued to be the language of the empire for several centuries. Moreover, the Romans were imitators rather than originators. Their art is largely Greek art, and other elements of their culture owe much to the Greeks who preceded them. Rome made a different type of contribution to the culture of the world; perhaps we could say it was more practical. Hellenism was an ideal. *Pax Romana* and *Lex Romana* were not ideals, they were realities; and because they were realities, the Hellenistic ideal was able to take even firmer root than it had, and the unity of which Alexander dreamed was realized in the Roman empire. Roman roads tied the empire together; Roman ships plied the lanes

[7] Arrian, *Anabasis of Alexander*, 7.4.4-8; Plutarch, *Life of Alexander*, 70.2. It is true that Alexander's soldiers conducted a burning and looting expedition, and some scholars have little sympathy with Alexander's pan-Hellenic ideal; cf. A. T. E. Olmstead, *History of the Persian Empire* (Chicago: University of Chicago Press, 1948), pp. 519-523. The attitude of Ghirshman, reminding us of Voltaire's words ("Alexander had built more towns than other conquerors had destroyed"), is a moderating viewpoint; cf. R. Ghirshman, *Iran* (Pelican Book A239; Harmondsworth, Middlesex: Penguin Books, 1954), pp. 212-219.

[8] S. Vernon McCasland has pointed out that this expansion of Greek influence had been under way for a long time and that Alexander's conquests only gave an impetus to it; cf. "The Greco-Roman World," in *The Interpreter's Bible* (New York: Abingdon-Cokesbury Press, 1951), vol. 7, p. 75. It is nevertheless true that the impetus was needed and Alexander provided it.

[9] Cf. John Pentland Mahaffy, *The Progress of Hellenism in Alexander's Empire* (Chicago: University of Chicago Press, 1905), p. 97.

of the Mediterranean; the Roman postal system made rapid communication possible; Roman citizenship not only protected the rights of individuals who were citizens, but made possible widespread travel. At the same time, the principle of colonial home rule added a sense of significance and individual value.

But a sense of human value can cause trouble! When a slave, or an ex-slave, suddenly realizes, "I, too, am a man," he can cause all sorts of difficulty for those who want to be masters. Slavery was a great problem in the Roman empire. It has been estimated that one-third to one-half of the entire population were slaves. Life was cheap. A master who was displeased with the way his slave served the table could throw him to the fish. A mistress could permanently disfigure her servant whom she caught brushing her hair. Emperors might send hundreds, even thousands, of slaves into the arena to engage in mass slaughter—just for entertainment! But others were thinking about these things. If human life has value, how can it be destroyed so easily? When life is cheap, immorality is rampant. In particular, immorality of a sexual nature is encouraged when human beings are insignificant. Roman writers have left us full, frank, and disgusting accounts of their day.[10] But Roman writers were also rebelling against such conditions. Cicero's orations against Catiline in 63 B.C., once known by every schoolboy Latin student, are only one example that could be cited.

There is a nobler side, even in fallen man, for which we ought to thank God. Men were grappling with serious matters. They did not always come up with the right answers, but they were making interesting suggestions. We still study their philosophies and find much of value in them. This is not the place to discuss them; I simply want to point out one fact: when God was ready to send His Gospel into the world, there were men who were ready to give it serious consideration.

The religious preparation. The four and a half centuries between the close of the Old Testament and the advent of Jesus Christ were

---

[10] For a graphic resumé, amply documented, see David R. Breed, *A History of the Preparation of the World for Christ* (New York: Fleming H. Revell Company, 1893), pp. 403-430. More restrained is McCasland's treatment, *art. cit.,* in *The Interpreter's Bible,* vol. 7, pp. 80-84. Paul refers to this condition in Romans 1:18-32.

years of great experience for the Jewish people. At the beginning of the sixth century B.C., they had been carried from Judah to Babylon in captivity. In 538 B.C., Cyrus the Great had granted to them the opportunity of returning to their land. Not all Jews, however, returned; as a matter of fact, some estimates of the number of Jews who seized the opportunity are as low as ten per cent.[11] Those who remained in exile made a new home for themselves. That home was the world. Such Jews were the "Diaspora," or the Jews of the Dispersion.[12]

Several things happened to the Jewish people in the Dispersion. For one thing, they developed a world view. Too long had they associated their God merely with the land of Palestine. By the rivers of Babylon they had wept because they had thought they could not sing the Lord's song in a foreign land (see Psalm 137:1-4). But now they had come to realize that the world was the Lord's. They not only could sing the Lord's song in foreign lands—they could even translate the song into foreign languages! In Babylon and the Mesopotamian region, as well as in the land of Egypt to which Jews had migrated in the time of Jeremiah and possibly earlier, Aramaic became the language of the Jewish people. Jews gradually spread to other parts of the world, and began to speak the Greek language. As their knowledge of the original Hebrew language decreased, it became increasingly necessary to have an explanation of the meaning of the Scriptures. Interpretations in Aramaic were at first preserved in oral form only, known as Targums, but later these were standardized in written form. Likewise Greek translations of the Old Testament Scriptures were made, which were far more significant for the New Testament period than were the Aramaic Targums.

Perhaps that statement needs a word of explanation. The reason why the Greek translations were important can be explained by the fact that the Jewish people were undergoing, consciously or unconsciously, a process of Hellenization. If they were not all participating in the games in the stadium—some indeed going so far as to have the visible signs of circumcision removed by an operation—at least their vocabulary was being expanded with Greek ideas. When the

---

[11] See my *Great Personalities of the Old Testament,* p. 174-183.

[12] Cf. F. J. Foakes Jackson and Kirsopp Lake, *The Beginnings of Christianity* (London: Macmillan and Co., 1922), vol. 1, pp. 137-168; and Robert H. Pfeiffer, *History of New Testament Times* (New York: Harper & Brothers, 1949), pp. 166-196. The latter has an excellent bibliography.

Hebrew Old Testament was translated into Greek, Hebrew words that had narrow meanings were often translated by Greek words that had broader meanings. Key theological terms had to be translated by words that had various nuances and connotations not present in the original. It could not possibly be otherwise. Our words are integrally part of our culture. When two cultures merge, the language has to become richer.[13] And the Jews had entered the Hellenistic stream of culture. The old wineskins were already being stretched; the new wine would require new wineskins. It is highly doubtful that Paul could have preached his gospel in the Gentile world if he had been limited to the concepts of the Hebrew Old Testament, and certainly impossible if he had been limited to the Hebrew language.

Another feature of the Dispersion was the development of the synagogue to serve as a partial substitute for, and later to take the place of, the temple at Jerusalem. While Jews lived in the land of Palestine, it was possible to fulfill literally the law requiring attendance at the annual feasts. When, because of distance, this could no longer be fulfilled, the synagogue provided a means of religious expression. It also provided a means of community, so that the Jews of the Dispersion continued to use the Scriptures of the Old Testament, and to a lesser and modified extent they preserved the elements of worship. It does not need to be argued that the preachers of the gospel found their first steppingstones into the Gentile world in the synagogues scattered throughout that world.

We could devote an entire study to the development of the Messianic expectation among the Jews, but here it is enough to point out that the hope that the day of deliverance was at hand was burning brightly. A whole literature was being produced centering largely about this theme.[14] False messiahs had arisen and would continue to arise for another century.

Nor was this sense of expectation limited to the Jews. There was

[13] One very familiar illustration is our own English language, which after the Norman conquest absorbed many French words to take care of new cultural elements. For example, Anglo-Saxon words were sufficient for the kitchen and barnyard, but French words were needed for the dining room, prepared food, and eating utensils (cf. *pig—pork, ox—beef, stool—chair; table* and *napkin* were additions, but not *knife* and *fork*).

[14] Cf. Charles F. Pfeiffer, *Between the Testaments* (Grand Rapids: Baker Book House, 1959), pp. 121-124; the entire book will provide an introduction to the intertestamental period. For a more detailed study, cf. Robert H. Pfeiffer, *op. cit.*, 561 pp.

in the Gentile world a sense of dissatisfaction with existing religions, and alongside this an expectation of something better. The Greeks had climbed Mount Olympus and found no gods there. The Latin writers Tacitus and Suetonius record the expectation of a powerful king.[15] All over the Gentile world many were becoming proselytes to Judaism, and it seems reasonable to suppose that it was the Messianic hope rather than the Mosaic law that was appealing to them.

This, then, is the fullness of time. God had prepared His world. Politically it was at peace under a stable government. Culturally it was united in the Greek language and the Hellenistic ideal. And the Jews, the people of God, scattered throughout the world, had at last come to the threshold and were ready to enter in to fulfill the promise made to Abraham, that they not only should be blessed, but that they should also be a blessing to the nations of the world.

[15] Tacitus, *History*, 5.13; Suetonius, *Vespasian*, 4.

CHAPTER II

John the Baptist

JESUS ONCE SAID, "Among those born of women none is greater than John" (Luke 7:28). If you go through the teachings of Jesus and note particularly the things He has to say about John the Baptist, you will probably be surprised at the unusually strong statements. Yet we frequently overlook John the Baptist. We know much about Paul and Peter and John, and less about some of the other Apostles. But what do we know about the Baptist? Some men can tell us that he wore a camel's hair coat, and that he lost his head when a drunken king made a rash promise to a dancing girl—usually they know her name—and that is about all. We confuse John the Baptist with John the Evangelist, and we are often not sure which John is referred to as we read the Scriptures.

I would like to try to correct that. If Jesus placed such a high estimate on John the Baptist, I think we should try to learn more about him.

John the Baptist and the Old Testament. John is the link between the Old and New Testaments. Jesus accepted this link. We shall see the significance, I trust, before we are finished.

The story of the birth of John is in itself startling. "In the days of Herod, king of Judea, there was a priest named Zechariah, of the division of Abijah; and he had a wife of the daughters of Aaron, and her name was Elizabeth" (Luke 1:5). Both of them were of priestly families, devout, "walking in all the commandments and ordinances of the Lord blameless. But they had no child" (Luke 1:6-7). Perhaps in our western society it is a little bit difficult to understand just how deeply the Semitic world felt childlessness. It was often looked upon as a curse, and was considered sufficient reason in some places for a man to divorce his wife and take another. Zechariah and Elizabeth prayed about the matter.

One day, as Zechariah was fulfilling his duty in the temple—as I understand it, it was given to each priest to minister in the temple and light the sacred fire once in his lifetime—the aged priest had a vision. An angel said to him, "Do not be afraid, Zechariah, for your prayer is heard, and your wife Elizabeth will bear you a son, and you shall call his name John" (Luke 1:13). Notice the devotion of the father and mother! They were continuing to pray for a son, even though they were past the prime of life. Is that not what the angel's words mean, for why else would the promise of a son be connected with the words, "your prayer is heard"?

The child was to be filled with the Holy Spirit. He was to bring joy and gladness not only to the family into which he was to be born, but to other people as well. He was to "turn many of the sons of Israel to the Lord their God . . . to turn the hearts of the fathers to the children, and the disobedient to the wisdom of the just, to make ready for the Lord a people prepared" (Luke 1:16-17). All the power of inspired prophecy was to be in him, for the Holy Spirit who inspired the prophets of the Old Testament was to come upon a human being once more that he might speak the word of God. All the hopes of a brighter tomorrow that had been hidden in the hearts of these people for several centuries were to be realized because of this child that was to be born.

There was no breach with the past. God was not saying, "I am through with My people. Those Scriptures that you have been reading for generations and that religion you have been following are now abolished, and We are going to start something new." Some may present Christianity as a breach with the past, but that is not the truth. Rather, God is saying, "We are continuing the old in the new. The same Spirit that came upon the prophets is going to come upon this child, and because of this fact, the people are going to be ready when I send My redeemer into the world."

And so "the time came for Elizabeth to be delivered, and she gave birth to a son" (Luke 1:57). This was just a little while before Jesus was born—perhaps six months. When the child was circumcised, they wanted to name him Zechariah after his father, but Zechariah, who had been dumb from the day of the vision in the temple, wrote, "His name is John." With that, his voice was restored, and he spoke the great song (the *Benedictus*) that includes the words: " 'You, child, will be called the prophet of the Most High; for you will go before the Lord to prepare his ways, to give knowledge of salvation to his people in the forgiveness of their sins, through the tender mercy of our God, when the day shall dawn upon us from on high to give light to those who sit in darkness and in the shadow of death, to guide our feet into the way of peace.' And the child grew and became strong in spirit" (Luke 1:76-80). This was the one who would later be known as the "Forerunner."

Christianity does not repudiate the Old Testament. It does not say that the Bible begins with the Gospel of Matthew. Christianity says that the Scriptures of the Old and New Testaments are the word of God. Jesus expressly said that He had not come to abolish the Old, but to fulfill it (cf. Matthew 5:17). John the Baptist rightly bridges the two; he is the prophet of the Old and the forerunner of the New.

John the Baptist and Judaism.[1] Judaism was in its formative period, and at that time was a house divided. In the New Testament we hear of the Pharisees and the Sadducees; there were also other factions not mentioned by name. Herod, who sat upon the throne, was an Edomite and could scarcely claim to be a Jew. The prophetic voice had been silent: the famine of the word of God that had been promised by the prophet (Amos 8:11). For centuries no prophet had spoken in Israel, and in the place of prophetic religion there had settled down upon the nation a curious mixture of formalism and rationalism and separatism. Not that these were all found in the same place: that is why I called it a house divided.

There were the Pharisees, the purists, who held to the letter of the law. Jesus was critical of the Pharisees, and pointed out that they were not instrumental in the redemptive work of God in the world. They had failed to bring men to realize that God was seeking to free them; rather they were binding men to a bondage that was far more rigid than God had ever intended. They were making men children of hell and not sons of heaven. They had reduced the glorious religion of the Old Testament to a system of ritual and rites and ceremonies, to things that should be done and things that should not be done, to tithes that should be given and tithes that were not required. They had paid attention to garden herbs, and ignored the more important matters of the Law (see Matthew 23:1-36). Fortunately, Judaism was able to break the bonds of Pharisaism and move beyond it.

[1] For a Jewish estimate of John the Baptist, see Josephus, *Antiquities,* 18.5.2.

Then there were the Sadducees, the old conservatives. That will strike some as a strange label, but a careful study of the Sadducees will justify it. They were the dead conservatives, so dead that they repudiated any notion that had come along since the time of Moses. They were not interested in the rest of the Old Testament, and if they did not find it in the Law, they wanted nothing to do with it. They were not only the starched traditionalists, but worse, they were hardened by rationalism. Having set down the lines within which truth as they understood it must conform, they had rationalized it until there was very little spirit left, and very little place for God's Spirit to work. They had taken over the priestly caste (the priests were the sons of Zadok, or Zadokites, which is probably the derivation of the name "Sadducees") and they sought to dominate the religious life of the nation.[2]

The Jewish historian, Josephus, mentions a third sect of Judaism, namely the Essenes. As I understand this movement, it was composed of those who had rejected the dead ritual of the Pharisees, who had grown tired of the starched conservatism of the Sadducees, and who sought the answer in asceticism. The Essenes wanted to get away from the world, to live in the desert, to have no part in the Jerusalem religion but rather to have their own true religion. The famous Dead Sea Scrolls were being produced in the century or so before the birth of John the Baptist. Most scholars working on the Dead Sea Scrolls are convinced that they were written by Essenes or by those very closely allied to Essenism.[3] The Qumran literature makes it quite clear that there were Jews who looked upon the Jerusalem priesthood as wicked, who repudiated the rest of Judaism, and who formed a separatist movement.

There were other divisions in Judaism, in addition to these three, but these will suffice to make the point that Judaism was no longer a single people worshiping God in God's way, but a set of factions, filled with suspicion, distrust, and hostility, so that it was possible to throw the Sanhedrin into a turmoil just by mentioning the word "Pharisee" (cf. Acts 23:6-10).

[2] It is difficult to evaluate the source material on the Sadducees, since it has come down to us only through Pharisee eyes and the New Testament. But the picture is much the same in these sources, and reasonably reliable. The new material added by a study of the Dead Sea Scrolls, in my opinion, strongly confirms this view.

[3] See my *Amazing Dead Sea Scrolls* (revised edition; Chicago: Moody Press, 1959), pp. 177-189.

Where does John fit into this? Well, John was apparently an ascetic, who drank no wine nor strong drink (Luke 1:15) and who was in the wilderness until "the day of his manifestation to Israel" (Luke 1:80). His food was vegetarian, or nearly so (locusts and wild honey), and his clothing was coarse (Mark 1:6). He was apparently not one of the Pharisees, and certainly not one of the Sadducees. He has often been identified as an Essene, and as often this has been denied.[4] Recently, he has been identified with the Qumran group.[5] Now, Qumran was certainly one of the few places in the wilderness of Judea capable of supporting life. John and the Qumranians both traced their origin to the priestly line. Both practised baptism. Both were ascetic. Both claimed Isaiah 40:3 as their keynote.

But on the other hand, there are important differences. The Qumran group was esoteric: only for those initiated into the group. There is nothing like this in John's preaching. The attitude of Qumran was to withdraw from the world. John, on the other hand, went back to the world to preach a message of repentance. The Qumran message was to withdraw from the world in asceticism. This certainly was not John's message. Rather, he said, in effect, "Conform your life to your faith in the world. Bring faith and life together." The soldier, asking what he should do, was not told to give up his military life; he could still be a soldier. The tax collector could still be a tax collector. The king could still be a king. But whatever he was, his service was to be rendered in accordance with the will of God. Finally, the Qumran group was waiting for a Messiah yet to come. John the Baptist was proclaiming that the Kingdom of God was present.[6]

John the Baptist and the world. One day, John left the wilderness to go to preach to the sinful world. Luke gives us the date. I suppose if you could ask the seven persons who are named what was

---

[4] For the identification, cf. K. Kohler, "Essenes," in *Jewish Encyclopaedia* (New York: Funk & Wagnalls Co., 1903), vol. 5, esp. pp. 231-232. For a thorough discussion of the opposite viewpoint, see J. B. Lightfoot, *St. Paul's Epistle to the Colossians and to Philemon* (London: Macmillan and Co., 1875), pp. 158-179.

[5] Cf. Jean Steinmann, *Saint John the Baptist and the Desert Tradition* (tr. M. Boyes; New York: Harper & Brothers, 1958), 191 pp.; but see also Millar Burrows, *More Light on the Dead Sea Scrolls* (New York: Viking Press, 1958), pp. 56-63.

[6] Several points here have been drawn from the very lucid discussion by Robert B. Laurin, article "John the Baptist," in *Baker's Dictionary of Theology* (Grand Rapids, Mich.: Baker Book House, 1960), p. 299.

the most important thing they had done in life, you would receive all sorts of answers; but so far as Luke was concerned, they were significant for dating the beginning of the ministry of John the Baptist: "In the fifteenth year of the reign of Tiberius Caesar, Pontius Pilate being governor of Judea, and Herod being tetrarch of Galilee, and his brother Philip tetrarch of the region of Ituraea and Trachonitis, and Lysanias tetrarch of Abilene, in the high-priesthood of Annas and Caiaphas, the word of God came to John the son of Zechariah in the wilderness" (Luke 3:1-2). It is almost as though John is saying, "Now I'm not sure which one of these men will be remembered, so I shall list seven and hope that one turns out to be significant." Fortunately, we know that the fifeenth year of Tiberius Caesar was about A.D. 27 or 28. It may have been a sabbatical year; if so, that would explain why the Jews were able to go to the Jordan in great numbers to hear this prophet.

John's message is a striking one. It has three major points.

First, the Kingdom is here.[7] To the Jews, the hope of the Kingdom was no mere academic subject to be discussed in theological schools, and perhaps to be preached by fanatical preachers. It had become their very reason for existence. How long had they hoped? A thousand years? Two thousand? They had hoped for glorious deliverance when Moses led them out of Egypt, but soon they were longing for something better than the wilderness hardship and the endless manna. They had hoped for a place in the sun when they got their first king. When he failed, they hoped David would be the one. Then David's son. And then the hope seems to have turned into a vague dream. David's son—would David's son never come? And suddenly, here comes a man out of the wilderness to proclaim that the Kingdom is here!

That called for an investigation, and Jerusalem sent its representatives. "Who are you?" they asked; and he confessed, "I am not the Messiah." "Then are you Elijah?" "I am not." "Are you the prophet?" "No." "Then who are you? Let us have an answer for those who sent us." "I am the voice of one crying in the wilderness, 'Make straight the way of the Lord,' as the prophet Isaiah said" (cf. John 1:19-23).

[7] For a clear discussion of the Kingdom, see George Eldon Ladd, *The Gospel of the Kingdom* (Grand Rapids, Mich.: Wm. B. Eerdmans Publishing Co., 1959), 143 pp.

Just a voice—but what a voice! And what a message! "The King-dom of Heaven is at hand!" If I could tell you today that the Kingdom of Heaven is here and all our troubles are over, all fears of war, all hatred and class struggle, all famine, sickness, and death, are forever ended, I would feel that I had the greatest privilege given to man. But it is not that easy!

The Jews had figured that when the Kingdom came, all Jews would be blessed, and all Gentiles would be put where they belonged. The prophets had tried to teach the people of God better than that. They tried to show that judgment begins at the house of God, that God was letting down a plumb line in the midst of Israel (Amos 7:7-9). Before there can be a Kingdom there must be righteousness. When Jesus began to lay the axe at the root, they protested: "We are Abraham's children." Abraham's children!—God can turn stones into Abraham's children (cf. John 8:39-40). The only heritage that counts in the Kingdom of God is spiritual heritage.[8] The Kingdom is here, and this means that the house of God, the people who have lived in the light of the revelation of God for these many years, will now have to face the judgment of God.

The New Testament says the same thing to us who are Christians. Judgment must begin with the house of God. We who have had the revelation most clearly are certainly going to be judged most severely. (See Romans 2:1-24; James 3:1-18.) If that disturbs your complacency, thank God that you have a Saviour who is able to keep you through it. But don't suppose for a minute that you are going to escape! There will be no man in heaven who has not had to stand before the judgment seat of God. And all those in heaven will be there because the blood of Christ has covered their sins.

With such a stern message, it is only logical that the people should ask, "What shall we do?" Listen to what John tells them. He does not say, "Attend the services more regularly; give tithes more faith-fully; pray more earnestly." Rather, he says, "He who has two coats, let him share with him who has none; and he who has food, let him do likewise" (Luke 3:11). If the Kingdom of God is here, it is time to begin living like members of the family of God. Tax collectors said,

[8] Even the command, "Be baptized," would underscore this, for baptism among the Jews had been only proselyte baptism, i.e., for Gentiles, and John is in effect saying, "You are the same as Gentiles; you must be baptized." See W. F. Flemington, *The New Testament Doctrine of Baptism* (London: S.P.C.K., 1953), p. 16.

"What shall we do?" John did not say, "Leave your job, you puppets of Rome!" He said, "Collect no more than is appointed you." Soldiers asked him, "And what shall we do?" How many times this verse has been overlooked by well-meaning Christians who seek to force non-violence on the world. John did not say, "Get out of the army; you cannot be a member of the Kingdom and bear arms!" No; rather, he said, "Rob no one by violence or by false accusation, and be content with your wages" (cf. Luke 3:12-14).

I suppose King Herod asked him one day, "What must I do?" It is clear that John told him, for later Herod had a guilty conscience about John. Herod had been responsible for the imprisonment and death of John, because John had told him, "It is not lawful for you to have your brother's wife" (cf. Matthew 14:1-12).

When the Kingdom comes, it is time to set our lives in order, for the coming of the Kingdom means the coming of judgment.

The third part of John's message was, "Repent!" The word, as everyone knows, means to turn around, change your attitude. Psychologists tell us that it is impossible in certain mental conditions for a person to be helped until first he decides he wants to be helped. They can do nothing with an alcoholic until the alcoholic definitely wants to be cured. That is why modern psychology puts so little emphasis on counsellor advice, and so much stress on client self-analysis and determination. First, there must be a change of attitude. Even so, before God can help us, we must repent.[9]

Repent! The things you are doing that cannot stand before judgment must go. You will have to make up your mind to do things in God's way, if you want to live in God's kingdom. Be baptized! Let your repentance be publicly declared. Take your stand in the world for God and His Kingdom. Bring forth fruits worthy of repentance! For after all, men will judge you, and not only you, but the Kingdom you represent, by your fruits.

John the Baptist and his followers. John won many followers, and they loved him. Some of them became Jesus' first disciples (John 1:35-42), but there were others who never followed Jesus. The teacher

[9] I am aware that some will insist that man can do nothing at all, not even repent, unless God's Spirit moves him. It is possible to be so logical as to be un-Biblical! I am glad that when they asked John, "What shall we do?" he did not say, "Wait until the Spirit moves you to repent."

is not always able to influence all his students. John taught his disciples to pray (Luke 11:1). He taught them to fast (Matthew 9:14). But more than religious acts, he taught them a religious attitude. They developed a tremendous loyalty, so much so that when Jesus put a question to the rulers about the source of John's baptism, they feared to answer because of the people (Matthew 21:25-26).

The ministry of John lasted possibly only six months. But twenty years later there were disciples of John the Baptist at Ephesus (Acts 19:1-7), and probably at Alexandria (Acts 18:24-25). There are still disciples of John the Baptist in the world; a few years ago I visited some of them in the silversmiths' bazaar in Baghdad.[10]

One wonderful day it was John's privilege to point to Jesus and say to his followers, "Behold, the Lamb of God, who takes away the sin of the world!" All his life was lived for that moment. From then on, it was, "He must increase, but I must decrease" (John 3:30).

[10] For a brief discussion and bibliography for further study, see my *Amazing Dead Sea Scrolls,* pp. 203-206.

CHAPTER III

Mary the Mother of Jesus

WHEN THE ANGEL Gabriel was sent from heaven to Nazareth, he greeted Mary with the words, "Hail, thou that art highly favored" (Luke 1:28, KJV). Elizabeth greeted her with the words, "Blessed are you among women"—or it could be translated, "You are the happiest of all women" (Luke 1:42).

In some areas of the Christian Church there has developed a body of fantastic superstition and tradition covering over the beautiful humanity of Mary until she appears as no one who ever lived on earth. In reaction against this fantasy, the rest of the Church has largely ignored her. It seems to me that we ought to recognize that she is the only woman in history chosen by God to be the mother of the God-man, Christ Jesus. She is unique. We should study Mary to find out what we can learn from her blessed nature, what examples we can use for our own spiritual growth, and what elements of womanhood there are that should be emulated by Christian women everywhere.

Mary and God. The angel addressed her as one who is highly favored. She was God's choice to be the mother of Jesus. Why? When you read the first chapter of Luke, let your mind wander back over the prophecies of the Old Testament that foretold the coming of a deliverer into the world. Think about God's choice of a people: it was the twelve tribes, the nation, the Jewish people, that God had chosen. Therefore, it had to be a Jewess who would be the mother of the child to be born (cf. Isaiah 9:6). I have heard that every Jewish woman in the world had the fond hope that she might be the mother of the Messiah. My mother never had that hope, nor did any other Gentile woman. That hope belonged to the Jewish people. Mary was one of the chosen race.

The coming redeemer had to be of the line of David. There are two genealogies of Jesus in the New Testament, one in Matthew, the other in Luke. Some scholars believe the one is Mary's, the other Joseph's; other scholars believe that both are Joseph's. Both go back to David. Whether Mary's genealogy is given in the New Testament, I do not know; but I believe that Mary was of the Davidic line, for the Scripture tells us that Jesus was born, according to the flesh, of the seed of David (Romans 1:3), and Jesus' human nature was not derived from Joseph, for Jesus was born of the Virgin Mary.

Girls married very young in that time and place, and tradition tells us that Mary was in her early or middle teens. She was a devout girl, and had been steeped in the Scriptures. We become aware of this fact as we listen to the beautiful words of the *Magnificat* that came from her lips (Luke 1:46-55). Every home has a Bible today, but that was not so when Mary was a girl. The Scriptures were hand written on large leather scrolls. I was called upon once to examine a scroll of the Pentateuch (the five books of Moses), and it was necessary for two of us to unroll it on the floor of a large room; I have no idea how long the scroll was. Imagine trying to study from such a Bible! the only practical way to use it was to keep it rolled on rollers, in a synagogue, and to work consecutively through it, in the manner in which some churches today have a lectionary with lessons from the Gospel and the Epistle. The student of the Scripture, since he would have access to the word of God only in the *Bêth ha-Sēpher,* committed large portions to memory, and when he wished to discuss a given matter, he would string together passages that were relevant. Even so Mary must have stored Scripture in her memory, for the *Magnificat* is composed entirely of parts of the Bible. The word she had indeed kept in her heart, and when the time came that she burst into a paean of praise, it came out spontaneously in the words of Holy Scripture.

There was no immorality in Mary. There was nothing that would make questionable the Saviour's birth. This is necessarily implied by God's choice of her. And yet there would be shame. When Mary asked the angel, "How can this be, since I have no husband?" (Luke 1:34), it was not, in my opinion, a question of doubt. Rather, the question was asked in a sense of awe—and perhaps in the back of Mary's mind there was also the question, "What will I tell people, since I have no husband?" Soon she must have asked herself, "What will I tell Joseph, the man I love, the man I am engaged to, the man I am planning to marry? What will I tell him when he learns that I am going to have a child, and he is not the father?" There would be shame. But Mary was brave enough to endure the shame and reproach, for her conscience was clear. And so she gave her consent: "Let it be to me according to your word" (Luke 1:38). Some call her the Mother of God;[1] she calls herself the handmaid of the Lord.

Mary and Joseph The picture of Mary and Joseph is not given to us in so many words in the Bible. Rather, we have to put it together from the first two chapters of Matthew and the first two chapters of Luke, and then we have to let our sanctified imagination think about some of the things that must have happened in the relationship between Joseph and Mary which the Holy Spirit has not seen fit to record.

We do not know much about Joseph. We do not know his mother's name, and in view of the problem of the two genealogies, we are not even sure of his father's name. There is a tradition that he was much older than Mary—but I am not sure that there is sufficient reason for accepting that tradition. For one thing, it seems to be part of the effort to support the concept of the perpetual virginity of Mary. According to this view, Mary never had any normal marital relations with Joseph, never had any other children besides the virgin-born Jesus. This would involve, of course, an equally unnatural celibate life for Joseph. But if Joseph had been previously married, if he had already raised a family, and if he had married Mary, at God's bidding, only in order that the child to be born would have a legal name and an honorable home, then, it is suggested, the concept of Mary's perpetual virginity does not involve Joseph. In effect, Joseph would look upon the girl Mary as a daughter rather than as a wife. In my estimation, this is an unworthy line of reasoning that belittles the Biblical view of marriage contrary to the explicit teaching of the Apostle (I Corinthians 7:2-5) and elevates the concept of virginity contrary to the Hebrew ideal of womanhood blessed in childbearing. A second reason for thinking that Joseph was an old man is suggested by the implication that he died between Jesus' twelfth and thirtieth year.[2] But even so, this does not prove that Joseph was an old man. If Joseph had been twenty-five when he married Mary, and died when Jesus

---

[1] The term "Mother of God" (*theotókos*), although used earlier, was not adopted by the Church until the Council of Chalcedon in A.D. 451. The Council of Ephesus in 431 condemned Nestorius, largely for his opposition to the use of the term.

[2] Since he is never mentioned after the visit to Jerusalem.

was fifteen (these figures are only for the sake of example), that would have made him forty—and certainly there is nothing unreasonable in that figure. I see no valid reason to accept the tradition that Joseph was an old man when he married Mary.

Was he previously married? This question has been raised as part of the problem of "the brothers and sisters" of Jesus. In Matthew 13:55-56 (and also in other passages), the brothers and sisters of Jesus are mentioned. The simplest interpretation of the expression is the natural one: they were children of Joseph and Mary, born after the birth of Jesus. This seems to be the earliest interpretation in Christian literature. But with the development of the idea of the perpetual virginity of Mary, other explanations were put forth. According to Epiphanius of Salamis (died A.D. 403), the brothers and sisters were the children of Joseph by a former marriage. According to Jerome (c. 340-420), they were the children of Mary's sister, also named Mary, the wife of Clopas. Helvidius, who was a contemporary of Jerome, defended the natural interpretation, which was opposed by Jerome.[3] Once again I feel that the attempt to escape the clear meaning of Scripture (including the use of "until" in Matthew 1:25, as well as the expression "brothers and sisters") is based on an unworthy view of marriage, an unholy view of the conjugal relationship, and an unscriptural doctrine of the perpetual virginity of Mary.[4]

Joseph, we know, was a carpenter, for Jesus was known as "the carpenter's son" (Matthew 13:55). By the offering for Mary's purification, we know that Joseph was poor (Luke 2:24; cf. Leviticus 12:8), hence he knew what it was to work with his hands, to work for low income, and, later, to have the responsibilities of a large family.

[3] The three positions are usually identified by the names of these three protagonists: Epiphanian, Hieronymian, and Helvidian. It should be added that this is not a difference strictly following Protestant and Roman Catholic lines, for a number of Protestant scholars defend the Epiphanian view. For full discussions, see article, "Brethren of the Lord," in Hastings' *Dictionary of Christ and the Gospels* (New York: Charles Scribner's Sons, 1924), vol. 1, pp. 232-237; and J. B. Lightfoot, *Saint Paul's Epistle to the Galatians* (rev. ed.; London: Macmillan and Co., 1881), pp. 252-291.
[4] In the *Catholic Commentary on Holy Scripture* (New York: Thomas Nelson & Sons, 1953), the Roman Catholic position is presented clearly and concisely, together with representative bibliography, §§ 672-673. The tendentious nature of the position is revealed in the closing statement, "Such an explanation [Jerome's] is the only one which safeguards both the dogma of the perpetual virginity of our Lady and the tradition of the Church as to the perpetual virginity of St. Joseph" (§ 673e).

Somewhere along life's way he had become engaged to Mary. We must be careful not to read back into the account our western customs of courtship—and yet we must avoid the other extreme of picturing the match as an Oriental transaction between the parents.[5] The young couple probably rarely had more than a passing glimpse of one another; they almost certainly were never together alone. They had no opportunity to plan together and dream together, as we think is necessary. And yet true love did develop—perhaps it was truer than the romantic type we have come to know. Then it happened! The angel told Mary that she was going to have a child by the Holy Spirit. She probably stayed around Nazareth a while, and then, before people would suspect and set their busy little tongues to wagging, she went to visit her cousin Elizabeth.

I suppose that she had not told Joseph what had happened. But when the time drew near for Elizabeth to have her baby, it was necessary for Mary to return home. According to Luke 1:56, Mary was by that time three months pregnant, and was beginning to show, or soon would, that she was with child. And she would have to see Joseph! I think it was at that point that the annunciation to Joseph took place. Read it carefully: "When his mother Mary had been betrothed to Joseph, before they came together she was found to be with child of the Holy Spirit; and her husband Joseph, being a just man and unwilling to put her to shame, resolved to divorce her quietly" (Matthew 1:18-19). Engagement, according to Jewish law and custom, was tantamount to marriage, and could only be broken by giving a bill of divorcement. "But as he considered this, behold, an angel of the Lord appeared to him in a dream, saying, 'Joseph, son of David, do not fear to take Mary your wife, for that which is conceived in her is of the Holy Spirit; she will bear a son, and you shall call his name Jesus, for he will save his people from their sins'" (Matthew 1:20-21).

[5] The thoughtful reading of David and Vera Mace, *Marriage: East and West* (Garden City, N. Y.: Doubleday and Co., 1960; 359 pp.), will help us to see that there is much of real value in the customs of the East. On the other hand, the Talmud makes it clear that a couple could not be married without the girl's consent (*Kiddushim*, 2a), nor was marriage permitted between fiancés who had never seen each other (*Kiddushim*, 41a); the same source provided for the possibility that the man could make his own arrangements for marriage; it did not have to be contracted for by the parents.

Joseph woke from his sleep, and proceeded at once to take Mary into his home as his wife—note the important words—"but knew her not until she had borne a son" (Matthew 1:25).

Mary and Jesus. So Mary gave birth to a little boy. Her body had been the tabernacle for His in the fetal stage, and her tender mother's care provided His nourishment and protection when He came into the world. She was His mother. She probably taught Him the first prayers, kissed away the tears, bandaged the bumps and bruises. The record clearly shows that she did an excellent job in bringing up Jesus. Joseph, no doubt, made his contribution, too. But the earliest years are mother's years.

There was another side, however, a side that Mary would find hard to understand. The *Nunc Dimittis* of Simeon included the enigmatic words, "a sword will pierce through your own soul also" (Luke 2:35). We usually refer this to the time of the crucifixion. But I think that sword began to pierce Mary's soul long before Jesus' death.

There was the time, for example, when Jesus was twelve and the family had gone to Jerusalem. By that time there were other children in the family,[6] and Mary and Joseph had their hands full of responsibility. They probably traveled in caravan, the men and older boys in one part, the women and children in another. And on their way home, when they halted for the first night's rest, probably at some caravanserai, it was discovered that Jesus was not with them. So they turned back to Jerusalem, where they found Jesus three days later, in the Temple, in the midst of the doctors of the Law. Mary said to Him, "Son, why have you treated us so? Behold, your father and I have been looking for you anxiously" (Luke 2:48). There is a trace of anxiety in the words, and perhaps a trace of rebuke. Mary seems to imply, "You know that we had to look out for the younger children; you are old enough to take care of yourself. You should have stayed with us, and not forced us to come back to look for you."

Jesus answered, "How is it that you sought me? Did you not know that I must be in my Father's house [or, about my Father's business]?" Did Mary understand those words? Put yourself in her place. Twelve years and more ago, the angel had told her something of the mystery of the child to be born. But during those twelve years, unless we be-

---

[6] Regardless of the interpretation of "brothers and sisters of Jesus," all agree that there were other children in the home.

lieve the fantastic accounts in the apocryphal gospels, He had been just like any other child. There had been no indication that He was different. Now, suddenly to say, "I must be about My Father's business" —what did He mean? Did a sword stab Mary's heart as she thought, "Joseph is not His father; God is"?

One day, not long after Jesus had begun His ministry, some eighteen years later, Jesus and His first disciples came from Jerusalem to Cana of Galilee, and there was a wedding there. Jesus was invited, and His mother was there. Perhaps they were related to the family, for Mary seemed burdened about details that would hardly concern a guest. Suddenly, Mary reported to Jesus, "They have no wine" (John 2:3). That is a beautiful touch! Let your mind play over it a moment. Jesus was a guest: what business was it of His? Yet, Mary felt that her Son would share her feelings and the feelings of the host, for the refreshments had run out and the party was not yet over.

Jesus said to her, "Woman, what have you to do with me?" (John 2:4). That was a harsh word. And the harshness is not in the word "woman," for in the Near East that can be used as a term of proper address. It is in the words that follow that Mary must have felt the sword's piercing thrust. The words that Jesus used were very likely *mâ lî w^elēk*—"What [is there] to me and to you," or "What do we have in common?" It is the kind of question that you put to a person when you want to say, "This is my business and that is your business."

As I sense the implication—and the expression is quite commonly used—it carries a mild rebuke. It is as though Jesus were saying, "For thirty years, now, I have been your son, and an obedient one. But now there is a gulf between us. Now that I have started My ministry, the accomplishment of My Father's business, it is time that you learn your place and My place." Jesus, of course, did not enlarge upon the statement, as I have done. His mother would have understood, without this. Then He went ahead and did what she wanted Him to do, quietly, without drawing attention to Himself (John 2:5-10). But the schism was developing none the less.

Then one day, a few years later, when Jesus began to run into opposition, Mary started to worry about Him. She was afraid for His welfare, and she and His brothers sought to take Him away from the endless crowds (cf. Mark 3:21,31). Word was passed to Jesus, "Your mother and your brothers are outside, asking for you." And Jesus said, "Who are my mother and my brothers?" Then, looking at those who sat at His feet, listening to His teachings, He said, "Here are my mother and my brothers! Whoever does the will of God is my brother, and sister, and mother" (Mark 3:33-35).

Now look at one more scene. Jesus was on the cross, and a heart-broken woman was standing at the foot. It was her firstborn son hanging there. Among the last thoughts that Jesus had in His dying hours was one for His mother. When Jesus saw His mother standing along-side her sister and her sister's son John—the disciple whom Jesus loved —Jesus said, "Woman, behold your son!" and to the disciple He said, "Behold your mother!" (John 19:26-27).

Why did Jesus do that? Could it be that He was already looking forward to the time when a great multitude from every nation and race would be standing around the throne; when severed friendships would be eternally rejoined? Mary will be there—but what will be her relation to the Lamb? Was Jesus already thinking of that moment, when He said, "Woman, John is your son, now, and you are his mother"?

Some say that Mary is closer to Jesus than anyone else, therefore ask her to get Him to help you. Jesus says, "He that does the will of God is my brother, and sister, and mother." Jesus Christ, the Son of God, will have no earthly ties in heaven. There will be no special in-terests and no pressure groups. A woman, looking at Jesus one day on the road, thinking, I am sure, how wonderful it would be to have a Son like that, said, "Blessed is the womb that bore you, and the breasts that you sucked!" Jesus said, "Blessed rather are those who hear the word of God and keep it!" (Luke 11:27-28).

Mary and the Church. Mary was at the foot of the cross when Jesus was crucified. She needed a Saviour. To talk about the immaculate conception of Mary, to say that she had no sin, is unscriptural. The idea was built logically upon a false view of sin that says, if sin is in-herited, and Jesus was without sin, then His mother must also have been without sin. No, Mary was a sinner, too, and faced the same sinful temptations in life as any of us. She needed a Saviour. Christ died for her sins.

Mary was in the Upper Room, with the Eleven, and Jesus' brothers, and the women who had attended Jesus in His earthly needs (Acts 1:14). They were waiting for the Holy Spirit. Mary needed the gift of the Holy Spirit, just as we all do. She was no more divine, and no less human, than the six score on whom the Spirit came at Pentecost. What happened to her after that we are not told, except that she lived in the house of John the son of Zebedee. Did she move to Ephesus with him, when he went there years later? According to one tradition, she did, and died there; according to another, her death occurred at Jerusalem.[7]

Mary will be in Heaven, but not as Queen of Heaven, and not as Mother of God. She will be there as a ransomed sinner saved, not by the blood of the child she bore, but by the blood of the infinite One, as a member of the Church which God purchased with His own blood (Acts 20:28).[8] When we cast our crowns around the throne and sing our praises to the Lamb, Mary, too, will hail Him as King of kings and Lord of lords. When He takes His power and reigns, she will reign with Him—but as a member of the Church which will be His glorious bride.

Hail, Mary, favored of God and happiest of women! But she has deserved better than she has gotten from the Church. For she is a woman, not a goddess; redeemed, not redemptrix—for there is only one Mediator between God and men, the man Christ Jesus (I Timothy 2:5)—the woman chosen by God in the fullness of time to be the mother of His son.

[7] These are, as a matter of fact, competing traditions at present in the Roman Catholic Church. At Ephesus I found a strong feeling in support of the Ephesus tradition. The "Assumption of Mary," the most recent dogma of the Roman Church (officially promulgated November 1, 1950), is the belief that after her death, Mary's body was taken up to heaven, where she was crowned as Queen of Heaven. It is admitted in Catholic writings that "there is no reference in Scripture to either of these events," but that they are logically inferred from the Immaculate Conception, which in turn is inferred from the Motherhood of God, which also is without scriptural foundation. See *A Catholic Commentary on Holy Scripture,* § 86e.

[8] "God" certainly has better manuscript authority in this verse than "the Lord," and greater intrinsic probability (*lectio difficilior!*).

CHAPTER IV

Jesus the Son of Man

THE CHRISTIAN CHURCH has always been faced with the problem of the nature of Jesus Christ: is He God, or is He man—or is He perhaps something other? The Church has fully debated the subject, and has given a clear answer. The answer sets forth four main points: (1) He is truly God; (2) He is truly man; (3) these two natures are not separate, but are truly one Person; (4) yet these two natures are not merged into one, but remain without confusion.[1] The Church has made it perfectly clear that He was not a man who became God, but God who became man without losing deity. He was in the beginning with God and was God, and then, at what human beings would call a "point in history," He laid aside the glory which He had with God the Father, and became fashioned as a man (cf. John 1:1-4,14; Philippians 2:5-8). Yet these two natures are so perfectly united in one person that it is impossible to say, now He is human and now He is divine; it is impossible to say, for example, that as God He walked on the sea, and as man He fell asleep.

Sometimes the Church has stressed one of these natures, and sometimes the other. It largely depends on the trend of thinking of the times. We are living in a day when the emphasis is on humanism, with a corresponding stress on the humanity of Jesus. Hence the Church, particularly that part which feels called upon to defend the historic faith, has reacted by stressing the divine nature of Jesus.

This is as it should be. But sometimes when we stress the one, we do it at the expense of the other. And in those churches today where the deity of Christ is being defended so very zealously—as it should be!

---

[1] Historically, the problem unfolded a step at a time. The "Arian" heresy, expressed by Arius (A.D. c.265-336), denying the true deity of Christ, was condemned by the Council of Nicea in 325. The "Apollinarian" heresy (Apollinaris, 310-390), denying the true humanity, was condemned by the Council of Constantinople in 381. The "Nestorian" heresy (Nestorius, died 451), asserting that the two natures were distinct, was condemned by the Council of Ephesus in 431. The "Eutychian" heresy (Eutyches, first half of fifth century), asserting

—we sometimes forget that Jesus was also a man, a man like ourselves. This results in a serious loss. God could have come to earth as God, but for our sakes He came as man. He took upon Himself our likeness in order that we might have some benefit from the incarnation, and that benefit is lost if we think of Jesus only as the Son of God.

One of Jesus' favorite names for Himself was "Son of man." What did it mean? There was an apocalyptic movement in the Jewish world when Jesus came into the world, and the title "Son of man" was used in the literature of that movement. The "Son of man" was to come from heaven and take over the rule of this world. But what did Jesus mean by the term? It is obvious, as H. H. Rowley has pointed out,[2] that the term could not have been synonymous with "Messiah" in the popular mind, for in that case it would have been meaningless for Jesus to charge His disciples to tell no one that He was the Christ (Mark 8:30) when He was constantly using the term "Son of man" of Himself. The term "Son of man," was also a common expression meaning simply "human being." Jesus certainly used the term in that sense. He also, beyond any doubt, used the term in a messianic sense. In fact, I am convinced that it was Jesus' use of the expression, "Son of man," that has given it its fullness of meaning. But when the words first fell from His lips, they probably conveyed little more than the use of the first personal pronoun would have done.[3]

The human beginnings of Jesus. The birth of Jesus occurred in an unusual way. According to independent testimony,[4] both Joseph and Mary were disturbed by the annunciations of the birth, for, as both records state clearly, there had been no union between them (Matthew 1:18 and Luke 1:34). By the Holy Spirit, Jesus was conceived in the womb of an intact virgin, hence we say He was "born of the virgin

---

that the two natures became one, was condemned, along with the Nestorian, by the Council of Chalcedon in 451. Cf. W. G. T. Shedd, *A History of Christian Doctrine* (3d edition; New York: Charles Scribner's Sons, 1883), vol. 1, pp. 392-408; Ronald S. Wallace, article, "Christology" in *Baker's Dictionary of Theology,* pp. 120-121.

[2] In *The Relevance of Apocalyptic* (2d edition; London: Lutterworth Press, 1952), pp. 30-31.

[3] Whether the first use of "Son of man" was in Mark 2:10 or John 1:51 makes little difference; we could substitute "I" or "me" respectively without changing the meaning.

[4] The first chapters of Matthew and Luke cannot be assigned to "Q" for they are entirely different accounts.

Mary." This is the historic faith of the Church;[5] I wholeheartedly subscribe to it and defend it vigorously.

But when we have said that, let us remember that Jesus was born just as any other child. Once He was conceived in Mary's womb, the processes were the normal life processes. Mary carried the child as all mothers do. When the time came, she gave birth to the child as all mothers do.

Jesus was born in Bethlehem,[6] due to a census or poll tax that required Joseph to appear in his ancestral town. We do not know the year, and we do not know the day.[7] Yet the event was of sufficient importance that a star appeared, leading Wise Men from the East to worship the child-King (Matthew 2:1-2), and a king became so agitated that he caused the massacre of baby boys in Bethlehem (Matthew 2:16). The event one day changed the calendars of the world to read "Before Christ" and "In the Year of Our Lord."

Jesus grew up in Nazareth in Galilee. There were other children in the home. Four brothers are named: James, Joseph, Simon, and Judas; and there were also sisters (at least two; some think "all" means at least three—cf. Matthew 13:55-56). He lived a normal childhood; there is no place for the fantastic accounts we find in the apocryphal gospels. There we read that the boy Jesus made clay birds, then caused them to fly away; He stretched boards to the right length for Joseph; He carried water from the well in His cloak when He broke a pitcher; He made a salted fish come back to life. Even worse, we read that He cursed one teacher, ridiculed another, and struck dead a boy who accidentally bumped Him, until the parents of the city begged Joseph, "Take away that Jesus of yours from this place."[8] Such stories are fantastic! The Church, Protestant and Catholic alike, has repudiated

[5] Cf. J. G. Machen, The Virgin Birth of Christ (New York: Harper & Brothers, 1930), 415 pp.

[6] Cf. W. M. Ramsay, Was Christ Born at Bethlehem? (2d edition; London: Hodder and Stoughton, 1898), 280 pp.

[7] Dionysius Exiguus (died c.550) established the present calendar "Anno Domini," calculating the birth to have occurred in the year 754 A.U.C. (from the founding of the City of Rome). We now know that Herod died shortly after an eclipse of the moon which occurred March 12-13, 750 A.U.C., and Jesus was born prior to that, perhaps 748 or 749 A.U.C.—6 or 5 B.C. The birthday was set at December 25 in the fourth century, without historical basis.

[8] In the Gospel of Thomas (to be distinguished from the recent Coptic find at Nag Hamadi), The Ante-Nicene Fathers, A. Roberts and J. Donaldson, editors (Grand Rapids, Mich.: Wm. B. Eerdmans Publishing Co., reprinted 1951), vol. 8, pp. 395-404

them.[9] There is no place for them historically or psychologically. When the time came for Jesus to take up His ministry, there is not the slightest indication that His fellow townspeople were either offended by His prior life or prepared for His miracles. They were simply amazed. "Where did this man get this wisdom and these mighty works? Is not this the carpenter's son?" (Matthew 13:54-55).

It was a poor home. Sometimes I get the feeling that incidental details in Jesus' teaching came from watching His mother. "Why don't you sew a new patch on that?" "Why don't you put the new wine in those old wineskins?" "Why are you sweeping the corners of the room so carefully?" "Why do you use only such a little bit of leaven?"

There would come a time when He would learn to read. Perhaps He was sent to the synagogue school.[10] He doubtless learned Aramaic, the common tongue, and Hebrew, the holy tongue; and, living in Galilee of the Gentiles, He probably learned some common expressions in Greek.

He loved the world of nature. He observed the birds, the flowers, the sower and his seed, the fisherman and his net, the clouds and storms, the stifling, blasting wind from the desert.

There was a saying, "Who does not teach his son a trade teaches him to steal." Joseph taught Jesus the carpenter's trade. He learned to work with His hands and arms until, I am sure, His hands were calloused and His arms were muscular. These paintings hanging in the museums of the world that make Jesus look like an emaciated weakling do not give the true picture! He could tramp the hills of Palestine with rugged men and keep up with the best of them.

He knew the Scriptures. He knew how to pray. He took part in the religious festivals, and it was His custom to attend synagogue on the Sabbath. When He visited Jerusalem in His twelfth year, perhaps for the *bar mitzvah* ceremony when He would take His place as a man in Israel, He amazed the doctors of the Law with His understanding and His answers. And He did not get those answers by being the Son of God! He got them by studying, just as you and I have to study. Then He went back to Nazareth with His parents "and he was obedient to them."

---

[9] Nevertheless they do hang on, in superstition, in ecclesiastical art, and often in anti-Christian writings.

[10] Elementary schools were started in Jerusalem by Rabbi Shim'on ben Shetach, c.75 B.C., but whether they had extended to Galilee by Jesus' day is not definitely known.

We know little of the eighteen years that follow, the "hidden years." We know that Jesus worked in the carpenter shop. It is quite probable that Joseph died, and that Jesus became the breadwinner of the family. We can be certain that He lived a perfectly normal life, from the reaction of the people; we can also be certain that He lived a perfectly pure life, from the reaction of God who said, "This is my beloved Son, with whom I am well pleased" (Matthew 3:17).

The beginnings of Jesus' ministry. One day, when John the Baptist had been baptizing for possibly six months, and the people were stirred to excitement by him, Jesus went from Galilee to the Jordan to be baptized by John. When John saw Jesus, he protested, "I need to be baptized by you, and do you come to me?" (Matthew 3:14). Did John know Jesus? John says, "I myself did not know him" (John 1:31). What was it then that made John protest? I think it was the clean appearance of One who had never sinned. At any rate, Jesus said, "Let it be so now; for thus it is fitting for us to fulfil all righteousness" (Matthew 3:15). I do not believe that Jesus was baptized in repentance for His own sins, for He had none; I believe He was baptized because He wanted to take His place with you and me. There was to be nothing to separate Him from the people He came to save.[11]

Following the baptism, John testified that he saw a dove descending upon Jesus, the sign that this was indeed the One for whom John was to prepare the way (cf. John 1:32-34).

Immediately, Jesus was driven into the wilderness to be tempted by the devil (cf. Luke 4:1-13). This deserves a study by itself; all we can do here is emphasize the fact that when Jesus was tempted, He was tempted as man; He faced both the subtle and the bold attacks of the Tempter in exactly the same way that you and I must face them. We get our ideas of sin hopelessly confused at times. We stress the fact that it is inherited, and we forget the fact that the greatest sin comes from our own hearts, our own wills. The great battleground of sin is in the human will. It is not the *temptation* that is sin, but what we will to do under temptation. It is not even the *deed,* but what we *will* to do. We may for one reason or another restrain the action; but the very fact that *we would like to do it* is sin. (Read carefully Matthew 5:21-

---

[11] On this, and on the temptations, see particularly G. Campbell Morgan, *The Crises of the Christ* (New York: Fleming H. Revell Company, 1903), pp. 107-210.

30.) When Jesus met the Tempter, He met him in the same freedom of will that you and I have as human beings. Moreover, Jesus faced the temptations under the worst possible conditions: in the wilderness, and alone.

I do not believe that Jesus' temptations ended at that time. Rather, I believe that He constantly faced temptation, for He "in every respect has been tempted as we are, yet without sinning" (Hebrews 4:15). On the last night of His earthly life, in the garden of Gethsemane, when He knew that He must drain the cup of death to its bitter dregs, He prayed in great agony, "My Father, if it be possible, let this cup pass from me" (Matthew 26:39). Not once, but three times He prayed this prayer. And every time He countered it with the prayer, "Nevertheless, not as I will, but as thou wilt." This was, in my opinion, the greatest temptation He ever faced: the temptation to save Himself. But He knew that if He saved Himself, He could never save others.

Jesus and His disciples. Somewhere I heard a saying, that if you would know a man, eat with him and sleep with him. Jesus ate and slept with His disciples. There are many teachers who get up in the morning, wash and put on their better clothes, go into the classroom or lecture hall and deliver their best lecture, and then go back home. Their students may never know how they live.

But Jesus did not teach that way. He did not get His disciples together for an hour or two a day in a lecture hall. He lived with them. They saw Him under all conditions: when He was hungry, passing through a field of grain; when He was tired, stretched out in the boat. They saw Him when religious officialdom prodded Him with sticky questions; they saw Him when a sinful woman washed His feet with tears of devotion because her sins had been forgiven. They saw Him bless little children; they saw Him drive money changers out of the Temple. They saw Him under every possible condition that could occur for about a year or more. Then one day Jesus said to them, "Who do you say that I am?" Peter spoke up, "You are the Christ, the Son of the living God" (Matthew 16:15-16). No man who has lived with me for a year is going to say anything like that about me—and I don't believe they will say it about you. But they said it about Jesus.

Jesus taught His disciples. Wonderful teachings! He used simple language, and drew upon familiar things for illustrations, and yet His teachings are so inexhaustible that men are still writing books about them, trying to get at the root of what Jesus taught. The subjects are of primary importance. Jesus is talking about God, about man, about sin and salvation, about righteousness and justice, about love and forgiveness. He is talking about the great central truths of life, the foundational matters on which all human relationships are built.[12] These are the things we need to know if we are to live together successfully in this world; and these are the things we must know if we are going to live with God in the world to come.

Comparisons are odious. I have had to study the scriptures of many other religions. It is impossible to get any real meaning out of the Bhagavad Gita unless some Hindu mystic explains it. When I studied the Qurân, my Arabic teacher assured me that it was impossible to understand it except in Arabic, and then only if you were an Arab. Even the apocryphal gospels of the Early Church present teachings, supposedly from Jesus, that are inconsequential. But when I read the Gospels, regardless of whether it is in Greek or in translation (and even the Greek is a translation of Jesus' original words), I know what Jesus is saying, and I know that it is significant. Little wonder that, when they listened to Him, they were astonished, "for he taught them as one who had authority, and not as their scribes" (Matthew 7:29). Little wonder that they said, "No man ever spoke like this man!" (John 7:46).

Jesus and His Father. Have you ever thought about Jesus and His Father? You probably have discussed the relationship between the First and Second Persons of the Trinity, but have you ever thought about the relationship between Jesus as a human being and His heavenly Father? In Philippians, Paul presents a subject that has evoked much discussion: theologians call it "kenosis." Speaking of Christ Paul says: "who, though he was in the form of God, did not count equality with God a thing to be grasped, but emptied himself, taking the form of a servant, being born in the likeness of men. And being found in human form he humbled himself and became obedient unto death, even death on a cross" (Philippians 2:6-8). This "emptying" is the kenosis. I do not pretend to know all that it means, but I am sure that it means at least this: while Jesus was in human

[12] One of the greatest books on this subject, in my opinion, is G. Campbell Morgan, *The Teaching of Christ* (New York: Fleming H. Revell Company, 1913), 333 pp. But, much as I value this book, having worked through it countless times, I feel it falls far short of exhausting the subject.

form He had the same relationship with God that you and I have as human beings.[13]

How did Jesus get along with God on this basis? It stands out clearly in the Scripture record: He pleased God. At the time of the baptism, that is, after about thirty years of life, He heard God say, "Thou art my beloved Son; with thee I am well pleased" (Mark 1:11). On the Mount of Transfiguration, when the public ministry of Jesus was all but over and He was about to set His face to go to Jerusalem, God declared again, "This is my beloved Son, with whom I am well pleased" (Matthew 17:5). Jesus could look His fellow men in the eyes and say, "which of you convicts me of sin?" (John 8:46), and He could stand before God and say unashamed and unafraid, "I always do what is pleasing to him" (John 8:29). He could pray, "Thy will be done," knowing that He would be happy with that will; when some of us pray "Thy will be done," I think we keep our fingers crossed!

On the last night of His earthly life, knowing that the next few hours would bring His death, He could say to God, "I glorified thee on earth, having accomplished the work which thou gavest me to do. . . . I have manifested thy name to the men whom thou gavest me. . . . I kept them in thy name. . . . I have given them thy word" (John 17:4, 6, 12, 14). He could look into His Father's face as He hung on the cross and say, "It is finished. . . . into thy hands I commit my spirit" (John 19:30; Luke 23:46).

This is how Jesus got along with God His Father. Do you want proof? Here it is: God raised Him from the dead. God has not raised anyone else from the dead.[14] But God, by the resurrection of Jesus Christ from the dead, said in effect, "This One does not deserve to die!" Therefore, Paul says, Jesus was "designated Son of God in power"—or it might be translated, "marked out as" or "declared to be the Son of God in power"—"by his resurrection from the dead" (Romans 1:4).[15]

---

[13] I did not say that He had *only* the same relationship. The mystery of His two natures, even though it may lie beyond our comprehension, enters at every point in His life.

[14] There have been other "resurrections," in which men and women, boys and girls, have been restored to this life, as recorded in the Scriptures. But none of them knew the resurrection by which they passed beyond death into the life of the world to come.

[15] The word *horisthéntos* has been variously translated, and is discussed extensively in commentaries on Romans. One thing it clearly can *not* mean is that

There is another nature about which we have said practically nothing: the divine nature of Jesus. Yet that was also manifest during His earthly life and ministry. We have not mentioned His knowledge of the innermost thoughts of men, nor His power to work miracles. These things were not used by Jesus to call attention to Himself, but only in the service of His fellow men. We have said far too little about His redemptive work, His substitutionary death, His resurrection and ascension, and His sending of the Holy Spirit. But these cardinal truths are so woven into the lives of the men and women yet to be considered, that we shall not ignore them. We have not mentioned the great purifying hope of the Church, the Return of Jesus Christ; that remains for another study.

We have confined our study to Jesus the man. He is the perfect man, the Adam who did not fall. He is the living proof that God's will is not impossible. If, in the judgment, Adam wants to stand up and say to his Creator, "You gave me something that could not possibly be done!" God can point to His Son who emptied Himself of His glory and took upon Himself Adam's likeness, who was tempted in all points as Adam was, without sinning, and God can say with finality, "He did it!"

But someone says, "I am not Adam; I inherited from Adam a fallen nature. I can't please God." Are you going to hide behind that excuse? God sent Jesus Christ into the world in order that we might hide behind Him and not behind Adam. In Christ that old man is crucified; you are a new man in Christ. No longer is Adam your example; now your example is Christ, that you should walk as He walked.[16]

But He is not a heartless and cold example, ready to destroy us if we fall. He is our help and encouragement. "Because he himself has suffered and been tempted, he is able to help those who are tempted" (Hebrews 2:18). He is not "a high priest who is unable to sympathize with our weaknesses, but one who in every respect has been tempted as we are, yet without sinning. Let us then with confidence draw near to the throne of grace, that we may receive mercy and find grace to help in time of need" (Hebrews 4:15-16).

Jesus *became* the Son of God by the resurrection; He *was eternally* the Son of God, but the great public declaration of the fact was accomplished by the resurrection.

[16] See I John 2:6; Ephesians 4:1; I Peter 2:21; Galatians 5:1; John 13:15—to which could be added many others.

CHAPTER V

Andrew the First Disciple

IN A SERIES on the Great Personalities of the New Testament, what shall we do about the twelve apostles? In one sense, all of them are great—great enough to have been chosen by Jesus. On the other hand, we know very little about several of them, and if we were to expand that in each case by what we know of the entire group, it would be repetitious. A few stand out with clear distinction: Peter, of course, and James and John. Is there one we can select to serve as a representative of the others? I think there is, and I have chosen Andrew for that place. Let me tell you why.

Andrew the disciple. How did Jesus begin His ministry? If you use the Gospel of Mark as a starting point (which is often used as a chronological basis for studying all the Gospels), you may get a mistaken idea that one day, when Jesus was walking along the Sea of Galilee, He saw two men fishing, and said, "Follow me and I will make you become fishers of men" (Mark 1:17), and that was it. Now tell me, would you give up your source of livelihood and follow a stranger? Neither would I. And I do not think Simon and Andrew did.

Most scholars today agree that it is impossible to harmonize the four Gospels (i.e. edit them so as to give one continuous and chronological account). Nevertheless I would like to try. You may not agree; but this is how I see it.

John the Baptist was baptizing, and the officials were sent to investigate his credentials. In the course of the conversation, John said, "Among you stands one whom you do not know, even he who comes after me" (John 1:26-27). The next day, he saw Jesus coming toward the group he was speaking to, and he said, "Behold, the Lamb of God, who takes away the sin of the world! This is he of whom I said, 'After me comes a man who ranks before me, for he was before me'" (John 1:29-30).

50

This was after the baptism of Jesus, as is clear from the verses that follow (31-34). And it was after the temptations; therefore at least forty days after the baptism. Meanwhile, John had continued his baptizing and preaching, and his disciples had continued to learn from him and to assist him. Hence it follows that they had had a chance to talk with John about this Figure who had come to be baptized, and on whom the dove descended.

The next day, John was talking with two of his disciples—I gather that the crowd was not present on this occasion—and seeing Jesus, John said, " 'Behold, the Lamb of God!' The two disciples heard him say this, and they followed Jesus . . ." (John 1:35-37). One of the two was Andrew; the other is not named, but the best solution to the problem is to recognize him as John the son of Zebedee.[1] The two went with Jesus and spent the rest of the day in His presence. Andrew went and found his brother Simon and brought him to Jesus (cf. John 1:39-42).

The following day, Jesus found Philip, who may have been another of the disciples of John the Baptist; and Philip found Nathanael, much as Andrew had found Simon. It is not incredible that John found his brother James. So, within a few days Jesus had gathered about Himself five or six of His first disciples.

But I do not think He began His ministry at that time. It seems that He waited until John the Baptist had finished his. According to John's Gospel, and it is corroborated by incidental details in the others, Jesus remained in the vicinity of John the Baptist, that is in Judea or in the region of the Jordan, but took no place of leadership. He must have engaged in some preaching (John records that Jesus Himself did not baptize, John 4:2), and it would seem that His following became increasingly larger. But the main effort, the start of the Galilean ministry, did not begin until Jesus had heard that John had been thrown into prison (Mark 1:14). It was then that Jesus declared, "The time is fulfilled, and the kingdom of God is at hand" (Mark 1:15).

How long was the interval between the identification of Jesus by John and the beginning of Jesus' ministry in Galilee? We cannot be

---

[1] One of the strongest arguments, it seems to me, is the fact that James and John, who in the other three Gospels are part of the "inner circle" (Peter, James, and John), are not mentioned in the first twenty chapters of John. This can only be satisfactorily explained as modesty on the part of the author.

sure, but it was probably not long. The traditional date of the baptism of Jesus is January 6. The forty days of temptation would bring us to the middle of February. According to John, a Passover occurred not long after the wedding in Cana (John 2:13), which would fall between the middle of March and the middle of April. The Galilean ministry of Jesus occurred soon after that. These dates are to some extent speculative—but they offer a reasonable approximation.

It is at this point that I would put the call of Andrew and Simon and a few minutes later the call of James and John, recorded in Mark 1:16-20. What about the call as recorded in Luke 5:1-11? Though many will disagree, I believe that occurred still later. In other words, as I reconstruct those days, soon after Jesus received word of the imprisonment of John the Baptist, He called His first disciples together. He had already gotten to know them, and they Him, in Judea several months earlier. But now He wanted them to enter into full-time discipleship. I believe they misunderstood His purpose and continued with their ordinary occupations. This made necessary the second call, recorded in Luke—and this accounts for Peter's reaction (Luke 5:8).

We have been using the word "disciples." Let us define our term before we go further. A *disciple* is one who comes under the discipline of another. The pupil is the disciple of the teacher; although this term is not generally used today when a pupil has several or many teachers. Jesus wanted these men around Him continuously, so He could teach them, by word and by deed. Only thus would they become His disciples.

Jesus had many disciples. Some of them, such as Andrew and the other who was unnamed, had been disciples of John the Baptist, and then had become disciples of Jesus. Others were added during the days of His ministry. Some became strongly attached to their teacher and His teachings. Others became impatient with His program, and turned away from Him (cf. John 6:66). Some of His disciples were trained by the method of learning-through-doing, as were the seventy disciples who were sent out two by two (Luke 10:1-20). So it is possible for us to speak of the twelve disciples, the seventy disciples, or the great multitude of disciples; it is possible to speak of active disciples and passive disciples; it is possible to speak of true disciples and false disciples.

Andrew was a disciple: he was under the discipline and instruction of Jesus. It is accurate to say that he was the first disciple, or at very least one of the first two disciples. He had been a disciple of John the Baptist and was turned to Jesus by John. He had been called into discipleship by the sea in Galilee. He was in the closest circle of discipleship, and remained a faithful disciple throughout the ministry of Jesus.

Andrew the apostle. The public ministry of Jesus can be divided into three main parts which can be characterized as follows: the proclamation of the Kingdom resulting in a wide following and then opposition; the organization and training followed by the separation of true and false disciples; the disclosure of the person of Christ.[2] It is impossible to attach definite dates to these periods, but it seems to me that it must have been at least several months, perhaps as much as a year, before the strong opposition to Jesus developed. If the baptism of Jesus is dated in the early part of A.D. 28, it was probably late in 28 or early in 29 when Jesus planned to meet the opposition by definite organization. The death of John the Baptist made it clear that death was the only probable outcome of Jesus' work, and there must be not merely disciples to carry on the work, but men organized under a program with a specific objective.[3]

So one night Jesus went into the hills to pray, and He prayed through the entire night. A serious decision had to be made and, humanly speaking, the fate of the world for all generations to come hinged upon the proper choice. The next day He called to Him His disciples, and out of the group He chose twelve. These He called "apostles" (Luke 6:12-13). The Twelve are named four times in the New Testament,[4] and while the order is not the same in these lists, it is remarkable that the grouping is the same. The first group contains the names Simon Peter, Andrew, James the son of Zebedee, and John. The second group contains the names of Philip, Bartholomew (usually identified with Nathanael), Matthew (usually identified with

[2] These correspond approximately to what have been called the First, Second, and Third Periods of the Galilean Ministry, respectively.

[3] This kind of expression may be objectionable to some who keep the deity of Christ prominent (see the preceding chapter). We must remember, however, that the entire ministry of Jesus, including His choice of Judas, comes within the mystery of His twofold nature. He acts, usually, as one who is not omniscient, but who must gather knowledge from experience.

[4] Matthew 10:2-4; Mark 3:16-19; Luke 6:14-16; Acts 1:13. Seven of the names appear in John, but no list.

Levi), and Thomas (also called Didymus, or the twin). The third group contains the names of James the son of Alphaeus, Simon (Zelotes, or the Canaanean), Judas ("not Iscariot"; or Thaddeus, also called Lebbeus), and Judas Iscariot (this name, of course, is omitted from the list in Acts). Not only are these three groups always the same, but the first name in each group (i.e., Simon Peter, Philip, and James the son of Alphaeus) is always the same.

We should notice the words, "he called his disciples, and chose from them twelve, whom he named apostles" (Luke 6:13). Some disciples were chosen to be apostles, and some were not. This is an important distinction. It was possible to be a disciple of Jesus without being an apostle; but it was not possible to be an apostle without being a disciple. A disciple, we have seen, is one who is taught by another. An apostle, as the word itself implies, is one who has been sent by another—but usually the word has a more specific meaning: one who is the officially delegated representative, one who has been sent on a specific mission in the name of the person or government who delegated him.

A few moments' reflection will show the logic and reason behind this move on the part of Jesus. He was sent into the world to represent the Kingdom of God; He was in turn sending into the world the Twelve who would represent the same Kingdom. They were to be the officially delegated representatives, the apostles, assigned to the task. They would receive their credentials in due time. But before they could even start on this work, they must be trained. And even before that, they must be carefully chosen. For that reason, Jesus gathered around Himself a large number of disciples. He trained them for several months. He observed them. He prayed about the matter. Then He chose twelve. The training would continue for at least another year.[5] They did not cease to be disciples, and indeed the expression, "the twelve disciples," is used in the Gospels. But once chosen, they were both disciples and apostles.

Mark makes clear the reason for the selection of the Twelve: "He appointed twelve, to be with him, and to be sent out to preach" (Mark 3:14). It seems that the Early Church understood this as a

---

[5] The length of the ministry of Jesus has been fully debated. I am convinced that at least two full years would have been necessary for the development of opposition, the training of the Twelve, and the other details recorded. This concurs with the view that finds three Passovers in the Gospel of John. I do not rule out the possibility of an additional year, but I do rule out the possibility of any less time.

principle for the apostolic office, for when they chose a successor to Judas, they first set forth the qualifications: "of the men who have accompanied us during all the time that the Lord Jesus went in and out among us, beginning from the baptism of John until the day when he was taken up from us" (Acts 1:21-22). Personal observation combined with discipleship was the first essential; to be based on this was the proclamation of what was seen and heard, or in the words of Acts, "one of these men must become with us a witness to his resurrection."

After appointing the Twelve, and ordaining them, Jesus delivered the "ordination sermon," which we know better as "The Sermon on the Mount" (Matthew, chapters 5 to 7).[6] As representatives of the Kingdom, they must know the ideals and principles of the Kingdom. John the Baptist came preaching, "The Kingdom of heaven is at hand." These men were to go out with this same proclamation, and men would certainly ask, "What is this Kingdom like? Is it like the other kingdoms of this world?" The Sermon on the Mount describes it.

Men say it will not work. Nor will it, while men believe that! Other men say they do not believe the rest of the Bible; they live by the Sermon on the Mount. Nonsense! They cannot live by the principles of the Kingdom and repudiate the King. When men truly accept the kingship of the Son of God, they will be able to live by His principles. If you say the Sermon on the Mount is idealistic and other-worldly, I thoroughly agree. Jesus Christ came into this world to bring ideals—heaven knows that this world needs ideals! And a Jesus Christ who is not other-worldly is not the Christ of the New Testament or the Christ of the historic Christian faith. He came into this world to bring heaven to earth, and ultimately to bring earth to heaven. The man who squirms under the teaching of the Sermon on the Mount sits in judgment on himself.

Jesus not only taught the Twelve;[7] He sent them out on a preaching mission (Matthew 10:5-33). That the details expressed in verses 9 and 10 were not intended to be applied literally throughout the age is clearly indicated in the words of Jesus Himself in Luke 22:35-36.

A beautiful summary of the apostolic office can be found woven

[6] Luke gives us the clue, in this case (cf. Luke 6:12-20); Matthew is obviously arranging his material logically and not chronologically.

[7] For a detailed study of this training, see A. B. Bruce, *The Training of the Twelve* (3d editon; New York: Richard R. Smith, Inc., 1930), 552 pp.

into the Lord's prayer in the seventeenth chapter of John: "I have manifested thy name to the men whom thou gavest me out of the world . . . I have given them the words which thou gavest me, and they have received them. . . . I have given them thy word; and the world has hated them because they are not of the world, even as I am not of the world. I do not pray that thou shouldst take them out of the world, but that thou shouldst keep them from the evil one. . . . As thou didst send me into the world, so I have sent them into the world. . . . I do not pray for these only, but also for those who are to believe in me through their word . . ." (John 17:6, 8, 14-15, 18, 20).

The full apostolic mission, however, was not to be accomplished until the death and resurrection of Jesus Christ had become historic reality. The specific testimony of the apostolic band was to be centered in the death and resurrection of Jesus Christ—not the cross alone, as so many stress, but the cross and the resurrection. A careful study of apostolic preaching in the Acts and Epistles will justify this statement. It is the "yea, rather" of Romans 8:34 (unfortunately lost in RSV).

Moreover, this completed apostolic proclamation of the crucified and risen Lord needed in addition the power of the Holy Spirit. For this the apostles were commanded to wait: "Then he opened their minds to understand the scriptures, and said to them, 'Thus it is written, that the Christ should suffer and on the third day rise from the dead, and that repentance and forgiveness of sins should be preached in his name to all nations, beginning from Jerusalem. You are witnesses of these things. And behold, I send the promise of my Father upon you; but stay in the city, until you are clothed with power from on high'" (Luke 24:45-49). And again: "To them he presented himself alive after his passion by many proofs, appearing to them during forty days, and speaking of the kingdom of God. And while staying with them he charged them not to depart from Jerusalem, but to wait for the promise of the Father . . . 'you shall be baptized with the Holy Spirit'" (Acts 1:3-5).

Andrew the missionary. The distinction between "apostle" and "missionary" as used here is the difference between theory and practice. My choice of words is probably not good; but I have been unable to do better. We have seen Andrew, as a representative of the Twelve, called and trained as a disciple, appointed and given the principles of the office as an apostle. Now we want to see how Andrew carried out his mission.

Perhaps that is not the picture you get when you hear the word "missionary." Perhaps you think of a strange person, rather out of touch with the modern world, who comes home once in seven years wearing clothes that are seven years out of style. Or perhaps you think of some idealistic do-gooder, or a meddling busybody poking into the affairs of people who would rather be left alone. Or you may have gotten a notion from some novel that missionaries are hypocrites who can sin unafraid in lands where sin is not so clearly labelled. (The novelist sins, too; he loves to wallow in indecency in his mind and to infect other minds the same way!) But have you ever thought of a missionary as simply a man or woman who is carrying out a mission?

Andrew had a mission; it was to tell people about the Lord Jesus Christ. And one of the reasons I have chosen Andrew for this study is simply because he was always finding someone and bringing him to Jesus.

The first day Andrew met Jesus, he had to tell somebody about Him. And the first person he thought of was his own brother. "One of the two who heard John speak, and followed him, was Andrew, Simon Peter's brother. He first found his brother Simon, and said to him, 'We have found the Messiah' (which means Christ). He brought him to Jesus" (John 1:40-42). There are several possible attitudes that a man can have toward his own brother. He can despise him; he can ignore him; he can want to help, but because of his approach, he offends his brother; he can have great influence over him. I can think of illustrations of each kind among men I have known, and you can, too. The most difficult relationship is the last mentioned: the man who has true love and ability to express that love in such a way as to influence his brother. Andrew was such a man. He was interested in his brother Simon. He thought first of Simon. He wanted to share his new blessing with Simon. That was good. But what a revelation it is of the relationship to read, "He brought him to Jesus"! I think it shows that they had a prior common interest in the religious faith and hope of their nation, that they had talked about this very subject on previous occasions. It is not easy to bring your brother to Christ under any conditions, but when there is no common basis of religious faith to start with, it becomes almost impossible.

I have often asked myself, What would have happened to the

Christian Church if Andrew had not brought Simon Peter to Jesus? Such a question is, of course, an improper question, and involves God's foreknowledge, will, and many other subjects. But just speaking from our human point of view, we would have to say that Peter was the key figure for the start of the Church, and without him, it is hard to see how the Church could have gotten started. But we do not have to answer the question, for Andrew carried out his mission and brought his brother to Jesus.

I wonder if Andrew also brought Philip to Jesus? It is pure speculation, I admit, but they were both from the same town (Bethsaida: John 1:44); they both had Greek names, whereas the rest of the apostles had Hebrew names; their names are often joined in the New Testament; and on two occasions Philip came to Andrew to get his help or advice on some problem. If Andrew did get Philip, then he was also responsible for Nathanael (John 1:45)—but that, I repeat, is speculation.

One day, at the height of Jesus' popularity, He was teaching by the sea and a large crowd had gathered. The wonderful words continued to flow, perhaps urged on by the eager assemblage, until the day was almost gone. Now, there had been no indication that the meeting would last so long, and the people were not prepared for such an eventuality. There was nothing for them to eat. Jesus asked Philip, "How are we to buy bread, so that these people may eat?" The author adds, parenthetically, that this was to test Philip (John 6:5-6). Philip saw the financial difficulties in the problem. Andrew, who must have been near enough to overhear the conversation, had a different approach. "There is a lad here who has five barley loaves and two fish; but what are they among so many?" (John 6:9). Obviously, Andrew did not see any solution to the problem, but he did see a personal angle: he brought the boy to Jesus, and we all know the wonderful way Jesus multiplied the boy's gift to take care of the entire crowd.

Some months later, in the last week of Jesus' ministry before His atoning sacrifice, the Twelve were with Jesus in Jerusalem. And in the throngs that were there to take part in the coming feast of the Passover were some Greeks, proselytes to Judaism from the Gentile world. They wished to have an opportunity to talk with Jesus, and they found Philip, whose name probably indicates that he was a Greek-speaking Jew. Once again, Philip took the matter to Andrew, and Andrew took Philip and the request to Jesus (John 12:20-22).

The author of the Gospel does not tell us the outcome; he has used the story to move into discussion of the "hour" that had come. We suppose that Jesus acceded to the request; we know that Andrew was busy trying to bring men to the Saviour.

In the calendar of the Church of England, Saint Andrew's Day, November 30, is the day on which it is customary to have a sermon on missions. George Milligan regards Andrew as the first home missionary, for bringing Peter to Jesus, and the first foreign missionary, for bringing the Greeks to Jesus.[8] Whether we agree with this terminology or not, I am sure we agree that in principle Andrew represents all missionaries, even as he represents the lesser known but equally important members of the apostolic band.

[8] Cf. "Andrew," in Hastings' *Dictionary of Christ and the Gospels,* vol. 1, p. 53.

CHAPTER VI

Lazarus, Mary, and Martha

WHAT HAPPENS WHEN Jesus comes into a home? Does He release the Christ-spirit that enables you to meet every difficulty with poise? Does He guarantee health and happiness and joy unbroken? Does He unveil the truth that sickness and death are only illusions? I hear things like this on the radio and read such statements in newspaper columns. Now I would like to take you inside a home where Jesus often visited; I want you to meet some people who loved Jesus and whom He loved: the family of Martha and Mary and Lazarus.

Perhaps you are wondering what Lazarus did that he should be included in the great personalities of the New Testament. Some men enjoy reflected greatness. It is not so much what they do, as it is what happens to them, that makes them great. Because of what happened in the home of Lazarus, particularly because of what happened to him, crowds came to see him and crowds came to see Jesus. Because of what happened, crowds thronged the way into Jerusalem on the day that has come to be known as Palm Sunday. Because of the sudden surge of popularity—and so near Jerusalem, too!—the rulers decided to put Jesus to death at once. Because of the embarrassing evidence that Lazarus himself had suddenly become, the rulers decided to put him to death likewise. In the light of these momentous events, who can gainsay a place of prominence, even greatness, for Lazarus?

The home of Lazarus. There were two sisters and a brother, and the Scripture lists them in the order: Martha, Mary, and Lazarus (John 11:5). This in itself is remarkable in a world where women are usually named last, if, indeed, they are named at all. (We recall that the sisters of Jesus were not named.) The suggestion is reasonable that Lazarus was the younger brother, and Martha the oldest member of the family. According to tradition, for what it may be worth, Lazarus was thirty years old when the miracle took place, and lived thirty years more. If so, we could suppose that Martha was in her late thirties or early forties.

It is generally stated that the brother and the two sisters lived in Bethany. This village is located on the eastern side of the Mount of Olives, a little more than a mile and a half from Jerusalem, and was the starting-point for the Palm Sunday procession. However, Luke tells a story about Martha and Mary (Luke 10:38-42) that seems to be located in Galilee. Bible scholars explain this as a story put out of its geographical context by Luke in order to bring out the point he is making—and this is a valid explanation. There is another suggestion, however, that merits consideration. According to Chase, the sentence in John should have been represented in translation somewhat as follows, "Lazarus was from Bethany, [having come] from the village of Mary and Martha."[1] In other words, Lazarus had moved to Bethany at some previous time, from Galilee where his sisters still were living.

Well, in either case, Jesus was closely tied to this family in the bonds of love. We get the impression that Jesus not only visited the family, but that He felt free to drop in at any time. During the last week of His life, when He spent no night in Jerusalem, He may have made Bethany His home. His love for this family is specifically stated thrice (John 11:3, 5, 36) and implied throughout the story. Now let us see what happens in a home where Jesus is a frequent visitor and an intimate friend.

The home was a home of love, but it was not without its quarrels. Luke tells us about a dinner that was being prepared for Jesus, in the account of which Martha and Mary are the principal characters. The two women have the same characteristics in John's Gospel as are recorded by Luke. Martha was the fussy type; Mary was a bit carefree. When she entertained, Martha wanted everything to be just right. We all know women like her: the living room must be immaculate, the window drapes must be just so, the flowers on the table must not clash in color with the table setting; the best china and silver must be used, and everything arranged exactly right. The house is referred to as Martha's (cf. Luke 10:38). This probably refers to proprietary rights, but we get the feeling—and I imagine any visitor would have gotten the same impression—that Martha was running things in that house, no matter who owned it.

Mary, it seems, cared little about details. She liked a house to look "lived in," and toys on the floor or disarranged cushions on the

---

[1] F. H. Chase, article "Peter," in Hastings' *Dictionary of the Bible* (New York: Charles Scribner's Sons, 1899), vol. 3, p. 757. Chase discusses John's use of the prepositons *apó* and *eb*.

sofa never bothered her. When they had interesting company, she would rather sit and listen than stir the soup. We are not told whether these women had been married, but if not, perhaps it was because Martha was too efficient, and Mary was too easygoing.

I have known women like Martha. Their husbands prefer to spend the evening at the club, for they never feel comfortable at home. No, there is nothing wrong with Martha! She is a wonderful woman. You can depend on her. She will make a most efficient president of the Women's Society. She is clever. She has a fine sense of balance, she is artistic, she is devoted. You cannot find anything about her to criticize—unless it is that you cannot find anything to criticize! I have known women like Mary. One such wonderful woman used to attend church every time the doors were open. She went to every Bible conference in the area. She was active in all sorts of Christian service. And she used to tell me, "I can't get my husband interested in church!" Poor man, he hardly ever had a home-cooked meal! And I just did not have the courage to say to her, "Perhaps if you were more interested in your home, your husband would be more interested in church!"

Martha and Mary! What happened when Jesus came into the home? Did they suddenly resolve their tensions? Did they fall into loving embrace? Did Martha stop fussing, and did Mary start spending more time in the kitchen? We know better than that. Mary sat at Jesus' feet, and Martha said to Jesus, "Don't you care that my sister has left me to do all the work? Tell her to help me!" (cf. Luke 10:40). If we could only hear the tone of voice in Jesus' answer: "Martha, Martha, you are anxious and troubled about many things; one thing is needful. Mary has chosen the good portion, which shall not be taken away from her" (Luke 10:41,42). There is a minor textual problem here, as our Bible notes in the margin. Jesus may have said, "Few things are needful" rather than "one thing." It makes little difference. If we may paraphrase, He is saying something like this: "Now, Martha, let's stop and think about life. There are really not many necessary things. You are concerned with a lot of details, but you could live without them, if you had to. On the other hand, there are a few things that you just cannot live without, and Mary has found one of these. It shall not be taken from her." Jesus does not really condemn Martha, does He? And He does not praise Mary for her indifference in the home. I certainly would not want anyone to think that Jesus will criticize a woman for keeping a neat house, or that He will bless a woman who sits all day at His feet and does nothing else. This is not the point. The point that Jesus wants to get across is simply this: there ought to be a place in the busy-ness of life for meditation at Jesus' feet.

Matthew records a beautiful story which I believe refers to Mary the sister of Martha and Lazarus.[2] It happened in the house of Simon the Leper in Bethany—some think that was Martha's father or husband, who had died some time before this, the house still being called by his name—and Martha, as usual, was serving. Mary took a pound of costly ointment; Judas estimated its value at three hundred denarii (about sixty dollars; cf. John 12:5), and since a denarius was a day's wage for a laborer that would make it worth a year's pay. Pouring the nard on Jesus' feet, Mary wiped them with her hair. Some of the disciples were indignant, and Judas Iscariot was quite outspoken. What waste! Jesus said, "Why do you trouble the woman? For she has done a beautiful thing to me. . . . In pouring this ointment on my body, she has done it to prepare me for burial. Truly, I say to you, wherever this gospel is preached in the whole world, what she has done will be told in memory of her" (Matthew 26:10, 12-13). Men still object to waste in religion: expensive churches, beautiful windows, magnificent organs, representative salaries, money and lives sent to mission fields, etc. The Lord Jesus has little patience with ostentatious spending; but He honors the beautiful extravagance of love.

The sickness and death of Lazarus. One day Lazarus became seriously ill, and they sent word to Jesus, "He whom you love is ill" (John 11:3). Then follows a very strange statement: "Now Jesus loved Martha and her sister and Lazarus. So when he heard that he was ill, he stayed two days longer in the place where he was." That little

[2] The number of times that Jesus was anointed, and the identification of the women, is a problem on which there is wide difference of opinion. The accounts are found in Matthew 26:6-13 (clearly parallel with Mark 14:3-9), Luke 7:36-50, and John 12:1-8. Origen (A.D. c.185-254) said there were three different anointings; others combine the Johannine account with Matthew and Mark and reduce the number to two; still others combine all accounts into one. This last view, *ipso facto,* makes Mary of Bethany the sinful woman of the city, and Simon the Pharisee, Simon the Leper. J. B. Mayor gives a good summary of the views, lists six points at which the Lucan account differs from the others; see article "Mary," in Hastings' *Dictionary of the Bible,* vol. 3, p. 279.

word "so" relates the sentence that follows to the sentence ahead of it, and it means that when Jesus heard of Lazarus' illness, because of His love for the family He delayed for two days before responding to the message. That is a strange kind of love, is it not? If I were to send word to a very dear friend, "I need you; come at once," and he were to reply, "I love you dearly, am leaving in two days," I would feel that our friendship was wearing thin. But think a minute! Can it be that Jesus is deliberately delaying for a reason? The teaching that God always answers prayer immediately needs rethinking.

There is another strange statement in this story: "When Jesus heard it he said, 'This illness is not unto death; it is for the glory of God . . .'" (John 11:4). Be careful how you read! The illness did result in death (John 11:14). But the purpose of the illness was that the Son of God might be glorified by means of it—that is, by means of the illness and the death.

There is a teaching abroad in the world that sickness is not the will of God in this world. This is a false teaching. The present world is a world of sickness and death, and to confuse this world with the world to come, where there is no sickness and no more death, is to bring confusion into the revelation that God has given us. Sickness and death are not unreal. They belong to this world. They are very much with us, and Jesus, in the story we are studying, wants to make this perfectly clear. Listen to Him: "Lazarus is dead; and for your sake I am glad that I was not there" (John 11:14-15). Why? Was it because if Jesus had been there, Lazarus would not have died? Possibly so. That is what the sisters thought (John 11:21, 32). But the main point is that Jesus wanted all who witnessed this to know, first, that Lazarus was truly dead, and second, that Jesus the Son of God had power over death.

Jesus and the disciples were beyond the Jordan when they received the news about Lazarus. The trip from Bethany to Jericho can be made in a day (it is a little over twenty miles, downhill), and Jesus was probably not far on the other side of the Jordan. The return trip is much more difficult, for starting about 1,100 feet below sea level the road climbs to nearly 2,700 feet above sea level; and to make a trip of perhaps twenty-five miles altogether, and climb 3,700 feet at the same time is a gruelling day's journey. It took, then, a day for the news of Lazarus to reach Jesus; He delayed two days; and it took at least a day for the journey to Bethany. When Jesus reached Bethany,

Lazarus was already dead four days; in other words, Lazarus, as Jesus knew (John 11:14), was already dead when the news reached Jesus. We are forced to conclude that Jesus delayed His visit, not in order to let Lazarus die, but in order that the full impact of that death and the resurrection that was to follow might be felt by all who were present.

When Jesus was nearing Bethany, news of His coming preceded Him, and Martha (the active one!) went out to meet Him. Mary sat in the house. For four days, they had doubtless said to each other, "If Jesus had only been here!" When Jesus came, they said it to him, "If you had been here, my brother would not have died" (John 11:21, 32). There was no false appearance of peace and calm. Their hearts were broken. Death means heartbreaks, even when there is faith. To say, "If you know the truth, death will not touch you" is sheer nonsense. To say, "There is no death; it is only illusion" is utter folly. Death will break your heart. It broke the hearts of Martha and Mary. It even broke the heart of Jesus: "Jesus wept" (John 11:35).

Jesus was touched by all human infirmities. I cannot believe that He ever looked at anyone who was ill, deformed, or handicapped in any way, without feeling compassion. I cannot believe that He ever looked at a passing funeral without grieving. Yet we know as a fact beyond any contradiction that He did not cure all the sick or raise all the dead. He had it in His power. As a matter of fact, He had it in His power to abolish all sickness and death, just as much at that time as in the age to come. What we must realize is the simple truth that it is not God's will to banish disease and death in this present age! Until sin is removed from God's universe, disease and death must remain. Death is the last enemy to be destroyed. It would be no blessing to give eternal life to men who do not know how to use it! That would be eternal hell!

But Jesus did heal some diseases and He did raise some from the dead to convince men that He has the power which He claims and which He someday plans to use on a universal scale. Lazarus is perhaps the supreme example.

Jesus said to Martha, "Your brother will rise again" (John 11:23). Martha believed in the general resurrection, but she did not dare to hope that Jesus was speaking of a special resurrection for her beloved brother. "I am the resurrection and the life," said Jesus; "he who believes in me, though he die, yet shall he live, and whoever lives and believes in me shall never die. Do you believe this?" (John 11:25-26). Martha believed that Jesus was the Messiah, the Son of God, the One who was to come into the world (John 11:27). That is splendid faith! There is not much more that anyone could believe. But it still fell short of believing what Jesus was planning to do for her. "Where have you laid him?" asked Jesus. Then, when they had come to the tomb, He said, "Take away the stone." That was too much for Martha, and she protested, "Lord, by this time there will be an odor, for he has been dead four days" (John 11:39).

Some tell us that there must be faith before there can be a miracle. Some tell us that sickness, disease, and death are not real; that if we have faith, these things disappear. Some tell us that if sickness is not healed, it is because faith is not sufficient. Read this passage over and over until you see that Martha did not have that kind of faith. If faith by itself could heal, there would be many persons alive and well today who died in faith. And if lack of faith prevented the work of God, there would be many others in misery. God asks faith—but He asks neither complete faith nor complete knowledge. He heals when and where He pleases. Some, whose faith is weak, He encourages by greater works than they would ever have believed possible. Others, whose faith is strong, He allows to drink the cup of bitter sorrow. What shall we say of the Lord Jesus Himself: was He lacking in faith? Yet He suffered and died!

The resurrection of Lazarus. After thanking God for hearing Him, Jesus cried with a loud voice, "Lazarus, come out" (John 11:43). And Lazarus came out, bound hand and feet in the grave bindings, and his face wrapped in a cloth. "Unbind him, and let him go," said Jesus— and we are reminded that Jesus did for Lazarus only what his friends could not do; He left the rest for them.

We call this "resurrection." But in a sense, it must be clearly differentiated from the resurrection to come. Jesus brought Lazarus back to this life: this life of sickness and death. There is an old tradition to the effect that when Lazarus was unbound, the first thing he said was, "Must I die again?" to which Jesus said "Yes." And from that time, Lazarus never smiled again. The tradition may not be true; but it contains a great truth. The resurrection of Lazarus was a mighty demonstration of Jesus' power over death; but it was not the resurrection unto life eternal. Only Jesus' own resurrection could demonstrate that.

What is death like? Lazarus did not tell. There are many who would like to know. Is it darkness, or light? Is it painful, or blissful? Do you see the Lord at once? Do you see any of your loved ones who have gone on? Lazarus, who might have told us the answers to some of our questions, remained silent. There are two things, and perhaps only two, that can be said with certainty. We know, from the words of Paul, that to be "away from the body" is to be "at home with the Lord" (II Corinthians 5:8), and "that is far better" (Philippians 1:23). We know too, from specific teachings of Paul, and also from the implicit meaning of all Scripture, that death is not the perfection for which we hope; only the final resurrection can bring the age of glory (cf. Romans 8:18-23). Whatever Lazarus may have seen or experienced in death was not even to be compared with the glorious experience that awaits us in the resurrection.

There is therefore little profit in asking Lazarus, or anyone else, what is death like? Suppose you could get in touch with those in the "world beyond"; suppose you could talk with them and ask them what it is like—what would that tell you? Neither they nor anyone else, except the Lord Jesus Himself, can tell you what it will be like in the resurrection, for the resurrection has not yet taken place. And all that the Lord Jesus wants us to know about the resurrection life, He has already told us in His word.

The resurrection of Lazarus, however, was of great importance for the disciples. In just a few days, their Master would be seized, tried, and put to death. Their faith would be dealt a shattering blow. He had told them, not once but several times, that it was necessary for Him to suffer, to die, and to rise again; but they were so slow to believe! Even after the experience of seeing Lazarus come out of the grave, they would have difficulty holding on to faith in Jesus. But it would help. In the years to come, when they went out into the world with the message of redemption, they might be inclined to ask themselves, "Was it all real? Did it really happen?" Then the resurrection of Lazarus would be one very important event, among many events, to reassure them.

But how would that make any difference? Simply from the whole sequence of events that the resurrection of Lazarus set off. Shortly after that event, there was a supper in Bethany, and when the news got around that Lazarus was there, a large crowd came (remember that they were very close to Jerusalem, and it was just a week before the great feast), "not only on account of Jesus but also to see Lazarus, whom he had raised from the dead" (John 12:9). The rulers had already decided, several times,[3] that Jesus would have to be put to death. The resurrection of Lazarus, however, was the climax. It was the miracle that sent Jesus to the cross. "The chief priests and the Pharisees gathered the council, and said, 'What are we to do?' . . . So from that day on they took counsel how to put him to death" (John 11:47-53). Moreover, it would be necessary to put Lazarus to death (John 12:10-11)—at least that was their plan. The day after the supper was the day of the "Triumphal Entry" into Jerusalem. While it is probably not correct to say that the crowd was there just because of the resurrection of Lazarus, still John makes it clear that there was a close connection between the two facts (John 12:18). The sequence of events may not greatly impress modern scholarship; but it would certainly have impressed those who lived through it.

The resurrection of Lazarus is a source of comfort to us also. When we are called upon to lay our loved ones in the tomb, we are in need of comfort, and it is consoling to hear the words, "I am the resurrection and the life." We need to be reminded that the Lord Jesus has the power over the grave, power demonstrated when He called Lazarus forth from the tomb. We need to be reminded, also, that death is not something foreign to the present world. It is a very real enemy that is with us and will be with us until Christ has put all enemies beneath His feet. But that day of triumph shall certainly come, just as surely as the Lord Jesus by His own resurrection became the first fruits of those who have fallen asleep (cf. I Corinthians 15:20-26).

This, then, is a home that Jesus loved, a home He graced with His presence, a home He blessed with His greatest miracle. There was no escape from the trials and tragedies of life. There was no false optimism, no unreal love. There were the normal quarrels and jealousies of a normal home; there were the sicknesses and anxieties; there was death and grief. The presence of Jesus in the home did not exempt

---

[3] The decision is noted in John's Gospel in the seventh, eighth, tenth, and eleventh chapters.

that home from these things. There was faith, deep, self-committing faith, in Jesus. There was also a limit to faith, beyond which it found itself unable to go.

How much is your home like this home? The presence of Jesus in your home will not remove the realities of life, but He will help you to live through them and to triumph over them.

CHAPTER VII

Simon bar-Jonah

PETER'S RIGHT TO a place in the hall of fame will not be denied anyone. In all the lists of the apostles in the New Testament he stands first. As the ready spokesman for the Twelve he assumes and is granted a place of leadership. In the first stage of the history of the Early Church he is clearly the leader, and continues to be until Paul comes into prominence.

Unfortunately, because of certain anti-Romanist reactions, Peter has often been ignored by Protestants. Statements made about him by Jesus Christ have been stripped of much of their meaning. So far as some Protestants are concerned, the Church would have gotten along perfectly well if there had never been anyone called Peter. Just a sidelight on this is reflected in the fact that whereas many Roman Catholic churches are named for Saint Peter, the name is uncommon among Protestant churches.

I believe we have made a mistake. There is a right of priority that belongs to Peter by Jesus' choice. He is the Rock with which Jesus began the building of His Church. He deserves careful study.

The great challenge. One day, passing along the shore of the Sea of Galilee, Jesus saw two men at their occupation of fishing. He said to them, "Follow me and I will make you become fishers of men" (Mark 1:17). One of the two was named Simon; the other was his brother Andrew. In another place, Simon is called "bar-Jonah," which is Aramaic for "son of John"; if he had been a Scandinavian, we would have called him Simon Johnson.

We have already devoted a study to Andrew,[1] and many of the things we have learned of Andrew are equally true of Simon. They should be reviewed in connection with the present study. When Andrew brought his brother Simon to Jesus, "Jesus looked at him, and said, 'So you are Simon the son of John? You shall be called Cephas'

[1] See Chapter V.

70

(which means Peter)" (John 1:42). We should add another parenthesis, "(which means Rock)." It would be clearer if we omitted the Greek and Aramaic words, and read it simply, "So your name is Simon? You shall be called Rock."

Now let us make sure that we do not misunderstand that statement. I do not think that Jesus intended simply to give a new name to Simon (although that is what it has amounted to); rather, I think Jesus was revealing a character. When Jesus called him "Rock," Simon was not very rock-like. Many times in his days of discipleship, he seemed more like shifting sand. But when we get to the end of his life, looking back over it, we are forced to admit that Jesus named him well. He was a Rock. But the development of that character took time; it took experience; it took trial. Most of all, it took a basic character that had to be there in the first place.

Perhaps an illustration will make clear what I am trying to say. It would be possible for a skillful worker to spend time and craft on a piece of wood, and for the finished object, because of the nature of the wood, to be of little value. The same worker could spend the same time on another piece of wood, and turn out a beautiful and valuable object. The difference is in the wood, for in one case it was soft, its grain was not suited to the purpose, it would not take the necessary finish, it would not stand the stresses and strains to which it would be subjected; in the other case the wood was hard, clear, straight-grained, strong and pliable, and just waiting for the artist to make something useful and beautiful out of it. Simon had the qualities in him that Jesus needed, and Jesus had the ability to fashion Simon into what was needed for the beginning of the Church. Therefore Jesus called him Peter—Rock.

Simon, like the others of the Twelve, was first a disciple, then an apostle. He, like them, heard the call and followed Jesus. He heard, observed, and talked with Jesus. But in addition, he had the opportunity of some special training.

The great confession. Jesus had been with His disciples for several months, possibly a year or more. The days of easy popularity and large following had turned gradually into days of stiffening opposition and hardening heart. Men who looked for a simple solution to the problems of the world were not sure that Jesus was offering the program they wanted. Ecclesiastical officials who cared more for political security than spiritual growth were afraid of the consequences of the words and works of the Galilean. Jesus had therefore chosen His Twelve, and started the intense training by which they would be ready to carry on the work when the time came. But they, too, needed sifting and testing.

One day Jesus took the Twelve away from Galilee into the region of Caesarea Philippi, located on the slopes of Mount Hermon. The Sea of Galilee is nearly seven hundred feet below sea level, and while it is beautiful to look at, because of the mountains and the prevailing winds it is usually sultry and enervating. On the slopes of Hermon, on the other hand, cool refreshing winds often roll down the mountain from snows that remain most of the year; many copious springs bubble forth from the mountain to form the rivers of Damascus or the tributaries of the Jordan. Moreover, the disciples were away from the milling crowds of Galilee and the suspicions of Judea.

Starting with a rather innocuous question, Jesus asked, "Who do men say that the Son of man is?" (Matthew 16:13).[2] That elicited interesting discussion which gives us some idea of the large and varied personality of Jesus who impressed men in so many different ways.

Jesus then asked, "But who do you say that I am?" Peter answered, "You are the Christ, the Son of the living God" (Matthew 16:15-16). Now, I cannot say certainly whether Peter was speaking for himself alone, or whether he was speaking for the Twelve. It is difficult to believe that the apostles had been with Jesus for so long, certainly having heard much discussion about Him and much speculation about His person, without discussing the matter among themselves. Personally, I believe they had talked it over many times, and had come to some sort of conclusion. I am sure that Peter would have participated in that discussion, and probably had a large part in reaching the conclusion. I cannot believe that it was a secret conclusion to which Peter had come independently—for Peter was not the kind of man to keep a secret. He was a talker. What happened at Caesarea Philippi, then, was probably what had happened earlier—only this time in the presence of Jesus. Peter had formulated the conclusions in his own words, having led the group in reaching those conclusions, and having the boldness to express in concrete terms what otherwise might have remained only in vague abstractions.

Jesus did not turn this statement aside; He accepted it. Those who

---

[2] Here again the expression probably conveyed little more than the force of a personal pronoun: "Who do men say I am?" See p. 42, above.

deny the Messianic consciousness and claims of Jesus seem to ignore Jesus' willing acceptance of this confession of faith. "Blessed are you, Simon Bar-Jona! For flesh and blood has not revealed this to you, but my Father who is in heaven" (Matthew 16:17).[3]

Then Jesus added the words that have been discussed almost without end: "I tell you, you are Peter, and on this rock I will build my church, and the powers of death [Hades] shall not prevail against it. I will give you the keys of the kingdom of heaven, and whatever you bind on earth shall be bound in heaven, and whatever you loose on earth shall be loosed in heaven" (Matthew 16:18-19).

There is a distinct play on words in the expression, "You are Peter [=Rock], and on this rock." Some have obscured it by pointing out that *Petros* (*Peter*) is masculine and *petra* (rock) is feminine. Some have tried to show that these two Greek words have different meanings, perhaps like "stone" and "rock." But Jesus doubtless spoke Aramaic—and Aramaic does not have masculine and feminine forms of this word. The distinction was a necessary one in Greek, because the man's name (*Petros*) had to have the masculine form. To the best of my knowledge and understanding, we are forced to admit that Jesus was designating Peter as the Rock on which He was beginning the building of His Church.[4] The subsequent work of Peter in Acts will substantiate this statement.

The words that follow, "I will give you the keys of the kingdom of heaven, and whatever you bind on earth shall be bound in heaven, and whatever you loose on earth shall be loosed in heaven" (Matthew 16: 19), have to be interpreted in the light of Peter's activities in the book of Acts.

The great revelation. "From that time Jesus began to show his disciples that he must go to Jerusalem and suffer many things from the elders and chief priests and scribes, and be killed, and on the third day be raised" (Matthew 16:21). Once the issue was settled, once the apostles were committed to faith in Jesus Christ as the Son of God, Jesus undertook to prepare them for the coming Passion. According

[3] That the Father had revealed it does not mean that a process of consideration and discussion had not taken place, such as I have tried to describe. God's revelations are often, perhaps most often, through historic situations; dreams and visions are, I believe, less common means of revelation.

[4] Some think "rock" refers to Peter's confession of faith; but according to

to the Gospel of John, both His messianic revelation and the prediction of His death were given in the earlier part of Jesus' ministry (the "Early Judean Ministry"). I see no necessary contradiction. The ideas may have been expressed, even with considerable clarity, and still not understood. That certainly was the history of the disciples' comprehension as portrayed in the Synoptic Gospels (Matthew, Mark, Luke). The full implication of the declared sacrificial ministry, however, would not be felt until there had been sufficient background of the revelation of the person of the Master, and this took time.

Even after the great confession at Caesarea Philippi, however, Peter was not ready to accept the necessity of the ministry of suffering, and had to be strongly rebuked by Jesus (cf. Matthew 16:22-23).

Something more was needed, and in order to reveal this to His disciples, Jesus selected the three who had made the greatest progress in comprehending His revelation. We usually refer to Peter, James, and John as the "inner circle." This term is only correct if we understand that it was not a clique, it was not a steering committee or a lobby, it was not even a favored few. There was nothing of the sort in Jesus' fellowship, and when two of the three misunderstood the purpose of the special training they had been receiving, and sought for places of honor in the Kingdom, Jesus promptly set them straight.[5] Any teacher who is truly interested in his calling will devote special teaching to his more serious students. So it was that Jesus took Peter, James and John up a high mountain,[6] where He was transfigured before them (cf. Matthew 17:1-8).

The transfiguration revealed Jesus in His heavenly glory. This was Peter's evaluation, after years of considered judgment: "We were eyewitnesses of his majesty. For when he received honor and glory from God the Father and the voice was borne to him by the Majestic Glory, 'This is my beloved Son, with whom I am well pleased,' we heard this voice borne from heaven, for we were with him on the holy mountain" (II Peter 1:16-18). Possibly this is what John referred

---

Acts, the confession by Peter at Caesarea Philippi was not a sufficient confession. After all, the devil himself could have subscribed to the truth of Peter's confession; there is no commitment involved.

[5] See Mark 10:35-45. In Matthew 20:20-28, it was the mother of James and John who actually made the request. The lesson is the same in either case.

[6] Traditionally, Mount Tabor. The setting of the story, however, makes this unlikely; I believe it was Mount Hermon.

to when he said, "We have beheld his glory, glory as of the only Son[7] from the Father" (John 1:14).

The transfiguration also set the prophecy of the coming death and resurrection against the background of the Old Testament revelation. Moses and Elijah, who appeared with the glorified Jesus on the mountain, were the representatives of the Law and the Prophets. Luke records for us the fact that Moses and Elijah "spoke of his departure, which he was to acccomplish at Jerusalem" (Luke 9:31). After the resurrection, Jesus likewise emphasized the truth, that the Law and the Prophets contained all the essential elements of the passion ministry (cf. Luke 24:27, 44-47).

It was as though Jesus were anticipating questions that would be asked and objections that would be raised—and I think He was. One question would certainly be, "How can You be the Son of God and talk about suffering and dying?" This is a major stumbling block to many: it was to Peter, when he said, "This shall never happen to you" (Matthew 16:22); it was to many Jews, as Paul realized (see I Corinthians 1:23). So, in order that the apostles would have a clear understanding of both His mission and His person, Jesus was revealed in the effulgent glory of deity, while at the same time His death and resurrection were declared. A second question, or perhaps an objection, would be that such a ministry of suffering is not part of the Old Testament revelation of the Messiah. The presence of Moses and Elijah, and their knowledge about and interest in the sacrificial work to be accomplished at Jerusalem, anticipated that objection.[8]

The great denial. It takes human beings so long to learn! As a teacher, I am constantly on the horns of a dilemma, whether to move more rapidly to cover the subjects that need to be taught, or to move more slowly to teach the students who need to be taught. And woe to the teacher who says, "I answered that question yesterday!" or "We covered that subject last week!" Peter was slow to learn, but sometimes those who learn slowly learn best. Perhaps that is why Peter is

---

[7] Some versions, through confusion of two similar Greek words, read "the only begotten of the Father." The word translated "only" means "unique, only one of its kind," and certainly does not weaken the doctrine of the deity of Christ.

[8] On the transfiguration, see G. C. Morgan, *The Crises of the Christ,* pp. 213-267, and A. M. Ramsey, *The Glory of God and the Transfiguration of Christ* (London: Longmans, Green & Co., Ltd., 1949), pp. 104-147.

such a helpful person to the rest of us. He learned well, when at last he grasped the lesson.

When Jesus asked, "Who do you say that I am?" Peter had the answer: "The Christ, the Son of the living God." Jesus said, "I must go to Jerusalem and be killed." Peter said, "Never!" But that is the Son of God you are talking to, Peter—you yourself just said so! When they went up to the mountain, and Jesus was transfigured before them, and Moses and Elijah were talking with Jesus about Jerusalem, Peter said, "It's nicer here; let's build three tabernacles [the word really means something like huts, lean-tos] and stay here." No wonder God spoke from heaven and said, "This is my beloved Son . . . listen to him!" (Matthew 17:5).

There was still time for Peter to learn, and in the weeks that followed Caesarea Philippi, Jesus returned to the subject of His death and resurrection more than once. Finally, the hour was at hand, and Jesus met with His Twelve for the Passover. The closing part of the ritual, which had to do with the messianic expectation, He directed toward Himself, thereby establishing the Lord's Supper. During the meal, probably before the institution of the bread and the wine, Jesus took a basin of water, after He had laid aside His clothing and put on a towel, and He began to wash the disciples' feet. It was a needed lesson in humility and service, for the disciples had gotten so far away from the heart of the Master that they were quarrelling over greatness (see Luke 22:24-27). Peter completely missed the point of the lesson, first by protesting, "You shall never wash my feet" (John 13:8), and then by asking that he be completely washed.

Patiently, Jesus explained the meaning of His action, and said, "If I then, your Lord and Teacher, have washed your feet, you also ought to wash one another's feet" (John 13:14). Then He declared that there was a traitor in their midst—a statement that seems to have truly hit each one of the Twelve at the depths of his conscience (see Matthew 26:22). Finally, Jesus was ready to turn to the closing teaching, and He said, "Where I am going you cannot follow me now; but you shall follow afterward." Peter had a ready answer for that, "I will lay down my life for you." Then it was that Jesus told him that before the crowing of the cock at the next dawn, he would deny Him three times (see John 13:37-38).

In the garden of Gethsemane, when Jesus asked the three to watch with Him as He entered into that last great agony, they promptly fell asleep—three times! Peter was one of them (see Matthew 26:36-46).

When the soldiers came to take Jesus for trial, Peter seized his sword and slashed away, hacking off the ear of the high priest's servant—as if the Son of God needed Peter, or any other human being, to defend Him! (see Matthew 26:51-54). What was Peter trying to do? Was he trying to prevent the death of Jesus, after Jesus had tried in so many ways to show that it was necessary?

The climax came while Peter was sitting by a fire in the courtyard of the house of Caiaphas the high priest. One of the maids saw him and thought she recognized him. "You also were with the Nazarene, Jesus." Peter denied it, and moved away. At the gateway, the maid said, "This man is one of them." Again Peter denied it. But one of the bystanders was impressed by the girl's accusation, and he noticed Peter's Galilean accent: "Certainly you are one of them for you are a Galilean." This was too much, and Peter collapsed under the strain. He not only denied knowing Jesus, but the record tells us quite clearly that He cursed and blasphemed.[9] At that moment the cock crowed, and Peter remembered the words of Jesus and broke down and wept (see Mark 14:66-72).

The great restoration. After Judas Iscariot betrayed Jesus, when he realized what he had done, he went out and hanged himself (see Matthew 27:3-10). Peter could have done the same thing. If there is any difference between Peter and Judas, it is not in the heinousness of their crime. Only our own attempts at self-justification lead us to judge Judas more harshly. To deny that you ever knew your best friend is utterly reprehensible. To deny the Lord Jesus, when you have been chosen for the express purpose of telling men about Him, is even worse. But whereas Judas went out and hanged himself, therefore denying with finality that God is willing to forgive, Peter held on to some slender thread of faith.

Three days later, when women brought the incredible report that the tomb of Jesus was empty, Peter and John ran to the garden, and saw the empty grave cloths in the place where Jesus had been laid (see John 20:2-10). It seems that Peter failed to comprehend the meaning of what he saw. According to an early tradition[10] preserved by the Apostle Paul (see I Corinthians 15:5), the risen Christ appeared

[9] Why so many expositors have tried to tone this down I fail to understand. The words in the Scripture are the strongest possible.

[10] The use of this word does not imply that it was not true; it had been handed down, probably by word-of-mouth, until Paul was led by the Spirit to record it; see I Corinthians 15:3.

to Peter first of the apostles. When this happened we are not told, but it must have been in the morning or early afternoon of resurrection day (cf. Luke 24:34), and it doubtless served to strengthen Peter's feeble faith. Likewise, the word of the young man to the women at the tomb, when it was reported to Peter, must have been a source of strength: "Go, tell his disciples and Peter" (Mark 16:7).

The great restoration of Peter, however, took place by the Sea of Galilee, some days later. Simon had returned to his occupation of fishing, and Thomas, Nathanael, James, John, and two others were with him. Jesus appeared on the shore and asked whether they had any fish. They had caught nothing. So Jesus said, "Cast your net on the right side of the boat, and you will find some" (John 21:6). When that resulted in a huge haul, John recognized Jesus (was it because of what had happened, rather than by sight?), and told Peter. Peter jumped into the sea, seemingly anxious to hurry to shore.

After they had eaten breakfast, Jesus turned to Peter and said, "Simon, son of John, do you love me more than these?" There was a time when Peter would have promptly said "Yes." "Though they all fall away because of you, I will never fall away" (Matthew 26:33). But now Peter will not compare himself with the others. He says simply, "Yes, Lord; you know that I love you." Jesus asked the question a second time, and a third time. Each time Peter replied in the affirmative, and each time Jesus gave him the commission to take care of His sheep.[11]

It has often been pointed out that, as Peter denied His Lord three times, Jesus gave him the chance to declare his love three times. This may well be the reason behind Jesus' threefold question. Certainly there can be no doubt that Jesus was stressing the fact that Peter was henceforth to be a shepherd of the flock of God.

How well Peter learned that lesson is reflected, I think, in his letter to the elders of the church of the dispersion: "Tend the flock of God that is your charge, not by constraint but willingly, not for shameful gain but eagerly, not as domineering over those in your charge but being examples to the flock. And when the chief Shepherd is manifested you will obtain the unfading crown of glory" (I Peter 5:2-4).

[11] Two different Greek words for "love" are used in the passage, and many scholars believe that there is a difference in the meanings of these words. I fail to find the difference, but have no strong conviction on the matter.

CHAPTER VIII

Peter the Rock

THE PRIMACY GIVEN to Peter by Jesus—using the word "primacy" in its fullest meaning, and not in the ecclesiastical sense used by the Roman Catholic Church—was accepted by Peter and the rest of the believers immediately after the ascension of Jesus. According to the record in the first paragraphs of the book of Acts, the risen Jesus met with His followers from time to time during a period of forty days, teaching them about the Kingdom of God, and impressing upon them that they must wait in Jerusalem until they were baptized with the Holy Spirit (Acts 1:3-5). At the end of the forty-day period, Jesus gathered His disciples to Bethany, and, with a parting word of instruction, ascended to heaven in their sight. The disciples thereupon returned to Jerusalem, to wait in prayer for the promised Spirit (Acts 1:6-14). It was there that Peter asserted his leadership, suggesting that a successor to Judas should be chosen and setting forth the qualifications for the office (Acts 1:15-22). Matthias was chosen by lot from the two who were qualified.[1] Peter did not make the selection and Peter did not ratify it. He presided, and the disciples acted.

Peter and Jerusalem. The disciples had waited for about ten days, when suddenly on the day of Pentecost there was a sound from heaven, tongues of flame appeared on each one, and they were filled with the Holy Spirit (Acts 2:1-4). The noise must have been heard not only in the house but throughout the city, for it brought a crowd

---

[1] Some believe that Peter erred in this suggestion, not having received the Holy Spirit as yet, and that Paul should have been the twelfth apostle. But Paul could not meet the basic requirement, which was set forth not only by Peter but by the Lord Jesus as well (if I correctly understand Mark 3:14), namely, that these men were to be eyewitnesses not only of the risen Lord, but of His previous ministry as well. If the Christian faith was to be rooted in the historical, it had to have witnesses to all that had happened historically. Moreover, the choice was not really a *successor* to Judas (no successor to James was chosen when he was killed), but rather the selection of an *alternate* who had been in exactly the same relationship to Jesus and the eleven as Judas had been.

79

to see what was happening. When they had gathered, they were amazed by the fact that the followers of Jesus were speaking "in other tongues," and each one heard them speaking "in his own language" (Acts 2:4, 6).[2] Jerusalem was filled with pilgrims from many lands for the feast of First-fruits or Weeks—the name Pentecost had come in with Greek influence, signifying that the feast occurred fifty days after Passover—and the speaking in tongues served a twofold purpose: to startle the crowd into recognizing that a miraculous act was occurring, and to present the message in a form that would be intelligible at once to all. The miracle, incidentally, was not confined to the Twelve, but involved the entire group of disciples, about one hundred and twenty (Acts 1:15; 2:4).

After the first reaction to the miracle, the crowd became more critical, and some said mockingly, "They're drunk!" Now, much as I dislike the heckler, I am forced to admit that it is a good thing to have him around. He often speaks out the doubts that lie unspoken in the minds of others, and he keeps the speaker or doer on his toes.

Peter, standing with the other apostles, accepted the challenge and spoke to the point. They were not drunk, but this was the fulfillment of the prophecy which God had given through Joel, the outpouring of the Spirit on all flesh, to the end that whoever would call on the name of the Lord should be saved (Acts 2:17-21; cf. Joel 2:28-32). That salvation, Peter hastened to point out, was made possible by the crucifixion of Jesus Christ (Acts 2:23). It took Peter a long time to learn that lesson: from Caesarea Philippi to Calvary! But he had learned it well, and never forgot it. This crucified Jesus God raised up; this crucified and risen Jesus had poured forth the Spirit (Acts 2:22-36).

Peter's sermon applied the sword to the consciences of his hearers. If Jesus was indeed God's Anointed, and they had been responsible for His crucifixion, what should they do? Peter replied in clear terms, "Repent, and be baptized every one of you in the name of Jesus Christ for the forgiveness of your sins; and you shall receive the gift of the Holy Spirit. For the promise is to you and to your children and to all

[2] The phenomenon has been called, from the Greek term used, "Glossolalia," and has come into prominence in modern times by the emphasis of the Pentecostal movement. More recently, some of the "staid old denominations," including the Episcopalians, have received publicity through the experiments of certain ministers with Glossolalia. In the absence of any Scriptural proof that the miracle has ceased, the Church should not deny the possibility that it continues, but rather try to bring it under the sound principles of I Corinthians 14:1-19.

that are far off, every one whom the Lord our God calls to him" (Acts 2:38-39). This is not all that Peter said—he used "many other words"—but this is quite sufficient. It opens the door wide for all who repent to come back to God through Jesus Christ. Some say that Peter and Paul, in their theology, were poles apart. Cullmann not only rejects this notion, but says, "Indeed, I should go even further and definitely assert that within the circle of the Twelve he [Peter] is the one who in this respect *stands closest to Paul."*[3]

One day, Peter and John were going to the temple to pray—we should take note of the fact that the Christian community did not break with Judaism. At the gate of the temple was a lame beggar more than forty years old: how many years his friends had been bringing him there we are not told, but it was a daily occurrence and he was well known by sight to the people. Peter was led by the spirit to heal the man (Acts 3:6), and the beggar's excitement over his new ability to walk quickly drew a crowd. Peter seized the opportunity to disclaim any power in himself and to declare that the miracle had been performed by the power of the crucified and risen Jesus. Once again Peter called on his hearers for repentance and faith in Jesus.

The crowd and the excitement at the gate of the temple brought the priests and the Sadducees, and these were annoyed because Peter and John were speaking about Jesus and the resurrection. Therefore, they took the apostles into custody for the night. Luke, who has recorded that three thousand were converted at Pentecost, adds that the number had now reached five thousand.

The following day the religious leaders assembled to question the apostles: "By what power or by what name did you do this?" (Acts 4:7). How could Peter help following up a lead like that? He proceeded to preach Jesus the crucified and risen Saviour (see Acts 4:10, 12). Peter never preached anything else except this message. It is important that we note how he weaves the crucifixion and the resurrection into every message, and comes to some kind of presentation of a call to repentance. This was too much for the officials; but they could not deny the miracle (Acts 4:16), so they settled for a stern admonition to the apostles to cease speaking and teaching in the name of Jesus. Peter and John rejected this as a violation of their conscience;

[3] Oscar Cullmann, *Peter: Disciple—Apostle—Martyr* (trans. by F. V. Filson; London: SCM Press, 1953), p. 65 (italics his).

they returned to their friends, and all joined in prayer, asking for boldness to meet the new threat (Acts 4:24-30).

Peter's disciplinary leadership, as well as his prominence in preaching, is indicated by the incident of Ananias and Sapphira (Acts 5:1-11). We should be thankful that God does not so deal with every hypocrite in the church!

Peter in Judea and Samaria. The death of Stephen was the signal for the start of violent persecution and the Church was scattered throughout the region surrounding Jerusalem, that is, Judea (principally to the south and west) and Samaria (principally to the north and northwest). The apostles, however, remained in Jerusalem (see Acts 8:1-3). The scattering could be likened to scattering fire in dry brush: instead of stamping out the new faith, the persecutors only caused it to spread farther afield. The Church had become large, and organization had become desirable. Seven men had been chosen to handle administrative details in order that the apostles could devote their entire time to preaching the gospel. One of the seven was named Philip, and following the outbreak of persecution he[4] became active in preaching the gospel in Samaria. When word of this reached the apostles at Jerusalem, they sent Peter and John to pray for the new converts that they might receive the Holy Spirit.

It is possible to read too much into this event, and likewise possible to read too little. There can be no doubt that the Early Church felt a sense of unity and a sense of responsibility that is lacking in many Christian denominations today. The apostles and, later, James the brother of Jesus, held a position of oversight at Jerusalem that has been likened to an episcopacy; James has in fact been called the Bishop of Jerusalem. The accuracy of the title and the extent of the authority are points on which there will be varying opinions, and this is not the place to discuss the matter. In my opinion, the extremes of independency and hierarchy are both dangerous and to be rejected.

Peter's work (his apostolic supervision of new churches?) led him to Lydda. At nearby Joppa there was a disciple named Tabitha, the Aramaic word for "gazelle." We know her best by the Greek form of her name, Dorcas. Dorcas was one of those wonderful Christian women who express their love and devotion to the Lord Jesus by good

---

[4] Some identify this Philip with the apostle of the same name; I think Philip the apostle remained in Jerusalem.

deeds. We sometimes forget, when we are discussing the gifts of the
Spirit, that these powers are not limited to preaching and teaching
and speaking with tongues. Paul lists service, liberality, giving aid, and
doing acts of mercy also as gifts of the Spirit (Romans 12:8), and
when speaking of the offices that God has appointed in the Church,
he mentions helpers and administrators along with prophets, healers,
and speakers in tongues (I Corinthians 12:28). Dorcas was a Spirit-
filled woman, doing the work that God had appointed for her by the
gift of the Spirit in her.

Dorcas became sick and died, and since the church in Joppa knew
that Peter was in Lydda, they sent for him. When he arrived, they
took him to the room where the body of Dorcas was lying, and the
heartbroken members of the Christian fellowship could not help but
show Peter some of the coats and garments that Dorcas had made for
them. Peter was led to put the mourners out of the room and raise
Tabitha from the dead (Acts 9:40)—and then he called the members
of the Christian community and restored her to them.

Why is this story told in Acts? Was it part of an effort by Luke to
reconcile the Peter–Paul tension in the Church? I do not think so.
That is largely the product of modern critical imagination. Was it the
Early Church constructing legends about its heroes? Then why was
there not more of this kind of material? For myself, I believe it happened as told by Luke in Acts. Perhaps if the Church today were to
spend more time in fellowship with the risen Lord and less in discussing human doubts, we too would have such power! But another
question deserves to be asked: why was it that on some occasions—not
many, but some—such deeds of power occurred? I can only give my
conviction. This was the Lord's way of demonstrating to the young
and tender Church the truth of His word, "I am with you always,
even to the end of this age."

While Peter was in Joppa, a man in Caesarea, about thirty-two miles
to the north, had a vision. The man, whose name was Cornelius, was a
Gentile, a centurion in the Roman army; he was moreover one of
those Gentiles who had despaired of the religion of paganism, and
who had found spiritual help in the religion of Israel: Cornelius was a
worshiper of God. In the vision, God told him to send to Joppa, to
the home of Simon the tanner, and to get Simon Peter to come to
Caesarea (see Acts 10:1-8).

The next day, Peter had a vision during a noonday prayer on the roof-top. In his vision, he was being commanded to kill and eat unclean, or non-kosher food. When he refused, the voice said, "What God has cleansed, you must not call common." The vision was seen by Peter three times (Acts 10:9-16). While he was puzzling over the meaning of the vision, the emissaries of Cornelius arrived, and the Spirit told Peter, "Go down, and accompany them without hesitation; for I have sent them" (Acts 10:20).

After giving them hospitality and a night's lodging, Peter went with them to the home of Cornelius, where he told what had happened to him, and Cornelius recounted his experience. Peter began to preach the gospel of Jesus Christ, including the crucifixion and resurrection (Acts 10:39-40), but before he had finished, the Holy Spirit came on the assembled group as He had on the day of Pentecost, and the Gentiles began to speak in tongues (Acts 10:46). Peter was convinced by this miracle that God had included Gentiles in the redemptive work, and therefore he baptized those who were present (Acts 10:47-48).

News of this reached the apostles and other members of the Church in Judea, and when Peter returned to Jerusalem an inquiry was held. The principal spokesmen are referred to as "the circumcision party" —a name which came to be used of them at a later time, and was used here proleptically (much as I have been using the term "Christian," although that name was not conferred until later). These men were sincerely convinced that Jews should abide by all the laws of *kashrût* (ceremonial cleanness), and that Peter had violated this principle when he went into a Gentile home and ate non-kosher food (Acts 11:2-3). Peter told the story of his vision and his experience in the home of Cornelius. His closing words summarized the argument: "If then God gave the same gift to them as he gave to us when we believed in the Lord Jesus Christ, who was I that I could withstand God?" (Acts 11:17).

This event is one of the most important in the history of the Early Church. It marked the opening of the discussion of a subject that was to ocupy the Church for perhaps twenty or twenty-five years, and which was to result in the establishment of a principle that the Church has not yet fully learned. The problem began with the simple question, was the Christian Church to continue as a sect within Judaism? In other words, was the Church required to observe the ceremonial laws of the Jews? The question, however, became larger:

Was the Church to consist of two groups, Jewish-Christians and Gentile-Christians? Ultimately, this has to lead to the discussion of the principle, are there second-class citizens in the Kingdom of God? We shall return to a fuller discussion of this subject in a later study. But it must be obvious, however, that the Church cannot settle for anything less than God's will, and in the case of Cornelius and his household, at least, God had willed that they should receive the gift of the Spirit.

This incident has often been referred to in such terms as "the Gentile Pentecost," "Peter's second use of the keys," etc. In the light of Acts 15:7 it is probably correct to say that Peter used the keys of the Kingdom to open heaven's gates to Gentiles as well as to Jews. We shall safeguard our ideas against extremes if we recall that Peter did not act unilaterally: he did only what God instructed him to do, and he had to account to the apostles and the brethren for his actions.

Peter unto the ends of the earth. Herod Agrippa I had gradually acquired control of Palestine, his most recent additions being Judea and Samaria. As a Jew (which Herod the Great was not), Agrippa soon became involved in the anti-Christian hostilities, and put to death James the brother of John (Acts 12:2), and when he saw that this pleased the Jews,[5] he proceeded to arrest Peter. The apostle escaped death only by a miraculous intervention of the Lord in answer to the prayers of the Christian community, and after reporting his deliverance to the Church, he "departed and went to another place" (Acts 12:5-17).

Some few scholars have taken this to mean that Peter died in prison, and his spirit visited the Church. This clearly is not what Luke intended, for Peter appears again in the account of the Jerusalem conference (Acts 15:7 ff.), and if we ignore this portion of Acts, we may as well ignore the twelfth chapter.

A more serious problem is, Where did Peter go after he departed from Jerusalem? The death of Herod Agrippa I occurred in A.D. 44. According to some Roman Catholic scholars who follow the tradition preserved by the church historian Eusebius, Peter went to Rome at

---

[5] I dislike to use the term, for it is misleading. At that point in the history of the Christian Church, it was almost 100 per cent Jewish. As Luke uses the term in Acts 12:3 it refers to that segment of Judaism that was hostile to the new movement.

this time; others hold that he went to Antioch, as indicated in Galatians 2:11, and at a later date went to Rome.[6] Protestant scholars are divided on the question of whether Peter was ever in Rome, probably the majority taking the negative position.[7] The problem is certainly not an item of essential faith.

Leaving tradition out of the consideration for the moment, we know from Scripture that Peter was in Antioch (almost certainly Antioch-on-the-Orontes, or Syrian Antioch) prior to the writing of Galatians. Whether that was written before or after the Jerusalem conference of Acts 15 is a problem in itself, which cannot be discussed here.[8] We also know that Peter was in Jerusalem for the conference. At some date between the founding of the Church in Corinth (probably A.D. 51) and the writing of First Corinthians (probably from Ephesus c. A.D. 56), Peter and his wife visited Corinth—at least this seems to be the implication of Paul's reference in I Corinthians 9:5; the statement in I Corinthians 3:6, on the other hand, makes it clear that Peter did not found the Corinthian Church. If we are not persuaded that Paul's statement implies that Peter visited Corinth, we must at least admit that it testifies to missionary activity on the part of Peter, and probably an itinerant activity rather than one that was settled in any particular place.

Scholars are not unanimous concerning the authorship of First Peter, but all would admit that it preserves an early tradition that Peter was an apostle "to the exiles of the dispersion in Pontus, Galatia, Cappadocia, Asia, and Bithynia" (I Peter 1:1). This area approximates the central, northern, and western portions of modern Turkey, extending from Kayseri to Efes (Ephesus) and north to the Black Sea, a sizeable and difficult territory that would occupy an apostle's time even if he limited his activities to the Jewish communities. At the end of the same epistle we read, "She who is at Babylon, who is likewise chosen, sends you greetings; and so does my son Mark" (I Peter 5:13). It is an early tradition of the Church that Mark was Peter's interpreter. The identification of "Babylon" is more of a problem. Some take it

[6] Both suggestions are noted in *A Catholic Commentary on Holy Scripture,* § 833g.

[7] For a good survey of the discussion of the question, see O. Cullmann, *Peter: Disciple—Apostle—Martyr,* pp. 71-77.

[8] For a full discussion and bibliography, see F. F. Bruce, *Commentary on the Book of Acts* (The New International Commentary on the New Testament; Grand Rapids, Mich.: Wm. B. Eerdmans Publishing Co., 1956), pp. 298-302.

literally: Babylon on the Euphrates. This seems highly questionable, for Babylon had been thoroughly ruined, scarcely repaired, and the capital had moved to Seleucia in 275 B.C. According to Strabo (first century B.C.), Babylon was almost entirely deserted.[9] The usual interpretation is to take Babylon as a figurative expression for Rome. If we accept the canonicity of First Peter, as I do, it seems that only a perverse anti-Romanism can refuse to interpret Babylon here, as in Revelation 18, to mean Rome.

Does accepting the primacy of Peter and his final location in Rome mean accepting the Roman Catholic view of Peter with reference to the papacy? I do not think so. To say that Peter was first of the apostles is one thing; to say that this primacy was passed on by apostolic succession is another. To say that Peter reached Rome toward the end of his life and was martyred there is one thing; to say that he was the first pope is something entirely different.[10] Protestants have done some muddy thinking at this point. There is no Scriptural support for the election of a successor to Peter; this is admitted by Catholic scholars who base their argument on tradition plus the question, Why would Jesus have instituted the office if He had not intended to continue it?—which is a misunderstanding, as I have tried to show, of the apostolic office. As for the primacy of the Roman See, both Jerusalem and Antioch have prior and more convincing claims. But above all, Peter drops out of Luke's story in Acts. Now Luke had one clear-cut objective in Acts: to tell the story of how the gospel got to Rome. Luke drops Peter, after keeping him in the center for many chapters, not because of any attempt to resolve a Peter–Paul feud, and certainly not because Paul was his personal friend (Luke was too honest a historian for that!), but because Peter was not the one who took the gospel to Rome. The conquest of the Gentile world for Christ was Paul's appointed task; Peter was responsible for reaching the Jews. The Petrine epistles support this view of his ministry.

According to an old tradition, when fierce persecution of Christians broke out in Rome, the Church there convinced Peter that he should flee. As he was leaving the city, he met the Lord Jesus who was walking toward Rome. *"Quo vadis, Domine*—where are You going, Lord?"

[9] Strabo, *Geography*, 16.1.5.
[10] After struggling with the problem for years and coming to this conclusion (not at all popular with many Protestants!), I was pleased to find that Cullmann comes to a similar position in his *Peter: Disciple—Apostle—Martyr.*

he asked. "I am going to Rome," answered Jesus, "to be crucified again for you." At those words, Peter returned to Rome where he was crucified, head downward, because he felt he was unworthy to die in the same fashion that His Lord died.[11] This tradition may have nothing more behind it than an early attempt to explain the words of John 21:18-19. But it seems so much like Peter that many of us are willing to accept it. Traditions can sometimes be right, you know.

[11] For the full story, cf. "Acts of the Holy Apostles Peter and Paul," *The Ante-Nicene Fathers,* vol. 8, pp. 844-845.

CHAPTER IX

Stephen the Protomartyr

ACCORDING TO A widely held modern heresy, preachers are responsible
for preaching, and deacons are responsible for financial matters in the
church. I used the word "heresy"; perhaps I should defend that.
Heresies develop from ignorance or denial of the Word of God. Sects,
on the other hand, develop from overemphasis of some part of the
Word and de-emphasis of some other part. The modern attitude
toward preachers and deacons is a heresy, and to correct it we must
study the Word of God, not just in part, but in full. We must search
out the entire body of Scripture until we have been corrected in our
thinking and instructed in what the Word of God teaches. Obviously, that is too large a task for this chapter,[1] but we hope at least
to make a beginning, and we shall do this by studying Stephen, the
first deacon and the first martyr of the Christian Church.

First steps in Church organization. In the sixth chapter of Acts we
have the account of the first steps in organization made by the Early
Church. The occasion is given: "Now in these days when the disciples
were increasing in number, the Hellenists murmured against the
Hebrews because their widows were neglected in the daily distribution" (Acts 6:1). Two words need to be explained, "Hellenist," and
"Hebrew." "Hellenist" is a technical term used in the book of Acts
meaning Greek-speaking Jews. That is not the usual meaning of the
word, and if you check it in an English dictionary you will get an entirely different impression; but the word is used enough times in Acts
that we can control the specialized sense in which Luke uses it. Jews
of the Dispersion who had given up the use of the Hebrew language
and had become Greek-speaking Jews are "Hellenists," whereas those

---

[1] A very fine approach to the problem is G. W. Bromiley, *Christian Ministry*
(Pathway Books; Grand Rapids, Mich.: Wm. B. Eerdmans Publishing Co.,
1960), 118 pp.

who had remained in the Land and continued to speak Hebrew or Aramaic[2] are called "Hebrews."

There were tensions between the two groups of Jews. The Hebrews had a pride of place and language. They were not subject to the uncleanness of the Gentile world. They were living in the land that God had given their Fathers. They were speaking the Holy Language. They were fulfilling obligations of the Law that could only be fulfilled by men living within easy traveling distance of Jerusalem. The Hellenists, on the other hand, were not without their own feelings of pride. Many of them had lived in the Gentile world long enough that now, having returned to Palestine to live, they had greater appreciation of the blessings of the Land. They were also more sensitive of the finer values of Judaism, the spiritual realities that were developed when ritual was impossible.

Conversions to Christianity had introduced serious difficulties that can be seen by reading between the lines. Pilgrims to Jerusalem who had heard the gospel and had accepted Jesus as their Messiah were reluctant to leave. This may have been largely due to the teaching that He was going to return from heaven and that this return would be localized at the Mount of Olives—and of course they would want to be nearby when that happened! Perhaps many of them were without employment; some may not even have sought employment, for why work when the Lord is coming back soon?[3] Others found it impossible to get work, for Judea was not an industrial area. The Early Church sought to meet some of the difficulties by a "daily distribution" —a bread line, soup kitchen, or something of the sort.

The Hellenists began to murmur because the Hebrews were getting fed and clothed and they were being neglected. That may or may not have been true. When men are in an unfavorable economic condition, minority groups feel that they are the victims of unfair discrimination. Usually they are; but sometimes the feeling is unjustified. However—and this is what modern politicians have too often forgotten—you cannot allow such discontent to continue to grow, whether it is justified or not. This is even more true in a group such as the

[2] Formerly it was generally accepted that Aramaic was the language commonly used, and that it was called in popular speech "Hebrew." Since the discovery of the Dead Sea Scrolls, however, it is recognized that Hebrew was much more widely used than had been believed, and it is possible that the word "Hebrew" in the New Testament means Hebrew as well as Aramaic.

[3] This heresy crops up even today; it is fully answered in the New Testament.

Early Church. The apostles therefore called together the disciples and made a suggestion.

Underlying the suggestion was an important principle: "It is not right that we should give up preaching the word of God to serve tables. Therefore, brethren, pick out from among you seven men of good repute, full of the Spirit and of wisdom, whom we may appoint to this duty. But we will devote ourselves to prayer and to the ministry of the word" (Acts 6:2-4). This is clearly a sensible distribution of responsibility, based not on privilege or rank, but on qualification. The men who had been with Jesus were the men who should proclaim the message. Since this task is of primary importance, and since it is of extremely large proportions (there is a world waiting to be evangelized), no time should be taken from the apostles to do the jobs that others could do equally well. The suggestion pleased the multitude, and they accepted it.

The qualifications for the office are sketched briefly in verse 3. The men were to be chosen from the fellowship of the Early Church ("from among you"). They were to be men of good reputation. They were to be Spirit-filled men. They were to be men of common sense.[4] No church should settle for less in its officers!

It is interesting to read the list of names of the men chosen for the task: Stephen, Philip, Prochorus, Nicanor, Timon, Parmenas, and Nicolaus a Proselyte (Acts 6:5). They are all Greek names; six of them are Hellenists, and one is a Proselyte (a Gentile converted to Judaism). That sounds as though they had been chosen from the group doing the complaining, therefore men in a position to know the situation at first hand. As a result—at least I think that is why Luke added the statement at this point—"the word of God increased; and the number of the disciples multiplied greatly in Jerusalem" (Acts 6:7).

From time to time we hear objections to church organization. Some say, "Oh, if we could only get back to the Church of the first century!" Men have even attempted to establish churches conforming to their ideas of first-century Christianity. But a careful study of the Early Church will clearly reveal an organization—not for the sake of

---

[4] The word *sophia*, "wisdom," has a wide range of meaning, from knowledge and skill in the common things of daily life to specialized learning. In the light of the kind of men whom Jesus chose to be apostles, I doubt that the word here means specialized or philosophical wisdom.

organization, however, but to meet the complex and growing needs of the Church. Our greater problem is that we fail to adjust organization to need, we impose American organization on missionary churches in Borneo and elsewhere, and we think of organization as an end in itself.

Stephen and his work. Stephen was chosen to take care of the temporal problems of the Church in Palestine. Nothing is said of how he fulfilled his office; I suppose he did a fine job, but it is taken for granted. We are told, however, quite a lot about other work that he did, "over and beyond his call to duty." Perhaps that is not the way we should say it. These are the things that he did as a Christian, and in addition to these things he fulfilled the office of deacon. He was a "witness." All Christians have been called to be witnesses. "You shall be my witnesses," said Jesus, and the book of Acts tells the story of some of the witnesses. The duty of a witness is to tell what he knows, "the truth, the whole truth, and nothing but the truth."

Stephen was not only a witness, he was also an advocate. He was not content merely to tell what he knew, but he got into active discussion with those who did not agree with him. "Some of those who belong to the synagogue of the Freedmen (as it was called), and of the Cyrenians, and of the Alexandrians, and of those from Cilicia and Asia, arose and disputed with Stephen" (Acts 6:9). The "Freedmen"[5] were those who had been taken captive (perhaps by Pompey) and later they or their children had been set free. Cyrenians and Alexandrians came from Africa; Cilicia and (proconsular) Asia were in Asia Minor. All of them were Hellenists.

What was it Stephen said that stirred them so deeply? Stephen was a Hellenist; how had he irritated these other Hellenists? We are not told in so many words, but I think we can reconstruct it from the story. They charged Stephen, for example, with speaking "blasphemous words against Moses and God," and "against this holy place and the law" (Acts 6:11,13). It seems obvious that Stephen had attacked the Temple (God) and the Law (Moses).[6] How? Where did

[5] King James Version reads "Libertines," a translation which should be rejected, since the word has come to have an immoral connotation.

[6] The identification of the Temple with God may seem farfetched, but as a matter of fact, the words became so closely identified that God is still called *ha-Maqôm* ("the Place") by Jews who seek to avoid using the word for God.

he get such an idea? Some tell us that it was his Hellenistic back-ground which had given him ideas foreign to Judaism. But a study of Hellenistic Judaism will quickly prove that this is fallacious. The supreme example of Hellenistic Judaism is Philo of Alexandria (c.20 B.C.—c. A.D. 50), and he is extremely positive in his attitude toward the Law, arguing that the laws of Scripture are like the laws of nature: they do not change. Moreover, Stephen was having his difficulties with Hellenistic Jews. Certainly it was not Hellenism that had led him to his position!

But if we study the teachings of Jesus, we soon discover where Stephen got his peculiar notions. Jesus denied the hereditary view of religion that said, Because our Father is Abraham, we are God's children. Jesus said, In order to be Abraham's children, you must have the vital faith that Abraham had (cf. John 8:39). Jesus denied the legalistic view of the Law. The Pharisees asked, "Why don't your disciples wash their hands before eating?" (cf. Mark 7:1-5). They were referring, of course, to ritual washing, and not to sanitation. The dis-ciples might have just washed their hands; but if it had not been done according to the correct ritual, they would still be "unclean." Jesus went on to point out that "there is nothing outside a man which by going into him can defile him; but the things which come out of a man are what defile him" (Mark 7:15). Jesus challenged the righteous-ness of the Pharisees (see Matthew 5:20). Jesus particularly and pointedly challenged their attitude toward the Sabbath, stating as a principle that "the sabbath was made for man, not man for the sabbath" (Mark 2:27). To illustrate this principle, Jesus on several occasions deliberately broke the Sabbath (as interpreted by the tra-ditions of the elders).[7] For example, one day in the home of a ruler of the Pharisees there was a man who had dropsy. Jesus had been invited there to dine, and it was the Sabbath. Jesus asked, "Is it lawful to heal on the sabbath, or not?" (Luke 14:3). According to their tra-dition, healing was work, and work was forbidden by the Sabbath commandment. Jesus deliberately forced the problem into the open, and then proceeded to heal the man.

Further, Jesus denied the view that worship was either limited to a particular place, or more advantageous if performed at a certain place. When the woman of Samaria raised the question by saying, "Our

[7] For a forceful study of the way Jesus dealt with the Sabbath, see A. G. Hebert, *The Throne of David* (London: Faber and Faber, 1951), pp. 143-163.

fathers worshiped on this mountain; and you say that in Jerusalem is the place where men ought to worship," Jesus replied, "The hour is coming when neither on this mountain nor in Jerusalem will you worship the Father . . . the true worshipers will worship the Father in spirit and truth . . ." (John 4:20-24).

According to tradition, Stephen had been one of the Seventy. If we prefer not to accept that tradition, we must still admit that Stephen had been taught by men who had been with Jesus. Stephen had begun to think, and the more he thought the more he realized the implications of Jesus' teachings. Law was a matter of the spirit and intent of the heart, and not mere ritual. Worship was a matter of spirit and truth, not geography. If we carry these principles to their logical conclusion, the Law can be replaced by the Spirit of God in the heart, and the Temple can be replaced by spiritual fellowship between redeemed man and his Saviour God.

To the Jew, brought up as he had been to think of the Law and the Temple as essential elements in his religion, this was a hard teaching. The Jewish Church in Acts had much difficulty at this point, and for many years the Church seemed about to be torn into two churches. Peter got into the struggle; so did James the Lord's brother, and Paul. We shall have to return to it again. For the present we simply wish to point out that Stephen was the first man to step out in faith into the deeper significance of the teachings of Jesus. And just as Jesus had run into serious difficulty and opposition, so did Stephen.

Stephen's defense. The accusation of blasphemy was serious enough to warrant a formal trial. Witnesses—false witnesses—were brought in (cf. Acts 6:13), as had been done in the trial of Jesus. When they had finished, Stephen was given the opportunity of speaking on his own behalf. The seventh chapter of Acts is usually referred to as "Stephen's defense."

It is strictly speaking not a defense of Stephen so much as it is a defense of his teaching. He is defending Christianity. He is defending the larger view presented by Jesus. It might better be termed an "apology," using the word in the original meaning, the defense of a cause or doctrine.[8] Stephen does not mention himself. He does not

---

[8] It is an interesting illustration of the way words change in meaning, that "apology," which formerly meant, "these are the reasons why I am right," now means, "I am sorry that I made a mistake."

mention the charges made against him. He stays with the central issue, which could be paraphrased, The prophetic view of Scripture versus the legalistic.

Let me make clear what I mean by the terms. The prophetic view of Scripture tries to get the truth out of Scripture; the legalistic view tries to force Scripture into a mold. The prophetic view says, God has spoken, now let us try to get the fullest and clearest possible meaning of what He said. The legalistic view says, God has spoken, and this is the way our fathers understood Him; this is therefore what God meant, and we shall resist any attempt to make it mean anything else.

There are many sincere people teaching the Bible today who follow in the tradition of legalism. If you were to suggest to them that they walk in the steps of the Pharisees, they would doubtless feel insulted. Yet it is quite obvious that they are not trying to let the Scripture lead them into all truth; rather, they are trying to jam the truth into the little molds which they received from those who taught them. "It was good enough for Mother, and it's good enough for me." They do not think that way of their washboard, their horse-and-buggy, or their medical doctor, but they do think it about their religion. Now it certainly must be obvious, in the light of what I have already said, that I am not challenging the fundamental doctrines of the Scriptures; I am speaking about interpretation of the Scriptures, about the application of the truth of God to the life of man.

Stephen undertook to meet the legalistic attitude by a long, involved argument. Some scholars think he missed the point; that it is not an argument at all, but simply a rambling, pointless speech. It seems to me that he has a very clear-cut argument. Let me sketch first the points I think he is making; then check them, if you will, in Acts.

He started by pointing out that the original covenant was made by God long before the time of Moses, long before the time of Solomon; it was made with Abraham, when there was no Law and no Temple. Yet Abraham could worship God acceptably. This covenant was not made in the land of Canaan; it was made in Mesopotamia. The law was not given in Jerusalem; it was given in Sinai. God's activity therefore had not been limited to Palestine. It had been operative on behalf of Joseph in Egypt, and again in Egypt for all of Israel. Now, if worship was acceptable to God and God's redemptive activity was available to men, before there was a Law and before there was a Temple, these things were not essential elements, certainly not essential forms. Moreover, God's revelation has been progressive. God has been dealing with the race as a parent deals with a child: a little at a time, increasing as the child increases in understanding. God's revelation increased as we pass from Abraham to Moses, and continued to increase as we pass from Moses to Solomon, and then to the prophets. Why, then, could it not continue to increase still more as we come down to the time of Jesus? If God's promise originally made to Abraham had included the blessing of the Gentiles, certainly it was not intended to stop with the Jewish people.

Now, I grant that Stephen did not say these things as I have said them. But check over his speech, and see whether I have misrepresented his train of thought. When he came to the matter of progressive revelation, he introduced the other side: human inertia. The great problem has not been that men have moved ahead of the prophets; the great problem has been that men have refused to move with the prophets. "Which of the prophets did not your fathers persecute?" (Acts 7:52). These prophets, who had announced the coming of the Righteous One, Stephen ties in with Jesus, and the Righteous One, the Messiah of Israel, he identifies with Jesus.

This was too much! A speech like this may make its point with thoughtful men, as they have time to sit down and ponder its subsurface truth. But the mention of the murder of Jesus was inflammatory, and men of inflamed passions do not take time to sit down and think. Stephen's defense is one of the great prophetic messages of the Early Church. It is a pioneer speech that moves out into unexplored territory of thought. But its immediate result was the death of Stephen.

The stoning of Stephen. Stephen was stoned for blasphemy. According to the Law, "He who blasphemes the name of the Lord shall be put to death; all the congregation shall stone him" (Leviticus 24:16). Stephen was stoned outside the city, in accordance with the Law, "Bring out of the camp him who cursed" (Leviticus 24:14). The witnesses stoned him first, for the Law said, "The hand of the witnesses shall be first against him to put him to death, and afterward the hand of all the people" (Deuteronomy 17:7).

Not only was the Law specific on the matter, but the tradition of the Fathers was clear and detailed. The Talmud says that after the witnesses have been heard, and sentence is pronounced, the condemned man "is led forth, while some one precedes him announcing: Such a one, son of so and so, is led forth to be stoned for such an offense; so and so are the witnesses; whoever has anything to produce in his favor, let him produce it." When they are about six feet from the place of execution, the condemned man is stripped, and "one of the witnesses casts a stone, and if this does not kill the man, then another, and then, if death has not ensued, the people take up the task" (*Sanhedrin,* 6).

"One of the witnesses casts a stone, and if this does not kill the man . . ."—think of that a moment! That stone was thrown so as to kill! I have seen an angry mob take up stones. I have seen stones fly. Once I thought we were going to get stoned, but we were able to get to a waiting car. Those stones come in with the force and accuracy of big-league pitching! In such a manner Stephen was stoned to death, and like his Lord, he died uttering the words, "Lord Jesus, receive my spirit. Lord, do not hold this sin against them" (Acts 7:59, 60; cf. Luke 23:46,34).

"And the witnesses laid down their garments at the feet of a young man named Saul" (Acts 7:58). "And Saul was consenting to his death" (Acts 8:1). Augustine observed, *Si Stephanus non orasset, ecclesia Paulum non habuisset,* "If Stephen had not prayed, the Church would not have had Paul."

So Stephen, whose name means "crown," received the crown of the martyr. And so the language received another word, for the Greek word *martys* (genitive, *martyros*) originally meant simply "witness," but because of the great crowd of witnesses who paid for their testimony with their blood, came to mean what our English word "martyr" means. Stephen is the protomartyr, the first Christian martyr.

> The martyr first, whose eagle eye
>   Could pierce beyond the grave,
> Who saw his Master in the sky,
>   And called on Him to save;
> Like Him, with pardon on his tongue,
>   In midst of mortal pain,
> He prayed for them that did the wrong:
>   Who follows in his train?

I like to think of Stephen, too, as the first great apologist for the Christian faith, the first to follow in the train of his Master in stepping from narrow Judaism into the prophetic message and ministry of world-wide Christianity. And he was only a deacon!

What kind of church officer are you? Are you content to leave the Christian witness for the minister? Or will you join the ranks of those who look to Stephen as their example of a true Christian layman?

CHAPTER X

Saul of Tarsus

IN THE New Testament there are two men; the one is the persecutor of the Church, the other is the apostle of Christ. The former, if he had not been crucified with Christ, would have done his best to destroy utterly the infant Church. The other, if he had not been born from above, would not only have failed to see the Kingdom of Heaven himself—you and I probably would not have seen it either. And yet, as any student of the New Testament knows, these two men are one. The first is Saul of Tarsus; the second is Paul the apostle.

These two are one; yet they are different men and we must study each separately. Saul of Tarsus is the man of the flesh; Paul the apostle, by the grace of God, is in his own words, ". . . the least of all the saints," but in the words of the historian John Lord, "After Jesus, the most colossal figure of the ages." We plan to spend two studies on this great figure, and we shall develop these studies about cities prominent in the record of his life and ministry.

Tarsus.[1] Tarsus had a long and rich history. Excavations have uncovered successive civilizations from c.4000 B.C. Situated in a rich plain, protected from the cold winter winds by the lofty Taurus mountains to the north, the region was an ideal place for a young civilization to get started. The Cydnus River, navigable as far as Tarsus for small boats, formerly emptied into the Rhegma a few miles south of the city, the Rhegma being a lake or harbor that served as a seaport for the Mediterranean. Two great trade routes passed through Tarsus, one from the Euphrates valley and the other from Egypt via Palestine and Syria; from Tarsus they proceeded first northward, to pass through the Cilician Gates (a natural pass, widened c.1000 B.C., through the Taurus range) thence to central Anatolia and the west. It is therefore no mere figure of speech to say that Tarsus was a meeting

[1] For a detailed study, see W. M. Ramsay, *The Cities of St. Paul* (London: Hodder and Stoughton, 1907; reprinted, Grand Rapids, Mich.: Baker Book House, 1960), pp. 85-244.

place of East and West, for commercial and military expeditions of scores of centuries passed through that city.

Antiochus IV (Epiphanes) visited Tarsus in 170 B.C. and made it an autonomous Greek city, probably planting a Jewish colony there at that time. It was made a free city by Mark Antony, and the privileges of a free city were confirmed by Augustus. To be able to claim to be a citizen of Tarsus was to claim proudly to be a citizen of "no mean city" (Acts 21:39).

Tarsus was a university city. Ramsay said it was one of the three great university cities of the Mediterranean world, but later modified that statement.[2] The two outstanding universities, it would seem from Strabo, were at Athens and Alexandria, but what Tarsus lacked in greatness, however, it made up for in zeal for knowledge.[3] The term "university" as used here does not mean what it probably implies to us today. It was not an institution with a faculty, curriculum, and student body. Rather, it was a place where lecturers who were passing through could give their lectures, where teachers could establish themselves, gathering around them townspeople and receiving from them fees by which they supported themselves. When we are discussing Saul's education, however, it is necessary for us to be reminded that there is no means of measuring the effect of this intellectual environment on Saul during his formative years.[4] He spoke Greek, the language of the city, and as Deissmann has pointed out,[5] it was the vernacular rather than the classical language of the rhetoricians. Saul was certainly acquainted with either the teachers or the writings of the Stoic school of philosophy.[6] His few quotations from the Greek poets, however, are very slender grounds on which to build a supposition of vast formal learning.[7] Tarsus was a prominent Roman

[2] The original statement was published in his article, "Tarsus," in Hastings' *Dictionary of the Bible,* vol. 4, p. 687, and corrected in *The Cities of St. Paul* (London: Hodder and Stoughton, 1907), p. 233.

[3] Strabo, *Geography,* 14.5.13.

[4] Cf. J. Strahan, "Tarsus," Hastings' *Dictionary of the Apostolic Church* (New York: Charles Scribner's Sons, 1915), vol. 2, p. 549.

[5] Cf. A. Deissmann, *Light from the Ancient East* (trans. by L. R. M. Strachan; New York: George H. Doran Co., 1927), pp. 238 ff. A careful critical reading is necessary to distinguish this great scholar's a priori judgments from objective scholarship.

[6] Cf. J. B. Lightfoot, *Saint Paul's Epistle to the Philippians* (4th ed.; London: Macmillan and Co., 1878), pp. 304 ff.

[7] Cf. J. B. Lightfoot, *Biblical Essays* (London: Macmillan and Co., 1893), p. 206. The entire essay, "St. Paul's Preparation for the Ministry," pp. 201-211, is worth reading. For a defense of Paul's classical background, see Evelyn Howell,

city,[8] and since Saul had been born to a Roman citizen, he could claim that he was a freeborn Roman citizen (Acts 22:28). The pride and the responsibility of his citizenship became, after his conversion, an ideal worthy of the gospel, and we find it expressed several times in his writings and speeches (cf. Philippians 1:27 and Acts 23:1; see also Ephesians 2:12; and Philippians 3:20).

Far more important, however, than the Greek or Roman heritage which was Saul's in Tarsus was the heritage which was his through his parents. Both father and mother were Hebrews (Philippians 3:5), hence Saul grew up to know the God and the Scriptures of the Jewish people, even though it was in the Hellenistic world.[9] Since his father was of the tribe of Benjamin, the young boy had been named after the first king of Israel, the Benjamite Saul. His upbringing had been according to the strictest sect of the Pharisees, doubtless antedating his formal training in Jerusalem, in a home where the Law was rigidly observed. The origin of Saul's second name (Paul) is disputed; some hold that it was probably derived from the well-known Pauli family in Rome, his father having been a manumitted slave who received his name and citizenship for some great service; others hold that it was taken by Saul in honor of Sergius Paulus, the proconsul whom he converted at Paphos (Acts 13:7).

So we see that Saul obtained from Tarsus the three elements so prominent in his life, and so important in the world of his day: Roman citizenship, the language and culture of Hellenism, and the religion of the Jews.

Jerusalem. Saul had a sister, and from the fact that her son lived in Jerusalem and had access to the barracks (see Acts 23:16), it is usually assumed that she lived in Jerusalem. It is further assumed that Saul went to live with this sister, probably not long after his twelfth year, becoming subsequently a disciple of the famous rabbi Gamaliel (see Acts 22:3).

"St. Paul and the Greek World," *Expository Times* 71 (August 1960), pp. 328-332.

[8] Shakespeare has reminded succeeding generations that it was here that Antony and Cleopatra met, the Egyptian beauty's bark navigating the river into the very city. *Antony and Cleopatra*, Act II, Scene ii, lines 192 ff.

[9] I have not seen the fact noted that, although Saul might accurately have been classified as a "Hellenist," he refers to himself as a "Hebrew." This implies that his Hebrew characteristics were deliberately emphasized above his Hellenistic characteristics.

This Gamaliel, known as "the elder" to distinguish him from two others of the same name, was the son of Simon and the grandson of Hillel. So highly was Gamaliel the elder regarded by the Jews that it is recorded in the Mishnah that "with the death of Gamaliel, the reverence for the law ceased and purity and abstinence died away."[10] He was the first of seven rabbis to be called by the highest title "rabban." He was of the school of Hillel, as opposed to that of Shammai, and therefore represented a broader and more liberal view among the Pharisees (cf. Acts 5:38-39). He was interested in Greek literature, and encouraged the reading of it. He also held a more spiritual view of the Law, and encouraged Jews to have friendships and social relationships with foreigners. At the same time, there can be no doubt that he was a strict Pharisee, and that the young Saul was given training in the tenets of this sect at the feet of the great rabbi (cf. Acts 22:3).

Saul was born about the beginning of the Christian era and probably came under the influence of Gamaliel sometime in the second decade of the first century. The conversion of Saul is usually dated between A.D. 33 and 36, and since Gamaliel did not die until c.57 or 58, it is a reasonable assumption that Saul was under the influence of Gamaliel for several years at a time when the young disciple was at a very impressionable age, and the master in the ascendancy of a very brilliant career.

It would be interesting to be able to trace in detail the development of young Saul for the next ten or fifteen years. From several references in his speeches or letters we can gather that he developed into an ardent Pharisee, extremely zealous for the Law. If Acts 26:10 means what it is generally interpreted to mean, Saul became a member of the Sanhedrin.[11] The statement is sometimes found that members of the Sanhedrin had to be married men, therefore Saul was married. This reasoning is unfortunately based on two uncertainties: first, it is not certain that Saul was a member of the Sanhedrin; and second, it is not clearly established that members of the Sanhedrin had to be married. It is certain from I Corinthians 7:7 and 9:5 that the Apostle was not married when he wrote this epistle, and the inference of the former reference seems to be that Paul had not been a married man. On the other hand, there is a tradition preserved in Eusebius,[12]

[10] Mishnah *Sota* 9.15.

[11] The ruling council of the Jews, consisting of 23 (the small Sanhedrin) or 71 (the great Sanhedrin) members. Cf. *Sanhedrin* 1, 6 .

[12] *Ecclesiastical History*, 3.30. Eusebius lived from A.D. 260-264 to c.340.

that the Apostle married Lydia at Philippi and refers to her later as "true yokefellow" (Philippians 4:3). The tradition does not commend itself.

If Saul was in Jerusalem between the years A.D. 26 and 30 the question naturally comes up, had he seen or heard Jesus? Scholars can be found on both sides of the question, and quotations of Scripture can be found to support either side. Speaking for myself, I get the general impression from reading Paul's letters that he had not known Jesus prior to the resurrection.

Saul became extremely active in his zealous endeavor to keep the Law of Moses, and gained sufficient reputation that he could refer to this as proof of his earnest devotion to Judaism (Acts 22:3; 26:5).

It is not clear that Saul had engaged in the persecution of the Church prior to the stoning of Stephen. Saul was present at that event, and consented to it (cf. Acts 7:58; 8:1). This is not quite the same, however, as what he says concerning his active persecution of the Church, "I cast my vote against them" (Acts 26:10). We might be justified in concluding that Saul was merely consenting inwardly to what was being done in the case of Stephen, and that at some later date he became a member of the Sanhedrin that took part in voting to persecute Christians unto death.[13]

The very fact that Luke has chosen the stoning of Stephen as an introduction to Saul seems to imply a logical connection. As I understand the story, it was the stoning of Stephen, or more accurately, the trial that preceded the stoning together with Stephen's strong words, that stirred in the heart of Saul an unholy zeal and led him to participate in the great persecution that broke out that day against the Church in Jerusalem (Acts 8:1-3).

The difference between the moderating view of Gamaliel and the zeal of his disciple which amounted almost to rage, has drawn comment from several writers. It would seem to me that two forces were struggling within Saul, even from boyhood. On the one hand, there was the Hellenistic ideal that must have influenced anyone born in the Dispersion; on the other hand there was the strong Judaism that enabled him to say later, "I am a Hebrew of Hebrews." On the one hand, there was the broad liberalizing tendency of his master, Gamaliel the elder; on the other hand, there was the rigid narrowness us-

---

[13] We have already seen that membership in the Sanhedrin is not definitely implied in Acts 26:10.

ually associated with those who were zealous for the Law. If these forces were struggling within Saul, the trial of Stephen made it clear what the logical implications must be. If Jesus had said and done the things which His followers attributed to Him, then indeed He was a blasphemer. If His followers attributed to Him the place of glory and honor which belonged to God alone, as Stephen had done in the closing part of his defense, then certainly these believers deserved to be put to death as blasphemers. And if the breadth and tolerance of Hellenism made it possible for a man like Stephen to accept the transiency of the Law and the Temple, then it was time for Saul to make up his mind! This was the logical position from which Saul seems to have been fleeing until this moment. But once it became clear, he knew what road he must take. He could no longer remain quiescent or passive; he had to become active in his zeal for the Law: he had to persecute the Church. There was no middle course.

Something of Saul's struggle with the demands of the Law seems to be preserved for us in the seventh chapter of his epistle to the Romans.[14] He was not finding in the Law the peace of heart that he sought, and, like Martin Luther, he had a deep struggle of soul for something which the Law could never provide. It is the nature of Law not to provide, but to demand. Law requires rigid obedience and it can neither tolerate short measures and partial fulfillment, nor provide satisfaction or forgiveness. The Law was driving Saul more and more in a relentless pursuit of something that would satisfy the deep yearnings of the heart, but it was not providing satisfaction for those yearnings. Saul's outburst of fanatical zeal against the Christian Church may be looked upon as one of the means by which he sought to satisfy the Law's demands.

This has been the experience of others who have been seeking truth, but who have begun by rejecting the basic claims of Jesus Christ. Having rejected those claims and being driven by a relentless zeal to do whatever it is that God wants men to do, they find outlet for their zeal, not in persecution of the Church, but in an effort to undermine the basis for Christian faith. They attack the credibility of the Gospel record and seek to prove that Jesus was a fraud or, at best, a deluded

---

[14] The debate whether this chapter refers to his preconversion experience or his soul-struggles after conversion can be studied in almost any commentary on Romans. Certain portions seem to me to reflect an earlier struggle, even though the chapter seems to refer to experiences after the conversion.

young visionary. In their own unbelief they seek to destroy the belief of others, and if this cannot be done by reason, they seek to do it by ridicule. Books that are the products of such mentality range all the way from little blue books to learned discourses in many languages by some of the world's greatest minds.

In Jerusalem, "Saul laid waste the church" (Acts 8:3). The persecution was thorough and the results are reflected in Acts at several points. Saul was not satisfied, but "still breathing threats and murder against the disciples of the Lord, went to the high priest and asked him for letters to the synagogues at Damascus, so that if he found any belonging to the Way, men or women, he might bring them bound to Jerusalem" (Acts 9:1-2).

It was on the road to Damascus, for the purpose of carrying out this project, that Saul had his great experience. Luke, who has demonstrated in many ways that he is a careful author and historian, felt it necessary to record this story at three different points in the Book of Acts (Acts 9:3-18; 22:6-16; 26:12-18). The accounts are sufficiently different that anyone looking for difficulties can find them; the accounts agree, however, in reporting the essential event. It was about the noon hour in the full strength of the sun, not far from Damascus, that Saul saw a brilliant light from heaven and fell to the ground blinded by it. He heard a voice saying to him, "Saul, Saul, why do you persecute me?" He replied, "Who are you, Lord?" The voice from heaven said, "I am Jesus, whom you are persecuting; but rise and enter the city, and you will be told what you are to do" (cf. Acts 9:4-6).

Damascus. At Damascus there was a disciple named Ananias, and the Lord said to him in a vision, "Rise and go to the street called Straight, and inquire in the house of Judas for a man of Tarsus named Saul; for behold, he is praying, and he has seen a man named Ananias come in and lay his hands on him so that he might regain his sight" (Acts 9:11-12). If you were Ananias, what would you do? Nothing has been said to indicate that Saul has been converted. Ananias knew, probably by the grapevine,[15] that Saul had come to Damascus to do to the Church there what he had done in Jerusalem. So Ananias began

[15] This amazingly rapid spread of rumors and news will astound the Westerner. I have experienced it in the Near East and the Far East, and have been in situations where we were traveling (by horse) thirty miles a day, with no means of

to make excuses. The Lord said, "Go, for he is a chosen instrument of mine to carry my name before the Gentiles and kings and the sons of Israel . . ." (Acts 9:15). Ananias went. As a result, Saul received his sight and was baptized (Acts 9:18). In the synagogues, Saul declared his faith, saying of Jesus, "He is the Son of God" (Acts 9:20).

Saul's hatred of Christ and the Church, if we have analyzed it correctly, was due to Saul's conviction that Jesus was blaspheming in making the claims He made, while the Christians were guilty first of failing to repudiate His blasphemy, and then of making equally blasphemous statements. This, then, is the key to Saul's new message. Jesus was either a blasphemer or He was the Son of God. Formerly, Saul had taken the view that Jesus was a blasphemer; after his conversion experience, Saul declared that Jesus was the Son of God. It is either the one or the other; there is no third position.

What made the difference? Saul makes it clear: he saw the risen Christ. If Jesus was alive, then God had raised Him from the dead. Certainly God would not raise up a blasphemer. By raising Jesus from the dead, God had declared Him to be the Son of God. It was as simple as that!

Men have written many books or parts of books about the conversion of Saul. They have tried to discover reasons for his conversion in all sorts of experiences: in psychological and emotional factors, the stoning of Stephen, sunstroke, a fall from a horse, epileptic fits, and other suggestions. To Saul it was a simple matter, and he never attempted to make it more complex: he had seen the risen Lord. That explanation can only be set aside on two grounds: it is insufficient to account for the change; or it is incredible because it is impossible. It is my personal conviction that it is sufficient to account for the change. A sunstroke or an epileptic fit would not be sufficient; many men have suffered such things, but where is a second Saul of Tarsus? But if Jesus actually appeared to Saul, if the credentials offered to Saul were unmistakable, as they had been when offered to Thomas and the other apostles, if Saul (who certainly must have been as hard to convince as Thomas) was convinced that he had seen the risen Lord, so that this appearance could be listed with the others (see I Corinthians 15:8),

---

communication except word-of-mouth; yet when we arrived at our destinations, word of our coming had preceded us. Our only explanation is that someone was always traveling, bearing the news, while we were halting for food, rest, and other incidents of the route. This is the "grapevine."

then we have a sufficient explanation of Saul's conversion. It does not need amplification, and any attempt to augment it only weakens it.

As for the other objection, that it is impossible, what man is so wise that he dares to say that it is impossible for God to raise His own Son from the dead? That man belongs in the category of those who said it was impossible to reach the East by sailing west, or those who said it was impossible to convert mass into energy. Arguments from human non-experience are no stronger than arguments from silence. It takes only one experience to overthrow them; and Saul had such an experience.

At some point, Saul made a journey to "Arabia," according to his own testimony (see Galatians 1:17). Personally, I am inclined to put this journey between Acts 9:21 and 22. In other words, before Saul was able to present compelling proof that Jesus was the Christ, he had to think over the implications of his new experience. Saul had come to his convictions concerning Jesus and the new Christian religion as a result of his careful study of Judaism. This could not be overthrown quickly. And while it is true that the simple experience on the Damascus road is sufficient to account for his conversion, it is also true that this experience had to be reconciled with all that he had been taught previously—or to put it the other way, his previous learning had to be rethought in the light of the data provided by this new experience.

We forget to take this factor into consideration, oftentimes, when we are seeking the conversion of a well-educated person. The "simple gospel" is sufficient for conversion (although we may in some cases refuse to admit that it is conversion), but many rational obstacles remain. For Saul, the Old Testament and the teachings of the rabbis were as authoritative as are the teachings of science to a young college graduate today. And to harmonize these things with the claims of Jesus Christ is not easy. How long it took, we do not know; the upper time limit, from Galatians 1:18, is three years, but it could have been, and probably was, less. Where Saul went we do not know. Some think he went to Sinai; it is far more likely that he went to some secluded place not far from Damascus. When he had finished, he had thought through his faith and was ready to offer it to the world. Saul's statements concerning the origin of his faith leave no doubt that it did not come from the apostles; it came from his training in the

Old Testament Scriptures and his personal experience of the risen Christ.[16]

After being driven from Damascus, Saul began preaching in the synagogues of the Hellenists in Jerusalem (Acts 9:29)—taking up the work, it would seem, that had been left by Stephen. Saul, of course, encountered the same opposition that Stephen had; the opposition turned to murderous hatred, and they sought to kill him. He was saved by the activity of the Christians in Jerusalem—what complete reversal of poetic justice!—and went to Caesarea, thence to Tarsus. But no longer was he the old Saul of Tarsus; now he was a new creation in Christ Jesus.

[16] For a fully detailed, scholarly and thoroughly documented study, see J. G. Machen, *The Origin of Paul's Religion* (London: Hodder and Stoughton, 1921), 329 pp.

CHAPTER XI

Paul the Apostle

YEARS OF STUDY in the Book of Acts and the epistles of Paul have impressed me with the excellency of Paul's strategy and method. There is a lesson here that has too often been overlooked by the Church in its mission, a lesson that is being learned again by some mission boards. The strategy of missions in recent centuries has been to try to get enough missionaries (preferably American or British, and certainly white) to spread all over the world in order to "preach the gospel to every creature." That method is doomed to fail, for at least two reasons: it exalts the white Westerner; and the population of the world increases far more rapidly than missionaries can be supplied. The Apostle Paul, on the other hand, did not try to do the work alone, and he did not try to cover the whole population of any region. He located in important strategic centers on the great trade routes, established schools where he trained the native men and women, encouraged them to develop their own leadership and to evangelize their own people, and once the local church was established, moved on to the next center.

The advantages of such strategy are obvious at once. Workers are multiplied. Instead of one Paul there are scores of fellow workers. These workers know the people, the language, the customs, etc., far better than any foreigner coming into the area can ever come to know them. The developed sense of responsibility helps strengthen the local church. Perhaps most important of all, there is no inference, stated or implied, that "we can do the job better than you can." But I am stating my conclusions before presenting my evidence. As we study Paul the Apostle, keep your eyes open, and watch him mastermind his program of evangelization.

The cities of Galatia. Paul's "first missionary journey" covered the island of Cyprus and the southern portion of the Anatolian plateau. The cities of Antolia, after leaving the coastal region of Perga, were

Antioch in Pisidia, Iconium, Lystra, and Derbe. To study these places on a map, or even to read about them in a modern guide, may leave you puzzled, for only Iconium (modern Konya) is of any importance. But a visit to Antioch (just outside modern Yalvach) will quickly convince you that this was an important and large city in the Roman period. Lystra was reasonably large. In fact, of all the cities of Paul that I have visited, Derbe is the only place that was not of sizeable importance.[1]

Antioch, Lystra, and Iconium were located in the area of Galatia, and Derbe was on its southern border.[2] Paul's letter to the Galatians was written to the churches in these cities, probably to the Church at Antioch in particular, and his first recorded sermon was delivered in Antioch. The apostle had first visited Galatia as the result of some sickness, perhaps malaria contracted in the Pamphylian plain.[3] The Galatians had received him with undue kindness—they would have plucked out their eyes for him (cf. Galatians 4:15)—and Paul was bound by a strong bond of affection to them. Their later defection from the faith disturbed him emotionally, as is evident from the language of his letter to them, and this again gives us some idea of the relationship between the missionary and the people he was serving.

His sermon in Pisidian Antioch gives us several indications of his method and approach. The area was, of course, Gentile, but Paul had gone to the Jewish community and had taken his place as a worshiper in the synagogue. I suppose that Paul wore the robe of a rabbi or some indication that he was a qualified teacher in Israel—although it is possible that this information had been given upon his arrival in the city. At any rate, after the reading of selections from the Law and the Prophets, the visitors were invited to speak a word of exhortation, and Paul accepted. He began with a historic survey of Israel which

[1] The site of Derbe as established by Ramsay is now questioned by the discovery of Michael Ballance. Unfortunately, although I covered the region thoroughly, I could find neither Ballance nor anyone who knew where he was exploring. See M. Ballance, "The Site of Derbe: A New Inscription," in *Anatolian Studies* 7 (1957), pp. 147-151.

[2] I accept the "south Galatian" theory as fully established, and suggest that travel in Galatia will convince all but the most stubborn. For discussion, see W. M. Ramsay, *A Historical Commentary on St. Paul's Epistle to the Galatians* (New York: G. P. Putnam's Sons, 1900), pp. 103-234; *The Church in the Roman Empire Before A.D. 170* (London: Hodder and Stoughton, 1893), pp. 16-89; and "Galatia," in Hastings' *Dictionary of the Bible*, vol. 2, pp. 81-89.

[3] Cf. Ramsay, *Galatians*, pp. 417-428.

led through the Davidic kingship to Jesus the promised Saviour. He told of the death of Jesus at the hands of the Jewish rulers. He proclaimed the resurrection and the post-resurrection appearances of Jesus, and declared that this was the fulfillment of God's promises to the Fathers. "Let it be known to you therefore, brethren, that through this man forgiveness of sins is proclaimed to you, and by him every one that believes is freed from everything from which you could not be freed by the law of Moses" (see Acts 13:14-41).

As in the case of Peter's preaching we notice the insistence on the historical. The apostles preached no vague message of personal encounter in a suprahistorical realm; they declared that the events of divine redemption took place in time and space. The crucifixion of Jesus, the resurrection, and the personal witness of these events, is intimately tied to the forgiveness of sin. In Paul, however, we find a note that is not found in Peter's first sermons (it is, however, in Peter's speech before the Jerusalem council, Acts 15:10), namely, that the Law of Moses cannot give deliverance. Was Paul speaking out of his own experience of the frustrating demands of the Law?

There were present in the synagogue when Paul spoke a number of Gentile Proselytes ("you that fear God" in 13:6). To me one of the most discouraging features of Judaism for a Proselyte would be the legalistic obligations; and some Jews would agree with me. Some have expressed themselves as not in favor of seeking to convert Gentiles in words like these, "Why make him exchange the seven commandments of Noah for the 613 commandments of Moses?" Jesus suggested that the Pharisees made it onerous for Proselytes (Matthew 23:15). Imagine the reaction, then, when Paul stated that Jesus had freed all that believe in Him from the Law (Acts 13:39)! "The next sabbath almost the whole city gathered together to hear the word of God" (Acts 13:44).

In the multitude that gathered were many Gentiles, and the sight of Gentiles (not Gentile Proselytes, who were acceptable) stirred up deep resentment among the Jews (Acts 13:45). This led to the great decision on the part of Paul: "It was necessary that the word of God should be spoken first to you. Since you thrust it from you, and judge yourselves unworthy of eternal life, behold, we turn to the Gentiles" (Acts 13:46).

If I understand Acts correctly, Luke has introduced this statement because it signals the beginning of a deliberate program to win Gentiles. Prior to this, if God wanted a Cornelius in the Church, there was no objection (there was a mild protest, but it was satisfactorily answered). If a few Gentiles here and there heard the message and were converted, there would be problems, but there was no overt objection. But there was no definite program to bring Gentiles into the Church. In other words, it was a Jewish-Christian Church. Paul is now launching out on a program that may make it a Gentile-Christian Church. Up to this point, the members of the Church, except for a small Gentile minority, continued to perform the ritual of Judaism. With the admission of large numbers of Gentiles, it will be only the small Jewish minority that will continue the practices of Judaism. The Gentiles "were glad" (Acts 13:48), but not the Jews.

Obviously this introduced a new problem in the young Church. When Paul and Barnabas returned to Syrian Antioch from their first journey, and told of their successes in this new Gentile campaign (Acts 14:27), they soon began to encounter opposition. Men from Judea had come and were saying, "Unless you are circumcised according to the custom of Moses, you cannot be saved" (Acts 15:1). Paul and Barnabas stubbornly rejected this doctrine, and the result was the appointing of a commission to go to Jerusalem to lay the problem before the apostles and presbyters (Acts 15:2).

This opens what is known as the Judaizer controversy, which continued in the Church for years, and its subcurrents are felt even down to the present time. The issue, bluntly stated, is simply this: *Must a Gentile become a Jew in order to become a Christian?*

We are amused by the question today. That is because we are a Gentile Church. But turn the question around: Must a Jew become a Gentile in order to become a Christian? Must an Oriental become a Westerner in order to become a Christian? Must a Negro become a white man in order to become a Christian? Basically, the question is one of second-class citizens in the Kingdom of God. Shall there be in the Church of Christ two groups: those who are saved and in addition they also keep the Law; and those inferior ones who are merely saved? Shall we erect a partition down the middle of the Church and put signs over the doors, admitting the special-class members to the one side and relegating the second-class members to the other?

It makes no difference what the "plus" is, the result will be the same. The church that establishes as a rule of membership, "In order to belong to this church, you must believe in the Lord Jesus Christ and——," regardless of what is written in the blank, comes under the Judaizer problem.

At the Jerusalem conference, the Judaizers, in reply to the report of Paul and Barnabas, stated their principle: "It is necessary to circumcise them, and to charge them to keep the law of Moses" (Acts 15:5). This was debated. Peter spoke, telling of the experience he had in the case of Cornelius, and asserting his principle, "We believe that we [Jews] shall be saved through the grace of the Lord Jesus, just as they [Gentiles] will" (Acts 15:11). Barnabas and Paul were given a chance to speak. Then James the brother of Jesus, sometimes known as the Bishop of Jerusalem, summarized the problem, and gave his judgment (Acts 15:19-20). The Church gave its answer, and appointed representatives to take that answer back to the Gentiles in Antioch of Syria. The answer: Gentiles are not to be forced to become Jews in order to become Christians! (see Acts 15:28-29).

There shall be no second-class citizens in the Kingdom of God.

The cities of Greece. Paul's new program carried him farther and farther into the Gentile world on his "second missionary journey," until he had crossed over into Europe and journeyed through Greece (Macedonia and Achaia) to Athens and Corinth. These two cities symbolize the best and the worst of the pagan world. We have seen Paul as the champion of the liberty of the gospel. Now let us see how he measures up to the problems of paganism.

Athens was in many respects the glory of Greece. Architecture, sculpture, philosophy: to say these words is to think of Athens. Standing in the Agora, proclaiming Jesus and the resurrection, Paul was looking up at the Acropolis crowned by the Parthenon. Around him were the magnificent temples and statues that today, except for the Hephaesteion, are only foundations and broken bits of marble. That is where Plato had his academy, Aristotle the lyceum, and Zeno his stoa or porch. Paul mentioned none of the wonders of the city or its history; he preached Jesus and the resurrection.[4] The council of learned men, the Areopagus, wanted to know more about this doctrine, and Paul made his address.[5]

---

[4] The word for "resurrection" in Greek is feminine and perhaps was misunderstood as a female deity (cf. the name Anastasia), which would explain the curious statement, "He seems to be a preacher of foreign divinities" (Acts 17:18).

[5] Whether the address was made before the large council or the smaller one

The two dominating philosophies at that time were Epicureanism and Stoicism. Epicureanism is atheistic and materialistic. There is no creation, no soul. Life has no higher moral purpose than self-gratification. From the Greek word for pleasure it is sometimes called hedonism, and in popular thought it is looked upon as a morally low system of thought and behavior. Actually, it can be either high or low. A person can find his highest pleasure in some of the fine things of life: nature, art, the theatre, music, literature, and the like; or he can find his highest pleasure in the base and sensual experiences. To be an Epicurean does not mean that you have to be immoral; it means that you find your greatest purpose in self-gratification. There is no God, no tomorrow, so live it up today.

Stoicism is pantheistic: everything is God. Matter is inseparable from Deity. Reason, not pleasure, should be man's guiding principle. The moral system is accordingly much higher, and scholars have found numerous points of contact between Stoicism and Christian ethics.[6] Since man is God (all is God), man is self-sufficient (to call on God for help is to call on yourself), which of course leads to pride and rugged individualism.

Paul faced these two philosophies in his address to the Areopagus. Some writers feel that Paul completely missed the mark; it seems to me that he subtly undercut the basic premises of both philosophies. He started well, by referring to "an unknown God," and proceeded to tell of the God who made the world and everything in it (certainly not the atheism of Epicureanism and not the pantheism of Stoicism!), who requires of men that they should seek Him (certainly not the self-gratification of Epicurus nor the reason or pride of Zeno's Stoicism), and who has appointed a day of judgment when the world will be judged (where is there room for a day of judgment in the no-tomorrow view of Epicureanism?). At this point, Paul moved into the presentation of Jesus (unnamed) and the resurrection (Acts 17:31).

Some mocked. Some wanted to hear more—but "later." But "some

---

of twelve men, whether it was made in the council chamber or on the hill facing the Acropolis (Mars Hill), I leave for classical scholars to debate. Except for those who demand to see "the exact spot" it makes little difference.

[6] S. V. McCasland, *art. cit., Interpreter's Bible*, vol. 7, p. 84, points out that the concept of universal brotherhood is not Pauline or New Testament, but Stoic, later becoming absorbed by Christian theology. J. G. Machen had already made the same observation, *The Origin of Paul's Religion*, p. 226.

men joined him and believed" (Acts 17:34). We are told that Paul failed; nothing happened, no church was founded, no epistles were written to Athens. But since when is the success of a preacher to be measured by the number of converts? If Paul had had only one convert in Athens, that one being Dionysius the Areopagite—which is the equivalent of invading a great university center and converting one of the intellectual leaders—his mission could not be called a failure. Far more important than numbers are key persons. If the Christian Church would stop measuring growth by numbers and set its sights on the political and intellectual leadership of the world, the influence of the gospel would be far greater—and the numbers would also increase.

If Athens was the glory of Greece, Corinth was its cesspool. Located on the trade routes, where ships from the west docked to transfer cargo to ships for the east (or, for smaller boats, to be rolled across the isthmus), Corinth was a typical liberty port. No, not quite typical, for on Acrocorinth, the hill behind the city, there was a temple of love with free prostitutes in great numbers for all who would worship the goddess of love. Look up the word "Corinthianize" in your English dictionary, and you will get a good idea of what Corinth was like. In Greek, the word is even more expressive of its sin.

The Church at Corinth was made up of men and women who had for the large part been rescued from sin. Read the letters of Paul to the Corinthians, and you will quickly learn that while the Corinthians had been taken from sin, not all sin had been taken from the Corinthians. No other church in the New Testament had the problems of immorality that we find in the Church of Corinth.

Would the Gospel of Jesus Christ meet the needs of the people in Corinth? Paul went there "in weakness and in much fear and trembling" (I Corinthians 2:3), but the Lord told him that He had many people there and Paul stayed a year and a half (Acts 18:9-11). I am sure that Paul soon lost his fear and trembling as he saw the power of the gospel at work in the lives of men and women redeemed from sin. The epistle to the Romans was written from Corinth on Paul's second (or third?) visit to that wicked city, and it is almost certain that Paul's picture of the sin of the Gentile world (Romans 1:18-32) was drawn from experiences such as he had in Corinth, as was his firm conviction that the gospel is the power of God for salvation to everyone that believes (Romans 1:16).

The churches in Asia. On his "second missionary journey," Paul had wanted to go into Asia, but was forbidden by the Spirit (Acts 16:6). "Asia" is used in Acts of the Roman province, and denotes a portion of southeastern Asia Minor. The principal city was Ephesus, an important seaport (although its importance in that respect was diminishing, due to the fact that the harbor was silting up), capital of the province, and terminus of the road that stretched across Asia Minor to the east, connecting with Syria, Palestine, and Egypt, with Mesopotamia, and with Persia and India. Paul not only visited Ephesus on his "third missionary journey," but even located there for an extended period, possibly as much as three years (Acts 19:8,10,22).

In some respects Ephesus is Paul. I am inclined to believe that Luke reserved his discussion of Paul's method until the story of Ephesus was to be told because Ephesus pictures Paul most fully.

As was customary, Paul began his work in the synagogue. Even though he had turned to the Gentiles years before (Pisidian Antioch was visited first c. A.D. 47; the Ephesian ministry began c.54), he never turned from the Jews. They were his brethren, his kinsmen, for whose conversion he could wish himself "accursed and cut off from Christ" (Romans 9:3). His invariable plan was to go to the synagogue and preach there as long as possible; at Ephesus this was about three months (Acts 19:8). Then, when that door was closed to him, he opened a school near by (at Corinth it was next door to the synagogue, Acts 18:7), taking his disciples with him.

His daily program was to teach his disciples for some period of the day, and to visit from house to house. At Ephesus he taught in the hall of Tyrannus, according to some ancient manuscripts of Acts between the hours of 11 A.M. and 4 P.M. (Acts 19:9). Some have pointed out that this is the least likely time of the day for a school; on the other hand, as visitors to the Near East know, shops are shut during these hours, the people eating their noonday meal (the main meal of the day) and taking their rest. It is precisely the time of the day that there would be no interference with the daily obligations. The house-to-house instruction is mentioned only incidentally (Acts 20:20).

At the end of two years, "all the residents of Asia heard the word of the Lord, both Jews and Greeks" (Acts 19:10). Strong churches were established at Colossae, Hierapolis, and Laodicea in the Lycus Valley almost a hundred miles to the east, and probably at Magnesia, Tralles, and Nyssa along the intervening route; it is almost certain that the other churches of Asia mentioned in Revelation were also founded at this time: Smyrna, Pergamum, Thyatira, Sardis, and Philadelphia; and there are several other places where strong churches were located early in the next century that can probably be traced to the same origin. Since Paul stayed in Ephesus to conduct his program of training, we can only conclude that Paul's disciples were busy in evangelizing the surrounding territory.

Ephesus was an important religious center, the location of the splendid temple of Artemis. This was one of the seven wonders of the ancient world, and attracted pilgrims from far and wide. The religion was a type of nature-worship,[7] honoring Cybele the mother goddess, and far removed from the Greek and Roman idea of the goddess Artemis or Diana who was the symbol of chastity. The religious concept at Ephesus had come from the east, and was spreading into the west, carrying with it grossly immoral sexual practices. The Apostle Paul, as a matter of principle, had to strike at the roots of this religious system. The way he did it is of considerable interest and importance.

The goddess Artemis was represented as a many-breasted woman, symbol of fertility. Small statues and shrines of the goddess were used in the home and probably carried on the person, perhaps as amulets, much as the more superstitious among us have small figurines of the Madonna on the dashboard of their cars. At Ephesus there was an important industry, involving a number of silversmiths, which thrived on the manufacture of silver shines of Artemis.

One day "there arose no little stir"[8] over the Christian opposition to Artemis. Demetrius, perhaps the leader of the silversmiths' union, agitated his fellow craftsmen with the words, "not only at Ephesus but almost throughout all Asia this Paul has persuaded and turned away a considerable company of people, saying that gods made with hands are not gods. And there is danger not only that this trade of ours may come into disrepute, but also that the temple of the great goddess

---

[7] It is hardly a mere coincidence that the concept of the "mother of God" (*theotókos*) entered the Christian Church at Ephesus via the Council of A.D. 431. For some stimulating ideas, see W. M. Ramsay, *Pauline and Other Studies* (London: Hodder and Stoughton, 1906), pp. 125-159.

[8] The careful reader of Acts will be aware of the fact that Luke often employs litotes, the figure of speech in which an affirmative is expressed by the negative of its contrary. Thus "no little stir" and "no small dissension" actually mean a large commotion and a heated argument.

Artemis may count for nothing, and that she may even be deposed from her magnificence" (Acts 19:26-27). Even allowing for understandable exaggeration such as is common in inflammatory speeches, we must understand that Paul had hurt the business of making Artemis shrines!

The riot got out of hand for a couple of hours, but finally the town clerk restored sufficient quiet to reason with the crowd. What he said should be carefully noted: After pointing out the place of honor that belonged to Ephesus because of the temple of Artemis, he went on to say, "You have brought these men here who are neither sacrilegious nor blasphemers of our goddess" (Acts 19:37).

Think of it! For two years Paul had been preaching in Ephesus. By driving home the principle that "gods made with hands are not gods," he had brought the silversmiths' business to a serious crisis. Yet in public assembly it could be said that he had never blasphemed their goddess!

That is preaching! It avoids name-calling, but gets down to the basic issues. It cuts clean with a sharp edge—but it cuts principles and not persons. Let every preacher and every missionary learn from the Apostle Paul!

CHAPTER XII

Barnabas and Mark

WE HAVE ALREADY learned that there were disciples and apostles among the followers of Jesus, and that before a man could become an apostle he had to be a disciple. We have learned that Jesus chose twelve of His disciples and commissioned them as apostles; they are the Twelve Apostles, or simply the Twelve.

There are other apostles in the New Testament. Matthias was chosen to fill the place vacated by Judas; Paul is called an apostle, likewise James the brother of Jesus, and Barnabas whom we shall study in this chapter. In Romans 16:7, Adronicus and Junias are mentioned in such a way that they may be called apostles,[1] and in I Thessalonians 2:6, it is probable that Silas (Silvanus) is included as an apostle. That seems to complete the list. Timothy is definitely excluded by the opening words of Second Corinthians and Colossians. Apollos is not named as an apostle in Scripture, and he seems to be ruled out by the words of Clement, who probably knew him, and who certainly knew the Corinthian Church.[2]

A clear understanding of the New Testament usage of the term "apostle" will help us better to understand the idea of "apostolic succession." If the first prerequisite of the office was that a man should have been an eyewitness to the resurrection, that establishes a clear dividing line. Timothy, who was converted in Lystra (or possibly

---

[1] The expression, "They are men of note among the apostles," according to James Denney, is as vague in Greek as in English, and may or may not mean that they were apostles; see *The Expositor's Greek Testament* (reprint; Grand Rapids, Mich.: Wm. B. Eerdmans Publishing Co., n.d.), vol. 2, p. 719. The Church Fathers understood it to mean that they were apostles; cf. W. Sanday and A. C. Headlam, *A Critical and Exegetical Commentary on the Epistle to the Romans* (International Critical Commentary; 5th edition; Edinburgh: T. & T. Clark, 1902), p. 423.

[2] The First Epistle of Clement to the Corinthians, *The Ante-Nicene Fathers*, vol. 1, p. 18 (chap. 47); as the passage is constructed, "towards apostles . . . and towards a man" can only refer to the apostles Paul and Cephas and the man Apollos.

Derbe), and Apollos, who came from Alexandria and was given
fuller instruction in Ephesus, obviously could not meet that qualification. Andronicus and Junias, on the other hand, who were Christians
before Paul's conversion (cf. Romans 16:7), could have had the opportunity of witnessing the risen Lord in Palestine. Most emphatic is
Paul's argument, "Am I not an apostle? Have I not seen Jesus our
Lord?" (I Corinthians 9:1). On this basis, the only apostolic succession
can be a succession in the work, and not a succession in the qualifications: in other words, a much looser usage of the term.[8]

Barnabas was, beyond all doubt, an apostle (Acts 14:14). He had
seen the Lord, and he had been commissioned by the Church at
Antioch for the work. There is no doubt that he was commissioned as
an apostle to the Gentiles (Acts 13:2; 15:12). Barnabas manifested the
signs of an apostle (II Corinthians 12:12). We might devote an entire
study to the apostolic office; but I prefer to look at a different side of
Barnabas: I would like to study him as a man who had faith in people.

Barnabas and the Early Church... We first meet Barnabas in the
fourth chapter of Acts. His name was Joseph, and the apostles had
called him "bar-Nabas," an Aramaic expression meaning "son of encouragement (or exhortation)" (Acts 4:36). He was a native of
Cyprus, a Levite, and he owned a field or possibly several fields (Acts
4:36-37)—which was contrary to the Law, for the tribe of Levi was not
supposed to have a land inheritance; but this law was not always observed. Barnabas was considered as a prophet and teacher by the
Church (Acts 13:1), and "a good man, full of the Holy Spirit and of
faith" (Acts 11:24). It is possible that he, like Paul, was not married—
but the reference is not clear (I Corinthians 9:5-6).[4]

Barnabas was probably robust and attractive. When he and Paul
were in Lystra, after Paul had healed a cripple, the people wanted to
honor the visitors, saying, "The gods have come down to us in the
likeness of men!" They thought Barnabas was Zeus and Paul was
Hermes (Acts 14:11-12). Statues of Zeus that have been preserved

[8] For an important discussion, see J. B. Lightfoot, *St. Paul's Epistle to the Galatians* (7th edition; London: Macmillan and Co., 1881), pp. 92-101.
[4] In the fifth verse Paul is discussing the apostle's right to be married, and in
the sixth verse, the apostle's right to work with his hands. Barnabas is mentioned in verse 6, hence it would seem that he is also included in the "we" of
verse 5.

from ancient times always present him as a big, husky, handsome man, the chief of the gods. Hermes was his messenger.[5]

Barnabas is introduced to us in an account telling that he sold a field and gave the proceeds to the apostles, to meet the needs of members of the Early Church. The Church's efforts in this difficult situation are sometimes called "communism," but this is a misnomer. In the first place, the practice was not applied to the State but only to the Church, and there is never any indication that the apostles intended either to extend it to other areas beyond the Jerusalem Church or to present it as an ideal for the State. In the second place, it was purely voluntary and in no sense compulsory, as the subsequent story of Ananias and Sapphira clearly states (Acts 5:4). The Church was attempting to solve a serious problem in a commendable way: those who had more than they needed sold their goods and gave the money to the apostles; those who had less than they needed received from the apostles to meet their needs (Acts 4:34).[6] Barnabas felt the sense of community, the oneness of the Church, and entered into this demonstration of Christian love.

That was an indication of his faith in the Church, and his faith in the people that make up the Church. In order to enter into a movement of this kind, you have to believe that men will not take advantage of the situation. Christian charity and all welfare efforts break down, or at least stagger, under the burden of freeloaders. I am perfectly willing to help the man who cannot help himself, but I am unwilling to make my productive abilities available to someone who is just as able to take care of his wife and family as I am. For the same reason I resent the intrusion of the State at this point.

Now I suppose the Early Church was more ideal in some ways than the Church of the modern day—at least this is what we are told sometimes. And yet as I study the Book of Acts, I think I can honestly conclude that even the Early Church was not without its share of men and women who wanted to take advantage of others.

But when we have expressed our negative feelings, and agreed that in this sinful society, even in the Church of the redeemed (which

[5] An early tradition of Paul, incidentally, describes him as short, bowlegged, bald-headed, with meeting eyebrows and a long nose. Cf. The Acts of Paul and Thecla, *The Ante-Nicene Fathers,* vol. 8, p. 487.

[6] The Marxist ideal is sometimes quoted, "From each according to his ability, to each according to his need." We have no objection to the ideal; it is the method of enforcing it that is significant: in communism it is the State; in the Church it is love.

is not without sin in this world), the idealism of the Early Church is not practical, we still rejoice to find someone like Barnabas. Whether or not his faith in people was always justified, he had something that we would like to have. The Church will be poor indeed when it has no men like Barnabas, men with great faith in their fellow man.

Barnabas and Saul. After Saul was converted, he went to Jerusalem and attempted to join the disciples (Acts 9:26). Saul had been in Jerusalem before, and the disciples knew all about him: he was the key figure in the persecution that had broken out following the stoning of Stephen (Acts 8:1, 3). Saul had become so personally involved in the anti-Christian movement that he had gone to Damascus to persecute the disciples in that city. As a result, the Christians in Jerusalem wanted nothing to do with him. We know, of course, that in the meantime Saul had been converted and had returned to Jerusalem to try to make amends for his former hatred and persecution. They did not know that, or if they had heard it, they did not believe it.

But Barnabas did believe it. He took Saul to the apostles (according to Paul's account, he saw only Peter and James the brother of Jesus; Galatians 1:18-19), and "declared to them how on the road he had seen the Lord, who spoke to him, and how at Damascus he had preached boldly in the name of Jesus" (Acts 9:27). The intercession of Barnabas on Saul's behalf was successful, and Saul was able to initiate a ministry that only had its beginnings in Jerusalem. I think we agree that it was a good thing there was somebody like Barnabas in the church at Jerusalem. Speaking from the human viewpoint, we would have to admit that if Saul had been unsuccessful in meeting the apostles in Jerusalem (even though, as he asserted, he received nothing to add to his gospel from them), he would have had an extremely difficult if not impossible task. For whether or not he received his gospel from the apostles, he still had to have their credential; his letter to the Galatians, as a matter of fact, depends in a large part for the force of its argument on the fact that his apostleship had been accepted by the apostles (Galatians 2:9).[7]

Again at Antioch, Barnabas demonstrated his faith in Saul of

[7] This side of the argument is often played down in the effort to stress the independency of Paul's gospel. But Paul's whole ministry, his periodic return to Jerusalem and to Antioch to report on his work, and particularly his part in the great discussion at the Jerusalem conference, deny any notion of independency. To him the Church was a body, and no part could say of any other, "I have no need of you" (I Corinthians 12:12-26).

Tarsus. After telling the story of the scattering of the Church by describing Peter's work in Samaria (Acts 9:32—11:18), Luke picks up another thread of the story: "Now those who were scattered because of the persecution that arose over Stephen traveled as far as Phoenicia and Cyprus and Antioch, speaking the word to none except Jews. But there were some of them, men of Cyprus and Cyrene, who on coming to Antioch spoke to the Greeks also, preaching the Lord Jesus. And the hand of the Lord was with them, and a great number that believed turned to the Lord" (Acts 11:19-21). News of this work reached Jerusalem, and the Church in Jerusalem sent Barnabas to Antioch to find out what was going on—at least I can only conclude that the mission was a kind of investigation, for as yet the Church felt no sense of call to a ministry of this type.

The word "Greek" needs to be defined.[8] We have previously seen that Luke uses "Hellenist" in a special sense, meaning a Jew who spoke Greek. He likewise uses "Greek" in a special sense, meaning Gentile. The classical use of the word "Greek" set it over against "barbarian" but this is found only once in the New Testament (Romans 1:14). In Luke the term "Greek" seems to include even barbarians (cf. Acts 14:1 and perhaps 16:1). This is another step outward, then, in the progress of the preaching of the Early Church. It is an emphasis, made by some, designed to reach Gentiles. We cannot yet describe it as a deliberate plan or program of the Church; that did not occur, as we have seen, until the first missionary journey a year or more later. Those who initiated the work among Gentiles were men from Cyprus and Cyrene, doubtless Jews of the Dispersion who were sufficiently Hellenized that they had a sense of mission to Gentiles and freedom to put it into practice. They had been converted to Christianity in Jerusalem (note that "some of them" refers back to "those who were scattered"), but their eyes were on the world. They had listened to the words of Jesus carefully, whether from His lips or from those of His faithful disciples, and they knew that the gospel was to be preached to all the world.

Barnabas saw the work in Antioch as a demonstration of the grace of God and he rejoiced. He not only rejoiced; he encouraged the work, and as a result, "a large company was added to the Lord" (cf. Acts 11:22-24). More than that, he saw the possibility of expanding the

---

[8] Some manuscripts read "Hellenists" in Acts 11:20. Internal evidence, however, requires "Greeks."

work still further if he could get the right man to help him—and Barnabas knew the right man, and he thought he knew where to find him. So he went to Tarsus to look for Saul (Acts 11:25). It took time, but it resulted in a wonderful year of Christian activity in Antioch, and more than that—but let us not run ahead of the story.

I wonder why Barnabas thought of Saul? We have a ready answer: "Saul was the apostle to the Gentiles." But is that the right answer? Did Barnabas know that at that time? Was Barnabas even thinking in terms of a Gentile ministry at that time? Antioch-on-the-Orontes was a huge city, perhaps one of the most beautiful ever built, and, as third largest city of the empire, capital of the East. There was a large Jewish population there. There were probably many Proselytes. Even without thinking of a Gentile ministry, Barnabas saw a great opportunity.[9] But why Saul? What had he been doing? Some tell us that after leaving Jerusalem (Acts 9:30), Saul went to Tarsus and spent about ten years making goat-hair cloth. I doubt it! Barnabas did not want a weaver, he wanted a preacher. The letter from the Jerusalem conference was addressed "to the brethren who are of the Gentiles in Antioch and Syria and Cilicia" (Acts 15:23). Syria-and-Cilicia was the name of the Roman province around Antioch, including Tarsus. At the start of his second missionary journey, Paul visited the Churches of Syria and Cilicia to strengthen them (Acts 15:41). Where did these Churches come from? Paul told the Galatians that after he left Jerusalem he went into "the regions of Syria and Cilicia" (Galatians 1:21). It is my belief that Saul had spent ten years or so preaching in the province around his home town.[10] I think Barnabas knew something of that work. I think it took Barnabas some little time to find Saul because he was out preaching; if he had been weaving, Barnabas could have found him quickly. Barnabas wanted a man with experience for the work that was opening up. Saul was the man.

The Church in Antioch was led by the Spirit to commission

[9] The fact that believers were first called "Christians" in Antioch is too well known to need repetition, Acts 11:26. I should point out, however, that the author of Acts is much more careful than I have been in the use of the term, and where I have spoken of "Christians" before this point in the history of the Church, Luke would have used one of several synonyms, "disciples," "believers," "those of the way," etc.

[10] R. C. H. Lenski, on the other hand, takes a strongly opposite view in *The Interpretation of the Acts of the Apostles* (Columbus, Ohio: Lutheran Book Concern, 1934), pp. 372-373, 615.

Barnabas and Saul for the work to which He had called them (Acts 13:2). This was the beginning of organized missionary activity by the Early Church. Their first journey took them to Cyprus and to the south-central portion of Asia Minor.

Why did they go to Cyprus? I think it is obvious: Barnabas came from there. He had friends, and probably relatives, who lived in Cyprus, and he wanted them to hear the gospel. It is a sound missionary principle to start where you have the most in common with your hearers. Failure to apply this principle is perhaps the greatest single reason for the vast number of missionaries (estimated at between 50 and 80 per cent) who do not return to the field after their first term of service. Before Barnabas and Saul set out on their first missionary journey, they had had at least twelve or thirteen years of Christian service. Even then, they went into an area that one of them knew, and among people with whom they had something in common.

Barnabas and Mark. Barnabas and Saul took with them on their missionary journey a young man named John (Acts 13:5) who was also named Mark (Acts 12:12). The expression, "And they had John to assist [or, minister to] them," is not clear; some think that Mark performed personal services, others think that he helped to catechize the converts.

John Mark was a cousin of Barnabas (Colossians 4:10). Mark's mother Mary (Acts 12:12) was a prominent woman in the Church in Jerusalem, and it was in her house that the disciples were praying for Peter when he had been seized by Herod. From this the inference has been drawn that Mary had a large house and the double inference that she was wealthy. Some have supposed that the Last Supper was held in an upper room in her house, and that the disciples waited in prayer for the Holy Spirit in that same Upper Room.[11] Mary the mother of Mark cannot be identified with any other Mary in the New Testament.

John Mark was called "my son Mark" by Peter (I Peter 5:13). On the strength of the parallel whereby Paul calls Timothy his son, many

---

[11] This guessing game goes even further. The young man who wore only a linen cloth and who lost it in the Garden of Gethsemane (Mark 14:51-52) was Mark. He knew where Jesus would be, because he overheard the discussion in his mother's house. He knew the soldiers had come for Jesus, for they came first to Mary's house. He wore only a sheet because he had not taken time to dress, but ran to warn Jesus. All guesses!

conclude that Mark was converted by Peter's preaching—and this is possible. We must point out, however, that it is not certain that Paul converted Timothy, for Timothy's mother and grandmother were believers (II Timothy 1:5); it is possible that "son" in the case of both Timothy and Mark refers to association and training in Christian service.

We first meet Mark in the year A.D. 44, when he is already a Christian and a respected member of the Church in Jerusalem. When Barnabas and Saul returned to Antioch, after their famine-visit to Jerusalem (cf. Acts 11:27-30), they took Mark with them (Acts 12:25). As we have seen, they subsequently took Mark on the first missionary journey.

Later, Mark was associated with Peter, and still later, he wrote the Gospel called by his name. According to an early tradition of the Church, Mark served as interpreter on Peter's missionary journeys, and after Peter's death Mark wrote down the words of Peter.[12] This would account for the graphic style of the Gospel of Mark. If the early Christian preachers used catechetical methods of instruction, as seems likely, and if Mark assisted the apostles in this instruction, this would account for formal elements of the Second Gospel, which in turn would account for some of the verbal agreements between Mark and other Gospel sources.[13]

When the apostolic mission reached Perga, John Mark turned back. We are not told why, but we know that it caused a serious breach between Paul and Barnabas (Acts 15:39). Various suggestions have been given concerning the cause of Mark's defection. Some think he had experienced a great deal of sickness; it is entirely possible in that part of the world. Some think he was worrying about his mother; that too is possible, and many men have had to give up work they would like to do for the sake of the parents they love. Some think he was afraid; I am inclined to doubt that reason. It seems to me that the "sharp contention" between Paul and Barnabas, however, requires a much more significant reason than any of these expressed. The only

[12] For a summary of the numerous sources of this tradition, see H. B. Swete, *The Gospel According to St. Mark* (3d edition; London: Macmillan and Co., 1927), pp. xxiii-xxiv.

[13] This is certainly not the place to get into a discussion of Source- and Form-Criticism. For a helpful introduction to the subject, see F. F. Bruce, *The New Testament Documents*, pp. 29-46. On the catechetical motives, see Vincent Taylor, *The Gospel According to St. Mark* (London: Macmillan and Co., 1952), p. 133.

reason that would have sufficient magnitude would be one arising from the Judaizer problem. Paul seemed to be able to tolerate almost anything else; but when anyone suggested that anything should be added to the gospel of grace, Paul could find no point of compromise. On this issue he was willing to censure Peter, yes, even Barnabas (Galatians 2:11-14). As I reconstruct the situation, Mark had found Paul's work with Gentiles contrary to his own view of the Law. When it became obvious that they were going to move into territory where Gentiles would predominate, Mark drew the line. He went home.

Barnabas still had faith in Mark. When the Jerusalem conference was over, and Paul said, "Come, let us return and visit the brethren in every city where we proclaimed the word of the Lord" (Acts 15:36), Barnabas said, "Fine; let's take Mark with us." When Paul stubbornly refused, "Barnabas took Mark with him and sailed away to Cyprus, but Paul chose Silas . . ." (Acts 15:39-40). That Mark justified the faith Barnabas put in him, even Paul would admit. Years later, when Paul was in prison waiting for the executioner's sword, he wrote to Timothy, "Get Mark and bring him with you; for he is very useful in serving me" (II Timothy 4:11). What would have happened if Barnabas had not had faith in Mark? Humanly speaking, it is possible that Mark would have dropped out of Christian work altogether. If we had not had his Gospel, we would not have had either Matthew's or Luke's Gospels, for they draw large portions from Mark. But God would not let a man like John Mark get away—that was one of the reasons why He had Barnabas!

Barnabas was not perfect; no one is. The Bible presents its characters without make-up; we see them as they really were—and that is encouragement for the rest of us. Barnabas lost sight of the need of preserving the pure gospel and Christian unity. Under the pressure of Peter and others, he "was carried away by their insincerity," and had to be sternly rebuked by Paul (Galatians 2:13). I am not trying to excuse Barnabas; I am convinced that Paul was absolutely right in his intransigence at this point. The purity of the gospel must be preserved at all cost. The unity of the Church cannot be denied by the erection of a special class of Christians. But I wonder if even at this point it was not Barnabas's faith in people that got him into difficulty. I wonder if he was not trusting the brothers who had come from Jerusalem, if he was not trusting Peter's hasty action, rather than pursuing cold logic.

Well, it did not destroy Paul's respect for him. Paul speaks of Barnabas only in terms of appreciation. Even in the situation described in Galatians, Paul mentions Barnabas, but he puts the burden of his argument on Peter. After all, you can't help loving a man like Barnabas!

CHAPTER XIII

Luke the Beloved Physician

THERE IS ONLY one Gentile author included in the Bible: Luke, who wrote the Third Gospel and Acts. That Luke was a Gentile is clearly indicated in Colossians, where Aristarchus, Mark, and Jesus Justus are distinguished from Epaphras, Luke, and Demas, the first three being "the only men of the circumcision among my fellow workers" (Colossians 4:11), and therefore the only Jews.[1] The writings of this lone Gentile, which comprise the largest part of the New Testament by any single writer, are magnificent literature. Even a man who is not interested in the spiritual values of the writings will appreciate the literary qualities, the composition, style, and other elements, of Luke's works. Luke's appreciation of beauty is evident often, but perhaps especially in the fact that he alone of the New Testament writers recorded the hymns, *Benedictus, Magnificat,* and *Nunc Dimittis,* hymns which have become part of the liturgy of the Church.

Luke the physician. Luke was a scientific man and a doctor. I used to love to make that statement to the college students in my course at Lafayette College. Naturally, it would raise an immediate objection. "Doctor? Witch doctor, maybe! How would you like to have Luke operate on you?" Well, now let us stop a minute and think.

The science of medicine has a great history, and it is worth our while to review some of the facts. When Galen of Pergamum (A.D. 130-200) wrote his medical treatises, medical science had reached a high point which it did not exceed for thirteen hundred years. In fact, no further advances were made in medical science until the nineteenth century. But medical science did not begin with Galen;

---

[1] In spite of the clear statement in Scripture, an occasional author, trying to defend the theory that Romans 3:2 requires that all Scripture writers be Jews, insists that Luke was a Jew. Romans 3:2 refers to the Old Testament. Moreover, if God was breaking down the wall that separated Jews and Gentiles, why would this not also apply to the writers of Scripture?

as a matter of fact, it ended with him in antiquity. Medicine achieved greater advances between the sixth century B.C. and the second century A.D. than at any other time in history until the last century and a half. But even that is not the beginning of medicine.

The origins of medicine are lost in antiquity. The Egyptians looked upon Imhotep (c.2700 B.C.) as a sort of patron saint of medicine. Egyptian medical texts go back to c.1700 B.C., but it is questionable, in my opinion, whether these deserve the term "scientific," for they are "a hodge-podge of home remedies based on a lore of herbs and of sympathetic magic, outright witch-doctoring in the forms of charms and incantations, and shrewd observation on the functions of the body."[2] It seems there was some knowledge of broken bones, and possibly the setting of them; and certainly the knowledge of the abdominal cavity and its organs had been learned from the process of mummification, but no scientific knowledge is recorded. In Mesopotamia medical skill was more nearly a science. A Sumerian text from c.2200 B.C. contains a collection of prescriptions which has been called "the oldest medical 'handbook' known to man";[3] it is notably lacking in magic spells and incantations. In the Code of Hammurabi (c.1700 B.C.), laws regulated the amount physicians could charge for operations and for bone-setting (§§ 215-225). One operation, the meaning of which is not entirely clear, seems to be for an ulcer or abscess of the eye, and some scholars think it means a cataract.[4] The penalty for destroying the eye, we should add, was the loss of the surgeon's hand—which certainly limited the number of failures the doctor could make! Grave excavations at Mycenae (dated 1650-1550 B.C.) have uncovered skulls that give clear evidence of skillful trepanation (brain surgery performed by removing a piece of the skull),[5] and in one instance, at least, the patient recovered, for the bone had partially grown back over the saw-cuts.

Strictly speaking, however, these were skills rather than science. The rise of science can be dated to the sixth century B.C., and was

[2] J.A. Wilson, *The Culture of Ancient Egypt* (Chicago: University of Chicago Press, 1956), p. 56. This work was published in 1951 under the title, *The Burden of Egypt*.

[3] Samuel Noah Kramer, *From the Tablets of Sumer* (Indian Hills, Colo.: Falcon's Wing Press, 1956), pp. 56-60.

[4] Cf. G. R. Driver and John C. Miles, *The Babylonian Laws* (Oxford: Clarendon Press, 1955), vol. 2, pp. 78-81 and 251-253.

[5] Cf. George E. Mylonas, *Ancient Mycenae* (Princeton: Princeton University Press, 1957), p. 138.

largely due to the Greek ability to abstract principles from empirical data.[6] In medicine, the name of Hippocrates (460?-377? B.C.) is significant, and the *Collection of Hippocrates,* dealing with wounds of the head, is a model of what succinct clinical records ought to be. Herophilus of Chalcedon is regarded as the father of anatomy, and Erasistratus of Chios as the father of physiology. The body had been dissected, and the brain, nervous system and circulatory system had been explored (although some of the theories make us smile today). The center of medical science was along the Ionian coast of the Aegean Sea—which is where Luke seems to have spent much of his life.

Luke was a scientist. Science is the process of observation, comparison, control, and deduction, or the abstracting of principles. That method was already well known in the Greek world and particularly in the medical world, and Luke was heir to a science of medicine that could compare favorably with any medical practice up to the early part of the last century.

According to some scholars, Luke was born in Syrian Antioch. He certainly shows great familiarity with Antioch and with the Church there. Others think that Luke came from Philippi in Macedonia. We first cross his trail in Troas (Acts 16:10; his use of "we" will be discussed shortly), and he is personally involved in the apostolic mission to Philippi. Luke was apparently a Christian before he met Paul, but we have no knowledge of his conversion. There is some rather convincing evidence that Luke was familiar with the sea and with ships; and the suggestion that he was at one time a ship's doctor would fit in with this evidence. We know that Paul had some kind of affliction that he refers to, and the suggestion has been made that Luke was called in to treat Paul. All these suggestions are attractive—but we must bear in mind that they are only suggestions, not established facts.

Some years ago one scholar made a detailed study of the medical language of Luke,[7] and was convinced (and convinced others) that

---

[6] For an illuminating treatment, see Benjamin Farrington, *Greek Science* (Pelican Book A142; Baltimore, Md.: Penguin Books, 1953), 320 pp. It is not generally known that, working from philosophy, mathematics, and observations, the Greeks had computed the circumference of the earth to within about two hundred miles and had conceived of its sphericity three centuries before Christ. See Strabo, *Geography,* 2.5.7 and 34 on size, and 2.5.2 and 10 on shape.

[7] William K. Hobart, *The Medical Language of St. Luke* (Dublin: Hodges, Figgis & Co., 1882; reprinted, Grand Rapids, Mich.: Baker Book House, 1954), 305 pp.

the evidence demonstrated that Luke was a physician. He proved too much, and modern scholars have reacted perhaps too far in the other direction; but at any rate it is safe to say that Luke's medical profession, if established by other evidence, would account for his use of technical terminology. There is other evidence. Luke shows great interest in healing. Of the four Gospel writers, he is the only one to tell of the Good Samaritan (Luke 10:25-37), the casting out of the demons (Luke 11:14-36), the healing of the man with dropsy (Luke 14:1-6), the healing of the woman with the unclean spirit (Luke 13:10-17), and the cleansing of the ten lepers (Luke 17:11-19). Likewise in Acts, he tells of the healing of the lame man at the Temple gate (Acts 3:1-8), the healing of Aeneas (Acts 9:33-34), the healing of the cripple at Lystra (Acts 14:8-10), the resuscitation of Eutychus at Troas (Acts 20:9-12), and the curing of Publius' father on Malta (Acts 28:7-10).

Luke shows a deep interest in women and children, which would also be true of a medical doctor. Of the Gospel writers, Luke alone records the details of the birth stories and the childhood details (Luke 1:5—2:52). He alone tells of the raising of the widow's son (Luke 7:11-17), of the anointing of Jesus by the sinful woman (Luke 7:36-50);[8] he alone tells the story of Martha and Mary (Luke 10:38-42), and the parable of the importunate widow (Luke 18:1-14). Likewise in Acts, women are included at numerous points in the story of the Early Church.

In the account of Paul's healing ministry on Malta there is an indication that Luke may have added his medical skill to Paul's miraculous healing. Two different Greek words are used: the first in the statement "and Paul visited him and prayed, and putting his hands on him healed him" (Acts 28:8), where the word conveys the idea of healing brought to its completion; the second word is used in the next verse, "the rest of the people on the island who had diseases also came and were cured" (Acts 28:9), where the word conveys the idea of the healing process from its beginning.[9] We might paraphrase by saying that Paul healed the first, Paul and Luke treated and cured the others. Is this why Luke records, "They presented many gifts to us"?

[8] See my note, p. 63, above.
[9] The first word is from *iáomai* "to heal," the second from *therapeúõ* "to treat medically, to cure."

Luke the historian. In the providence of God this man with scientifically trained powers of observation became the historian of the Early Church. The opening of his Gospel gives an idea of his method and purpose: "Inasmuch as many have undertaken to compile a narrative of the things which have been accomplished among us, just as they were delivered to us by those who from the beginning were eyewitnesses and ministers of the word, it seemed good to me also, having followed all things closely for some time past, to write an orderly account for you . . ." (Luke 1:1-3).

Luke states at once in the Gospel that he was not an eyewitness; he used available sources. There are some believers who hold such a narrow view of inspiration that they feel we dishonor the Holy Spirit when we speak of sources. The historic view of inspiration teaches that the Holy Spirit inspired men in their use of materials, including sources.

In the case of Acts, on the other hand, Luke was an eyewitness of some of the things he had recorded. In Acts 16:10, the first person pronoun "we" slips unobtrusively into the record, and continues to verse 17; the account then is told in the third person ("he" or "they"). In Acts 20:5 another "we" section occurs, continuing to Acts 21:25; and a third "we" section is found from Acts 27:2 to 28:16. Now the name of Luke does not occur in the Book of Acts. The question therefore naturally arises, How do we know that "we" is intended to include Luke; is there any way to check on this? There is. The periods covered by the "we" passages are the following: from Troas to Philippi on the second missionary journey, from Philippi to Caesarea on the third journey, and from Caesarea to Rome on the first journey to Rome. We can find in the writings of Paul indications of these periods and references to his associates. Luke is mentioned in the New Testament only three times: two of these references are from the Roman imprisonment (Colossians 4:14; Philemon 23), which agrees with the third "we" section.

Have you ever heard of Aristarchus? He was not a very important person, so far as the record goes; he is mentioned only five times in the New Testament. Paul mentions him twice: each time in connection with Luke (Colossians 4:10; Philemon 24). The other three references are in Acts (19:29; 20:4; and 27:2)—in each instance in a "we" passage. It is clear, then, that when Aristarchus was present Luke was also present. Speaking for myself, I am convinced that this is no mere coincidence, and that Luke was Paul's companion for the parts of Acts indicated.[10]

For the balance of the material in Acts, Luke used sources. From the itinerary sketched by the "we" sections, we can tell with reasonable certainty what some of these sources may have been. There was Paul, of course, who could have told Luke all about the stoning of Stephen, his own conversion, the first missionary journey, the Jerusalem conference, and all the other details that involved Paul when Luke was not present personally. There was Silas, who certainly knew important details of the Jerusalem Church, for he was one of the leaders there (Acts 15:22). At Caesarea there was Philip the evangelist (Acts 21:8), who surely knew the details of the choosing of the Seven (the deacons) and the conversion of the Ethiopian, as well as the story of Simon Magus and other incidents in Samaria (Acts 6 and 8). Since Luke was present in Caesarea both at the end of the third journey and at the beginning of the journey to Rome, it is a reasonable supposition that he remained in the general area for the intervening two years, and it is also reasonable to suppose that he used some of this time to collect material for the Third Gospel. The sources for this material would be able to furnish information for the remainder of the early chapters of Acts.

Luke has gathered together in Acts an amazing mass of detail. According to one scholar, one hundred and ten persons are named in Acts.[11] Place names, geographical details, official names and titles, with other factual data, are found on every page. In 1880, William M. Ramsay made his first visit to Asia Minor, the beginning of research that was to occupy him for the next thirty-four years. He was a classics scholar, with a critical view of the Scriptures. As he became acquainted with detail after detail, fact after fact, he came to realize that Luke was the master historian. In 1911 Ramsay stated: "Every person is found just where he ought to be: proconsuls in senatorial provinces, asiarchs in Ephesus, strategoi in Philippi, politarchs in Thessalonica, magicians and soothsayers everywhere."[12] Ramsay's

---

[10] For a recent and full discussion, see A. H. McNeile, *An Introduction to the Study of the New Testament* (2d edition, revised by C. S. C. Williams; Oxford: Clarendon Press, 1953), pp. 103-110.

[11] Lenski, *Interpretation of the Acts of the Apostles*, p. 5.

[12] W. M. Ramsay, *The Bearing of Recent Discovery on the Trustworthiness of*

many volumes have had considerable effect on many scholars, and have convinced not a few of the general correctness of his conclusions.

Luke has preserved the color, the character, the verisimilitude of widely different persons and situations. The speeches he has preserved retain the personal characteristics of the speakers. The local customs are accurately reflected. Life is filled with endless variety; Luke has observed that variety, and recorded the details with unerring eye and ear. Peter is Peter and Paul is Paul; Antioch is Antioch and Athens is Athens. Try to record the details of your travels sometime (I have tried, often!), and you will appreciate Luke as never before. Try to portray an imaginary journey, and you will realize how empty is the argument that Luke wrote fiction. Hollywood hired technical advisors for the production of a Biblical film and when they were finished, scholars in the audience laughed at the errors in detail. Luke had no staff of technical advisors, no research library, no electronic equipment. And Sir William Ramsay, who had few peers in classical studies and none in the historical geography of Asia Minor, could find no flaw in Luke's production! Luke was a scientifically trained historian.

Luke the evangelist. Luke wrote his books not just to write, but to save a soul. Scholars are generally convinced that he had in mind a larger circle of readers—and possibly he did. But the undeniable fact is that he addressed both works to Theophilus for the express purpose of setting the truth before Theophilus. He wanted to present the story of Jesus Christ in the most convincing form, which was to tell the truth with beauty and clarity; likewise he wanted to present the story of the origin of the Christian faith. There are some who believe that Theophilus was a dignitary in a place of authority, and that Luke was using this means of writing Paul's defense. This may be so. I feel, however, that as a defense of Paul the works are too subtle to accomplish the purpose. That Theophilus was a person entitled to be addressed with honor and respect is evident from the words of Luke, "most excellent Theophilus."

Luke is called "the Evangelist" because he wrote the Gospel that

---

the New Testament (2d edition; London: Hodder and Stoughton, 1915; reprinted Grand Rapids, Mich.: Baker Book House, 1953), pp. 96-97. The lecture was delivered in 1911.

bears his name. I am using the term here, however, in the broader sense: Luke was at heart an evangelist. He wanted to proclaim the Evangel, the Good News. When Luke first met Paul, Silas, and Timothy, they were at Troas. That is the last place in Asia: before you lies the narrow water that separates Asia from Europe, and Europe can be seen very clearly. We read that Paul saw a vision in the night, a man of Macedonia, urging Paul, "Come over to Macedonia and help us" (Acts 16:9). Some think this vision was caused by the plea which Luke had been making on behalf of Macedonia. It is an interesting suggestion. We know that the subconscious often works at night on problems that we have tried to thrust aside during the day.

Philippi was "the leading city of the district of Macedonia" (Acts 16:12). Named for Philip II of Macedon, the city overlooked the Plain of Drama, where in 168 b.c. the Roman general Aemilius Paulus had overcome the last of the Macedonian kings, and where in 42 b.c. Brutus and Cassius were slain and the hopes of the Roman Republic died before a rising Empire. But most important, it was from Philippi that Alexander the Great went forth to conquer the world. Luke was proud of Philippi; that is one reason why he is often identified with the city. Perhaps he looked upon it as the place to defeat the empires of the world and to start a kingdom not of the world. Perhaps he thought that a Greater than Alexander had come. But we are only speculating. One thing we do know: Paul and his party went into Europe, to Philippi, and Luke was with them.

There, by the river outside the city, for there was no synagogue (which means that there were not ten male Jewish property-owners in the city), a woman from Thyatira in Asia Minor, a business woman, a Gentile woman who had come to worship the God of the Jews, heard the gospel and was converted. She was Lydia. Her house became the meeting place of the Church in Philippi (Acts 16:11-40). At Philippi a slave girl was delivered from a spirit of divination (Acts 16:16-19). The Church there grew and came to be known as one of the most generous of the Pauline churches (Philippians 4:14-18). Every morning the Jew blesses the Lord who has not created him a Gentile, a slave, or a woman (*Talmud Berakoth* 60b).[18] Paul may have had

---

[18] The reference is taken from Philip Birnbaum, *Daily Prayer Book* (New York: Hebrew Publishing Company, 1949), pp. 16, 18. The prayer runs, "Blessed art thou, Lord our God, King of the universe, who hast not made me

such a prayer in mind when he wrote, "There is neither Jew nor Greek, there is neither slave nor free, there is neither male nor female; for you are all one in Christ Jesus" (Galatians 3:28). At Philippi, the conversion of the Gentile woman Lydia and the healing of the Gentile slave girl testify strongly to this principle of oneness in Christ.

Luke remained at Philippi when Paul and the others moved west to Thessalonica. He rejoined Paul perhaps four or five years later when Paul was enroute to Jerusalem. In the meantime it is possible that Luke had been sent to Corinth. In II Corinthians 8:18 there is a curious verse that has puzzled Biblical scholars for centuries. Paul was planning to send Titus to Corinth, and he adds, "With him we are sending the brother who is famous among all the churches for his preaching of the gospel." Who is this brother? As early as the time of Origen (A.D. 185?-254?), he was identified as Luke. (This would explain, in my opinion, the absence of the name Titus from Acts, if he were Luke's brother.) In a colophon at the end of II Corinthians, found in some manuscripts of the eighth and ninth centuries and in some English editions, are the words, "Written from Philippi by Titus and Luke." This would support the view that the brother sent with Titus was Luke. Once again, it is interesting speculation, and may indeed be true.

Luke's interest in the gospel of salvation, however, is not speculation. It is firmly established. His Gospel alone records the parables of the lost coin, the lost sheep, and the prodigal son and his lost brother (Luke 15). His Gospel alone tells the story of Zacchaeus, who climbed a tree to see Jesus, and whose house Jesus graced with the words: "Today salvation has come to this house. . . . For the Son of man came to seek and to save the lost" (Luke 19:1-10). The Book of Acts is the message of salvation from beginning to end. The disciples waited until they had received the Holy Spirit; then they began the preaching of the gospel. Stephen was chosen to serve tables, but he preached the gospel. Saul was the persecutor of the Church, but when the risen Lord appeared to him he began at once to preach the gospel. To see this truth is to know Luke the Evangelist.

In my ministry I have known three physicians who were fine Bible teachers with important Bible classes. I have known several others who

---

a heathen . . . who hast not made me a slave . . . who hast not made me a woman."

were active witnesses to the power of the gospel both in their churches and in their medical practices. They are following in the footsteps of Doctor Luke. Luke should be an inspiration and a challenge to any medical doctor, in fact, to any man of a scientific mind, for he combines the rare gifts of scientific training and evangelical passion, the care of the body and the care of the soul.

CHAPTER XIV

Priscilla and Aquila

PREVIOUSLY WE VISITED the home of a brother and two sisters where Jesus was often present, and we learned a little about that home. Now let me take you to a home which was often visited by Paul. In fact, he lived with this man and wife for months, probably for years, and a friendship developed between them that stretched across sixteen or seventeen years. I refer, as I am sure you have guessed, to Priscilla and Aquila.[1]

Priscilla and Aquila. We first meet this couple in Corinth at the time of Paul's second missionary journey: "After this he [Paul] left Athens and went to Corinth. And he found a Jew named Aquila, a native of Pontus, lately come from Italy with his wife Priscilla, because Claudius had commanded all the Jews to leave Rome. And he went to see them; and because he was of the same trade he stayed with them . . ." (Acts 18:1-3).

Aquila, then, was a Jew, born in Pontus, which is in the north-central part of Turkey, toward the eastern end of the Black Sea. We do not know the age at which he moved to Rome, or the reason. He could have been taken as a slave while still a boy. Priscilla and Aquila are mentioned six times in Scripture and Priscilla's name stands first four of the six times. Perhaps this is not significant; some scholars, however, feel that it indicates that Priscilla was of a higher social standing than her husband. The name Aquila is found among Roman slaves of the period (it is also found among the freemen, so we cannot make too much of the point). Therefore, it is possible that Aquila had been a slave in a Roman household and had married one of the daughters of that family. We know that manumitted Roman slaves had come to be regarded as equals.[2] The name Priscilla[3] is purely a

---

[1] This name is frequently mispronounced; it is accented on the first syllable: ăk′wĭ-luh.

[2] See Jérôme Carcopino, *Daily Life in Ancient Rome* (New Haven: Yale University Press, 1960), chapters III-IV.

[3] The name means "little old lady"—how this came to be given to babies

138

Roman name, hence Aquila's wife was not a Jewess. Again we may surmise that Priscilla had become attracted to Aquila's God, and perhaps had even become a proselyte to Judaism before she married Aquila.

We are not told when this married couple first became Christian. Paul makes no mention of the fact and gives no indication that he was instrumental in their conversion, so it is safe to suppose that they were already Christians when he first met them. If so, they were already Christians when they came from Rome.

Priscilla and Aquila had been forced to leave Rome by the edict of the emperor Claudius. Suetonius, the Roman historian of the second century A. D., records that "since the Jews constantly made disturbances at the instigation of Chrestus, he [Claudius] expelled them from Rome."[4] According to Ramsay, the edict is to be dated in the end of A.D. 50, and the arrival of Priscilla and Aquila in the early months of A.D. 51.[5] The name "Chrestus" has been discussed many times, and while no compelling conclusion has been reached, it seems reasonable to suppose that this word is to be linked with "Christ" or "Christian," and that the disturbances in Rome were due to disputes between Christian Jews and non-Christian Jews, such as occurred at Jerusalem and elsewhere. The Claudian edict was not rigidly enforced for very long, and soon the Jews began to return to Rome.

Paul was in Corinth when Gallio was proconsul (Acts 18:12), and Gallio became proconsul in July, A.D. 51. Priscilla and Aquila had come to Corinth early that same year, hence Paul's arrival must have been at approximately the same time. According to Acts 18:11, Paul stayed in Corinth for eighteen months, and if Acts 18:18 is to be added to that, the period was a bit longer. Nothing is said of Priscilla and Aquila during that time, but when Paul left for Syria, he took with him Priscilla and Aquila, and left them at Ephesus (Acts 18:18-19). That would have been early in A.D. 53, probably as soon as the sea lanes opened. Whether Paul returned to Ephesus that fall or early the

---

(the masculine form also occurs), we can only guess. Probably someone said, "Why, she looks just like a little old lady!" hence the name.

[4] Suetonius, *Claudius*, 25.

[5] Cf. W. M. Ramsay, *St. Paul the Traveller and the Roman Citizen* (10th edition, London: Hodder and Stoughton, 1908; reprinted Grand Rapids: Baker Book House, 1951), p. 254.

following year cannot be determined. By the time he reached Ephesus, Apollos had already been instructed by Priscilla and Aquila and had gone on to Corinth (Acts 18:26—19:1). Luke does not tell us anything else about the couple, but we can add a few details from incidental references in Paul's writings.

Paul wrote his first letter to the church in Corinth toward the end of his stay in Ephesus. The length of this Ephesian ministry is not exactly determined, but the following time references are given by Luke: three months in the synagogue (Acts 19:8), two years in the hall of Tyrannus (Acts 19:10), plus an additional period (Acts 19:22). His arrival in Ephesus was dated late in A. D. 53 or early 54; hence the close of the Ephesian ministry must be dated in A.D. 56 or perhaps even 57.[6] First Corinthians, then, was written perhaps in A.D. 56, and according to the closing chapter, Prisca (the more formal name, invariably used by Paul) and Aquila joined in sending greetings, "together with the church in their house" (I Corinthians 16:19). It is therefore possible to conclude that this Christian couple had spent three years or more in Ephesus, had opened their home to the young Church there, had devoted themselves to Christian instruction, and had been generally useful in assisting Paul.

Toward the end of Paul's third missionary journey, when it was obvious that he could not go on to Rome at that time, he wrote the epistle to the Romans. The letter was written from Corinth, and almost certainly was sent to Rome by the hand of Phoebe, "a deaconess of the church at Cenchreae" (Romans 16:1). At that time, Priscilla and Aquila were back in Rome and a Church was meeting in their house (Romans 16:3-5).[7] When they had returned to Rome we are not told, but it had to be between the time Paul left Ephesus (A.D. 56/57) and the time he was ready to leave Corinth (A.D. 57/58).

Only one other reference remains; that is in Paul's last letter. At that time, when he was awaiting his execution, writing his last words to Timothy who was then at Ephesus, he added, "Greet Prisca and Aquila" (II Timothy 4:19).

Putting these details together, we can reconstruct the outline of the

[6] F. F. Bruce comes to a slightly earlier date; cf. *The Book of Acts,* p. 405.
[7] I accept the conclusion of Romans as an original part of the epistle. Many modern scholars think it was originally part of the letter to Ephesus; but the preponderance of Roman names rather supports the Roman destination. For discussion see James Denney in *The Expositor's Greek Testament,* vol. 2, pp. 580-582, and, conversely, T. W. Manson, "St. Paul's Letter to the Romans—and Others," *Bulletin of the John Rylands Library* 31 (November, 1948), pp. 1-19.

life of Priscilla and Aquila rather completely from beginning to end. For the period from our first meeting with them, about the year A.D. 51, to the time of Paul's last letter, perhaps A.D. 67, they traveled from Rome to Corinth to Ephesus, thence to Rome, and a second time to Ephesus. They spent about two years in Corinth, about three years in Ephesus, and from five to ten years in Rome before returning to Ephesus again. In each case they were active in Christian work and their home was open to the local Church for its meetings. Church buildings, of course, had not yet come into existence. Aquila was a weaver of goat's hair tent cloth. It is hardly likely that this provided sufficient income for travel; we can suppose that Priscilla had some personal wealth that made their journeys possible.

Priscilla and Aquila and Paul.   Paul first met this Christian man and wife in Corinth. What brought them together was their trade of weaving goat's hair cloth. This material, also known as *cilicium* from the fact that it originated or became prominently known at Cilicia, is usually made on long looms set up along the street in a certain part of the town; sometimes the looms are fifty feet or more in length. It is difficult for the average American, unless he has traveled through the Near or Far East, to think of areas of commercial concentration, such as a street of basketweavers or silversmiths, an area where each shop will sell identical items and where nothing else is sold. To our way of thinking, this is unnecessary and useless competition, but to the Oriental there is a splendid camaraderie, and the coppersmith who does not have an item to please you will cheerfully direct you to one of his fellow craftsmen in a nearby shop. I suppose Paul found his way to the street of the tent-cloth weavers, as Aquila had done a few weeks or months earlier, and there he began to work at his trade. There he doubtless met Aquila. They probably soon found that they were believers in the same Saviour, and the next thing, Paul was invited to stay at the home of Aquila and his wife (cf. Acts 18:3).

Since Luke does not say much about Priscilla and Aquila, we have to read between the lines; but we have little difficulty doing this, for we know Paul's interest, and we soon get to know the interests of his friends. Aquila had recently come from Rome. Not long after the account of the meeting of Aquila and Paul, Luke records Paul's decision, "I must also see Rome" (Acts 19:21). This suggests only one thing to me: Aquila and Priscilla had told Paul about the Christian community in Rome.

We know little or nothing about the origin of Christianity in Rome. According to the view held by some, Peter founded the Roman Church c. A.D. 44. This seems unlikely.[8] But if we are correct in surmising that Priscilla and Aquila were Christians before leaving Rome, and if we are correct in identifying "Chrestus" with Christ and the Christian movement, then the gospel had reached Rome prior to the Claudian edict of A.D. 50. This is borne out, to some extent, by Paul's strong statement in his epistle to the Romans, "your faith is proclaimed in all the world" (Romans 1:8)—a statement which certainly requires some prior period of development.

I suppose that Priscilla and Aquila told Paul of the developments in Roman society. Slavery was passing through a strange process of democratization, and so many slaves had been set free that two things had become necessary: first, more and more slaves had to be sought in the outlying regions of the Empire, and second, the laws of manumission were made more rigid by Augustus.[9] Men were shocked by the free rein that was being given to youth, and by the cheapness of human life.[10] Things had reached such a state that many were ready for something like the gospel. Moreover, Rome was the center of the empire. The future belonged to the West. And certainly Paul was enough of a strategist that he could visualize the importance of locating a strong Christian training center in Rome.

Paul also had his heart on Ephesus. Early in his second journey, he had seen it as a strategic place to locate the gospel but he had been prevented from going there by the Spirit's direction (cf. Acts 16:6). It became clear to him that Ephesus had to precede Rome in his itinerary and so he hit upon a clever plan. It was his custom, as a good Jew, to return to Jerusalem as often as possible to participate in the religious festivals. He had been away long enough, so he planned to make his pilgrimage from Corinth, before taking up the work in Ephesus. But meanwhile, he could get the work there started; and this he did by the simple expedient of taking Priscilla and Aquila to Ephesus and leaving them there while he went on to Jerusalem (Acts 18:18-19).

It is quite clear to me that Paul acted out of his experience. For a period of about two years Paul had worked and lived with Priscilla and Aquila in Corinth. He knew the kind of work they could do. He knew their zeal and devotion, their knowledge of the Scriptures, their

---

[8] See p. 86, above.
[9] Suetonius, *Augustus*, 40.
[10] Cf. Carcopino, *Daily Life in Ancient Rome*, pp. 58, 79f.

knowledge of the basic facts of the Christian faith. If Aquila was a manumitted slave, he had Roman citizenship; Priscilla probably was freeborn. They could settle down in Ephesus in their trade, perhaps support themselves from independent resources, and lay the groundwork for Paul, when and if he could get to Ephesus (cf. Acts 18:21). I can see no other possible reason for rooting them up from their important work in Corinth.

Priscilla and Aquila were in Ephesus during all of Paul's extended stay in that city. The Church met in their home. Then suddenly a few months later Priscilla and Aquila were in Rome when Paul wrote the epistle to the Romans, toward the end of his third missionary journey. Why? I can think of only one satisfactory reason: Paul was using the same strategy for Rome that he had used for Ephesus. He was sending Priscilla and Aquila on ahead in order that the groundwork would be laid for his arrival. What he did not know at the time was that a two-year delay would be occasioned by his imprisonment in Caesarea.

We are often told that Paul was a woman-hater. Where does this idea come from? I suppose it arises partly from some of the things that Paul says about women in First Corinthians and in his letters to Timothy. But are we right in judging Paul by what he said in these writings? The one was addressed to Corinth, the other to Ephesus. Corinth was a wicked city, and the women in Corinth, for the most part, had a terrible name, so that the word "Corinthian" had come to mean harlot. Ephesus was not so overtly wicked, but its religious life was just as objectionable from a Christian viewpoint. So when Paul expressed his feeling that he did not want women to be active in the Church, that he did not want them to teach or to pray in public, that he wanted them to keep their heads covered, I think we must understand these things against the background of the cities involved.

There is another side to the story of Paul and his attitude toward women. This is expressed by Priscilla and the work she was doing. It is expressed by Lois and Eunice of Lystra, by Lydia of Philippi, by Euodia and Syntyche of Philippi, by Tryphaena and Tryphosa of Rome, and by other women mentioned either by name or in general statements in Paul's letters. For a woman-hater, Paul certainly had a long list of female fellow workers!

Priscilla and Aquila and Apollos. Apollos is introduced to us by Luke as "a Jew . . . a native of Alexandria . . . an eloquent man, well versed in the scriptures" (Acts 18:24). Alexandria was one of the largest cities of the Empire, and it had a large and vigorous Jewish quarter. The Jews of Alexandria seem to have been characterized by a love of philosophy and by an allegorizing tendency in interpreting the Scriptures. It seems likely that there was a John-the-Baptist sect of Jews in Alexandria, and that Apollos was influenced by this movement.

When Apollos arrived in Ephesus, he participated in the worship of the synagogue, and it was there that Priscilla and Aquila heard him. They were not only impressed with his eloquence and knowledge of the Old Testament, but also with his knowledge of details of the life of Jesus. He knew only the baptism of John, however, and was apparently ignorant of the facts of the baptism of Christ which is baptism of the Holy Spirit (cf. Acts 18:25). If I may be permitted to expand this, as I understand it, Luke is telling us that Apollos knew the messianic hopes of the Jews; he knew the declaration of John the Baptist that the Kingdom of God was at hand, therefore these hopes were to be realized; he knew that Jesus was designated by John as the One who should come; he may have known the story of the crucifixion of Jesus. But he did not know the fundamental nature of the Church. He did not know that baptism by the Holy Spirit was necessary for entrance into the Kingdom, or that the Church was the body of those who had received this baptism. He probably did not know that the death of Jesus Christ was redemptive in atonement for sins, or that it was by faith in this divine act that man received the benefits of God's gracious redemption.

Priscilla and Aquila realized that Apollos was a gem in need of a bit of polishing, and "they took him and expounded to him the way of God more accurately" (Acts 18:26). They must have been satisfied that he understood what they were trying to teach him, for they encouraged him to go to Greece, and wrote letters of recommendation on his behalf (Acts 18:27-28). Some indication of the work done by Apollos in Corinth can be drawn from a statement which Paul makes in First Corinthians: "I planted, Apollos watered" (I Corinthians 3:6). Paul might have said, "I started the church in Corinth; Apollos continued to nourish and develop it."

There are some scholars who think that Apollos was responsible for a factious spirit in the Church of Corinth. It is obvious that Paul wrote First Corinthians because there was trouble in that Church. "For it has been reported to me by Chloe's people that there is quarreling among you, my brethren. What I mean is that each one of you says, 'I belong to Paul,' or 'I belong to Apollos,' or 'I belong to Cephas,' or 'I belong to Christ.' Is Christ divided? Was Paul crucified for you? Or were you baptized in the name of Paul?" (I Corinthians 1:11-13).

Now it could be that Apollos, the Alexandrian, with his love of philosophy and his allegorizing of the Scriptures, had started the people of the Church in Corinth thinking in a slightly different way than Paul had led them to think. To be committed to the inspiration of Paul's writings is not to be committed to the infallibiliy of Paul's preaching—if this were so, then we should have to accept Peter's infallibility as well; and that would include Peter's dissimulation at Antioch when Paul rebuked him. No, Paul was not infallible as a preacher; he was only a human being. He developed and used the gifts that were in him, and I am sure Apollos did the same. It is possible that Paul had something of Apollos' preaching in mind when he wrote, "When I came to you, brethren, I did not come proclaiming to you the testimony of God in lofty words or wisdom" (I Corinthians 2:1). Perhaps Paul is reflecting something of the difference between the two men when he says: "I fed you with milk, not solid food; for you were not ready for it; and even yet you are not ready. . . . For when one says, 'I belong to Paul,' and another, 'I belong to Apollos,' are you not merely men?" (I Corinthians 3:2-4). Some think that Apollos was deficient in his doctrine of the Holy Spirit, which would account for Paul's emphasis upon the subject in his Corinthian correspondence.

It seems to me, however, that the party spirit that developed in the Church at Corinth did not result from any deliberate act on the part of Apollos. Rather, it was the result of human factors common to all men. Some liked Apollos' preaching; some liked Paul's. That happens in churches, does it not? Some like the "simple gospel"; some like philosophy. Some like simple language; some like rhetorical preaching.

Paul's reaction, as I understand it, was an effort to override the personal elements. Listen to him carefully: "This is how one should regard us, as servants of Christ and stewards of the mysteries of God. Moreover it is required of stewards that they be found trustworthy. But with me it is a very small thing that I should be judged by you or by any human court. I do not even judge myself. I am not aware of anything against myself, but I am not thereby acquitted. [This statement helps us put the accent on the right words; Paul is not emphasizing the "I's."] It is the Lord who judges me. . . . I have applied all this to myself and Apollos for your benefit, brethren, that you may learn by us to live according to scripture, that none of you may be puffed up in favor of one against another" (I Corinthians 4:1-6).

You see, Paul is not suggesting that he is right and Apollos wrong. Rather he is saying, in effect, "Now I am bringing this out into the open so that you can see that Apollos and I are mere men trying to do the job God gave us to do." Paul does not criticize Apollos and his method of preaching; he does not defend his own method other than to claim that it is suited to the spiritual maturity (or immaturity) of his hearers. He simply stresses the importance of preserving the unity of the Church in Christ Jesus while forgetting the human leaders.

Further on Paul says, "As for our brother Apollos, I strongly urged him to visit you with the other brethren, but it was not at all God's will for him to go now. He will come when he has opportunity" (I Corinthians 16:12). Does this sound like a man who is trying to defend his own viewpoint and who is afraid to have his opponent come into the church and stir things up anew? It sounds rather like a man who feels that the best thing that could happen would be to have Apollos return and straighten up the Corinthians on this matter of human leadership and divided loyalties.

We know nothing else about Apollos. Some think that he wrote the Epistle to the Hebrews; Martin Luther did, for example, and A. B. Bruce was content to say, "Apollos is the kind of man wanted" for such an assignment.

Priscilla and Aquila, husband and wife! As McGiffert says, "They furnish the most beautiful example known to us in the Apostolic Age of the power for God that could be exerted by a husband and wife working in unison for the advancement of the Gospel."[11] Their home was always open for the Church that met in their house. They were always ready to go wherever God needed them. They were willing to lose themselves in the footnotes of history. But their influence was clearly felt in the greatest cities of their day. Here is an example for any young couple to follow.

[11] A. C. McGiffert, *A History of Christianity in the Apostolic Age* (revised edition; New York: Charles Scribner's Sons, 1906), p. 428.

CHAPTER XV

Timothy and Titus

THIS STUDY SHOULD be dedicated to mothers and grandmothers, for it is the story of a young man, perhaps little more than a boy when we first meet him, who was brought up in the faith by a believing mother probably over the opposition of an unbelieving father. The mother was aided in her faith by her mother, the boy's grandmother. One day the Lord laid His hand on this young man for full-time Christian service, and the mother, in splendid faith and sacrifice, gave him to the Lord. The young man was Timothy, and his story can be told in connection with his associates in Christian work.

Timothy and Paul. In his customary manner, Luke gives us a brief description of Timothy when he first appears in Acts: "And he [Paul] came also to Derbe and to Lystra. A disciple was there, named Timothy, the son of a Jewish woman who was a believer, but his father was a Greek. He was well spoken of by the brethren at Lystra and Iconium" (Acts 16:1-2). The way the statement is worded, Timothy may have been living at either Lystra or Derbe.[1] The time was early in the second missionary journey, perhaps A.D. 50. Luke's sentence structure—an important point when reading an author who is so careful in such matters—suggests not only that Timothy's father was a Greek, whereas his mother was a Jewess, but also that Timothy's father was not a believer. Since Timothy had not been circumcised (cf. Acts 16:3), we may suppose that the father was not sympathetic to the mother's religious views and perhaps had even forbidden the religious rite.

Paul had visited Lystra and Derbe on his first missionary journey a few years earlier. At that time he was accompanied by Barnabas, and

---

[1] F. F. Bruce, for example, chooses Lystra on the basis of its occurrence in both sentences (*The Book of the Acts,* p. 321). It would be equally logical to assume that Derbe was Timothy's home, since his reputation at Lystra and Iconium is mentioned. See also Acts 20:4. The point is hardly worth debating.

147

at Lystra they had performed a miracle on a man who had been
crippled from birth (Acts 14:8-10). The wonderful work of mercy
quite naturally caused widespread excitement, and created a keen interest in the apostles. Paul of course used this as an opportunity to
preach the gospel. Luke does not fill in the details, but it is obvious
that effective preaching led to conversions as well as to opposition;
news of what was happening reached Antioch and Iconium; Jewish
opposition to the apostles came from these cities and stirred up mob
action, and as a result, Paul was stoned and dragged out of the city
for dead (cf. Acts 14:19-20). Some of the converts gathered about him,
and he revived and entered the city; the next day he and Barnabas
went to Derbe.

Luke does not mention the conversion of Timothy's mother, Eunice,
but it is reasonable to believe that it occurred at that time. Some have
suggested that Paul may have been taken to her home, and his wounds
may have been bathed and bandaged there. The suggestion is based
on Paul's reminder to Timothy that he had observed Paul's persecu-
tions and sufferings, and what befell him at Antioch, at Iconium, and
at Lystra (cf. II Timothy 3:11).[2] It is an attractive suggestion, and we
would like to think that young Timothy came to know the gospel at
that time. However, this is far from certain. We can safely conclude
that Timothy's grandmother Lois was also converted to the faith at
that time or soon thereafter, and finally he himself (cf. II Timothy
1:5).

It is generally assumed that Timothy was converted to Christianity
by Paul. This is based on the way Paul refers to his young colleague;
for example, "my true child in the faith" (I Timothy 1:2), and "my
beloved and faithful child in the Lord" (I Corinthians 4:17). Once
again, however, I would suggest that we do not accept as an established
fact what is only a very good suggestion. In II Timothy 3:15 there is a
suggestion that Timothy may have received his faith from his
mother. Paul's references to Timothy as his "child in the faith" would

[2] The question of Pauline authorship of the Pastoral Epistles (I and II Timothy and Titus) is very complex, and many scholars are firmly convinced
that Paul did not write them. I follow the traditional view, hence use material
in the Pastorals for these studies. All scholars, I believe, would admit that the
Pastorals contain an early tradition, and whether it had been written down by
Paul or by someone else would not greatly affect the use we are making of it
here. For a full discussion, with references to recent literature, see Donald
Guthrie, *The Pastoral Epistles* (London: The Tyndale Press, 1957), pp. 11-53,
212-228.

be sufficiently explained, I believe, by the fact that Paul trained Timothy in Christian doctrine and practice.

How old Timothy was at the time we are not told. Nearly twenty years later Paul addressed Timothy as a young man—but what is a "young man"? To a twenty-year-old, a man of forty is not young; to a man of sixty or seventy, the forty-year-old man is still young. We suppose that Timothy was in his teens when Paul first visited Lystra and Derbe; that he was perhaps in his early twenties at the time of Paul's second visit—which would make him forty or forty-five when the Pastoral Epistles were written.

When Paul returned to Timothy's home town on his second missionary journey, he was impressed with the reports of Timothy's Christian faith and life, and desired to take Timothy along with him. On the first journey, we remember, Paul and Barnabas had started out with young John Mark as their helper. Timothy would stand in the same relationship to the team of Paul and Silas. Timothy's mother agreed, obviously, and the Church ordained the young man by the laying on of hands (compare II Timothy 1:6 with I Timothy 4:14).

Because Timothy was the child of a mixed marriage, Paul circumcised him (Acts 16:3). This action has caused a great deal of discussion on the part of Biblical scholars, and many think that Paul at this point displayed a serious inconsistency. Just a year or so earlier, at the time of the debate in Jerusalem over the Judaizer problem, Paul had refused to permit Titus to be circumcised (cf. Galatians 2:3). Paul was standing on the principle that a Gentile should not be required to take upon himself the obligations of the Law of Moses.[3] Now Paul was violating that principle, it is charged, by circumcising Timothy.

It seems to me that two entirely different principles are under consideration. Titus was a Gentile born to Gentile parents. Circumcision in his case would be a violation of Paul's principle concerning Gentiles. Timothy, on the other hand, was part Jew. Moreover, Paul wanted to use him in Jewish evangelism in the synagogues. As a Jew, even of a mixed marriage, Timothy would be an offense to other Jews if he did not keep the Mosaic Law, and this would become an unnecessary

[3] It should be pointed out that circumcision in itself was not the issue. The implication of the act was what mattered, for by submitting to this rite the male was obligated to perform all of the Law. Whether a present-day Christian Gentile should have his male children circumcised as a matter of personal hygiene is entirely another question and has no theological implication.

stumbling block to his fellow Jews. Paul therefore applied a different principle, which is described by him as follows: "To the Jews I became as a Jew, in order to win Jews; to those under the law I became as one under the law . . . that I might win those under the law. . . . I have become all things to all men, that I might by all means save some. I do it all for the sake of the gospel . . ." (I Corinthians 9:20-23). Timothy, a Jew by birth and therefore no hypocrite in taking on himself voluntarily the obligations of Judaism, was a demonstration of this principle.

We can trace Timothy's itinerary with some detail. He went to Europe with Paul, Silas, and Luke, but was apparently not jailed with Paul and Silas in Philippi (Acts 16:19). Luke seems to have stayed in Philippi when the other three moved west along the Egnatian Road to Thessalonica. When Paul and Silas were sent off to neighboring Beroea by night, Timothy seems to have remained in Thessalonica, but later joined the apostles in Beroea (cf. Acts 17:10,14); Timothy and Silas stayed there when Paul moved on to Athens. Later Paul sent Timothy to Thessalonica (it would seem that Timothy had meanwhile rejoined Paul at Athens, but this is not clear), in order to get news about his recent converts and to establish them in the faith (I Thessalonians 3:1-2). After that, Timothy and Silas joined Paul in Corinth (Acts 18:5), and Paul sent the first of his letters to the Thessalonians (I Thessalonians 3:6), rejoicing over the news which Timothy had brought. It is possible that Timothy acted both as Paul's amanuensis and emissary, writing the letter for Paul and delivering it; then returning with a reply that occasioned the second letter to Thessalonica.

The next time we hear of Timothy he was in Ephesus with Paul, and Paul was sending him and Erastus to Macedonia, where Thessalonica is located (Acts 19:22). Still later, Paul sent Timothy from Ephesus to Corinth to handle some of the difficult matters in that Church (I Corinthians 4:17). The last time Timothy is mentioned in Acts is at Troas with the group that was planning to carry an offering from the Gentile churches to the needy Jewish Christians at Jerusalem (Acts 20:4).

According to the salutations of the Prison Epistles, Timothy was with Paul during the first Roman imprisonment (cf. Colossians 1:1; Philippians 1:1; Philemon 1). Then, if we are correct in following the tradition that Paul was released from prison, Timothy went to Ephesus with Paul and was left there to carry on the work in that city

(I Timothy 1:3). He was imprisoned, where and when we do not know, and subsequently released (Hebrews 13:23), and later, according to tradition, martyred at Ephesus under Domitian after having served as the first bishop of Ephesus.[4]

Timothy was doubtless the closest of Paul's associates, with perhaps the exception of Luke. He is mentioned in the opening salutation of six of Paul's epistles as co-author, and two others are addressed to him. He was young, somewhat timid, possibly not physically strong (cf. I Timothy 5:23). Some scholars seem to think that he experienced a moral degeneration in the years he was on his own, and that Paul had to warn him against temptations of the flesh, the love of money, and laziness. I do not get this impression; rather, it seems to me that Paul is reacting as a father would react to the snares and temptations of the world. When I encourage my children it is not because I have lost confidence in them, but rather because I feel that we all need to be reminded constantly to be on guard against the wiles of the devil. In such a way Paul exhorted Timothy.

Timothy and Titus. Titus is one of the outstanding men in the New Testament Church, and yet he is not mentioned by name in the Book of Acts. The only satisfactory explanation of this omission would be either that Titus was another name for Luke, or that Titus was a relative of Luke and was not named because of family modesty. Are there any indications that would support either of these theories? A cursory reading of II Timothy 4:10-11 quickly proves that Titus (who had gone to Dalmatia) was not Luke (who was with Paul in Rome). When there was trouble in the Church at Corinth, Paul sent Titus to work it out, and he wrote, "With him we are sending the brother who is famous among all the churches for his preaching of the gospel" (II Corinthians 8:18). Again he said, "I urged Titus to go, and sent the brother with him" (II Corinthians 12:18). This is not much to build on, but the supposition that Titus was Luke's brother is attractive —at least to me.

Titus was of Gentile parents (Galatians 2:3), and was taken to Jerusalem by Paul at the time of the Judaizer controversy (Galatians

---

[4] Eusebius, *Ecclesiastical History* 3.4; Nicephorus, *Ecclesiastical History* 3.11. The latter reference is from *The Fathers of the Church,* edited by R. J. Defarrari, vol. 19, *Eusebius Pamphili, Ecclesiastical History* (New York: Fathers of the Church, Inc., 1953), p. 142, n. 6; I have been unable to verify the reference.

2:1). Titus was "Exhibit A"—evidence that could be examined; living proof that a Gentile who had not come under the Law of Moses could still demonstrate the fruits of the Spirit that were the sign of a regenerate man in Christ.

Titus comes into our story about Timothy in connection with the problems in the Corinthian Church. Timothy, we learned, had been sent to Corinth by Paul to take care of grave difficulties in that Church, difficulties of moral, doctrinal, and administrative nature. To read the letters to the Corinthians is to discover how complex the problems were. And Timothy failed in the mission. He failed not because of any lack of ability, but because of lack of experience: he was just too young. The Church in Corinth despised his youth, and were hostile because Paul himself had not visited them (see I Corinthians 4:17-18 and compare I Corinthians 16:10-11). Perhaps that was why Paul on a later occasion said to Timothy, "Let no one despise your youth" (I Timothy 4:12).

If we take the trouble to check the chronological details, we shall find that this was about A.D. 55. Timothy had been in Paul's company almost constantly for about five years. He had traveled widely, had undergone all sorts of experiences with Paul and with Silas; he had even been sent on missions alone by Paul, such as those to Thessalonica. He was by this time probably twenty-five years old, and a veteran of five years' service. In our modern day, we take young fellows and girls who have had little or no training in Christian service and send them into some of the most difficult situations in the world—then we wonder why they sometimes fail. They fail because we are expecting young people to do the work of mature and experienced workers. With far more preparation and experience, Timothy failed. But failure under such circumstances is no disgrace.

Titus, however, succeeded. Paul was comforted by the news that Titus brought and by the fact that he had been so well received in the Corinthian Church (cf. II Corinthians 7:5-7). Titus was probably somewhat older than Timothy (compare Titus 2:15 with I Timothy 4:12), and he had had a few more years' experience. Possibly he had certain personal qualifications that Timothy lacked, as, for example, self-confidence or boldness. It is even possible that Timothy had, knowingly or unknowingly, prepared the way for Titus; the Corinthians had had time to regret how they had treated Timothy and may have determined to act toward Titus in a more Christian manner. Whatever the reasons, we know that an affection developed between Titus and

the Corinthian Church that brought joy to Paul's heart (cf. II
Corinthians 7:13-14; 8:16).

After Paul was released from the Roman imprisonment, he took
Titus and Timothy on some part of his further travels. He left Timothy
in Ephesus, as we have seen; and he left Titus in Crete (Titus 1:5).
That in itself is to me an amazing testimony of Paul's confidence in
these two men. Ephesus was, by Paul's own estimate, one of the most
strategically important cities of the Empire. It was not without its
difficulties, particularly with reference to the hostility of those who
were devoted to the goddess Artemis. Later, as we find from Second
Timothy and corroborated by Revelation 2:2-6, strong reaction set in
against the gospel. Yet Paul was willing to entrust the situation to
Timothy. Likewise Crete was one of the more difficult regions in the
Empire, as we know from references in the literature of the day. Paul
was willing to place the work there in the care of Titus.

Timothy and the Church. We are beginning to get, through the
experiences of Timothy, a different view of the Church. Up until
this point, we have been seeing the Church of the first generation. It
was the Church of the apostles, the Church of those who had known
Jesus according to the flesh, or had (in the case of Paul) been granted
a personal experience of the risen Christ. But with Timothy, and
doubtless also with Titus, we are moving into the next generation: this
is "second generation Christianity," with all its new problems. The
Church that we see in the experiences of Timothy is the Church in
its on-going history, after the apostles have begun to depart from the
scene.

Of course the apostles were not yet gone; but Paul was anxiously
making preparations for the day when he would be. He was setting up
Timothy and Titus (and were there others, of whom these are
typical?) in strategic locations because he knew that the hour of his
departure was at hand. He was writing letters to them (and shall we
not assume that he expected others to read these letters?) in order to
strengthen them for the work of the next generation.

Timothy was not an apostle; that is made clear in Colossians 1:1. He
was never looked upon as a successor to Paul, and he was never
portrayed as having the authority of an apostle. Read the letters to
Timothy and Titus, and notice that such authority remained in the
apostolic office and was not conferred on younger ministers. Yet there
is authority (cf. I Timothy 4:11, 14): it is the authority of the gospel.

Through Timothy we learn something about the nature of the Church. It is God's family (I Timothy 3:5, 15). Its members are called "brothers" (I Timothy 4:6), "believers" (I Timothy 4:12; 5:16), and "holy ones" (or "saints," I Timothy 5:10). These words define their relationship to one another: they are brothers; their relationship to God: they are believers; and their relationship to the world: they are holy, set apart from sin for lives of purity.

In the Church are certain officers, whose duties and qualifications are described in the Pastoral Epistles. We call them "bishop," "priest" or "presbyter," and "deacon." I think these high-sounding names have confused us. Originally they were common Greek words that could be translated "overseer" or "supervisor," "elder," and "minister" or "servant." But hierarchies do not develop from such commonplace words, therefore we have bishops, priests, and deacons. Two other "offices" are described in the letter to Timothy, but we tend to ignore them. These are "women" or "wives" and "widows." As we read through the qualifications from I Timothy 3:1 to 5:22, particularly if we read them in some modern language translation, we get the feeling that we are not reading about ecclesiastical offices, but about normal family life. "Bishops" are described in their relationship to their households and their children, "deacons" likewise; their "women," or better, "wives" (cf. I Timothy 3:11-12) are to refrain from gossipy slander; the duties of the "widows" concern the religious obligations they have to their own children (I Timothy 5:4). Do not misunderstand me; I am not opposing organization within the Church, nor am I seeking to belittle the offices instituted by God. But I think these offices, in some cases, have gotten far away from the divine intention. Let the Church be the family of God and the officers the members of that family.

We learn quite a bit about the beliefs of the Church in the Pastoral Epistles, but I shall reserve that for another study.

Finally, and notably, we observe that Paul is very much concerned about false teachers and apostasy. "Understand this," says Paul, "that in the last days there will come times of stress. For men will be lovers of self, lovers of money ... lovers of pleasure rather than lovers of God, holding the form of religion but denying the power of it" (II Timothy 3:1-5). "Now the Spirit expressly says that in later times some will depart from the faith" (I Timothy 4:1). As long as apostolic eyewitnesses are present, they can controvert error by their personal testimony, but what can Timothy do? What can you and I do?

Our first responsibility, as was Timothy's, is to guard the faith that is in us. "You then, my son, be strong in the grace that is in Christ Jesus" (II Timothy 2:1). If you are concerned by apostasy in the world, look to your own spiritual life. Make sure that it is strong.

The second responsibility that Paul laid upon Timothy was to train up faithful successors. "What you have heard from me before many witnesses entrust to faithful men who will be able to teach others also" (II Timothy 2:2).

The third responsibility was to trust God. "God's firm foundation stands, bearing this seal: 'The Lord knows those who are his,' and 'Let every one who names the name of the Lord depart from iniquity' " (II Timothy 2:19).

The fourth responsibility, and by no means the least important, was to stay out of arguments. "Have nothing to do with stupid, senseless controversies; you know that they breed quarrels. And the Lord's servant must not be quarrelsome but kindly to every one, an apt teacher, forbearing, correcting his opponents with gentleness. God may perhaps grant that they will repent and come to know the truth . . ." (II Timothy 2:23-25). Righteousness, faith, love, and peace will have far greater effect upon the opponents than argument (cf. II Timothy 2:22).

All these responsibilities can be summarized in one charge: "Preach the word, be urgent in season and out of season, convince, rebuke, and exhort, be unfailing in patience and in teaching" (II Timothy 4:2).

This is the Church and its responsibility in the post-apostolic age, as I see it in Timothy: officers to divide up the duties according to ability, and not just to be officious; preachers to preach the word handed down by the apostles, and witnesses to tell what they have experienced personally; and always teachers, everywhere teachers, to train up the next generation in the faith.

You and I shall never stop the attacks on faith that our young people must face in the world. That is an impossibility. And if we seek to shun our responsibility by sheltering our young people in some other-worldly school or college, we merely delay the day when they must face the anti-Christian forces in the world. Our only defense of the faith is to stengthen the faith that is in us and to train our children and their friends in the Word of God. Our responsibility ends when we have passed on the truth to the next generation. After that, we must trust God to do the rest—and He is faithful.

CHAPTER XVI

Thomas Who Believed

WE USUALLY SPEAK of Thomas as a doubter: "doubting Thomas." I would like to present him as the believer. The words of his faith constitute the fullest statement of faith expressed in the Gospels: "My Lord and my God" (John 20:28).

We are not sure of his name. You say, "Why, it was Thomas!" But that is only because we have made the word "Thomas" into a name —at first it was only a common noun. The Gospel writer knew that, and translated the word for us: "which means Didymus" and Didymus means "twin." Need we point out that one does not usually name a child "Twin"? What would you name the other one?

An early and widespread tradition tells us that his name was Judas. If, so, there were three of the Twelve with the same name: Judas Iscariot, Judas "not Iscariot," and Judas "the Twin." That would not be improbable, for Judas was a very common name. Another tradition that is preserved in the writings of the Church in the Middle Ages tells us that Thomas was the twin of Jesus. How such a notion started is probably to be explained from the words of the Lord Jesus in the Acts of Thomas, where Jesus appears in the likeness of Thomas and, when asked if He is Thomas, replies, "I am his brother!"[1] It is easy to see how such an idea, once started, could have become the source of much confusion. Thomas is usually portrayed as the Apostle to India; the earliest tradition, however, locates his field of labor in Parthia (modern Iran). So much for tradition.

Thomas and Jesus. Thomas was a doubter; I would not deny that. But even his doubts must be set against the background of his faith. Thomas was one of the Twelve, but before he became one of the Twelve, he had to be one of the disciples. Let the implications sink in, and you will realize that somewhere along the way, and it must have

---

[1] Acts of the Holy Apostle Thomas, *The Ante-Nicene Fathers*, vol. 8, p. 537.

been early in Jesus' ministry, Thomas had heard the call of Jesus and had cast his lot in with Him. Jesus had observed him carefully, as He had observed the others, and after a night in prayer had chosen Thomas as one of that group to whom would be given the tremendous and awful responsibility of evangelizing the world. This should convince us of the worth of this man.

There are three short references to Thomas, all of them in John. The first is in the eleventh chapter, in connection with the illness of Lazarus and the events pertaining to it. Jesus and His apostles were beyond the Jordan, safely beyond the reach of those who were seeking to destroy Him; for, as we know, Jesus had a sense of timing whereby His death must occur on the day of the great sacrifice, the Passover. Word had been sent to Jesus that Lazarus was ill, and Jesus had delayed going to Bethany. Then He announced to the disciples that "Lazarus is dead . . . let us go to him" (John 11:14-15). At this point, Thomas comes into the picture, saying, "Let us also go, that we may die with him" (John 11:16).

It is clear that Thomas did not understand Jesus, and I am not sure I understand Thomas. Thomas may have thought that by the expression, "Let us go to him," Jesus was implying that they should join Lazarus in death. Such an idea he would have gotten, I think, from Jesus' teachings about the suffering and death that must occur at Jerusalem. Or it may be that Thomas was simply referring to the danger that a trip to the vicinity of Jerusalem would incur: it would be sealing their own death warrants. But regardless of what Thomas implied, there can be no doubt that Thomas was declaring his loyalty to the Master, and his willingness to die, if necessary, for the Master.

I rather like Thomas for this, don't you? There is no bravado; no boasting that he was able to face dangers that would cause the rest of them to run. Quite the opposite, Thomas includes the rest in the decision: "Let us also go." There is a gloomy outlook, true; but there is a quiet and deep devotion. If Jesus feels that He must return to the place of danger, let us not desert Him. Let us stay with Him, even if it means our death.

The second reference to Thomas is found in the fourteenth chapter of John. This was only a short time after the resurrection of Lazarus, and the dinner given in honor of Jesus had brought a crowd of people to see Lazarus also (cf. John 12:9). The following day had been exciting, with the triumphal entry of Jesus into Jerusalem; that had been

followed by two days of activity in Jerusalem, as Jesus sought desper-
ately to bring the city to its senses, while the religious leaders sought
to trap Him into some statement or action that could be used as a
capital charge against Him. The sands of time were running out
rapidly, and Jesus had gathered His own in the Upper Room for the
parting words of instruction.

"Let not your hearts be troubled," He said; "believe in God, believe
also in me. In my Father's house are many rooms; if it were not so,
would I have told you that I go to prepare a place for you? And when
I go and prepare a place for you, I will come again and will take you
to myself, that where I am you may be also. And you know the way
where I am going" (John 14:1-4). Thomas interrupted: "Lord, we
do not know where you are going; how can we know the way?"

I am puzzled to know what lay behind Thomas' question. He
may not have understood what Jesus was talking about—but I find
that hard to believe. In view of the events of the preceding days, added
to the teachings of Jesus, it seems that they all should have known that
Jesus was talking about His imminent death. Still, there is that word
spoken later, "Ah, now you are speaking plainly, not in any figure!"
(John 16:29). But then again, Thomas may have understood that
Jesus was referring to His death, and may have been seeking more
light on the "where" and the "way." If Jesus had intended to follow
up this line of inquiry, He was interrupted by Philip's question (John
14:8 ff.). Most of us, I am sure, wish that Jesus had said more about
His Father's house—but He told us all He wants us to know, and all
we need to know.

The third reference to Thomas is in the twentieth chapter of John.
The resurrection of Jesus had taken place. It was the evening of resurrection day, the first Easter Sunday, and there was much excitement
among the Eleven—Judas had removed himself not only from the
apostolic band but from this life as well—for there were strange reports
that Jesus was alive. He had been seen by Peter. Two disciples from
Emmaus reported walking and talking with Jesus. The women's
stories about the empty tomb and the angelic messages were being re-
counted. And as a result, the apostles, who had been scattered by the
terrible tragedy of the cross, had gathered together, still fearsome of the
spirit of hostility in the city. Suddenly, Jesus was in their midst. His
first words were, "Peace be with you." Then He showed them the

tokens of His passion, His hands and side.[2] Thomas was not present.

When the disciples found Thomas, they told him, "We have seen the Lord." Thomas said, "Unless I see in his hands the print of the nails, and place my finger in the mark of the nails, and place my hand in his side, I will not believe" (John 20:25).

Thomas and his doubts. Have you ever thought about the different kinds of doubt? There is one word,[3] sometimes translated "doubt," that means "perplexity, inability to comprehend." Like the Latin word *dubitare,* from which we get our word "doubt," it has a basic meaning related to "way," except that the Latin literally means "to go two ways," whereas the Greek means, "without a way." This is the word used of the women at the empty tomb: they were "perplexed" (Luke 24:4); this is the word used of the disciples when Jesus announced, "One of you shall betray me" (John 13:21); a similar but stronger word is used of Herod, when he heard reports that John the Baptist was alive again (Luke 9:7), and again of the crowd in Jerusalem when they heard the apostles speaking with tongues (Acts 2:12). In all cases, they were stopped, they did not know which way to turn for a solution to the situation confronting them.

A second word for "doubt" has more the meaning of "weakening or loss of faith."[4] Faith was already present, but then began to fail. The word is used of Peter, after he had started to walk on the water, and then asked himself, "What am I doing here?" Jesus said to him, "Why did you doubt?" (Matthew 14:31). The word is also used of the disciples, when they met with the risen Lord: "And when they saw him, they worshiped him; but some doubted" (Matthew 28:17).

The third word originally meant "to discriminate, decide," and in Hellenistic Greek came to mean "to be divided in mind, hesitate, doubt."[5] It is used when God instructed Peter concerning the men sent by Cornelius: "accompany them without hesitation"—I suppose we might translate it, "without allowing your critical judgment to hold you back by doubting My word" (Acts 10:20).

---

[2] Traditionally, there were five wounds: the hands, the side, and the feet. Strangely enough, Scripture nowhere mentions any nailing of the feet of Jesus!

[3] In Greek, *aporô.* Quite similar in meaning is *diaporô.*

[4] The Greek word is *distázō,* which is somewhat like the Latin *dubitare* in its formation from the word for "two."

[5] In Greek, *diakrínō.*

None of these words is used about Thomas, and none of them truly fits the situation.

If we turn to the idea of "unbelief," we find again that there are several kinds of unbelief, although in this case we do not find the distinction in the use of different Greek words. Rather, the differentiation must be sought in how the word is used.[6] There is a kind of unbelief that might be termed scientific skepticism. It says, "I do not believe, because there is insufficient evidence to convince me." It is a judgment that may be challenged by others who are convinced that there is sufficient evidence, but we must recognize the fact that the scientist has been trained to verify his observations, and the once-for-all (the miracle, the unique Son, the single resurrection, etc.) is not repeatable and therefore not verifiable by the scientist. The historian, on the other hand, must accept hearsay evidence; his verification is only an effort to check the accuracy of the witnesses. This skeptical unbelief is perhaps illustrated by the disciples, when the women reported their experiences at the garden tomb to the apostles: "but these words seemed to them an idle tale, and they did not believe [literally, they disbelieved] them" (Luke 24:11).

A second kind of unbelief is deliberate rejection. Paul uses the noun form of the word, "unbelievers," quite often in his Corinthian letters, to designate non-Christians (see I Corinthians 7:12-15; II Corinthians 6:14-15, etc.), but the deliberateness of the rejection is more sharply etched in a statement such as that reported at the close of Acts: "And some were convinced by what he said, while others disbelieved" (Acts 28:24). Paul's use of a quotation from Isaiah (6:9-10) serves to define further the kind of disbelief that is intended.

A third kind of unbelief is perhaps best illustrated by the father of the demon-possessed boy. Jesus said to him, "All things are possible to him who believes," and the father replied, "I believe; help my unbelief!" (Mark 9:23-24). It is almost like saying, "I have faith; but I haven't yet come to the place where I have real faith." There is nothing essentially wrong with this kind of unbelief, provided we do not become established in it. But if we become content with unbelief, we shall one day find ourselves confronted with the horrible judgment prepared for the cowardly, the faithless, murderers, liars, and others like them (see Revelation 21:8).

[6] In Greek, the word is *ápistos* ("without faith") and its derivatives.

What was Thomas' characteristic? It was not doubt. It could hardly be called skepticism. In the light of what happened when he was confronted with the evidence, we cannot call it deliberate disbelief. The best term is simply unbelief. Jesus confronted Thomas, and said, "Put your finger here, and see my hands; and put out your hand, and place it in my side; do not be faithless, but believing" (John 20:27).[7]

Thomas and his faith. The resurrection of Jesus Christ is central in the faith of the Christian Church. Carefully defined and clearly understood, it would be possible to say that without the resurrection of Jesus Christ there is no Christian faith. This is what the Apostle Paul says in his great chapter on the resurrection. Read it carefully: "If Christ has not been raised, then our preaching is in vain and your faith is in vain. . . . If Christ has not been raised, your faith is futile and you are still in your sins" (I Corinthians 15:14, 17).

This has always been the unwavering and unquestioned faith of the Church. There has never been a doctrinal controversy on the subject of the resurrection of Christ.[8] The Church discussed the natures of Christ, the Trinity, the procession of the Holy Spirit, and many other subjects, but it was unanimous in the declaration that on the third day Christ rose again. The person who denies the resurrection of Christ places himself outside the faith of the historic Christian Church just as surely as does the man who denies the incarnation.

In the hazy thinking and careless usage of words that characterize too much of modern religious thought and writing, immortality is often confused with resurrection. Immortality is a state of being not mortal, not subject to death. Resurrection is an act, a change, a rising from the dead to newness of life. What could the statement "on the third day He was immortal" possibly mean? If He was immortal on the third day, He was equally immortal on the second and the fourth. Moreover, what is the significance of the resurrection appearances of Jesus to His apostles? And that brings us back to Thomas. Thomas was

[7] The play on words in Greek (*ápistos* and *pistós*) would be better brought out if translated, "do not be believing-less, but believing" or "do not be without faith, but with faith."

[8] An examination of R. Seeberg's two-volume *Text-Book of the History of Doctrines* (Philadelphia: Lutheran Publication Society, 1904), for example, will show that the word "resurrection" is not even in the index. The only discussions on the subject of resurrection that took place concerned the nature of our bodies in the final resurrection. I do not consider modern unbelief to be in the category of a doctrinal controversy.

not convinced by the accounts that he heard. He wanted evidence before he was willing to commit himself in faith. What kind of evidence was available?

First, either Jesus died on the cross, or He did not die. If He did not die, then what happened to Him? The "swoon" theory supplies the answer: He revived in the cool of the tomb. Pushing aside the stone,[9] He made His way to the apostles, who nursed Him back to health. Apart from the hypocrisy involved in apostles who would report His resurrection knowing the truth, how does this fit with the experience of Thomas?

Second, if Jesus died on the cross, either His body was found in the tomb, or the tomb was found empty. His body was not found in the tomb: that is the testimony of the women and also of Peter and John (see Mark 16:5; John 20:6); further, it is corroborated by the fact that His enemies did not produce the body.

Third, if an empty tomb was found, it was either the wrong tomb or the right one. The right one was identified by a seal and a guard of soldiers (Matthew 27:66). Independent groups or individuals found their way to a common point: Mary Magdalene, very early in the morning, then Peter and John, and still later the women mentioned in Mark (see John 20:1 ff.; Mark 16:1 ff.)—and their testimony concurs. They could not all have made the same mistake. Moreover, the testimony of the soldiers substantiates this point (Matthew 28:11).

Fourth, if the tomb was found empty, the body either was taken or rose. If it was taken, it was taken either by enemies or friends; if by enemies, they would have produced it and silenced the apostolic preaching of the resurrection; if by friends, then we have, as many have recognized, the psychological impossibility of apostles suffering martyrdom for what they knew was not true. The story that the disciples had stolen the body was tried at the very outset (see Matthew 28:11-15), and convinced no one. Except for some cheap pulp writings or some anti-Christian movements, this theory has been given up. And again, we must ask, what about Thomas? Can we suppose that he who refused to be convinced by apostolic testimony could be convinced by apostolic fraud?

That brings us to the last step of the logical process: Jesus Christ

[9] The theory was first proposed in ignorance of the nature of such stones. They roll in deep-cut grooves, and fall into a socket when closed. It would take two healthy men to move such a stone, as the women knew (Mark 16:3).

rose from the dead. Either He was seen thereafter, or He was not seen. Peter says he saw Him; the two from Emmaus claim they saw Him; the women saw Him; the rest of the apostles saw Him. Paul, having started out as a bitter opponent of the movement, declared that Jesus appeared "to more than five hundred brethren at one time," most of whom were still alive when he wrote those words (I Corinthians 15: 6). But what about Thomas? Thomas refused to believe the testimony of anyone else—even that of his closest friends. Then came the night when Jesus appeared to him, challenged him to put his unbelief to the test by touching the wounds still visible, and Thomas yielded: "My Lord and my God!"

I suppose one other objection should be faced here. All that I have said is based on the Gospel record; but how do we know that this record is true? This is a study in itself.[10] Suffice it to say here that as a result of nearly two centuries of critical study, the Gospels are as firmly entrenched as ever. Critical scholars have now despaired of trying to find a "historical Jesus" (by which they mean non-supernatural) by critical study of the Gospels; they admit that these Gospels are products of the first century and represent the convictions of the Early Church; they now concentrate their efforts on trying to explain the faith that produced the Gospels. It seems fair to say that the evidence for the resurrection of Jesus Christ is as historically trustworthy as any evidence for any event in the past. If on the basis of critical judgment applied to the study of historic documents we cannot believe in the resurrection of Jesus Christ, then we cannot believe anything. Alexander's Empire can be explained away as the projection into the past of Hellenistic ideals, and Napoleon's campaign to Egypt as an attempt by his followers to make him as great as Alexander.

Thomas and his followers. Thomas faced the problem of faith for all honest unbelievers. Jesus knew that there would be others like Thomas: "Have you believed because you have seen me? Blessed are those who have not seen and yet believe" (John 20:29).

Some doubters do not deserve to be classed with Thomas: those who are superficial and are not interested in the evidence; sophomoric persons who are proud of being skeptics and do not want to see any

[10] See, for example, F. F. Bruce, *The New Testament Documents: Are They Reliable?* (fifth revised edition; Grand Rapids, Mich.: Wm. B. Eerdmans Publishing Co., 1960), 120 pp.

evidence that will force them to change their minds; and the disbelievers, who flatly reject all evidence.

But there are others who can be called honest doubters. They do not believe the evidence is sufficient, or they have not considered the evidence. They are willing to consider it, and Thomas would be the first to invite them to sit down while he tells them his experience.

You and I shall probably never have the opportunity in this life of seeing the Lord Jesus Christ. Paul claimed that he was given such an experience—we have seen this in an earlier study—and there have been others who have claimed to have had a vision of Christ. But for most of us, God requires us to rest content with the apostolic testimony. I believe in the resurrection of Jesus Christ because I believe in the reliability of the record; because I believe the testimony contained in the record is that of reasonable men, rational men, who were convinced against their first doubts that their Lord was alive again. I believe their testimony is not only historically supported, but also psychologically supported, for their subsequent course of life and action can only be explained on the basis of their experience. I believe in the resurrection because it is consistent with the nature of God, who could not let such a One as Jesus be conquered by death. Finally, I believe in the resurrection of Jesus Christ because only such a faith can account for whatever spiritual power I can find in my own self. Is this your faith too?[11]

[11] For an excellent article, see W. M. Smith, "Resurrection," *Baker's Dictionary of Theology*, pp. 448-456.

CHAPTER XVII

John the Theologian

WHEN I VISITED Ephesus, I found that a portion of the modern city is known as Ayasuluk—a corruption of the name Hagios Theologos, "Holy Theologian." This name was given to Saint John, who lived in Ephesus, according to a strong tradition, in the closing years of his life.

Theologians today are not high on the list of the world's most popular figures. Let a preacher announce that he is planning to give a series of theological lectures, and the people stay away in droves. Scientists, on the other hand, are quite popular. Yet the strange and simple fact is that theologians are, or ought to be, scientists. That statement needs explaining, I know. A scientist is one who has learned to apply scientific method, which is to observe, record, compare, control, and draw whatever conclusions are valid. The theologian ("theology," as the word implies, is the orderly study of God) should observe, record, compare, control, and draw conclusions concerning what he can learn about God.[1]

The Bible, we are told, does not contain theology. In a sense, this is true. Neither does the world contain geology or chemistry. But the world does contain the data which the scientist can arrange into the science of geology or chemistry; and the Bible and the world likewise contain the data which the theologian can arrange in orderly and systematic manner—which is theology. Theology, by its very nature, is fraught with the dangers of subjectivism. The theologian, if he is not extremely careful, will record his impressions or opinions about God and the spiritual world, and think that these are objective data; and the scientist, of course, becomes impatient with him.

The theologian, therefore, should have a long life, for he has many observations to make; he should be intimately acquainted with God,

[1] There is a different viewpoint, according to which the theologian is a philosopher. The difference, in my estimation, arises from a man's methodology: if he works at the problem from deductive processes and speculation, he is more of the philosopher; if he works inductively from what God has revealed, he is more of the scientist.

not only in mystical immediacy, but also in some way that is sensuously verifiable; and he should be gifted in ability to make known his conclusions in such a way that others will understand him.

John had these qualifications.[2] He lived to about one hundred years of age. He was a mystic, and yet he knew the Incarnate Son of God in the flesh (cf. I John 1:1). His Gospel is, beyond any argument, a beautiful book, a book that presents theological concepts in the simplest form, a book that men have read and loved and understood—at least sufficiently to give them satisfaction of soul.

John and the Holy Spirit. The most extensive, and in fact the only satisfactory teachings on the Holy Spirit in the Gospels are in the Gospel of John. This omission in the other Gospels may seem strange in the light of the emphasis placed upon the subject of the Holy Spirit in the Early Church as portrayed in the book of Acts. I cannot explain it; I can only record it. I cannot explain it any more than I can explain the fact that the great creeds of the Church are deficient in their statements concerning the Holy Spirit. The Westminister Confession, for example (adopted A.D. 1643), had no satisfactory statement on the Holy Spirit, and the Presbyterian Church, which adopted the Westminster Confession in 1729, added the chapter on the Holy Spirit in 1903.

On the last night before His death, Jesus said, "These things I have spoken to you, while I am still with you. But the Counselor, the Holy Spirit, whom the Father will send in my name, he will teach you all things, and bring to your remembrance all that I have said to you" (John 14:25-26). Perhaps John did not particularly notice those words when they were spoken—no one else recorded them—but sixty-five years or so later, he remembered them as clearly as if they had just been uttered. Why? To reply that this is how the mind works, that as we grow older we tend to remember details of our earlier life, is only part of the answer. John remembered because the Holy Spirit helped him to remember. That is what the Holy Spirit is for.

---

[2] This is not the place to enter into a discussion of the Johannine problems. I am personally convinced that the simplest and most satisfactory solution to the problem is to accept the traditional view that John the son of Zebedee, the "disciple whom Jesus loved," wrote the Gospel of John, the Epistles, and the Apocalypse. This chapter proceeds on that assumption. For a discussion of the problem see R. V. G. Tasker, *The Gospel According to St. John* (Grand Rapids, Mich.: Wm. B. Eerdmans Publishing Co., 1960), pp. 11-20, and William Temple, *Readings in St. John's Gospel* (London: Macmillan and Co., 1950), pp. ix-xxxiii.

This certainly does not mean that the Holy Spirit leaves us free from any responsibility or effort to memorize. Students in my Hebrew classes who feel that they can depend upon the Holy Spirit to take the place of memorizing vocabulary soon discover the heretical nature of such a theory. Moreover, it does not mean that John's records of Jesus' teachings will be in the exact words that Jesus used. Six decades had perhaps taken away some of the words, but had added understanding and depth of meaning. "Memory, reflection, and the incubative work of the Spirit enabled the writer to penetrate to the heart of the Lord's person and mission and so elicit truth which he perceived only dimly, if at all, in his earlier days."[3]

Jesus had said also, "I will pray the Father, and he will give you another Counselor, to be with you for ever, even the Spirit of truth" (John 14:16-17). John had lived long enough to see the forces of falsehood begin to oppose the truth of the gospel. Men were denying that Jesus was the Christ, that He was possessed of the Father (I John 2:22-23); men were teaching that gratification of the fleshly appetites was not sin, that the fleshly nature of man was not real, that only the spiritual nature was real (I John 3:4-9); men were teaching that the Son of God could not therefore have taken a true human nature (I John 4:2-3). But the Holy Spirit, the Third Person of the Godhead who was sent to dwell in all who believe in Christ, is the Spirit of truth. He was the source of John's spiritual discernment of truth and error (I John 4:13; 5-7; cf. 2:26-27).

Some will say that this is not a very sure defense of truth; that it is too "subjective," and cannot be trusted. Two things need to be kept in mind: The Spirit who guides us in truth, who helps us discern between truth and error, is the same Spirit who inspired the Holy Scriptures; therefore truth will always be consonant with Scripture. In the second place, the guidance of the Spirit today extends to the entire Church, hence every individual is obligated to check his spiritual discernment with that of other Christians—including those of previous generations whose testimony is recorded in the great creeds and theological works of Christendom.

Jesus had further said concerning the Spirit, "And when he comes, he will convince the world of sin and of righteousness and of judgment" (John 16:8). He is the *Holy* Spirit, or the Spirit of holiness.

---

[3] Everett F. Harrison, "The Gospel and the Gospels," *Bibliotheca Sacra* 116 (April, 1959), p. 114.

John had had many years in which to learn the lessons of holiness. He knew that Jesus had once told Nicodemus, "Unless one is born of water and the Spirit, he cannot enter the kingdom of God" (John 3:5). He knew that access to the Kingdom under the symbol of the Holy City was denied to all evildoers (Revelation 21:8; 22:15). He knew that "any one born of God does not sin, but He who was born of God keeps him, and the evil one does not touch him" (I John 5:18). To John this was no mere academic discussion. He knew from experience that the One who was most completely possessed of the Holy Spirit could not be convicted of any sin. Jesus was holy as God was holy, and the Holy Spirit was the Spirit of Jesus.

Yet once more, Jesus had said, "When the Counselor comes, whom I shall send to you from the Father, even the Spirit of truth, who proceeds from the Father, he will bear witness to me" (John 15:26). The Spirit does not witness to Himself. For this reason Christians sometimes ask, "How do I know whether I have the Holy Spirit?" The Spirit witnesses to Jesus, just as the apostles witnessed to Jesus (cf. John 15:27).

The Holy Spirit is no mere doctrine: He is an experience. Every Christian in the Early Church knew that he possessed the Spirit of God, for he had an experience of the presence of the Spirit. That very same Spirit who dwelt in Jesus dwells in you and me, and we know it—or else He is not present (I John 3:24). He works through the Scriptures as we read or meditate upon them. He reminds us of God's will when we are tempted to wander away into sin. He tells us of Christ and His redeeming work. He warns us of error when we hear some false gospel. He helps us discern between error and truth. He does all these things—if we let Him. But we must learn to become sensitive to His leading. The Apostle John had developed that sensitivity; that is why John was Christlike, for he had let the Spirit of Christ dwell in him. Did John speak in tongues? Did he have the gift of healing? Very little is said about these gifts in connection with John. But he did have the best gift of the Spirit, the gift of love. He learned that "if God so loved us, we also ought to love one another" (I John 4:11). In fact, "Love one another" could be described as John's life-text.

John and the Son of God. John was one of the first to heed the words of John the Baptist and follow Jesus (John 1:35-39). John was the last (and perhaps the only) disciple at the foot of the cross (John 19:26). Between those two events, John was with Jesus during most of His ministry. As one of the "inner circle" of the apostles (Peter, James, and John), he witnessed some of Jesus' works and experiences that the rest of the Twelve did not behold. Perhaps that is why he was the first to believe in the resurrection (John 20:8).

John was one of the sons of Zebedee (Matthew 4:21), and from the fact that Zebedee had "hired servants" (cf. Mark 1:20) it is assumed that he had a sizeable fishing business on the Sea of Galilee. Zebedee's wife was Salome[4] (compare Mark 15:40 with Matthew 27:55-56), who was one of the women who ministered to Jesus and the disciples and one of those who went to the tomb to care for His body. According to what seems to me to be the normal reading of John 19:25, there were four women at the foot of the cross (it would be contrary to all experience for two sisters to have the same name); and if this is compared with the passages in Matthew and Mark just cited, we may reasonably infer that Salome was the sister of Mary the mother of Jesus. If so, then John was a cousin (or near relative) of John the Baptist, as well as a cousin of Jesus. This may explain some of the evidences of familiarity displayed by James and John and by their mother. We have already seen that Jesus did not tolerate demands based on earthly relationships.

In the Fourth Gospel, John does not refer to himself or his brother by name, but five times he does refer to "the disciple whom Jesus loved";[5] the only identification that meets the requirements in all of these texts is John himself. Some think that it would display gross egotism to call oneself "the disciple whom Jesus loved." But let us think about it a bit. Jesus did show some sort of preference for Peter, James, and John, when He took them with Him on certain occasions. Jesus did choose Peter and John to prepare for the Passover that was to become the Last Supper (Luke 22:8). Jesus did commend His mother into the care of John (John 19:26-27). There are indications that Jesus did love John in a way that was just a little different from His love for the others.

But let us look at this from a different angle. Jesus had given to

---

[4] To be distinguished, of course, from the daughter of Herodias who was instrumental in having John the Baptist beheaded. The name is pronounced suh-lō'me.

[5] John 13:23; 19:26; 20:2; 21:7, 20.

James and John the name "sons of thunder" (Mark 3:17). What led to that name we are not told; but some of the events that occurred later may give us a clue. One day—and it was late in the ministry, toward the time of the crucifixion—Jesus and His disciples were on their way to Jerusalem, and He sent disciples on ahead into a Samaritan village to make arrangements probably for their lodging. The village refused to give them hospitality. James and John said, "Lord, do you want us to bid fire come down from heaven and consume them?" Jesus turned and rebuked them (Luke 9:54-55). Another time, John said, "Master, we saw a man casting out demons in your name, and we forbade him, because he does not follow with us." Again Jesus rebuked him with the words, "Do not forbid him; for he that is not against you is for you" (Luke 9:49-50). On still another occasion, Salome brought her sons James and John to Jesus, and said, "Command that these two sons of mine may sit, one at your right hand and one at your left, in your kingdom" (Matthew 20:21; cf. Mark 10:35-41). Once again a rebuke was in order, and Jesus administered it kindly but firmly.

That John thought of these events many times I have no doubt—and I suppose that whenever he did, he grew red around the ears. He probably thought, "How He loved me, to put up with such a man!" John never told any of these stories in his Gospel—but he did write, "If we say we have no sin, we deceive ourselves . . ." (I John 1:8).

Son of God! John walked with Him, lived with Him, listened to Him. John heard Him make statements that sounded like the great "I Am": Jehovah Himself (cf. John 8:58). John saw Him perform miracles the like of which the world had never heard (cf. John 9:32). John heard Him pray in Gethsemane. John saw Him die on Calvary. John saw the grave cloths in the empty tomb. And John wrote, "The Word became flesh and dwelt among us, full of grace and truth; we have beheld his glory, glory as of the only Son from the Father" (John 1:14), and again, "That which was from the beginning, which we have heard, which we have seen with our eyes, which we have looked upon and touched with our hands . . . that which we have seen and heard we proclaim also to you, so that you may have fellowship with us; and our fellowship is with the Father and with his Son Jesus Christ" (I John 1:1-3).

To John the essence of antichrist was the denial of the Sonship of Jesus Christ: "Who is the liar but he who denies that Jesus is the

Christ? This is the antichrist, he who denies the Father and the Son" (cf. I John 2:18-24). To John the great divide was the witness to the incarnation: "Every spirit which confesses that Jesus Christ has come in the flesh is of God, and every spirit which does not confess Jesus is not of God" (I John 4:2-3).

To John the way God made His love known to the world was the incarnation: "In this the love of God was made manifest among us, that God sent his only Son into the world, so that we might live through him" (I John 4:9). The propitiation for our sins, the satisfaction of divine justice necessary because of our guilt, the removal of divine wrath against all unrighteousness, was possible only by the act of God's love: "In this is love, not that we loved God but that he loved us and sent his Son to be the expiation [or better, propitiation][6] for our sins" (I John 4:10). "He appeared to take away sins, and in him there is no sin" (I John 3:5).

John wrote his Gospel to set forth his convictions: "these are written that you may believe that Jesus is the Christ, the Son of God, and that believing you may have life in his name" (John 20:31). Some would tell us that the Son of God of the Fourth Gospel is not the simple Carpenter of the Synoptics. But did John make Jesus, or did Jesus make John? Did the son of Zebedee turn the Carpenter of Nazareth into the Son of God, or did the One who came that we might have life turn the Galilean fisherman into the Holy Theologian? For myself, I find it easier to believe the second alternative.

John and God the Father. In the symbolism of the Christian Church, John is often portrayed as an eagle, which is meant to imply that as the eagle is said to be the only bird able to look directly into the sun, so the Apostle John is the only evangelist able to look directly upon God. I am not sure that either the symbolic identification or the explanation is true—but there is a great truth behind the symbolism. Philip spoke for all of us: "Lord, show us the Father, and we shall be satisfied." Jesus answered, "He who has seen me has seen the Father" (cf. John 14:8-9). John has attempted to portray Jesus in such a way that we shall see the Father. It can be summarized, I think, in one word: love.

"God so loved the world that he gave his only Son, that whoever

[6] For a study of this great theme, and in particular the words used to describe it, see Leon Morris, *The Apostolic Preaching of the Cross* (Grand Rapids, Mich.: Wm. B. Eerdmans Publishing Co., 1955), pp. 125-185, especially pp. 177-180.

believes in him should not perish but have eternal life. For God sent the Son into the world, not to condemn the world, but that the world might be saved through him" (John 3:16-17). Love is the only sufficient reason for the redemptive work of God in Christ. You and I have no claim on God. He owes us nothing. We are not by natural birth His children—that is a Stoic idea that has forced its way into Christian (or should we say sub-Christian?) thought. At this point the scientist is absolutely right when he ridicules the notion that this microscopically insignificant bit of the vast universe should presume to identify himself with the Creator. But what the scientist has not been able to discover, God has revealed in Jesus Christ: God loves us. And by receiving this incarnation of God's love into our hearts and lives, we can become God's children (cf. John 1:12).

Some men object to this doctrine. They seem to think that God must treat all men exactly alike. But it is not God who is to be condemned for His love, but man for his unbelief: "He who does not believe is condemned already, because he has not believed in the name of the only Son of God. And this is the judgment, that the light has come into the world, and men loved darkness rather than light, because their deeds were evil" (John 3:18-19).

Only love is sufficient to explain the sacrifice of Jesus. Why did God let His Son die? What kind of divine justice is it that allowed wicked men to torture and kill One who went about doing only good? Or was God unable to stop it? Men struggle with the problem, seeking an answer; but the answer that God has given is sufficient: He loved us, even while we were sinners. "In this the love of God was made manifest among us, that God sent his only Son into the world, so that we might live through him" (I John 4:9). Jesus willingly went to the cross because He knew that only in this way would the Father be glorified. "Now is my soul troubled. And what shall I say, 'Father, save me from this hour'? No, for this purpose I have come to this hour. Father, glorify thy name" (John 12:27-28). After John had pondered the mystery of divine condescension for many years, he realized at last, "We have seen and testify that the Father has sent his Son as the Savior of the world. . . . So we know and believe the love God has for us" (I John 4:14, 16).

Love is sufficient to express obedience to divine commandments. "This is my commandment, that you love one another as I have loved you. . . . This I command you, to love one another" (John 15:12, 17).

Every law in the Decalogue can be obeyed by simply this: Love one another. The summary of the Law was expressed by Jesus in the two commandments, to love God, and to love your neighbor. John says, "Beloved, let us love one another; for love is of God, and he who loves is born of God and knows God. He who does not love does not know God; for God is love" (I John 4:7-8).

To John the example of divine love is sufficient to compel human love. "Beloved, if God so loved us, we also ought to love one another" (I John 4:11). To John the demonstration of love was a manifestation of God: "No man has ever seen God; if we love one another, God abides in us and his love is perfected in us" (I John 4:12). In fact, so essential is the demonstration of love on our part that John writes with great emphasis, "If any one says, 'I love God' and hates his brother, he is a liar; for he who does not love his brother whom he has seen, cannot love God whom he has not seen. And this command-ment we have from him, that he who loves God should love his brother also" (I John 4:20-21).

When man and woman are joined in perfect love, there is unity. Oneness is the ultimate realization of love. Because of the love of the Father for the Son and the Son for the Father, Jesus could say, "I and the Father are one" (John 10:30). Using a different figure, Jesus described this perfect unity as vine and branches, and immedi-ately He passed from speaking of abiding in the vine to speak of abiding in love (cf. John 15:1-10).

The most perfect expression of this unity in love is found in Jesus' prayer. "I have manifested thy name to the men whom thou gavest me out of the world. . . . I have given them thy word; and the world has hated them because they are not of the world, even as I am not of the world. I do not pray that thou shouldst take them out of the world, but that thou shouldst keep them from the evil one. . . . I do not pray for these only, but also for those who are to believe in me through their word, that they may all be one; even as thou, Father, art in me, and I in thee, that they also may be in us, so that the world may believe that thou hast sent me. The glory which thou hast given me I have given to them, that they may be one even as we are one, I in them and thou in me, that they may become perfectly one, so that the world may know that thou hast sent me and hast loved them even as thou hast loved me" (John 17:6-23).

This is John the Theologian. Many have summarized his theology in the key words: light, life, love. Life, I think, would characterize what he tells us about the Holy Spirit, for He is the source of life. We are born anew by the Spirit. We live by the Spirit. We have holiness of life by the Spirit. Light characterizes the Son, the true Light that came into the world. In His light we see light. God the Father is invisible, but the Son has manifested Him. Love characterizes the Father. God is love. We do not even know God if we do not know what love is, and to say that we love God without loving our brother human being is hollow mockery. Yet these three are one, and what is said of any one Person can be said of the others. We therefore say that these three are one God.

You thought theology was supposed to be dry and lifeless? Not so. Theology brings God into daily life. It derives concrete realizations from the abstract. It gathers together diverse teachings into useful categories and applies them to life situations. At least that is what John the Theologian did with theology.

CHAPTER XVIII

The Triumphant Christ

WE PREVIOUSLY DEVOTED a study to the human nature of Jesus Christ, pointing out at the time that there is also a divine nature to be considered (see Chapter IV). I have saved the study of the divine nature of Jesus Christ to the end because it can best be understood against the background of the Early Church. For the Early Church is, as I hope we have seen, the work of Jesus Christ the Son of God through the Holy Spirit whom He sent following His own death, resurrection, and ascension to heaven. To try to explain the Church as merely the work of men who had caught the vision of what the Galilean Carpenter was trying to teach them is to fail to understand either the Galilean or those who claim to be His apostles.

Christ in the midst of the churches. In His great commission, when the risen Jesus sent His apostles out into the world to make disciples of all nations, He added the promise, "and lo, I am with you always, to the close of the age" (Matthew 28:20). In the exquisite, if often misunderstood, symbolism of the Book of Revelation, this promise of Jesus' abiding presence is expressed in a different way. There John says, "I turned to see the voice that was speaking to me, and on turning I saw seven golden lampstands, and in the midst of the lampstands one like a son of man" (Revelation 1:12-13). John fell as one dead before the vision, but the Speaker, who identified Himself as the One who died and is alive for evermore, explained the symbolism: "the seven lampstands are the seven churches" (Revelation 1:20). Christ, then, is portrayed symbolically as standing in the midst of the churches.

Too often we seem to have the idea that Jesus has gone to heaven, where He is seated on the right hand of God, and whence some day He shall return to earth; meantime we are left to run things in our own wisdom and strength. Now it is true that Jesus has returned to heaven and maintains a session of intercession. It is also true that He is coming again. But it is not true that He has left us alone in the meantime. He has sent us One who is like Himself, who has all the power of the Godhead, who remains with us and in us during all this age; and these two are so completely identified that we can speak either of the Holy Spirit or the Spirit of Christ.

The seven churches are seven historic churches: Ephesus, Smyrna, Pergamum, Thyatira, Sardis, Philadelphia, and Laodicea. I have visited each of these sites. They are not just mysterious names put in a strange book; they are the locations of churches started when Paul was in Ephesus, and continuing during the ministry of Timothy and John and for centuries afterwards. They form approximately a circle, moving clockwise from Ephesus, the most distant being less than one hundred miles.

The Lord Jesus once said, "I will build my church" (Matthew 16:18). In the Book of Acts we see Him building His Church, working in and through men such as Peter, Stephen, Paul, Barnabas, and others. But that was only the beginning. The Book of Acts, as many have noted, has no true ending. In a sense we might say that it is still being written, for Christ is still building His Church.

The first of the seven churches in Revelation is the Church at Ephesus. Jesus tells John to write to the "angel"—the Greek word also means "messenger," and almost certainly refers to the pastor or minister—of the church and say, "I know your works" (Revelation 2:2). These words are spoken by the One "who holds the seven stars in his right hand, who walks among the seven golden lampstands." The "stars" are the "angels" or "messengers" (Revelation 1:20), and the lampstands, as we have seen, are the churches. The number seven, used so frequently in Revelation, suggests the idea of completion—not that the seven churches are the only churches, but that they are symbolic or representative of all churches. In other words, putting the symbolism into prosaic language, Jesus says, "I who hold the messengers in my hand and who walk in the midst of the churches—I know your works."

That is a beautiful thought, is it not? He knows the toil, the patient endurance, the impatience with false teachers (Revelation 2:2). He knows the tribulation and poverty (Revelation 2:9). He knows every detail of the life of every church.

But it is also a frightening thought, for He who knows the faith and patience, love and good works, also knows the unbelief, the lack of vitality, and the lukewarmness. He who stands in the midst of the lampstands, holding the stars in His right hand, is also the One out of whose mouth issues the two-edged sword (Revelation 1:16). The sword coming from the mouth can only be the Word, and its two edges can only symbolize its ability to cut both ways, in praise and in blame.

The Church in Ephesus was a church of toil and patience, but it was also a church that had abandoned the love it had at first (Revelation 2:4). That is a terrible thing to have to say to a church or to an individual. It indicates the lack of a sense of judgment. When you abandon what formerly you loved, it means either that you had poor judgment when you developed that love, or that you have poor judgment in leaving it. In other words, you sit in judgment on yourself either way. It indicates a lack of maturity, a basic inability to make up your mind, an absence of a true sense of values, a vacillating spirit. What can be done about it? "Remember then from what you have fallen, repent and do the works you did at first" (Revelation 2:5). Think back to the beginning, think of what led to that first love; then repent, turn your mind about, think the way you once thought; go back to the works you did in that previous way of thinking. And what if you do not? "If not, I will come to you and remove your lampstand from its place, unless you repent" (Revelation 2:5). The lampstand is the church. Christ is saying, if the church refuses to do the work of the church, if it refuses to demonstrate the love of the church, it is no church. By removing the lampstand, He takes away its right to call itself a church.

Approximately forty years earlier, Paul had expressed his great concern about the Church at Ephesus. "I know that after my departure fierce wolves will come in among you, not sparing the flock; and from among your own selves will arise men speaking perverse things, to draw away the disciples after them. Therefore be alert . . ." (Acts 20:29-31). No church can say that it has not been warned. What Paul said to the elders of the Church at Ephesus the Holy Spirit is saying to every church. What Christ said to the angel of the Church at Ephesus, the Spirit is saying to all churches. "He who has an ear, let him hear what the Spirit says to the churches" (Revelation 2:7).

What has been said about Ephesus can be said, *mutatis mutandis,* about the other churches. The letters to the seven churches are letters that search out specific points of praise or blame, so that "all the churches shall know that I am he who searches mind and heart, and I will give to each of you as your works deserve" (Revelation 2:23). We call this judgment. Judgment begins at the house of God.

Some men do not like the idea of judgment, and quite often the preacher hears an objection to sermons on the subject. I think that is because of a faulty notion of what judgment is. When we say, "He is a man of good judgment," no one shudders; but when we say, "God is a God of judgment," men cringe. But are we not saying the same thing? Men sometimes think of judgment as the final act, the ax that falls on the neck of mankind, ending the drama. There is indeed a finality in the Last Judgment, but we should think first of judgment as a process. God is a good Judge who discriminates between the good and the bad, between that which has value and that which has no value, between the ephemeral and the eternal. He judges His Church, not just at the end but at each stage along the way. Like a careful viticulturist, He prunes away that which is not good, in order that the good will be better. Like a skilled surgeon, He removes that which is diseased in order that life may be preserved.

There are those who seem to think of heaven as a cosmic junkyard, as though God is interested in collecting broken and rotten lives. Anyone who has been a failure can, if he will only attend the evangelist's rally, get into heaven. This is a travesty on the grace of God and a denial of His judgment. God saves sinners—but there will be no sinners in heaven, only ex-sinners. In beautiful symbolism, heaven is described for us, and we read: "They shall bring into it the glory and the honor of the nations. But nothing unclean shall enter it, nor any one who practices abomination or falsehood, but only those who are written in the Lamb's book of life" (Revelation 21:26-27). God's judgments in this age are gracious acts, whereby we who name His name are prepared for the Holy City.

Christ in the midst of the churches is also the Christ of rewards. To each of the churches He has some word concerning the reward He will give to those who overcome. Not all of His rewards are reserved for the age to come; even in this life we experience the benefits of serving the Lord in His Church.

Christ on the throne. In His great commission, Jesus said: "All authority in heaven and on earth has been given to me" (Matthew 28:18). This is expressed symbolically in the Book of Revelation in the following terms: "I was in the Spirit, and lo, a throne stood in heaven, with one seated on the throne! . . . And I saw in the right hand of him who was seated on the throne a scroll written within and on the back, sealed with seven seals; and I saw a strong angel proclaiming with a loud voice, 'Who is worthy to open the scroll and break its seals?' . . . And between the throne and the four living creatures and among the elders, I saw a Lamb standing, as though it had been slain . . . ; and he went and took the scroll from the right hand of him who was seated on the throne. . . . And they sang a new song, saying,

'Worthy art thou to take the scroll and to open its seals,
for thou wast slain and by thy blood didst ransom men for God
from every tribe and tongue and people and nation,
and hast made them a kingdom and priests to our God,
and they shall reign on earth'" (Revelation 4:2; 5:1-2, 6-7, 9-10).

The seven-sealed book is the book of destiny; it is the book of the future, the history that must yet take place on the earth. Who is able to open the book and lay bare the secrets? Who is able to control the destiny of the world? No one. No one in heaven, or on earth, or in the underworld. No one but the Lamb that had been slain, the Lion of Judah, the Root of David (cf. Revelation 5:3-5).

Men have varying views of history. Some are naïvely optimistic: things are getting better all the time. Give man enough knowledge, enough science, enough technical achievement, enough medical wisdom, and he will solve all his problems and bring in the golden age. Some are pessimistic: civilizations reach their peaks and then decline. No civilization can maintain the vitality necessary to dominate forever. History must ever be a series of rise-and-decline. Some look upon history as an endless cycle, a universal carrousel ride with its perpetual "here we go 'round again." History repeats itself. The Bible takes the truth in each of these systems and combines it into a complex idea that says that without God man is doomed to decline, but with God's redemptive power man shall reach the skies. God is in it with us, for when Jesus Christ came into this world God became incarnate, and He has never relinquished that human nature. He took it to heaven, and in so doing, He made it possible for man to become like God. He is totally involved in history, for the Church is His body, and whatever happens to the Church happens to Him; moreover, whether or not men admit it, He sits on the throne and rules the nations with a rod of iron.

The inability of anyone else to solve the riddle of the seven-sealed book is moral inability: "No one was found worthy to open the scroll or to look into it" (Revelation 5:4). Think about that for a minute or two, and you will realize how true it is. The problems of this world are moral problems. Wars, social inequities, class hatred, lust—these, and all other matters that constitute the riddle of history, are moral problems. The Christian businessman tells his pastor, "I cannot compete in this world and hold to my Christian convictions. I have to lie and cheat, I have to cut the corners, or I'll go out of business." On a vaster scale, the leaders of nations cannot operate according to the principles of the Kingdom of Heaven—the incident of the U-2 demonstrated that. While men or nations lie and deceive, all must use the same principles, or perish. Perhaps this is what Jesus had in mind when He said, "If my kingship [or kingdom] were of this world, my servants would fight" (John 18:36). This may have been what He meant when He said, "Behold, I send you out as sheep in the midst of wolves; so be wise as serpents and innocent as doves" (Matthew 10:16.[1] This is a sinful world, and there is no way out of the mess except to get rid of the sin—and that is possible only by the way of the cross. It is the Lamb that was slain who is able to break the seals and open the book.

When the seals are opened and the scroll is unrolled, what do we see? What is to be the history of the world? Well, at first it is not pleasant to behold: there is war, famine, pestilence (cf. Revelation 6:1-8, note verse 8); there is terrible persecution, and fearsome calamities (Revelation 6:9-17)—these are described as "the wrath of the Lamb." When we were looking at the picture of Christ in the midst of the churches, we saw that He visits judgments upon His own. Those judgments are in order to cleanse, to purify, to make His Church glorious, without spot or wrinkle. But in the symbolism of the

---

[1] It is possible, if the western world collapses under the godless impact of communism, that historians will one day write, "They tried to apply idealistic principles in a world that refused to adopt the same ideals." And the blindest of the blind are those ministers, who should be the interpreters of God's Word, who accept and repeat all that Jesus said about principles that are intended to apply to the Church, but who refuse to accept what Jesus said about the unbelief and the sin of the world, or the fundamental separation between the Church and the world. It is not wise for sheep to pretend that wolves are sheep!

central portion of Revelation are set forth the judgments of God on the world.

As a general principle it can be said that the judgments of God are bound up with His laws, particularly with the inexorable law of cause-and-effect. Men have war because they have rejected the way of peace. Men have famine because of the selfishness and greed of men. When empires refuse to treat their colonials like human beings, when they refuse to place confidence in them, train them, and prepare them for self-rule, empires can expect the colonies one day to rise in revolt. When the white man exalts himself as lord of the human race and treats his fellow men of different pigmentation as beasts of burden, he can expect them one day to rise up against him and seek to destroy him. When greedy capitalists exploit labor and manifest a public-be-damned attitude, they can expect a public reaction and a revolt of labor. When nations oppress nations they can be certain that war will follow.

These are the judgments of God, and they are just. When the bowls of wrath are being poured out on earth, the angel is heard to say,

"Just art thou in these thy judgments,
thou who art and wast, O Holy One.
For men have shed the blood of saints and prophets,
and thou hast given them blood to drink.
It is their due!" (Revelation 16:5-6).

But don't close the book! Read it through to the end. Men have missed the value of the Book of Revelation because they have gotten lost in the maze of details and have failed to see the progress. After the judgments comes triumph. After the failure of man comes success. "Then I saw heaven opened, and behold, a white horse! He who sat upon it is called Faithful and True. . . . On his robe and on his thigh he has a name inscribed, King of kings and Lord of lords. . . . Then I saw an angel coming down from heaven, holding in his hand the key of the bottomless pit and a great chain. And he seized the dragon, that ancient serpent, who is the Devil and Satan, and bound him for a thousand years. . . . Then Death and Hades were thrown into the lake of fire. . . . Then I saw a new heaven and a new earth . . ." (Revelation 19:11,16; 20:1-2,14; 21:1).

This is the story of the seven-sealed book. After the wars and the famines, after the horrors caused by man in his godless efforts to rule the world, comes the victory of the King of kings and the glory of His Kingdom.

Christ in the Holy City. The Lord Jesus, on the last night before He was betrayed, told His disciples, "When I go and prepare a place for you, I will come again and will take you to myself, that where I am you may be also" (John 14:3).[2] In the beautiful language of Revelation, this is set forth as follows: "I saw the holy city, new Jerusalem, coming down out of heaven from God, prepared as a bride adorned for her husband; and I heard a great voice from the throne saying, 'Behold, the dwelling of God is with men. He will dwell with them, and they shall be his people, and God Himself will be with them . . .'" (Revelation 21:2-3).

It is a beautiful city. All attempts to describe it fail because of the limitations of language. John saw it "having the glory of God, its radiance like a most rare jewel, like a jasper, clear as crystal" (Revelation 21:11). He saw a wall of jasper, and gates of pearl, a city of gold with streets of pure gold. The city was as high as it was wide and long —was it a cube, or a pyramid?—and it had a river flowing from the throne, nourishing the tree of life that grew along its banks. There was no need of the sun or moon or any artificial means of light, for the Lord God is its light (Revelation 21:11—22:5). Some men find it hard to get an intelligible picture from this description. This is because we are trying to visualize in our minds what we have never seen with our eyes. Perhaps the language is more symbolic than we think. Perhaps John himself was at a loss for words, trying to record the glories of the Holy City in expressions drawn from earth's vocabulary.

It is God's city. Centuries ago Abraham set out to find the city "whose builder and maker is God" (Hebrews 11:10). This is it. The wall of the city has twelve gates, "and on the gates the names of the twelve tribes of the sons of Israel were inscribed" (Revelation 21:12). The wall also has twelve foundations, "and on them the twelve names of the twelve apostles of the Lamb" (Revelation 21:14). It is only

---

[2] Some scholars do not think this passage refers to the Lord's return at the end of the age. I shall not debate the point, for whether in this passage or some other, the Scripture clearly teaches the return of Christ for His own at the end of the age.

one city, and only one wall; and a wall would be of no use without gates, and gates would be meaningless without a wall. It is one city, but Jew and Gentile, old and new alike have been brought together and fashioned into one to form the wall. They are one in Christ.

There is no temple in the city (cf. Revelation 21:22). When the Book of Revelation was written (perhaps A.D. 96), Jerusalem had long since been destroyed. The Temple was a heap of rubbish and ash. I have no doubt that many Jews were saying, "How can we worship the Holy One without the Temple? Without the Temple there can be no sacrifice, and without the sacrifice there can be no atonement." But what is the Temple? and what is the sacrifice of bulls and goats? These things are symbols behind which stand the greater realities. The Temple is the symbol of God's presence. There is no need of a temple in the Holy City, "for its temple is the Lord God the Almighty and the Lamb" (Revelation 21:22). And there is no further need of the sacrifice of bulls and goats, which can never take away sin, for the Lamb has been slain once for all and sin is no more.

It is a holy city. There will be no unholiness there, and no unholy beings. There will be multitudes of redeemed sinners, but all their sins will have been washed away. "Nothing unclean shall enter it, nor any one who practices abomination or falsehood, but only those who are written in the Lamb's book of life" (Revelation 21:27). "There shall no more be anything accursed, but the throne of God and of the Lamb shall be in it, and his servants shall worship him" (Revelation 22:3). God is holy, and His word has ever been, "therefore you shall be holy" (cf. Leviticus 19:2).

Sickness, sorrow, and death will never be present in the Holy City. God "will wipe away every tear from their eyes, and death shall be no more, neither shall there be mourning nor crying nor pain any more, for the former things have passed away" (Revelation 21:4). When Jesus brought Lazarus back from the grave, Lazarus returned to this world of sickness and sorrow and death. But this is not so in the City of God. No crippled children will limp in its streets, tearing the heartstrings of mothers and fathers. No loved ones will waste away consumed by suffering and disease. There will be no institutions crowded with men and women suffering from mental and nervous disorders. No heartbroken husband and father will lay his beloved wife and newborn baby in the grave. No drunken drivers will race through its streets, and no gangsters will lurk in its shadows; there will not even be shadows, and the gates will never have to be closed. No bombs will burst over the Holy City, and no air-raid sirens will ever wail. There will be no war, for the leaves of the tree of life will be for the healing of the nations (Revelation 22:2).

But before this is possible, there must be a final judgment. "Do not seal up the words of the prophecy of this book, for the time is near. Let the evildoer still do evil, and the filthy still be filthy, and the righteous still do right, and the holy still be holy. Behold, I am coming soon, bringing my recompense, to repay every one for what he has done" (Revelation 22:10-12). Here is the awfulness of the final judgment: it is so terribly final! While it is the day of grace, the evildoer can repent of his evil, and the filthy can turn for cleansing. Men can be changed! But when the last judgment is finished, there is no further day of grace. From that moment forever, men will be what they are. Inside the Holy City are those who have washed their robes, "that they may have the right to the tree of life." Outside are "the dogs and sorcerers and fornicators and murderers and idolaters, and every one who loves and practices falsehood" (Revelation 22:14-15).

Today it is still the day of grace. "The Spirit and the Bride say, 'Come.' And let him who hears say, 'Come.' And let him who is thirsty come, let him who desires take the water of life without price" (Revelation 22:17).

Bibliography

(A number of titles in my *Great Personalities of the Old Testament* are likewise pertinent to the New Testament, such as Bible Dictionaries, Atlases, etc. I have not repeated them here in the interest of space.)

BIBLE DICTIONARIES (articles on persons, places, terms, etc.)

A Dictionary of the Bible, edited by James Hastings. New York: Charles Scribner's Sons, 1898 ff. 4 vols. and extra volume. [In spite of need of revision in many places, plus presuppositions that are questionable, this work is still valuable for its many excellent articles on New Testament subjects.]

A Dictionary of Christ and the Gospels, edited by James Hastings. New York: Charles Scribner's Sons, 1924. 2 vols. [Not so well known as the previous work, but in many respects superior for work in the Gospels. Some of the articles are the finest treatments of their respective subjects that I have found.]

A Dictionary of the Apostolic Church, edited by James Hastings. New York: Charles Scribner's Sons, 1915. 2 vols. [Probably the least known of the three titles given here and of somewhat lower quality. Still, when I was teaching The Beginnings of Christianity I combed it thoroughly and found it amply rewarding.]

Baker's Dictionary of Theology, edited by Everett F. Harrison, Geoffrey W. Bromiley, and Carl F. H. Henry. Grand Rapids, Mich.: Baker Book House, 1960. 566 pp. [A very useful volume for ready reference on any subject included by the broad term Theology. The viewpoint is conservative but the scholarship is fully aware of competing views.]

(See also *The Westminster Dictionary of the Bible, Harper's Bible Dictionary,* and *The International Standard Bible Encyclopaedia,* full bibliography for which is in my previous volume.)

BIBLE GEOGRAPHIES, ATLASES, AND SIMILAR HELPS

Gustaf Dalman, *Sacred Sites and Ways.* Translated from 3d edition by Paul P. Levertoff. London: Society for Promoting Christian Knowledge, 1935. 397 pp. [Background material for studying the Gospels, based on the land, language, literature, and tradition.]

Paul Bruin and Philipp Giegel, *Jesus Lived Here.* Translated by William Neil. New York: William Morrow and Company, 1958. 239 pp. [A splendid collection of photographs to help you visualize the Holy Land.]

Asia Minor, with 160 pictures in photogravure, 8 colour plates, and introduction by Maxim Osward. Translated by Norma Deane. London: Thames and Hudson, 1957. 32 pp. + 160 plates. [A magnificent volume of pictures, not all of which pertain to Biblical backgrounds.]

Nelson Beecher Keyes, *Story of the Bible World*. Maplewood, N. J.: C. S. Hammond & Company, 1959. 192 pp. [Descriptive text, many pictures, also many maps in color.]

Henri Metzger, *Les routes de saint Paul dans l'Orient grec*. (Cahiers d'archéologie biblique, No. 4.) Paris & Neuchâtel: Delachaux & Niestlé S.A., 1954. 62 pp. [A useful study in the light of modern discovery.]

L. H. Grollenberg, *Shorter Atlas of the Bible*. Translated by Mary F. Hedlund. New York: Thomas Nelson & Sons, 1960. 195 pp. [This is a condensed version of the Atlas which I have recommended most highly. Get the larger edition if you can afford it.]

(See also *Westminster Historical Atlas* and George Adam Smith, *The Historical Geography of the Holy Land,* in my previous volume.)

ART AND LITERATURE

George Ferguson, *Signs & Symbols in Christian Art*. 2d edition. New York: Oxford University Press, 1955. 346 pp., 96 plates, XV color plates. [The symbols are illustrated by line drawings alongside the text; arrangement is by subject; the plates provide a general introduction to the great religious art of the Renaissance.]

Cynthia Pearl Maus, *Christ and the Fine Arts*. 5th edition. New York: Harper & Brothers, 1938. 764 pp. [A storehouse of illustrative material in pictures, poetry, music, and stories.]

The Story of Jesus in the World's Literature, edited by Edward Wagenknecht, illustrations by Fritz Kredel. New York: Creative Age Press, Inc., 1946. 479 pp. [A fine selection, arranged by subjects.]

DAILY LIFE IN ANCIENT TIMES

Everyday Life in Ancient Times. Highlights of the Beginnings of Western Civilization in Mesopotamia, Egypt, Greece, and Rome. Washington, D.C.: National Geographic Society, 1958. 368 pp. [Paintings, illustrations, and text illustrating the life and customs in various periods and areas of the Bible world.]

A Dictionary of Life in Bible Times, by W. Corswant, completed and illustrated by Édouard Urech, translated by Arthur Heathcote. New York: Oxford University Press, 1960. 309 pp. [An excellent work to help bring the Biblical characters to life.]

ARCHAEOLOGY

G. Ernest Wright, *Biblical Archaeology*. Abridged edition. Philadelphia: Westminster Press, 1960. 198 pp. [A condensation, in an inexpensive edition, of the larger work by the same title.]

John A. Thompson, *Archaeology and the Pre-Christian Centuries*. Grand Rapids, Mich.: Wm. B. Eerdmans Publishing Co., 1958. 139 pp.

John A. Thompson, *Archaeology and the New Testament*. Grand Rapids, Mich.: Wm. B. Eerdmans Publishing Co., 1960. 151 pp. [This and the preceding title are brief but reliable works.]

William M. Ramsay, *The Bearing of Recent Discovery on the Trustworthiness of the New Testament*. 2d edition. London: Hodder and Stoughton, 1915; reprinted 1953 by Baker Book House, Grand Rapids, Mich. [Sir William Ramsay wrote many books and articles and I cannot begin to list the important ones here. I have selected this title because it gives the author's summary of the results of his life's work. Unfortunately, Ramsay's works lack splendid organization, and the scholar has to roam through many of Ramsay's works to find material on any desired subject. We are indebted to Baker Book House for reprinting several of the more important titles.]

THE BACKGROUND OF JUDAISM

George Foot Moore, *Judaism*. Cambridge, Mass.: Harvard University Press, 1927. 2 vols. [The classic on the subject of Judaism in the first centuries of the Christian era.]

Josephus. Complete Works, translated by William Whiston. Grand Rapids, Mich.: Kregel Publications, 1960 (reprint). [The serious New Testament student should often look into Josephus for insights and sidelights. A bit of a critical approach to Josephus is, of course, necessary.]

Robert H. Pfeiffer, *History of New Testament Times*. New York: Harper & Brothers, 1949. 561 pp. [Valuable for a study of the intertestamental period and its literature; the work contains a magnificent bibliography.]

Floyd V. Filson, *The New Testament Against its Environment*. (Studies in Biblical Theology, No. 3.) London: S C M Press Ltd., 1950. 103 pp. [An excellent summary of the background of the New Testament, with footnote references to the significant publications.]

LIFE OF CHRIST

A Harmony of the Gospels, edited by William Arnold Stevens and Ernest de Witt Burton. Boston: Silver, Burdett & Company, 1897. 237 pp. [I fail to understand how anyone can study the Life of Christ without a harmony of the Gospels. This one uses the text of 1881 (English Revised Version), but in my opinion its arrangement of the events in the four Gospels is superior.]

Ralph D. Heim, *A Harmony of the Gospels for Students*. Philadelphia: Muhlenberg Press, 1947. 209 pp. [Uses the RSV text.]

Alfred Edersheim, *The Life and Times of Jesus the Messiah*. Eleventh impression. London: Longmans, Green and Co., 1901. 2 vols. [In many ways, still the best Life of Christ. There seems to be no inclination in modern scholarship to attempt a synthesis of the subject as Edersheim has done; yet much in Edersheim needs to be revised or rejected.]

William Manson, *Jesus the Messiah*. The Synoptic Tradition of the Revelation of God in Christ, with Special Reference to Form-Criticism. Philadelphia: Westminster Press, 1946. 267 pp. [Useful for an understanding of how the Gospel record is handled by modern Form-critics; Manson is quite a conservative representative of modern scholarship.]

J. Gresham Machen, *The Virgin Birth of Christ*. New York: Harper & Brothers, 1930. 415 pp. [A classic. The scholar who ignores this work lays himself open to the charge either of ignorance or of unwillingness to face the facts as presented by the best of conservative scholarship.]

G. Campbell Morgan, *The Crises of the Christ*. New York: Fleming H. Revell Co., 1903. 477 pp. [One of the finest works by one of the greatest of recent Bible expositors. Everyone who teaches or seriously studies the Life of Christ should read this work not once but often.]

G. Campbell Morgan, *The Teaching of Christ*. New York: Fleming H. Revell Co., 1913. 333 pp. [An excellent study; there are, however, areas of Christ's teachings that are not covered.]

A. B. Bruce, *The Training of the Twelve*. 3d edition. New York: Richard R. Smith, Inc., 1930. 552 pp. [A well-known and highly praised work that is rich in its insights.]

Richard Chenevix Trench, *Notes on the Parables of Our Lord*. 8th edition. New York: D. Appleton & Company, 1856. 425 pp. [A classic, but why has no one given us an up-to-date study of the same proportions?]

Richard Chenevix Trench, *Notes on the Miracles of Our Lord*. Eleventh edition. London: Macmillan and Co., 1878. 515 pp. [Again, a classic, and very rich, but in need of revision.]

A. G. Hebert, *The Throne of David*. London: Faber and Faber, 1941. 277 pp. [A modern effort to deal with Christ in the typology of the Old Testament.]

H. V. Morton, *In the Steps of the Master*. 23d edition. London: Methuen & Co., 1953. 388 pp. [This is a beautiful combination of geography, travelogue, religious devotion, and interesting anecdotes. I have carried it with me in the steps of the Master, and the opinion I had previously formed about the work was not dimished.]

THE BEGINNINGS OF CHRISTIANITY

F. J. Foakes Jackson and Kirsopp Lake, editors, *The Beginnings of Christianity*. London: Macmillan and Co., 1922. 5 vols. [A masterful work, at some places based on presuppositions which I not only cannot accept but which I feel are unwarranted. Nevertheless, it must be studied—particularly the first volume—by anyone working in Acts.]

F. F. Bruce, *A Commentary on the Book of Acts.* (The New International Commentary on the New Testament.) Grand Rapids, Mich.: Wm. B. Eerdmans Publishing Co., 1956. 555 pp. [Of all the commentaries on Acts that I have used, this is in many ways the most satisfactory. The scholarship is massive; the viewpoint is conservative; the application is devotional and helpful.]

J. Gresham Machen, *The Origin of Paul's Religion.* London: Hodder & Stoughton, 1921. 329 pp. [A thorough work on a subject that perhaps does not claim the attention today that it did formerly. Nevertheless, many of the points in this book are still valid and need to be repeated for the problems of Pauline study that are raised today.]

Bernard Ramm, *The Witness of the Spirit.* Grand Rapids, Mich.: Wm. B. Eerdmans Publishing Co., 1960. 140 pp. [A fine study of the Holy Spirit and His place in the believer's life.]

Daniel J. Theron, *Evidence of Tradition.* Grand Rapids, Mich.: Baker Book House, 1958. 135 pp. [Selections of source material, in the original languages, with English translation, for the study of the New Testament canon, the history of the Early Church, and other matters that require a knowledge of the earliest non-Biblical evidence.]

F. F. Bruce, *The New Testament Documents: Are They Reliable?* 5th revised edition. Grand Rapids, Mich.: Wm. B. Eerdmans Publishing Co., 1960. 120 pp. [A useful handbook on the basic problems of New Testament Introduction, from a conservative and scholarly viewpoint.]

H. V. Morton, *In the Steps of St. Paul.* New York: Dodd, Mead & Company, 1955. 499 pp. [Originally published in 1936, this work, like Morton's companion volume on the Master, is charming. It contains quantities of background material, unforunately without documentation—which annoys the scholar who wants to know where he got some of his material.]

WORD STUDIES

Leon Morris, *The Apostolic Preaching of the Cross.* Grand Rapids, Mich.: Wm. B. Eerdmans Publishing Co., 1955. 296 pp. [A splendid work, combining thoroughly scholarly word studies, well-rounded theology, and deep devotion. Highly recommended!]

J.-J. von Allmen, *Vocabulary of the Bible.* English translation by a group of scholars, edited by Hilda A. Wilson. London: Lutterworth Press, 1958. 479 pp. [Contains a breadth of scholarship. When studying words we need to be reminded that the context governs the meaning of words at least as much as the reverse. Always study words in context!]

Index

Abraham, 29, 95f
Acts of Peter and Paul, 85
Acts of St. Paul and Thecla, 120
Acts of Thomas, 156
Adam, 49
Alexander the Great, 15ff, 135
Alexandria, 17, 31, 93, 99, 143f
Ananias, 105; and Sapphira, 82, 120
Andrew, 50ff, 70
Andronicus and Junias, 118
Antichrist, 170
Antioch (in Pisidia), 109, 115
Antioch (in Syria), 86, 111, 121ff
Apocryphal Gospels, 38, 43, 48
Apollos, 118f, 140, 143ff
Apostasy, 154
Apostle, 53ff, 71ff, 118, 153
Apostolic succession, 118
Aquila, 138ff
Aristarchus, 128, 132
Artemis, 116f
Asia, 115f
Assumption of Mary, 40
Athens, 99, 112f, 150

Babylon, 86f
Ballance, M., 109
Baptism of Jesus, 45, 53
Barnabas, 111f, 118ff, 147ff
Bethany, 61, 65, 68, 79
Bethlehem, 43
Blasphemy, 96f, 103, 105
Breed, D. R., 19
Bromiley, G. W., 89
Brothers and sisters of Jesus, 35, 38, 43
Bruce, A. B., 55
Bruce, F. F., 86, 125, 140, 147, 163
Burrows, M., 27

Caesarea-Philippi, 72
Calendar, 43
Childhood of Jesus, 42ff
Children of God, 172
Chrestos, 139, 142
Christ, 72, 175ff
Christian, 123; "second generation," 153
Christology, 41

Church, 39, 73, 84, 119ff, 154, 175ff; buildings, 141; organization, 89, 154
Circumcision, 84, 149
Citizenship, 100, 111, 143
Claudius, 139
Clement, 118
Commandments, 172
Communism, 120
Conversion of Saul, 104ff
Corinth, 86, 112, 114f, 139, 142ff, 150; Church in, 86, 152; Epistles to, 86, 114, 140, 144
Cornelius, 83f, 111, 159
Courtship, 36
Council of Chalcedon, 34, 42; of Constantinople, 41; of Ephesus, 34, 41; of Nicea, 41
Cross, 56, 73f; crucifixion, 80, 110, 172
Cullmann, O., 81, 86
Cyprus, 108, 119, 122

Deacons, 89ff, 154
Dead Sea Scrolls, 26, 90
Death, 60, 63ff, 75, 183
Deissmann, A., 100
Denney, J., 118, 140
Derbe, 109, 147
Diana, 116 (see also Artemis)
Disciple, 50ff, 71; —whom Jesus loved, 39; disciples, 46
Dispersion (Diaspora), 20f, 89, 122
Dorcas, 82f
Doubt, 159f
Driver, G. R., 129

Elizabeth, 23f, 32, 36
Ephesus, 31, 40, 115f, 139, 142ff, 150, 153, 164, 176f
Epicureans, Epicureanism, 113
Epiphanius, 35
Essenes, 26
Eunice, 143, 148
Euodia, 143
Eusebius, 85, 101, 151

Faith, 66; faith-healing, 67
Father, 47ff, 73 (see also God)

190

Flemington, W. F., 29
Foakes Jackson, F. J., 20
Foot washing, 76
Fullness of time, 13ff, 51

Galatia, 108ff; Epistle to, 86, 109, 121
Galen, 128
Galilee, 43, 72, 78; Galilean ministry, 52f
Gallio, 139
Gamaliel, 100ff
Genealogies of Jesus, 32f
Gentiles, 83f, 110ff
Gethsemane, 46, 76f, 124
Ghirshman, R., 18
Gifts of the Spirit, 83
God the Father, 47ff, 171ff
Gospel of Thomas, 43
Grace, 178
Greco-Roman World, 18; language, 18, 20
"Greeks," 58, 122
Guthrie, D., 148

Harrison, E. F., 167
Heaven, 29, 40, 57, 178ff
Hebert, A. G., 93
"Hebrews," 89f, 100; Epistle to, 146
Hedonism, 113
Hellenism, 17; Hellenist, 89f, 92, 100, 107, 122; Hellenistic Judaism, 20, 93
Helvidius, 35
Herod the Great, 23, 43; Antipas, 28, 30; Agrippa I, 85
Hippocrates, 130
Hobart, W. K., 130
Holiness, 167f, 183
Holy City, 168, 182ff
Holy Spirit, 36, 39f, 56, 79, 166ff, 176
Home, 60ff, 138ff

Immaculate conception, 39f
Immortality, 161
Incarnation, 42, 171
Infallibility, 145
Inner circle (Peter, James, John), 51, 74
Inspiration, 132, 145

James, brother of Jesus, 82, 94, 112, 118, 121; son of Zebedee, 52, 85, 169
Jerome, 35
Jerusalem, 37f, 40, 69, 100ff, 125; Conference, 86, 112, 126
Jesus, childhood, 37f; deity, 49, 175ff; humanity, 41ff; ministry, 38, 50ff, 156f
"Jews," 85
John the Baptist, 23ff, 45, 51f, 144
John Mark, see Mark
John, son of Zebedee, 40, 51f, 74, 78, 81, 165ff, 176; Johannine authorship, 166
Joseph, 34ff, 44; see also Barnabas

Josephus, 25ff
Judaism, 25, 81, 93, 111; Judaizer problem, 84, 111, 126, 149ff
Judas Iscariot, 77; Thomas, 156
Judgment, 25, 55, 112f, 178ff

Kenosis, 47
Keys of the Kingdom, 73, 85
Kingdom of God, 27ff, 54f, 111f, 168, 182
Kohler, K., 27
Kramer, S. N., 129

Ladd, G. E., 28
Lamb, 31, 39, 50, 179
Laurin, R. B., 27
Law, 92ff, 101ff, 173
Lazarus, 60ff, 157, 183
Legalism, 93, 95
Lenski, R. C. H., 123, 133
Lightfoot, J. B., 27, 35, 99, 119
Lois, 143, 148
Love, 63, 168, 171f
Luke, 102, 128ff, 150f
Lydia, 102, 135, 143
Lystra, 109, 147

Mace, D. and V., 36
Machen, J. G., 43, 107, 113
Mahaffy, J. P., 18
Manson, T. W., 140
Mark, 86, 124ff, 128, 149
Marriage, 33, 36, 119
Martha, 60ff
Martyr, 89, 97
Mary, mother of Jesus, 32ff, 169; mother of Mark, 124; of Bethany, 60ff
Matthias, 79, 118
Mayor, J. B., 63
McCasland, S. V., 18f, 113
McGiffert, A. C., 146
McNeile, A. H., 133
Medical science, 128f
Messiah, 42, 66, 75; hope of, 21, 27, 76
Milligan, G., 59
Ministry, 89, 91, 176
Miracles, 66; apocryphal, 43f
Missionary, 56ff; methods, 108f
Morgan, G. C., 45, 47, 75
Morris, L., 171
Mother of God, 34, 116
Mylonas, G. E., 129

Nathanael, 51, 58
Nature of Christ, 41f, 49, 53, 175
Nestorian heresy, 34, 41
Non-violence, 30

Officers (church), 91
Old Testament, 23f, 75

Olmstead, A. T. E., 18
Ordination, 149
Organization, 89ff, 154f
Origen, 63, 136

Passover, 54, 76
Pastoral Epistles, 148
Paul, 79, 81, 83, 97ff, 108ff, 126, 131, 139, 141, 147ff, 151, 176
Pentecost, 79, 84f
Perga, 108f, 125
Peter, 70ff, 79ff, 110, 122, 124f, 142
Pfeiffer, C. F., 21
Pfeiffer, R. H., 20f
Pharisees, 25, 94, 101, 110
Philip (apostle), 51, 58f, 82; (deacon), 82
Philippi, 135f, 150
Phoebe, 140
Piper, O. A., 13
Preaching, 51, 80f, 84, 109f, 117, 155
Priest (Presbyter), 154
Primacy of Peter, 79, 87
Priscilla (or Prisca), 138ff
Prophetic view of religion, 25, 95
Propitiation, 171
Proselytes, 22, 58, 91, 110

Queen of Heaven, 40

Rabban, 101
Ramsay, W. M., 43, 98f, 109, 116, 133f, 139
Ramsey, A. M., 75
Redemptrix, 40
Repentance, 30, 81, 177
Resurrection, 48, 56, 66ff, 73ff, 77f, 81, 105, 110, 112, 158, 161ff
Revelation, Book of, 175ff
Rewards, 178
Roman Empire, 16, 18; society, 142
Rome, 85ff, 141, 143; Epistle to, 114, 140, 143; imprisonment(s) at, 150, 153
Rock, 71, 73
Rowley, H. H., 42

Sabbath, 44, 93
Sadducees, 26
Salome, 169
Salvation, 80, 136
Sanday, W., 118
Sanhedrin, 101f; *Sanhedrin*, 96f, 101
Saul (see also Paul), 97ff
Science, 128f; scientists, 165
Scriptures, scroll, 33
Second Coming, 90
Sermon on the Mount, 55
Seven, The, 82, 91; seven-sealed book, 179
Shedd, W. G. T., 42
Sickness, 60, 63f, 183
Silas (Silvanus), 118, 149f

Simon Peter, 51f, 57, 70ff (see also Peter)
Skepticism, 160
Slavery, 19, 138, 142
Smith, W. M., 104
Son of God, 39, 46, 48f, 76f, 105, 168ff, 175ff; Son of Man, 42
Sources, use of, 132f
Stephen, 82, 89ff, 102, 107
Stoics, Stoicism, 99, 112
Strabo, 87, 99, 130
Strahan, J., 99
Suetonius, 22, 139, 142
Swete, H. B., 125
Symbols, 171, 175, 183
Synagogue, 21; school, 44
Syntyche, 143
Syria-and-Cilicia, 123

Tabitha (Dorcas), 82f
Talmud, 36, 96, 135
Targums, 20
Tarsus, 98ff
Tasker, R. V. G., 166
Taylor, V., 125
Teachings of Christ, 46f, 93f
Temple, 21, 92ff, 183
Temple, W., 166
Temptations, 45f
Thessalonica, 150; Epistles to, 150
Thomas, 156ff
Throne, 178f
Timothy, 118, 125, 147ff, 176
Titus, 139, 149, 151ff
Tongues, speaking with, 80, 83f
Transfiguration, 48, 74f
Triumphal Entry, 60f, 68, 157
Troas, 130, 135, 150
Truth, 167
Tryphena and Tryphosa, 143
Twelve, The, 52ff, 55, 58, 70, 79

Unbelief, 160
Unity of the Church, 126, 146, 173, 183
Upper Room, 40, 124, 158

Virgin birth, 42f
Virginity, perpetual, 34f

Wallace, R. S., 41
War, 183
"We sections," 132
Westminster Confession, 166
Wilson, J. A., 129
Wisdom, 91
Witness, 56, 92, 97, 155, 168
Woman, 38
Worship, 93f; Worshiper, 83

Zechariah, 23
Zeus, 119f